M. + J. Walzer
July 1990
Princeton

A RIGID SCRUTINY

IVAN ENGNELL

A RIGID SCRUTINY

Critical Essays on the Old Testament

By Ivan Engnell

Translated from the Swedish and edited by

John T. Willis

With the Collaboration of

Helmer Ringgren

VANDERBILT UNIVERSITY PRESS   NASHVILLE, 1969

Contents

	Foreword	ix
	Preface	xiii
1	The Traditio-Historical Method in Old Testament Research	3
2	The Science of Religion	12
3	Old Testament Religion	35
4	The Pentateuch	50
5	The Book of Psalms	68
6	Prophets and Prophetism in the Old Testament	123
7	New Year Festivals	180
8	The Passover	185
9	The Exodus from Egypt	197
10	The Wilderness Wandering	207
11	The Messiah in the Old Testament and Judaism	215
12	The Son of Man	237
13	The Figurative Language of the Old Testament	242
	Index	291

To question all things;—never to turn away from any difficulty; to accept no doctrine either from ourselves or from other people without a rigid scrutiny by negative criticism; letting no fallacy, or incoherence, or confusion of thought step by unperceived; above all, to insist upon having the meaning of a word clearly understood before using it, and the meaning of a proposition before assenting to it;—these are the lessons we learn from ancient dialecticians.

John Stuart Mill, *Inaugural Address as Rector, University of St. Andrew, February 1, 1867*

Foreword

THOUGH Ivan Engnell energetically denied the existence of an "Uppsala school" in Old Testament exegesis, he himself was the primary reason that such a term was created and that it spread in the circles of biblical scholarship. Undoubtedly, more than anyone else, he has contributed to the particular approach to most Old Testament problems that is characteristic of several young scholars from Uppsala, as well as from other parts of Scandinavia. It was a grave loss to biblical scholarship when he died unexpectedly on the tenth of January, 1964, at the age of 57.

Ivan Engnell was fortunate to have begun his scholarly work at a time when the Ugaritic texts were relatively newly discovered and their full importance for biblical studies was about to be realized by scholars. He did not hesitate to seize the opportunity. So his doctoral thesis, *Studies in Divine Kingship in the Ancient Near East,* which was originally intended to deal with sacral kingship in Israel, came to place the main stress on the Ras Shamra material, and the application of its results to the Old Testament had to be condensed into three pages of concluding remarks. But in their marvellous concentration, these pages contain Engnell's views on most Old Testament problems. They are pages which one must always consult when he wishes to find out Engnell's opinion on a special question.

In his dissertation, Engnell appears as a follower of the method launched by S. H. Hooke in the collection of essays entitled *Myth and Ritual* (London: Oxford University Press, 1933), in which the concept of "pattern" plays a decisive part. This implies that a common myth-and-ritual pattern can be traced all over the ancient Near East, a pattern in which the sacral function of the king is an essential element. This conscious association with the scholarship of the English-speaking world, at a time when Swedish theology in general, and exegesis in particular, was dominated by German works, is a typical feature in Engnell. Unfortunately, in a corresponding degree, most German scholars adopted a negative attitude toward his ideas. The theory of "divine" kingship was heavily criticized, and "the Uppsala school" soon became like a red flag for most traditional exegetes. It is interesting to observe that, today, even rather conservative and cautious scholars accept more and more the idea of a sacral kingship in Israel without paying attention to the way it all began.

Sacral kingship and the messianic ideology connected with it formed one focus of Engnell's scholarly work. The other was oral tradition. Here, he took up a casual statement by his teacher in Semitic languages, H. S. Nyberg, in his *Studien zum Hoseabuche* (Uppsala: Almqvist and Wiksell, 1935), and applied it energetically and consistently to Old Testament literature in general. The results were first presented in the "traditio-historical introduction" published under the title *Gamla Testamentet* (Stockholm: Svenska Kyrkans Diakonistyrelses Bokförlag, 1945), of which unfortunately only the first volume appeared. Here it is obvious that, to Engnell, the traditio-historical method meant much more than placing emphasis on the oral transmission of the Old Testament texts. It also implied paying regard to the mythical and cultic traditions which have contributed to shaping the texts, to the technique of composition, and to ideological factors, and not least to comparative material from Israel's neighbors.

It is to be regretted that this sensational work is extant only in Swedish. To some extent, this resulted in a certain distortion of the international discussion of Engnell's ideas, since the opponents of his theses almost without exception had to rely on secondary reports of this work and on other articles by him which for the most part were also written in Swedish. This means that the somewhat modified view which Engnell maintained in his later works has not been duly appreciated. The sharpness of the discussion may be due partly to the fact that, from the beginning, Engnell formulated some bold and challenging theses, which he did not develop, himself, but left for his students to prove and work out in detail. On the other hand, this stimulated both friends and opponents to further work on these problems, which might otherwise have been overlooked.

Many of Engnell's original ideas were never put into writing, never appeared in print. They were presented in his teaching and remain sealed in the heart of his disciples, like the words of Isaiah. But Swedish readers have a monument of his life-work in *Svenskt Bibliskt Uppslagsverk* (Stockholm: P. A. Norstedt and Söner, 1962), a biblical encyclopedia of high quality which he edited and to which he contributed a large number of articles. In spite of the variety of contributors, he managed to maintain a certain ideological homogeneity in this work. His own articles, which sometimes developed into small monographs, have a considerable part in this result. The second edition of this encyclopedia, published only a year before his death, was thoroughly revised, to a great extent by Engnell himself, and represents, so to speak, his latest views on most questions. In order to present the essence of Engnell's ideas to the international public, it has seemed convenient to translate some of his contributions to this work. Comprehensive articles have been selected and supplemented with explanatory footnotes from other articles which are not translated in full. Quite naturally, the translated parts include the article on "Figurative Language," written for the second edition, for in a characteristic way it deals with everything but figurative language. It is, so to speak, the scholarly last will of its author.

It is the wish of the translator and of the writer of these lines that this little work may further a better understanding of Engnell's contribution to Old Testament scholarship.

Uppsala University
December 1968

HELMER RINGGREN

Preface

The thirteen essays by Ivan Engnell appearing here are translations from the two-volume biblical encyclopedia of which Engnell
was editor, *Svenskt Bibliskt Uppslagsverk*, second edition (Stockholm: P. A. Norstedt & Söner, 1962.)

In order to achieve a readable English translation of Engnell's
essays, it has been deemed best to relegate to notes some material
which appeared in the body of the Swedish text and, in a few cases,
to eliminate sentences or whole paragraphs which have no appeal to
English-speaking audiences and are irrelevant to the author's line of
argumentation. Engnell's versification follows the Hebrew text in
most instances, and I have decided to adopt this, assuming that the
main interest in these essays will come from scholarly circles. In the
very few exceptional cases which seemed to warrant it, the verse
numbering of both the Hebrew and the English texts is given. Quo-
tations from the Bible are from the Revised Standard Version, except
in those cases where Engnell's argument depends on his own translation, in which his wording is given in English. It is felt that the critical
reader can easily detect these variations from the Revised Standard
Version without our using additional space in notes to call attention
to them.

All references to scholarly works in the notes were initiated by

Prof. Helmer Ringgren of Uppsala Universitet and were completed by the translator according to the specifications of Vanderbilt University Press. We regret that in some cases we are unable to supply complete bibliographical information.

I am greatly indebted to Professor Ringgren for reading the entire manuscript to assure an accurate rendering of Professor Engnell's intention into English and for constantly promoting the completion of this work. I am also grateful to Mrs. Engnell for allowing us to proceed with this project and for providing photographs of the late Professor Engnell.

Special acknowledgment is made to the firm of P. A. Norstedt & Söner, who granted permission to translate and publish these thirteen essays.

Finally, I should like to express my deepest thanks to Prof. Walter Harrelson of the Vanderbilt University Divinity School for his enthusiastic support, and to Miss Martha I. Strayhorn of Vanderbilt University Press for suggestions, patience, and complete cooperation throughout the entire process of this undertaking.

John T. Willis

Nashville, Tennessee
February 1969

A RIGID SCRUTINY

1

✦

The Traditio-Historical Method in Old Testament Research

THE term *traditio-historical method* refers to an approach which has gained prominence in relatively recent exegesis. This scholarly method is parallel to earlier methods, to some extent but, at the same time, seeks to go beyond them. The term *traditio-historical* or, simply, *history of tradition* itself is not new but has been in use for some time, especially as a self-designation by exegetes who, in one way or other, emphasize the role of oral tradition. This is true of some of the adherents of the form-critical school—for example, of H. Gunkel, of Germany. It is also true of literary-critical scholars such as H. Gressmann and M. Noth, also of Germany, and of S. Mowinckel, of Norway.

In order to achieve a consistent traditio-historical view and a history of tradition which is genuinely worthy of the name, it is necessary that we free ourselves from the modern, anachronistic book-view and that we view the Old Testament realistically as a product of the ancient Near Eastern culture, of which Israel and its

A portion of an earlier version of this essay was published as part of the author's essay, "Methodological Aspects of Old Testament Study," *Supplements to Vetus Testamentum,* 7 (1959), pp. 13–30. As "Traditionshistorisk metod," it was published in Vol. II of *Svenskt Bibliskt Uppslagsverk,* 2d ed., cols. 1254–1261.

national literature, the Old Testament, are a part. But in doing this, of course, we must not lose sight of the importance of determining peculiar Israelite characteristics. Such a thoroughgoing reorientation is necessitated by a changed situation in Old Testament exegesis. With the help of recent discoveries, contemporary archaeological and philological research has disclosed completely different perspectives with regard to the problem of the text and tradition. Recent literary-historical research has worked out more accurate linguistic and stylistic laws and has gained deeper psychological insights into the Hebrew language, especially its syntax.[1] Newly oriented research in the history of ideas and history of religions has freed itself from the evolutionary doctrinarianism of an earlier period.

The basic characteristics of the traditio-historical method may be summarized briefly as follows.[2]

In the first place, the traditio-historical method is an *analytical* method which demands a thoroughly unprejudiced reconsideration of all aspects of the entire material. Its particular task is to delineate as far as possible the tradition works, the tradition collections, the tradition complexes, and individual tradition units, as well as possible strata within the oral tradition. It also includes the task of comparing different tradition works with each other in order to ascertain their individual peculiarities and of analyzing the different complexes and units within each particular tradition work to determine their place, function, and possible different original order of material. These tasks might be summed up under the concepts of *form analysis* and *composition analysis*.

In this analysis, all available criteria must be used—not only criteria of language and phraseology, so characteristic of literary criticism, and of form and style, so basic to form-criticism, and including arrangement and syntactical structure, but also of content: subject matter, the occurrence of the so-called leitmotifs, and purpose. The

1. Engnell was particularly interested in the problem of tenses. See his *Studies in Divine Kingship in the Ancient Near East* (Oxford: Basil Blackwell, 1967), pp. 207 ff., and his *Grammatik i gammaltestamentlig hebreiska* (Stockholm: Norstedt, 1960). He was especially attracted by the psychological approach to the Hebrew language as advocated by Johannes Pedersen, *Israel, Its Life and Culture*, I–II (London: Oxford University Press, 1964), pp. 107–133.

2. Cf. H. Ringgren, "Literarkritik, Formgeschichte, Traditionsgeschichte," *Theologische Literaturzeitung*, 91 (1966), cols. 641 ff; R. A. Carlson, *David, the Chosen King* (Uppsala: Almqvist and Wiksell, 1964), pp. 9–19.

analysis of tradition technique, the combination of different complexes according to particular cognate words and similar themes, is very important. This analysis is often conclusive for determining whether the transmission is oral or written. In other words, traditio-historical investigation must deal with form and content at one and the same time and must use all available data: literary, ideological, psychological, sociological, archaeological, and cultural. Religio-historical interpretation which takes into account the contemporary views is also of great importance for the traditio-historical analysis. One of the most important of these views is that of the modern "myth and ritual" school, or "patternism," which is centered around the belief in the high god and sacral kingship.[3]

The analysis must be accompanied by the *synthesis*, the interpretation of the smaller units in relationship to their context. Merely the separating out of the different literary units does not solve the whole problem of the tradition. On the contrary, a one-sided analytical procedure which neglects the synthetical dimension can entirely distort the understanding and interpretation of the text. Literary-critical and form-critical exegetes have excelled in subjective interpretations of literary units precisely because they have taken liberties with or have failed to show proper respect for the context and continuity of thought. This statement will be completely vindicated, in spite of the fact that some of these scholars now accept and pretend always to have accepted the exegetical principle that "The context is the guide to interpretation, and disregard of the context leads to chaos," formulated by E. J. Kissane, who otherwise is by no means a traditio-historical critic.[4] As obvious as this exegetical norm seems to be—and indeed *is*, for an advocate of the traditio-historical method—still, up until now, most critics have flagrantly neglected it.

A correct evaluation of the scope of oral tradition[5] is also of fundamental importance for a consistent traditio-historical method. In spite of assertions to the contrary, it is still true that the form-critical

3. See chap. 2 of this volume, "The Science of Religion."

4. E. J. Kissane, *The Book of Isaiah*, II (Dublin: Browne and Nolan, 1943), p. lxviii.

5. For this question, see E. Nielsen, *Oral Tradition* (Chicago: Alec A. Allenson, 1954); A. H. J. Gunneweg, *Mündliche und schriftliche Tradition der vorexilischen Prophetenbücher als Problem der neueren Prophetenforschung* (Göttingen: Vandenhoeck und Ruprecht, 1959). For Engnell's own position, see also *The Call of Isaiah* (Uppsala: Lundequist, 1949), pp. 55 ff.

school has failed to present proper evaluation of the scope and significance of oral tradition.[6] This fact is not least apparent in the obvious disinclination to draw inevitable consequences from the traditio-historical view of oral transmission.

However, for an advocate of the traditio-historical method, it appears incontrovertible that, to a large extent, Old Testament literature—although greatly varying within different literary types—has the character of an oral literature which was written down only at a relatively late period. Not only the smaller units, but also larger complexes—partly, whole collections or tradition works—had already reached a fixed form in the oral tradition stage, so that the writing down implies nothing new or revolutionary. This means that, whereas the units and complexes of the oral tradition, their combination and development, their history, could be traced, to some extent, even in the final form of the written texts, still, the process of combining this material and making it uniform had already taken place basically in the oral stage. Thus, the analytical task of delimiting the units and following the development of the tradition is extremely difficult, in most cases, and the result which is reached can be only more or less hypothetical. Therefore, it should go without saying that an intensive and meticulous analysis must be coupled with great discretion and sound, temperate judgment.

Thus, it is clear that oral transmission has played a fundamental rôle in the origin and growth of the Old Testament. This is also confirmed by the striking uniformity of language in the Old Testament. If the Old Testament had been written down early, this would have been reflected in a greater variety of language. However, certain parts of the Old Testament were undoubtedly written down early. This is the case above all with various documents which have an official character. In the royal chancellery, legal transactions of various sorts and codes of law were written down from the very first. It is also likely that sacral texts, such as the Psalms, were written down early— in this case, in order to aid the memory, but primarily in order to facilitate a normative control and to give the sacred texts canonical sanction. However, in actual use and in application to the "life situation," undoubtedly remembrance and oral transmission of the codes of law, the psalm rituals, and similar items were predominant, all

---

6. In New Testament exegesis, the situation is different.

along. Of course, there are exceptions, such as those laws which never had their *Sitz im Leben* in connection with oracular and legal usage in the temple but are secondary and were written down from the first for literary purposes. This applies to some laws in the "P work" and even more to some in the "D work."[7] It seems obvious that both of these works in their present form did not gain canonical authority until they were written down.

From what has already been said, it should be clear that oral and written transmission are not to be set over against each other as mutually exclusive alternatives, but are to be interpreted as parallel methods which complement each other. To equate the traditio-historical method with the theory of a one-hundred-percent process of oral tradition is to give a harsh caricature, as is also the assertion that the traditio-historical method consciously abandons all attempts at analysis which lead to a study of the history and development of the tradition.[8]

Closely connected with this is the question of the *reliability of the oral tradition,* the question of the extent to which the traditional material was preserved authentic and intact in the stage of oral transmission. The attempts which have been made in certain circles (recently by G. Widengren)[9] to minimize the worth of the oral tradition are not convincing, because they fail to recognize properly the absolutely unique character of the Old Testament as a body of sacred literature throughout, rooted in a most particular and homogeneous cultic *Sitz im Leben.*

Regarding the relationship between the internal and comparative interpretations in determining the role of oral tradition and factors on which the forms of the tradition depend, only the following observations may be made: first, the internal investigation of the literature of the Old Testament is the obvious place to begin in order to determine the question of the tradition, and it is the typology of the Old Testament literature itself which ultimately must decide in favor of the importance of oral tradition. In pursuing this internal in-

7. Cf. chap. 4, "The Pentateuch."

8. S. Mowinckel, *Prophecy and Tradition* (Oslo: J. Dybwad, 1946), pp. 18 f.

9. G. Widengren, *Literary and Psychological Aspects of the Hebrew Prophets* (Uppsala: Lundequist, 1948), chapters I–III; "Oral Tradition and Written Literature among the Hebrews in the Light of Arabic Evidence, with special regard to Prose Narratives," *Acta Orientalia,* 23 (1959), pp. 201–262.

vestigation, one must depend not only on the basic principle of association,[10] but also on such criteria as the occurrence of doublets and variants, the application of so-called epic laws (especially for the narrative portions of the literature), the compositional technique of the so-called alternating pattern—the pattern in which doom and hope alternate (especially for portions of the prophetic literature), the occurrence of iterating and retarding elements, the intertwining strophic structure in different patterns (a-b-a, a-b-c-c-b-a, etc.), and the technique of *parallelismus membrorum* in both poetry and prose.[11] However, this does not mean that a comparative critical approach has no value, but only that it must be tempered with proper discrimination. In order to avoid doing any violence to the contents and unique position of the Old Testament, it is necessary to observe carefully all possible differences in the comparative material with respect to time, place, environment, and—above all—"the life situation," as well as other related matters. In this connection, it needs to be emphasized that the manner of transmission is determined partly by the *Sitz im Leben,* motifs, and tendencies of the traditional material, and partly by the conservatism which was practiced in the transmission of the tradition itself. Those responsible for passing on the bulk of tradition adhered closely to the form of the tradition which they had inherited. But at the same time, remarkably enough, this tradition exhibits a relatively great independence from environmental cultural factors. Therefore, for example, "the argument from culture" that the prophets were literary authors is wholly unconvincing, as is also the contention that the oral and written transmission of the tradition is to be assigned to the pre-Conquest and the post-Conquest period, respectively. These views are combined with an erroneous evolutionary view of cultural development, and are actually based on wrong interpretations of crucial texts, such as Jeremiah, chapter 36.[12] Therefore, comparing Israelite material with relatively far-distant lands and cultures—India and Iran, for instance—actually can be more fruitful than comparing it with closer regions, such as Arabia. As a matter of fact, the latter can even be characterized as distinctly dangerous. In any case, it is applicable only to

10. I.e., the way different tradition units are linked together by means of associations of ideas or words.
11. Cf. chap. 13, "The Figurative Language of the Old Testament."
12. Cf. chap. 6, "Prophets and Prophetism in the Old Testament."

limited areas in Old Testament literature and even there with great reservations. On the other hand, ancient Greece does contribute to an understanding of the Old Testament. But above all, it is the Sumerian and Accadian literature which contains the most valuable material for comparison with the Old Testament. This is especially true because of the strong points of contact in content, literary types, and *Sitz im Leben.*

Also, within Judaism, the tradition which was inherited was passed on according to very conservative principles. This fact is often overlooked but is certainly not insignificant. The extraordinary significance of the oral tradition for Judaism is reflected both in the Mishna and in the Talmud.[13] Furthermore, the recitation of Old Testament passages as liturgical texts in the synagogue to a large extent relied on memorization, and had the character of oral recitation, not of reading.

Finally, it should be pointed out that although it is clear that oral tradition implies a certain living transformation of the inherited traditional material, still, in all essentials, the tradition remained fixed and reliable, especially because of the unique position of the Old Testament as cultic-religious literature. From all this, which could only be dealt with very briefly here, a fundamental principle of the traditio-historical method can be deduced: *confidence in the tradition,* even where oral tradition is involved. This principle is diametrically opposed to the viewpoint of literary criticism, which in reality implies a fundamental censure of the tradition and text.

In connection with this, it must be emphasized briefly that the traditio-historical method has important consequences for principles of textual criticism. The whole task of textual criticism is confined to *recensio* in the broad sense: to the restoration of the Massoretic text. Also, to a certain degree, one must keep in mind the possibility that errors of hearing were made in transmission.[14] However, it is more important for the traditio-historical critic that the principle of confidence in the tradition based on the realization of its stability be combined with a strong, positive attitude toward the Hebrew Massoretic text, which, after all, constitutes the only firm basis for text-critical

13. Cf. B. Gerhardsson, *Memory and Manuscript* (Lund: C. W. K. Gleerup, 1961).

14. Cf. H. Ringgren, "Oral and Written Transmission in the Old Testament," *Studia Theologica,* 3 (1950), pp. 34–59.

work. At the same time, he must consider the versions, the old translations, to have a relatively modest value. All in all, he must be very temperate in making emendations and other manipulations of the text, which have been so typical of previous methods.[15] This conservative viewpoint has clearly had an unexpected and sensational confirmation in the rather recent discovery of the scrolls from Qumran near the Dead Sea, some of which are more than one thousand years older than the oldest extant manuscripts previously known. These scrolls prove that the Massoretic text is based on a continuous older tradition and is by no means a creative and standardizing work of the type which P. Kahle, especially, wished to maintain.

It has already been suggested that the so-called form-critical investigation is far from insignificant and that, handled cautiously and with sound judgment, it renders an important service to the traditio-historical method. That this approach has now gone far beyond Gunkel's position is a different matter. On the other hand, the question of whether literary criticism can and should be undertaken along with the traditio-historical method is still much debated. With regard to this, it may only be suggested that it is best not to use *literary criticism* as a term for a certain method, but to reserve this designation for the tendency or school which, considered from a historical perspective, inaugurated the scientific, critical investigation of the Old Testament and advanced the different hypotheses of primary written sources. The advocates of this approach worked on the presupposition of a developed book-view which understood the Old Testament as written literature throughout, the work of various authors. It is true that, to the extent that we have to do with written sources in the Old Testament—although, as has been suggested, there are no continuous sources for the Pentateuch—a traditional, analytical method of the written literary type must be applied. This method might be called the *written literary method.*[16] It is one of the methods of investigation which the traditio-historical critic has at his disposal. It is useful, for example, in the "Chronicler's" work (which, however, by no means is based on written sources throughout), in certain parts of the Deuteronomistic historical work, namely—to some ex-

---

15. Engnell here follows the principles laid down by H. S. Nyberg in his *Studien zum Hoseabuch* (Uppsala: Almqvist and Wiksell, 1935), and since then applied by several Swedish Old Testament scholars.

16. Carlson, *op. cit.,* p. 11, note 1, uses the term *documentary-literary method.*

tent—in legal materials, annals, etc., and, to a smaller extent, in the "P work."[17] But it must be emphasized most resolutely that this written literary method is of very limited value because of the actual nature of the material and the manner of its transmission. One cannot vindicate the necessity of this method *ex analogia* with Tatian's *Diatessaron* (a position still defended by Mowinckel and others[18]) or by extending the situation in Chronicles to other portions of the Old Testament. Furthermore, this approach is completely out of place in dealing with the prophetic literature. Thus, the fact that one uses the written literary method in certain cases in no way obviates the validity of the thesis that the traditio-historical method is an exclusive alternative to the literary-historical view. The traditio-historical critic must completely do away with the anachronistic book-view of the literary-historical method. Thus, the traditio-historical method carries its *criterium veri* within itself, if it is true that the scientific working hypothesis which solves the most problems and leaves the least number of questions unanswered and, at the same time, on the basis of general considerations regarding the history of research, appears to emphasize that which is most realistic and is therefore the most trustworthy, is always the best. Therefore, this method is the necessary prerequisite for that which is now usually referred to as a realistic view of the Bible, which seeks to give a realistic historical picture of both the Old and New Testaments, an unprejudiced and objective picture, and so requires a method which approaches its subject from a positive viewpoint.

It is impossible here to describe even the most elementary results of the traditio-historical method. Some of the most significant of them are discussed in the following essays. It hardly seems necessary to point out that the traditio-historical method is still in the first stages of its development and that, therefore, in a great many cases, its results must be regarded as preliminary. Such is the nature of all genuine research which may be called progressive. The predecessors of the traditio-historical method, even when they stood in sharpest opposition to previous research, still directly or indirectly built upon the contributions which had been made under constant difficulties and with untiring patience by earlier generations of scholars.

17. See chap. 4, "The Pentateuch."
18. Mowinckel, *op. cit.*, p. 20.

2

๛

The Science of Religion

Questions concerning the science of religion and terminology. The origin and development of religion. The phenomenology of the idea of God.—The term *science of religion* can be taken in a broad or a limited sense. In the former sense, it embraces all theological disciplines; but in the latter sense, it is equivalent to what is generally called *comparative religion* in English,[1] as distinguished, for example, from biblical research (or exegesis), church history, or dogmatics. It is in the limited sense that the term is used here.

Judging from its presuppositions and method, though belonging both to the theological and the humanistic realms, the science of religion is essentially humanistic. It is a branch of the science of history but, at the same time, one of the most important auxiliary sciences for a historico-critical theology. This is true especially for the exegesis of the Old and New Testaments or, if one prefers, for biblical research.

Judging from the subjects which it investigates and from the different problems with which it deals, the science of religion may be said to include four subdisciplines: the history of religion (strictly

---

This essay appears in *Svenskt Bibliskt Uppslagsverk*, 2d ed., Vol. II, cols. 708–723, under the title "Religionsvetenskap, religionshistoria."
1. Thus, the discipline called *Religionsgeschichte* in German.

speaking), the phenomenology of religion, the sociology of religion, and the psychology of religion.[2] Of course, the dividing lines between these disciplines are quite flexible. The task of the history of religion, in the narrower sense of the term, is primarily the historico-genetic investigation of the various historically distinct forms of religion: the religions of primitive peoples, Iranian religion, the religions of India, Sumero-Accadia, and that of the Graeco-Romans. On the other hand, the phenomenology of religion has a more systematic character. It seeks to provide a synthetic comparison of the relevant data in the history of religions, for example, with regard to the phenomenology of the idea of God, the cult, myth. The sociology of religion deals with social forms, different types of communal organizations in which religion appears, the mutual relationships of these forms, and their relationships to profane social units. Finally, the psychology of religion, as its name specifically implies, deals with religion as a manifestation of the human mind.

All four branches of the science of religion may be of equally great significance for the comprehensive theological discipline which is called by the more popular name of biblical research. Thus, in Old Testament exegesis, the history of the religion of the Old Testament—or, rather, of Israel—constitutes an organic and important part or subdiscipline. Seen in this light, it is at the same time comparative and internal in nature: while the primary object of research is Israel's religion, an understanding of this religion is dependent on an understanding of religion in the ancient Near Eastern milieu to which it belongs. The phenomenological aspect of the Old Testament science of religion has become more and more important: for example, the problem of the phenomenology of the idea of God, the content and purpose of the cult, its structure and peculiar character belong to this structural and morphological investigation, as it may also be called. The sociological aspect of Israel and its several collective bodies, such as the tribes, the amphictyony, and the people, is extremely important and must never be neglected. The same is true of religio-psychological research which deals with collective and individual aspects of different phenomena in Israel's religion, especially the prophetic. Among all the auxiliary sciences which Old Testa-

---

2. Cf. H. Ringgren and Å. V. Ström, *Religions of Mankind* (Philadelphia: Fortress Press, 1967), pp. xxii ff.

ment exegesis has at its disposal, including archaeology and philology, the science of religion—which itself makes use of a group of auxiliary sciences such as anthropology, archaeology, philology, sociology, psychology, and the study of folklore—in many respects holds a unique position and is an integral and always indispensable part of all Old Testament research. The same is true in New Testament exegesis.

Despite the fact that it is one of the youngest members of the great family of historical sciences, the science of religion has itself undergone a series of fast-changing developments, in the process of which it has suffered several "childhood diseases." On the whole, and in perhaps a higher degree than the natural sciences, the so-called spiritual sciences are time-bound, influenced by contemporary currents and ideals. This is equally true of the science of religion, which is going through a period of great transition, and this has not failed to have its effect on biblical research. Just as modern critical science appeared in earnest during the golden age of the hypothesis of evolution, so the science of religion has got its impetus above all from just this doctrine and has come to stand under the curse of a strong a priori concept of the "origin of religion" and of its logical development which ran its course in process of time.[3] Theories, particularly with regard to the origin of religion or of the belief in God, have superseded one another only to be taken up and arranged in a hard-and-fast system which is basically defective because it does not agree with the complexity and richness of reality.[4]

The first general theory which was advanced to explain the nature and origin of religion was the animistic,[5] the basic element of which is belief in the soul, which in turn emanates partly from observing the difference between death and life and partly from the phenomenon of dreams. Animism is undoubtedly a factor in the religious world, as well as in the biblical world, but it cannot be regarded as having primary importance. Animatism—or pre-animism, as it is called—has been suggested as a complement to and a preparatory stage for animism.[6] It considers the basic phenomenon to be

3. Cf. G. Widengren, "Evolutionism and the Problem of the Origin of Religion," *Ethnos* 10 (1945), pp. 57 ff., Ringgren and Ström, *op. cit.*, pp. xxvii ff.
4. Ringgren and Ström, *op. cit.*, pp. xxiii ff.
5. E. B. Tylor, *Primitive Culture* (New York: Harper, 1958).
6. R. Marett, *The Threshold of Religion* (New York: Macmillan Co., 1914).

impersonal power, the positive aspect of which is designated by the Melanesian word *mana*, and the negative aspect by the Polynesian *tabu*. This belief in power is admittedly a significant phenomenon, but more recent research has greatly modified the whole theory, so that the relationship of power with personal beings is now emphasized more strongly—it is no longer understood "magically," without religious qualifications—and most significantly so that the evolutionistic form of the theory has been abandoned.[7] Belief in power is no longer considered to be the earliest phase of religion, the first stage in a successive uniform development expressed most simply in three stages: *mana*, animism, and theism, or the belief in power, in the soul, and in the divine character. Further, *tabu* is neither inherently nor necessarily the opposite of *mana* as a negative and dangerous power but is a negative manifestation of the unapproachable deity and, in any case, *can* immediately be explained religiously or sociologically—as can be done most often in the Old Testament, even if a more undifferentiated concept of *tabu* does occur, for example, in Lev. 5:2 f.

Closely connected with this is the question of holiness and its character.[8] In recent years, the earlier idea that the concept of *tabu*—which itself grew out of *mana*—developed partly in a positive direction into holiness and partly in a negative direction into "uncleanness" has been opposed energetically and, without doubt, justifiably. Actually, this idea falls with the *mana* theory itself. Holiness, in this mechanical, impersonal form, is no longer regarded as the basic phenomenon of religion, but "holy" is now considered to be a religious idea indicating that which belongs to the divine sphere and is therefore inviolable, that is, *tabu*. But by its very nature as a quality rooted in the deity, holiness is two-sided, ambivalent: in a positive sense, it is synonymous with "blessing" and "purity;" negatively, with "curse" —this is very clearly the case in the Old Testament.

In light of this "revolution against evolution," the question of religion and magic also appears to be considerably different from what

7. Ringgren and Ström, *op. cit.*, pp. xxx, 18, 37 f.
8. The discussion here is conditioned by the debate reflected in G. Widengren, *Religionens värld*, 2d ed. (Stockholm: Svenska Kyrkans Diakonistyrelses Bokförlag, 1953) [German edition in preparation], chapter on "Holiness"; the same is true of H. Ringgren, *The Prophetical Conception of Holiness* (Leipzig: Otto Harrassowitz, 1948).

it was before.[9] This is especially true since magic cannot or must not in any sense be interpreted as a primary stage out of which religion grew by a slow process of evolution. On the contrary, magic often can appear as a "degenerate product" of religion. This can be observed distinctly in the fact that religious texts are used in magical contexts: prayer degenerates into incantation. As a matter of fact, religion and magic exist side by side and, looked at from a psychological point of view, represent two different attitudes toward the deity: religion is characterized by a feeling of dependence; magic, by exploiting and attempting to control the deity and the divine powers. Thus, the dividing-line between religion and magic is extremely flexible and often difficult or completely impossible to determine.

Thus, the old, established theory of an orderly chain of evolution,[10] with its more or less fixed and uniform stages following each other in gradually ascending order—belief in *mana*, animism, polydemonism (belief in a number of spiritual beings), polytheism (belief in many gods), henotheism or monolatry (belief in several gods but worship of only one), and monotheism (belief in one God), which in its ethical form is the ultimate in religion brought forth through a long process of evolution by abstraction, generalization, and unification—is no longer tenable.

The consequences of this for the Old Testament are summarized in the essay *The Religion of The Old Testament*. In addition to what is said there with regard to the Old Testament idea of God, here it shall only be emphasized that the idea of Yahweh as originally a power, a type of *"mana* reservoir," bound to Sinai, or as a so-called animistic god—in a way, all gods are animistic: for example, "the spirit of the spring," in Kadesh[11]—makes it impossible to understand how he later developed into a creator god and sky god in Israel. In other words, such a view presupposes a phenomenological metamorphosis which lacks the necessary prerequisite of a similarity and continuity of nature. From the viewpoint of a historical development, therefore, it is very unsatisfactory, not least with regard to the

9. Cf. Widengren, *Religionens värld*, pp. 9 ff.; Ringgren and Ström, *op. cit.*, pp. xxi ff. For an excellent discussion of the problem, see C. G. Diehl, *Instrument and Purpose* (Lund: C. W. K. Gleerup, 1956), pp. 13 ff., 335 ff.

10. See Widengren, "Evolution and the Problem of the Origin of Religion."

11. S. Mowinckel, *Religion und Kultus* (Göttingen: Vandenhoeck und Ruprecht, 1953), p. 43, cf. p. 38.

amalgamation of the pre-Canaanite, Israelite Yahweh and the Jerusalemite sky god *'el 'elyôn,* "God Most High," which is a basic fact in the history of Israelite religion.

In more recent religious research, another extreme alternative has been advanced against the evolutionary pattern mentioned above: the so-called primitive monotheism.[12] It is true that different scholars mean different things by this term but in the particular formation of this thesis by Father Schmidt of Austria,[13] it is in its own way just as much an a priori approach. It presents the idea of a single all-inclusive sky god with ethical qualities as a starting point and, consequently, as the origin of religion. The belief in a high god among primitive peoples represents degenerate remnants of this belief. In Israel, the sky god has retained much of his original character and, through Jesus and the New Testament, he regains it completely, so that he is, ultimately, the Christian God. Examined scientifically and critically, the theory of primitive monotheism in this form must be rejected. Furthermore, one must completely refrain from idle speculations concerning the origin of the belief in God, and it would be wise to avoid the term *primitive monotheism* and retain the expression *high god.* The belief in so-called high gods or sky gods is a well-testified and inescapable phenomenon in the world of religion. Such high gods and the complex of beliefs and ideas connected with them obviously reach as far back in time as the source material on the whole permits us to go. In other words, the belief in a high god is contemporaneous with the "lower vegetation" of religion, which consists of the belief in powers and demons, in magic and fetishism.

Thus, the problem of monotheism is very complicated. A monotheistic form of religion can be original to the extent that it goes back to a primitive belief in a high god, but it can also be secondary if it originated by the fusion of different local deities. Such a fusion can also have a political character, but as a rule it presupposes that the gods in question are phenomenologically similar. Furthermore, it is important to keep clearly in mind the difference between a belief in a high god in the sense just mentioned and a monotheism which can be partly of an emotional type, that is, one which has grown out of a

12. Ringgren and Ström, *op. cit.,* pp. xxvi f.
13. W. Schmidt, *Der Ursprung der Gottesidee,* 1–12 (Münster: Aschendorff, 1926), *Handbuch der vergleichenden Religionsgeschichte* (Münster: Aschendorff, 1930).

genuine religious attitude, for example, in prayer (corresponding most closely to henotheism or monolatry), partly of a theoretical, speculative type with a religio-political or even a philosophical orientation.

Just as the origin of monotheism has several possible explanations, so also a polytheism, a pantheon, can arise in more than one way, one of which is through syncretism. Often, polytheism is actually secondary to monotheism: that is, a pantheon, an assembly of gods, can originate when different functions and attributes of the high god are splintered off and hypostatized and become independent deities alongside the high god.[14] Undoubtedly the most important of the deities originating in the splintering-off process is the so-called god of vegetation or fertility, the youthful god, or whatever he may be called, at the moment.

The characteristics of a high god which lie behind this phenomenon deserve careful consideration. In essence, the high god is a sky god, a creator god, a god of fate, and a giver of fertility. As a sky god, the nature aspect of the high god, that is, his identity with the sky itself, has at times been overemphasized, according to Pettazzoni;[15] however, it is obvious that this aspect contains an important element of truth. As sky god, the high god appears in different forms: as a sun god, moon god, or god of the atmosphere—of the winds, the clouds, the thunder, the lightning—and, consequently, as a god of rain and fertility.[16] In his character as creator god, the high god is connected with a mythology of creation, which is often expressed in a creation epic. This epic usually occupies a central place in the ritual of the annual festival. It should be observed that, when one focuses on the high god as a god of fate, actually, in essence, he seems to be ethically indifferent. He distributes good fortune and misfortune to men solely on the basis of his absolute authority.[17] But as the sky god, particularly as the solar sky god, he also clearly tends toward

14. Cf. H. Ringgren, *Word and Wisdom* (Lund: Ohlssons, 1947), "Introduction" and "Conclusion"; I. Engnell, *Studies in Divine Kingship in the Ancient Near East*, 2d ed. (Oxford: Basil Blackwell, 1967), pp. 9, 19, 54 f.

15. Especially in his earlier works, for example, *Dio I, L'essere celesto nelle credenze dei popoli primitivi* (Rome: Perrella, 1922); cf. also his essay "La formation du monotheisme," *Revue de l'Histoire des Religions*, 88 (1923), pp. 193 ff., and his work *The All-Knowing God* (London: Methuen, 1956).

16. G. Widengren, *Hochgottglaube im alten Iran* (Uppsala: Lundequist, 1938), p. 85.

17. Emphasized by Widengren, *op. cit.*, pp. 77 ff.

ethical differentiation. He is the judge with the all-seeing, all-piercing eye (sun rays or stars), inclined to punish or reward, all according to man's works.[18] When different, more positive characteristics of the high god are splintered off, often the negative, sterile fate aspect tends to develop. This happened to Yahweh in certain circles, as well as, for example, to Islam's Allah.

With regard to the high god as giver of fertility, it may be observed that when this side of his character is greatly emphasized,[19] the result is a clearly active high god that is an object for a regular cult. But as this aspect of fertility is naturally the most important aspect for primitive man, there is also a need and a tendency to splinter off this element of the original character of the high god. And so, to the extent that the greatly active god of fertility or god of vegetation—the youthful god—increases in importance, to that same extent the high god loses more or less entirely his most active function. And even if the other primary characteristics remain—his celestial character, his function as creator, and the fate aspect—still, he assumes the more or less pronounced character of a so-called *deus otiosus*, or resting god, who at best is the object of worship rather sporadically or at greater intervals. This cult is often associated with the annual festival. Such a *deus otiosus* is often connected with a high mountain or a volcano. Evidently, the god of the fathers, who, through Moses, became Yahweh, the Israelite god of the amphictyony, was of this type. Certainly it is not imperative that all gods of vegetation originated in this way, by splintering off from a high god. But there seems to be no doubt that here we have a real and frequent religious phenomenon which presents an important alternative to the mechanical, evolutionistic view of the animistic theory which assumes that the god of vegetation is the personified soul of the plants, originating by a process of abstraction and unification out of a countless number of local beings of this type. It should be observed, however, that basically there is only a tendency to splinter off, but that this has not necessarily occurred everywhere. When the tendency to splinter off is accomplished only rather imperfectly, the dividing lines between the high god and the god of vegetation (often inter-

18. The Israelite or Mosaic Yahweh, as well as the Jerusalemite *'el 'elyôn*, from the very beginning, belong to this ethically differentiated type.

19. As is true also of the closely-related idea that the high god is particularly a war god: victory is a prerequisite for prosperity and fertility.

preted as the son of the former) become very flexible, and the two gods become more or less identical.[20] It is also important to recognize the fact that an inactive high god can be reactivated by the personal activity of a religious leader who binds a cultic community, a tribal league, or a people to him. This happens with the Persian Ahura Mazda, through Zarathustra; with Allah, through Mohammed; with "El of the fathers," through Moses—and also, to some extent, with the God of Judaism, through Jesus.

The importance of the fertility aspect of this youthful god is, to a great extent, dependent on certain cultural and social factors. Thus, it is emphasized more in an agricultural milieu and in a culture dominated by sacral kingship. Also at work in this connection is the ineradicable human instinct to visualize and materialize the most essential needs, not least the instinct for food. Consequently, the god of fertility is embodied in a very special way in the person of the sacral king, who, at the same time, personifies his people according to the principle of "corporate personality." The exceedingly important religious phenomenon which is called sacral kingship is, to some extent, a corollary to the belief in the high god and will be discussed in another essay. Only a few remarks may be made here for the sake of illumination.

It should be observed that, even when one speaks of the identity of the sacral king and the deity, whether referring to the high god or to the god of vegetation, this expression has a limited meaning.[21] Primarily, it denotes two things which are closely related: on the one hand, that the sacral king in the cult—originally, to be sure, imitatively and dramatically—plays the rôle of the respective god (or, in many cases, gods); on the other hand, that in this connection he has the same divine qualities and is credited with the same epithets which characterize the deity. But, of course, his deification must be understood in a relative way. Such relativism is characteristic of the so-called primitive way of thinking. Thus, obviously, the king is not thought to become divine in the sense of becoming non-physical, metaphysical, immortal. Such an idea—which, amazingly enough, has

---

20. This is clearly the case at Ras Shamra, as well as in other parts of Canaan, with El and Baal.

21. This is one of the main theses in *Studies in Divine Kingship;* cf. Engnell's defense of his thesis against J. de Fraine in *Svensk Exegetisk Årsbok,* 18–19 (1955), pp. 204 f.

its representatives in many religious historians and exegetes (of the "anti-patternistic" type[22])—is an anachronistic modern philosophical concept.

As mediator between gods and men, especially in cases in which the high god is inactive, the so-called culture hero often appears. Sometimes, the sacral king can also be understood and depicted in these categories, although this is not the case in Israel. Sometimes, this realm of ideas is associated with the figure of the so-called Primal Man, but such a concept plays no prominent rôle in Israel, either.[23] In some religions, the previously mentioned splintering process is carried out so consistently that an immense pantheon of special deities emerges—particularly in Roman religion. In Israel, there were some tendencies toward such splintering processes and hypostatization, for example, as regards righteousness, grace, and, particularly, wisdom. But these tendencies could not be carried to their end.[24] Yahweh's original high-god character and the exclusive nature of the Yahwistic idea of good prohibited this.

A third major concept of deity, called pantheism, is usually placed alongside monotheism and polytheism. The predominant characteristic of this concept is that a mystical identity exists between the deity and the cosmos or between the macrocosmos and man as the microcosmos. The pantheistic form of religion is completely foreign to the Old Testament. It only appears much later in connection with the spread of Gnosticism. By means of the latter, it has left some traces in the New Testament, where, however, the church has replaced the natural world as bearer of the identity.

The Nature of the Cult; Sacrifice, Myth, and Ritual. The Problem of "Patternism."—Not the least important of the various manifestations of religion is the cult.[25] Therefore, the phenomenology of the cult is a very fundamental object of research in the science of religion. Here, sociological and psychological aspects are of great importance: above all, the cult is a community experience. It is strongly connected with the group and has the common interest of the community in view. Nevertheless, within the framework of the community, the

22. Cf. *Svensk Exegetisk Årsbok*, 18–19, pp. 204 f.

23. See I. Engnell, "Die Urmenschvorstellung und das Alten Testament," *Svensk Exegetisk Årsbok*, 22–23 (1958), pp. 265 ff.

24. H. Ringgren, *Word and Wisdom*, pp. 89 ff.

25. Cf. Ringgren and Ström, *op. cit.*, pp. xxxvi ff.

individual viewpoints can be emphasized very strongly, and the individual experiences reach their full expression there and only there.[26] The purpose of the cult is to establish communion with the deity and, by this means, to attain and revive blessing and life and ultimately to create and maintain the cosmos itself in its perpetual battle against chaos in all its manifestations.

Sacrifice is of fundamental importance in the cult. It involves a number of different aspects, especially gift, communion, and expiation. The latter is based on the concept of sacrifice as giving oneself, which is its deepest meaning. In turn, sacrifice is a part of the ritual, which is composed of strongly traditional and conservative cultic acts which take a number of forms beside sacrifice, as, for example, the cultic drama,[27] the daily service, purification ceremonies, initiatory rites, rites for the dead, rites for the newborn, but also—and not least—prayer, in all its different forms. The natural complement of ritual is myth, the holy "word" which gives content to the ritual, gives it meaning, and is made visual in it.[28] Sometimes myth, as a ritual text, can completely dispense with or supplant the ritual, while, on the other hand, the ritual or cultic act often supplies elements which are missing in the myth. As a cultic myth or ritual text, the myth can assume a number of different forms, the most important of which is the myth of creation, which also often plays a central rôle in the annual festival.[29] But there are several types of myths other than specific cult myths, such as myths concerning the establishment of the cult, social myths, myths concerning death, and myths concerning the destruction of the world. It is debated whether one is to assume the existence of so-called aetiological myths (myths which explain things) and fictional myths as particular types, more or less detached from the cult. As the spoken word in the ritual, myth is actually a creative cultic act. At the same time, it often ambiguously places that which is done in the cult in the divine sphere and presents it as a reflection of what was done once and will be done again in that sphere. It should

26. Cf. H. Ringgren, *The Faith of the Psalmists* (Philadelphia: Fortress Press, 1963), pp. xi ff., 1 ff.

27. Mowinckel, *Religion und Kultus,* pp. 73 ff.

28. For the question of myth and ritual, see B. Malinowski, *Myth in Primitive Psychology* (London: K. Paul, Trench, Trubner and Co., 1926), and cf. V. Grønbech, *The Culture of the Teutons* (London: Oxford University Press, 1931), II, pp. 260 ff.

29. See chap. 7, "New Year Festivals."

be observed that not only is it impossible to answer the time-bound evolutionary question whether myth precedes ritual, or vice versa, but actually the question is meaningless: myth and ritual are mutually interdependent and cannot be separated.

In recent years, the comparative, phenomenological investigation of the myth-and-ritual complex has led to the question of how the actual similarities which appear in different cultural areas should be interpreted. Standing at the center of this debate is the hypothesis which has come to be called "patternism," although this term has acquired a disparaging emphasis from the opponents of this approach. "Patternism" can be said to have originated in the certainly very diffuse so-called myth-and-ritual school in England, represented especially by S. H. Hooke;[30] but, in reality, it is based on a folkloristic research, dating approximately a decade earlier, represented by E. O. James and especially A. M. Hocart.[31] In recent years, it has found its most avid exponents in the Scandinavian countries, not least in Sweden. To put it briefly, as far as the ancient Near East is concerned, patternism implies the assumption of a rather homogeneous culture, a high culture dominated by the institution of sacral kingship, and a common cultic pattern recurring in an annual festival. In reality, the opinions of the different "patternists" differ so greatly that it is difficult to establish, more than what has already been said here, that which is common to them all. Opinions also differ with regard to the concrete manifestations of the cultic pattern and the different elements which it is thought to include. In Hooke's opinion, it contains the following elements: the dramatic representation of the death and resurrection of the god; the recitation or symbolic representation of the creation myth; the ritual sham battle which re-enacted the victory of the god over his enemies, the powers of chaos; a *hieros gamos* (sacred marriage); and a triumphal procession in which the king played the rôle of the resurrected and victorious god.

With some justification, the critics of patternism have objected

---

30. The basic work is S. H. Hooke, editor, *Myth and Ritual* (London: Oxford University Press, 1933); see also S. H. Hooke, *Myth, Ritual and Kingship* (Oxford: Clarendon Press, 1958).

31. E. O. James, *Christian Myth and Ritual* (London: J. Murray, 1933) and *The Old Testament in the Light of Anthropology* (New York: The Macmillan Co., 1935); A. M. Hocart, *Kingship* (London: Oxford University Press, 1927).

that this pattern is an oversimplification and disregards fundamental differences between its different manifestations.[32] But it must be observed that Hocart (according to whom the patternistic model includes considerably more elements) has already clearly maintained—although this fact seems to have escaped the attention of some of his followers—that the pattern is actually an invention, since a complete set of all the parts is not known to occur anywhere.[33] In other words, it ought to be clear that any mystical a priori concept of an original and complete unity is out of the question.[34] However, that certain real and central similarities exist within the various forms of the ancient Near Eastern cultural milieu is an inescapable fact: there are the Egyptian—admittedly distinct, but by no means essentially different from the rest, as Frankfort thinks[35]—the Sumero-Accadian, and the various western Semitic. How these similarities are best to be explained—by contact (*diffusion*), whether of a pre-historical (which, of course, is purely hypothetical) or historical sort (through trade or conquests); by historical inheritance or an original similarity in nature (J. G. Frazer, in *The Golden Bough* [New York: Macmillan, 1910], had already spoken of a "cultural phylogenesis" reflecting an original unity)—is after all an academic and less important question.[36] The essential thing is that the similarities are there. And if one can speak of a "cultural pattern," as even the aggressive anti-patternists Frankfort and Mowinckel do,[37] certainly one can speak of a "cultic pattern." This is true as surely as the cult is an essential part of a certain cultural sphere and provided that, by *pattern,* one intends *that which is characteristic, that which unifies,* but, at the same time, that which

32. H. Frankfort, *The Problem of Similarity in Ancient Near Eastern Religions* (Oxford: Clarendon Press, 1951). H. Birkeland, *The Evildoers in the Book of Psalms* (Oslo: J. Dybwad, 1955), pp. 16–23; cf. the rejoinder by Hooke in *Myth, Ritual and Kingship,* pp. 3 ff.

33. Hocart, *op. cit.* p. 70, with reference to the coronation ceremonies.

34. Of course, one must completely abandon the idea that one and the same "pattern" lies behind all religions.

35. See H. Frankfort, *Kingship and the Gods* (Chicago: University of Chicago Press, 1948), passim.

36. Cf., however, Hooke in his introductory essay in *Myth and Ritual,* where he argues in favor of the diffusion theory.

37. Frankfort uses "pattern" in the sense of social anthropology; cf. R. Benedict, *Patterns of Culture* (New York: Houghton Mifflin Co., 1934). In *He that Cometh* (Oxford: Basil Blackwell, 1959), Mowinckel uses the term only in a polemic sense; in *The Psalms in Israel's Worship* (New York: Abingdon Press, 1962), I, pp. 134, 145, he accepts the theory of a pattern to a certain extent.

differs from other cultural and cultic spheres. Further, it is obvious that the pattern cannot be a postulate: that is, one cannot supply an element which actually is missing, for example, into Israel's religion by a deduction based on analogy with Babylonian-Assyrian, as sometimes is done, as when Yahweh is made a dying god.[38] Also, it is clear from what has been said that the pattern cannot be understood as a doctrinaire model demanding conformity in every detail—this is a caricature of patternism to be found only with its bitterest adversaries.

Finally, it must be emphasized strongly that patternism by no means aims only at finding similarities, an affirmation which one may often hear. On the contrary, patternism is—or, at any rate, should be —analytical: ultimately, it may serve the purpose of finding those things which are characteristic and those things which are different in the various forms within common cultural areas. But in order to attain the desired goal, one must begin by recognizing those things which different cultural areas have in common and which are similar in character. In other words, a correct patternism is *the* correct comparative method. It restricts itself to a distinct cultural area and does not cross all borders of time and space, as is true of the comparativism of J. G. Frazer. It must also be free from a priori evolutionism which runs throughout Frazer's method. It must not use comparative material for "proof" by analogy but primarily for illustration and for offering suggestions for new interpretations, which is quite sufficient. Further, within the particular forms of the undeniably uniform culture of the ancient Near East, the work must be carried on *inductively:* it must begin with the extant historical material. This phase of the problem is particularly delicate when it concerns Israel and the Old Testament, because the material involved is so heterogeneous—or disintegrated, to use the patternistic term.[39] To a very large extent, this disintegration depends on the tendentious selection, the "censorship," and the ideological transformation to which Israel's traditional materials have been subjected in the proc-

---

38. G. Widengren, *Sakrales Königtum im Alten Testament und im Judentum* (Stuttgart: W. Kohlhammer, 1955), pp. 67 ff.

39. When the disintegrated material sometimes comes together again around the "pattern" or one of its details, scholars speak of "re-integration." Cf. Hooke, *Myth and Ritual*, p. 6. For re-integration, see H. Riesenfeld, *Jésus transfiguré* (København: E. Munksgaard, 1947), p. 14.

ess of transmission by the different tradition-bearing circles, such as "the P circle," "the D circle," and different prophetic circles.[40] However, undoubtedly, there is enough similarity to warrant the assertion that the primitive Israelite cultic pattern is, as a matter of fact, of the same type as that of the ancient Near East in general. The extreme to which opponents of patternism can go may be seen, for example, in H. Frankfort's denial of any sacral character in Israelite kingship, which he designates throughout as a chieftainship of the so-called nomadic type,[41] quite contrary to the clear evidence of the texts. Neither is the problem so simple as S. Mowinckel, another of patternism's bitterest adversaries, wishes to make it, although at the same time he strongly acknowledges the ancient Near Eastern *cultural* unity as such. In order to demonstrate how completely different and wholly unique the situation was in Israel, Mowinckel simply refers to the Passover as a primitive cultic fact of a wholly different sort.[42] There can be no doubt that the Israelite Passover is a specific form but, nevertheless, a form of the common ancient Near Eastern annual festival.[43] Finally, it should be emphasized that the cultic pattern has to do with the annual festival in particular, and by no means with the cult in its entirety—a fact which apparently has not always been recognized. Thus, when one uses sound judgment and handles the materials correctly, patternism remains the only correct method. But as always, the person is just as significant as the method, which, taken by itself, does not effect the result.

Soul and spirit; the concept of death. Eschatology and Apocalyptic.—The concepts of the soul in the different cultural milieux with which the science of religion has to deal are often very complicated, and the belief in several different souls in one and the same person is not a rare phenomenon.[44] A "life soul" or "body soul," in particular, often identical with the "breath soul" or with the blood, the heart, or the pulse, usually appears as one of the so-called functional souls. The belief in a heavenly "twin soul," with which the body soul is

40. See chap. 4, "The Pentateuch."
41. Frankfort, *Kingship and the Gods*, pp. 338 f.
42. Mowinckel (quotation not identified).
43. See chap. 8, "The Passover."
44. For questions of principle, see A. Hultkrantz, *Conceptions of the Soul among North American Indians* (Stockholm: Statens etnografiska museum, 1953). For the Old Testament, see, above all, J. Pedersen, *Israel, Its Life and Culture,* I–II (London: Oxford University Press, 1964, reprint), passim.

united after death, is often encountered. To the extent that the dead appear, one speaks of an "image soul" or "ghost soul," which clearly refers more or less to the memory picture that one has of the dead. When this completely disappears, one can speak of a "second death." Another image or manifestation of the soul is the "dream soul," which in the dream frees itself from man, reappears somewhere else or subjectively experiences extraordinary things. Typical of so-called primitive cultures is the collective emphasis which is also expressed in the concept of a "collective soul" in which a person is merged after death, when he "is gathered to his fathers." Several of these ideas are also encountered in a typical way in the Old Testament world.

Closely related to the "soul," and often impossible to distinguish from it, is the "spirit," which in most cases can also be characterized as a "functional soul." Otherwise, the spirit is the special life principle in man; and, in itself, the concept of the spirit seems to have an organic connection with the wind as divine life principle and life bearer, a fact which is especially prominent in Israel, as well as in the New Testament world. In the individual, *nᵉshāmāh*, "the breath of life," corresponds to *rûaḥ*, "wind," "spirit," as movable, energy-filled life-bearer.

Basically, there are two main types of concepts of man, the monistic and the dualistic. The Israelitic concept is typically monistic: soul and body are identified. The Greek concept is just as strongly dualistic: the soul dwells in the body, is imprisoned within it, and struggles for release. Consequently, their soteriologies, or doctrines of salvation, are typically different: the former is characterized by a belief in the bodily resurrection; and the latter, by a belief in the eternal existence of the soul after its release in death.

It is natural that, on the whole, the concept of the soul is always intimately connected with the concepts of death. As a general rule, there are no absolute boundaries between life and death in so-called primitive thought,[45] but in a typical way, the concept is relative. However, this does not mean that death was considered to be natural or inevitable. On the contrary, it was to be avoided by all means, and life retained. However, within some religions, especially those of great antiquity which have a pessimistic stamp, the basic attitude

45. *Primitive*, according to the modern religio-historical view, does not imply any derogatory value-judgment, but simply means *peculiar, influenced, original,* as characteristic of a distinct culture or cultural area.

toward death may have changed completely, and death may be regarded as the highest good, as salvation itself. As to what happens when one dies, it is usually said that the functional soul or the life soul leaves the body, after which the dead exists in a more or less empty or powerless form, in a shadowy form—obviously, a reflection of the surviving memory-picture, the "ghost soul."

The attitude toward the deceased, typically characterized by ambivalence and ambiguity, reflects at one and the same time terror and veneration, fear and devotion. The mourning customs and rituals associated with death in different cultures also express this ambivalence: some are intended to defend the living against dangerous ghosts (formerly overemphasized); others are intended to establish communion after death and so express affection for and solidarity with the dead, as well as the wish that in the future the living might share in the power and blessing of the deceased. From this perspective, mourning rituals could develop into a veritable cult of the dead, which naturally is directed particularly toward great and powerful personalities, such as kings, ancestors, or prophets. Here, the conservatism of the ritual plays a prominent rôle: it is a duty to preserve and fulfil the etiquette handed down in the tradition. Two primary ways of disposing of dead bodies—burial and cremation—are of great typological interest. A third which sometimes occurs is exposure to wild animals. Positive ideas seem to be associated predominantly with burial, which is not the least verified precisely by the occurrence of the ancestor cult in cultures which practice burial in the earth.

Myths which seek to explain how death came into the world occur in widely different cultures, which usually reject so-called natural explanations, including that of old age. These myths include references to a hostile power of one sort or other, to the fault of a beast, to the vengeance of the gods, or to a sin against some divine commandment.[46] There are also typical complexes of ideas and myths dealing with what lies beyond death; that something *does* lie beyond death seems to be a universal or almost unexceptional idea in the religious world. However, in and of themselves, these ideas are

46. This appears among some American Indians and among people in the South Pacific. But these parallels can in no way alter the uniqueness and peculiarity of the Old Testament.

undifferentiated and ambivalent: life after death is both good and evil. Sometimes it is understood as a gloomy and shadowy existence in the realm of the dead, the Sheol of the Old Testament; sometimes, as a happy and advantageous continuing existence in a land where eternal youth prevails; and sometimes, predominantly as a continuation of this life with its rejoicing, work, and gloominess. However, in most religions, there seems to be a clear tendency toward ethical differentiation: life after death is conceived as being directly related to man's conduct in this life. Virtue is rewarded, but vice is punished. Life after death is often painted with great richness of variation and with phantasy, especially in its descriptions of bliss. All the ideas and complexes of belief connected with death and life after death open up a rich field of investigation for the science of religion, including problems such as the "second death"; the transmigration of souls and reincarnation (rebirth); and the theory of apokatastasis, the doctrine of the restoration of all things. In several religions, these ideas have been brought together and worked out into a veritable doctrine of the last things, producing an eschatology both individual and collective in nature. Sometimes, eschatology has developed into apocalypticism (properly *revelation*); that is, speculation about and attempts to predict and describe the coming of the last time and the consummation of the world. Apocalypticism often contains a fixed chronological pattern and a detailed doctrine of the ages, together with a particular redeemer-figure who is sometimes of the so-called Primal Man type. In this connection, the question of possible influences of Iranian and Persian religions on the Old Testament, Judaism, and Christianity is of great importance for biblical research, although it is undoubtedly exaggerated in most cases. The question of Gnosticism, its type and development, and its influence on the biblical world and Christianity, also belongs here.

Religious Ecstasy: Mysticism.[47]—The concepts of soul and spirit are also naturally associated with the concept of the ecstatic phenomenon—a problem which belongs to the psychology of religion, since ecstasy is a state of "intense exaltation of mind and feelings" and has its origin in the psyche as bearer of the emotional elements of man's physiological life.

47. The Swedish discussion of this topic has been dominated by T. Andrae, *Mystikens psykologi* (n.p., 1926), and J. Lindblom, *Prophecy in Ancient Israel* (Oxford: Basil Blackwell, 1962). A later work is E. Arbman, *Ecstasy or Religious*

Ecstatic phenomena occur in most religions, both among primitive peoples and within different high cultures. The view that ecstasy was originally an arctic phenomenon (shamanism) which has been disseminated to various cultures like a contagious disease is erroneous. Also, all theories that certain races have a special ecstatic disposition are erroneous: among other things, it has been asserted that the Semitic race is bereft of an ecstatic disposition. On the other hand, it seems to be a universal fact that ecstasy is predominantly associated with the cult, where it can be induced with the aid of music, song, dance, or asceticism. Ecstasy is a psycho-physical phenomenon, not merely psychic and not merely physical or physiological (for example, a state induced by using poison). As to external behavior, ecstasy can be divided into two types: quietistic and motory. The former is tranquil and introverted in nature, and the latter is accompanied by more or less violent movements. This latter type especially explains why ecstasy is decidedly ambivalent, why it attracts and repels at one and the same time. Its psychological character consists of both a strong intensification of the emotional life and a constriction of the sphere of consciousness, so that the ecstatic centers his attention entirely on a single idea. The psycho-physical state fluctuates between pure hypnotism and a light trance. Thus, from a psychological point of view, the authentic form of ecstasy is *hallucination,* while, from the point of view of faith, it is considered to be divine *revelation.*[48] Often hallucinations are accompanied by specific phenomena, such as sensations of taste, photisms (light phenomena), and levitation (sensations of moving; compare the common so-called ascension). External symbolic actions often accompany the ecstatic experience, and by these it is exhibited as a creating of something real. With regard to internal sensations, ecstasy can also be divided into two types: a visionary or eidetic type, which has to do primarily with the faculty of sight; and an auditory type, which has to do primarily with the faculty of hearing. However, the dividing line between these two types is flexible and, actually, a mixed type is the most common.

The question of the relationship between ecstasy and inspiration

Trance in the Experience of the Ecstatics and from the Psychological Point of View, I–II (Boston: Universitëtforlaget, 1963, 1968).

48. Thus, it should be observed that the former term does not imply any value-judgment, and therefore it should not be considered derogatory by anyone making a faith-judgment.

is much debated. It is impossible to make any clear dividing line on this issue; the distinction that is to be made is not one of character, but of degree. As an intermediate type between these two, some scholars speak of a "sub-ecstatic" phenomenon, the so-called revelatory state. However, this term expresses a value judgment and should be avoided in a descriptive approach. A specific problem presents itself when one is forced to make the difficult decision as to whether a real ecstatic experience or merely a literary form is present in a particular instance. Also, one must be careful not to apply modern standards when evaluating ecstasy: by its very nature and particularly for the primitive man, ecstasy is by no means a morbid phenomenon. On the contrary, it is the natural expression of the experience of the divine rapture and of the powers which it bestows.[49]

Religious ecstasy as such is characterized by the religious commitment of the ecstatic: he relates his experiences to God, to a deity, or to the divine, and justifies his pursuit of ecstasy by its quality of experience. In this capacity, ecstasy plays a particularly prominent rôle in what is usually called mysticism, the goal of which is to attain complete unity with the deity, the *unio mystica*. Depending on whether the religious world view of the mystic is theistic or pantheistic, there are two different types of religious mysticism. The theistic type maintains a certain distance between the human and the divine, while the pantheistic type identifies the two. Both forms are well known from different religious milieux, the latter being represented, for example, by Sufism and by certain Syrian Christian mystics; the former—to the extent that one can speak of mystical piety in the Old Testament at all—represented by Israel's prophets. Further, mysticism as speculation and its connection with Gnosticism is a vast and important field belonging to the science of religion, and it is of utmost importance for biblical research.

Religion as Ethos; Collective and Individual. Matriarchy. Totemism.—A fundamental, inherent aspect of religion as a phenomenon is its ethos, its ethical commitment. Although it belongs to a particular theological branch of science, ethics, the ethos of religion must always be included in a scientific study of religion, because religion is never a purely individual matter, but always implies various community relationships. Consequently, as has already been sug-

49. See, further, chap. 6, "Prophets and Prophetism in the Old Testament."

gested in the introduction, these questions are connected, especially with the subdiscipline, sociology of religion, to which more recent research has given more and more attention. This discipline has developed its own special terminology: for example, it distinguishes between social forms established on the basis of "life fellowship" and those established on the basis of "interest fellowship."[50] It analyzes the relationship between the individual and the group and between the cultic and the more purely social communities. It investigates the social organization of different primitive peoples, of the civilized people of antiquity, and the modern, strongly diversified societies, with interest concentrated, for example, on men's societies, mystery societies, orders, etc.

In this connection, two special phenomena deserve brief mention: matriarchy and totemism. Both are undeniably real phenomena in the world of religion, the former referring to descent traced in the female line; the latter, to a specific organizational connection between a tribe or a clan and a distinct species in the vegetable or—usually—animal kingdom, a connection expressed partly in particular rituals, partly in special exogamic marital precepts. Totemism is indeed a richly variegated and elusive phenomenon, having sociological, magical, and religious dimensions, all at the same time. Here, as elsewhere in religious research, scholars make the fundamental mistake of concluding that these phenomena represent stages of a developmental pattern—well-defined stages through which all religions must pass in their course of development.[51] Scholars who combine the now antiquated doctrine of cultural areas of the Vienna school with the theory of matriarchy can still be found. Also, there are still those who think that they are able to trace historically the ongoing struggle

50. These terms were introduced by A. V. Ström in a Swedish work, *Religion och gemenskap* (Uppsala: n.p., 1946), and could be rendered in German as *Lebensgemeinschaft* and *Interessengemeinschaft*, respectively. The former denotes a group into which the individual is born, while the latter is organized to promote special interests, the individuals joining the group because of choice or invitation. Ström compares his classification with E. S. Bogardus's [*Sociology* (New York: The Macmillan Co., 1934), p. 5] "genetic group" and "congregate group" and R. M. MacIver's "community" and "association" [*Society* (New York: Farrar and Rinehart, Inc., 1937), pp. 8, 11]. In terms of the sociology of religion, J. Wach [*Sociology of Religion* (Chicago: The University of Chicago Press, 1944), p. 57] speaks of "natural groups" and "specifically religious groups."

51. With regard to Semitic religion, this has been maintained particularly by Robertson Smith.

between an original patriarchal pastoral culture and a matriarchal agricultural fertility culture in the ancient Near East and in Israel. However, these theories of matriarchy and totemism which are connected with an evolutionistic approach have completely failed and, in reality, no trace of any such idea occurs in Israel at all. But there is one thing which the more recent religious research has come to emphasize more and more strongly, which is necessitated by the material: the very strong collective quality characteristic not only of the religions of primitive peoples, but also of the ancient Near East. At the same time, it has become clear that the relationship between the group and the individual is not to be interpreted from a narrow, evolutionistic viewpoint: individualism is not a later stage which supersedes an earlier collectivism, but there is an organic connection between the group and the individual, so that the individual functions normally precisely within the framework of the group. These insights are of utmost importance in reconstructing the picture of the religion of both the Old and New Testaments. In addition, the extreme idea of *la mentalité primitive*[52] has been modified considerably. Even if this view in its extreme form contains a rather large amount of truth, still scholars now generally realize that there is no fundamental, qualitative, psychological difference between the primitive and the modern man, with regard to their manner of thinking and of facing reality.

The issues and problems which the science of religion faces are by no means exhausted by the ideas suggested in this essay. Actually, we have been able to discuss only those ideas which have a particular bearing on the biblical world. One final warning seems to be appropriate: the advocate of the science of religion is always faced with great dangers, especially that of exaggerated systematization and oversimplification in the synthesis, particularly with regard to the phenomenology of religion. Moreover, it is very important that one restrain himself from assuming too great a uniformity behind the different religions and an underlying uniform way in which all human beings react religiously. Of course, there is some truth in this view, but it is always necessary to describe every culture or cultural sphere as an entity in its own right on the basis of its own presuppositions. This is especially true of the biblical world, and more and

52. Developed in the French sociological school by Lévy-Bruhl.

more scholars have come to realize the correctness of this claim in biblical research and have attempted to put it into practice. In the Old Testament field, attempts have been made to do justice to Israel's own presuppositions—for example, with regard to the Mosaic religion, in the area of skepticism, etc.—while, in the New Testament field, there is now a growing emphasis on Israelite and Jewish elements, together with a denial of the idea that Hellenism is the solution to all New Testament religio-historical problems. Thus, one's eye should always be open to peculiar characteristics—for every form of religion *has* unique characteristics—and possibilities of variation, to differences in time and place, to inward cultural and outward material conditions. This is not least a mark of true "pattern research."

3

৫৬৩

Old Testament Religion

THE first prerequisite for understanding Old Testament religion is to understand *Canaanite religion* correctly, since the former is so dependent upon it. A detailed description of the Canaanite background falls outside the scope of this essay. Here, we can only point out that this collective title includes a very diversified phenomenon, which, however, can be divided appropriately into two major aspects: the popular and the official. But we must keep in mind that the boundaries between the two are quite flexible. The former consists primarily of a simple bāmāh cult, with its concepts. It bears the same stamp as other forms of so-called primitive religions in similar cultural periods. Perhaps the main reason that genuine Yahwism considered this cult to be foreign was its predominantly orgiastic nature. For this same reason, it became the object of a sharp polemic by the prophets. On the other hand, the religion of the Old Testament received many of its sets of ideas for all future time from the "official" religion, with its center at the great sanctuaries. These include certain essential features of the idea of God, messianism, and the belief

Most of this essay reproduces pp. 109–167 of Engnell's book *Gamla Testamentet* I (Stockholm: Svenska Kyrkans Diakonistyrelses Bokförlag, 1945). As "Gamla Testamentets religion," it appeared in Vol. I of *Svenskt Bibliskt Uppslagsverk*, 2d ed., cols. 762–773.

in the resurrection, to name only the most important. All of these, but particularly the last two, are intimately connected with sacral kingship and its festival calendar with its typical, dominant enthronement festival or New Year festival.

With regard to the idea of God, it is very important to recognize that, in pre-Israelitic Canaan, there was a typical high god figure bearing different names compounded with *'el,* "god." The Mosaic high god, Yahweh, came to be completely united with this Canaanite high god, especially with his most important form, the Jerusalemite *'el 'elyôn,* "God Most High" (or "God in the Highest," short form *'al*).[1] This seemed natural, not only because both gods were phenomenologically of the same type, but also because they had a common origin: they were both forms of the great west Semitic sky god.

The Canaanite cult pattern is completely dominated by sacral kingship, which was taken over in Israel, and especially in Jerusalem, by David. He—and to an even greater extent, Solomon—gave it its final shape in Israel in a syncretism,[2] which, however, unmistakably bore a clear, unique Israelite stamp. Similarly, all the cult forms—the temple and its equipment, the sacrificial system, different types of officials, priestly guilds, orders of singers, as well as cultic prophets—were taken over almost entirely from Canaan, which was superior to Israel in culture and organization. By far the most important festivals of the Canaanite festival calendar were the Annual Festival or "Enthronement Festival" in its double aspect, of which the Passover (Heb. *pesaḥ*) and the Feast of Booths (Heb. *sukkôth*) are the Israelite continuation.[3] As far as we can tell, the same elements which are regarded as characteristic of the ancient Near Eastern cultic pattern occur in the reconstructed pattern of this annual festival: cultic sham fights, the "passion" and "death" of the divine king, his "resurrection" and victory over the power of chaos, his enthronement and sacred marriage and "fixing of destiny"—that is, the "creating" of fruitfulness for the time to come and its necessary prerequisite, rain.

1. For *'al,* see H. Ringgren, *Israelite Religion* (Philadelphia: Fortress Press, 1966), p. 98 (following Nyberg).

2. Cf., G. W. Ahlström, *Aspects of Syncretism in Israelite Religion* (Lund: C. W. K. Gleerup, 1963).

3. In a way, the spring festival and the autumn festival both mark the beginning of something new (a new season); therefore, both have New Year character.

The primary goal of all this was to re-establish cosmos out of chaos, and this is the ultimate goal of every cult.

The second factor of basic importance to a correct understanding of the development of Israel's religion on Canaanite soil—to the extent that one can speak of its uniformity—is that which is usually called the Israelitic or, preferably, the pre-Israelitic nomadic or desert religion. This can include the religion of the so-called patriarchal period. But here we are on very uncertain ground. In fact, we are actually dealing with a reconstructed age because, in most cases, the real information which we possess comes to us, not through the greatly idealized snapshots of the Pentateuch and prophetic writings—however, the prophetic literature also expresses a strong critical attitude— but rather through analogy which is based on similar conditions among Bedouins of later times. Furthermore, our basis for reconstructing this age is rather poor, since, unfortunately, there is relatively little archaeological material which sheds light upon it.

One feature in this imperfect picture is the tribal religion. It has a powerful social stamp, whose religio-ethical consequences are drawn from the law of the vendetta. It also has tribal gods characterized by epithets such as 'ābh, "father," 'āḥ, "brother," who are ancestors of the respective tribes, their *heroes eponymi*.[4]

Still more significant, however, is the occurrence of the figure of the sky god or high god *'el* in the pre-Canaanitic "nomadic strata," where he is known principally by the comprehensive Amoritic name, *'el-Shadday*.[5] We also meet this great high god of the patriarchal period in the Mosaic stratum of immigrants bearing the name *Yahweh* (-'el). According to the tradition in Exod. 3:6, he is identical with the *'el* of the fathers. If we reject this tradition and consider the identification of Yahweh with the God of the fathers to be a late innovation, then we have no way of tracing the crucial continuous line in the earliest history of Israel's religion. Also, contrary to the usually accepted view, it should be emphasized that the cultural and religious

4. Such tribal gods are, according to Engnell, to be found in the names of several of the sons of Jacob: Judah, Zebulon, Dan, Gad, and Asher, who "at the same time denote the tribal god, the tribe, and the territory of the tribe," *Gamla Testamentet* I, p. 123. Cf. T. J. Meek, *Hebrew Origins*, Harper Torchbook (New York: Harper and Row, 1960), pp. 110 f.

5. J. Lewy, "Les textes paléo-assyriens et l'Ancien Testament," *Revue de l'Histoire des Religions*, 110 (1934), pp. 29–65.

conditions of the patriarchal period cannot be regarded as identical with those of a nomadic society.

We should study Moses against this background. The basic elements in the Mosaic religion may be outlined as follows. The *'el* of the fathers, of whom Moses had personal experience, is the great western Semitic high god, whose original home, in all probability, was Sinai or, according to another tradition, Horeb, the location of which has not been determined and apparently never will be. This El is an atmospheric sky god, the giver of fertility, and an ethically differentiated god of judgment. But at the time of Moses, he evidently had acquired something of the character of the type of deity which is usually characterized as the *deus otiosus,* a "resting," inactive god. However, in his personal experience of this god of the fathers who was somewhat remote from men, Moses "activated" him, and in doing so, bound him to an *amphictyony,* a tribal league, and formed a well-organized cult. On this point, there is no reason whatsoever to question the unanimous tradition of the Old Testament. From the time of Moses on, this god is called Yahweh, whether Moses is responsible for the origin of this name or not. Just as he is an ethically differentiated god, so the cult which Moses organized is also ethical in character. This is expressed theologically by the idea of the "covenant" (Heb. *berîth*).

Thus, finally, the creative or transforming personal experience of God is a factor of crucial importance to an understanding of the riddle of the Mosaic religion. We do not solve this riddle by introducing more or less unknown factors, such as the influences of the religions of the Kenites, the Midianites, the southern Arabians, or the Egyptians. This only moves the riddle back a step in time. The Mosaic religion just cannot be explained without assuming the existence of an initial figure of Moses's stature. Therefore, nothing can be more misleading than to regard Moses as merely a mythical creation or a collective name embodying the ideals of priestly speculation.

However, it is obvious that the Midianites actually played a big rôle in the amphictyony established by Moses. But precisely what tribes originally belonged to it is uncertain. No doubt great changes occurred during the periods that followed. And yet, the primitive existence of the tribal league is well established. In Canaan, the cultic community of the amphictyony is extended to a people, the people of Yahweh's own possession, who are bound to him by his election and love which he manifested in the covenant whose requirements the people are obligated to observe. But to say this is not to say that we know these requirements in their primitive form, since we have no possible way of reconstructing it. Originally, they were both cultic and ethical in nature, just as they are in the form in which they have been summarized in the laws of the Pentateuch, the *tôrāh*, even though their literary form is late. But these laws, including the Decalogue, are of a composite character and for the most part reflect conditions in an agricultural society. But in spite of the fact that these materials have thus been Canaanized, it is significant that the entire *tôrāh*, even in its final form, is presented under the authority of Moses.

In recent research, the hotly debated question of whether the Mosaic religion was monotheistic appears in a different light from the earlier view. There is no monotheism, as it was understood in the old schematic doctrine of evolution, but belief in a high god, in a divine figure, characterized by a strong exclusivism. The deeply personal experience of Yahweh makes him a god who can tolerate no other gods beside him. But this does not prevent Yahweh from assimilating *similar* divine forms at a later time. On the contrary, as has already been suggested, the complete identification with the Jerusalemitic high god leaves its mark on the whole succeeding development.

The next stage in the development of Israel's religion is the *period of syncretism*. This period is characterized by the encounter between the Mosaic religion, with its alleged, so-called wilderness character and the religious forms of an agricultural society. On the whole, the result was peaceful assimilation, a fusion of Israelite and Canaanite elements, although now and then, and in different places, this encounter takes the form of violent conflicts. The superior Canaanite culture triumphs in this encounter, both in the material and cultural sphere, and, to some extent, also in the religious and cultic sphere. As to the idea of God, this era is characterized by the transformation of Yahweh into a national deity. In this process, certain typical features of the Canaanite El are transferred to him. Also, he comes to be connected with the great cultic centers of the land, greater emphasis is placed on his original fertility character, and the forms and furnishings of the Canaanite cult are associated with him. Apparently the wilderness perspective vanishes completely.

The argument that Israel took over the Canaanite cult and all its external furnishings, but not the ideas associated with this cult, cannot be successfully defended. This argument implies an abstraction which cannot be assumed in an era when cult and religion were to a great extent synonymous ideas. In opposition to this, it should be pointed out that the usual picture of the Canaanite cultic religion needs to be radically revised. We are not to think of a sensuous and amoral cult which is supplanted by the elevated and pure faith of the Mosaic period. Behind its partly highly orgiastic cult, as is often the case in strongly emotional forms of religion, the Canaanite religion had room for profound and valuable ideas which, after having been sifted through the mind of the Israelite people with its unique religious talent, later came to be the most important concepts which the Old Testament had to give to the New Testament. The two most important of these have already been mentioned: the messianic expectation and the belief in the resurrection. The inferior ideas and practices which were present in the early stages of the fusing process were later eliminated by a series of more or less violent convulsions during the period of the Yahwistic reaction.

The above-mentioned transformation of Yahweh, the god of the Mosaic tribal league, into a national god was carried out in such a way that he was completely fused with the Jerusalemite sky god, who was also a creator-god, a god of judgment, and a god of fate. This deity, whose character was similar to Yahweh's, was known principally by the name *'el 'elyôn*, but he is also called *ṣedheq*, "Righteousness," and *shālēm*, "Peace."[6] However, El Elyon was of a clearly *solar* character,[7] while Yahweh represented the atmospheric high-god type. From the very beginning, this natural fusion was organic and indissoluble, but it received its final form through the brilliant work of David, who combined the pre-Canaanite Israelite traditions with the traditions of the agricultural society in Canaan, so that Yahweh-El Elyon became *the* Israelite God from then on.[8]

This type of fusion also took place with regard to other, similar divine figures, as, for example, with the northern Bethel figure[9] and

6. Cf. H. Ringgren, *Word and Wisdom* (Lund: Ohlssons, 1947), pp. 83 ff.

7. It is not quite clear what is the basis for this statement; the references given by G. Ahlström, *Psalm 89* (Lund: Ohlssons, 1959), p. 95, are inconclusive. Hollis, in *Myth and Ritual*, edited by S. H. Hooke (London: Oxford University Press, 1933), pp. 87 ff., refers to "sun-cult" in the temple at Jerusalem, but does not mention El Elyon. See also Ringgren, *Israelite Religion*, p. 43.

8. Cf. Ahlström, *Aspects of Syncretism in Israelite Religion*, pp. 13 f.

9. Ringgren, *Israelite Religion*, p. 23 with references.

with different Baal figures of the sky-god type. But there was no such fusion with divine figures of an alien type, and cultic forms which were interpreted to be alien to Yahwism were repudiated.

Crucial to the syncretistic development was the adoption of the sacral kingship, with all the functions and concepts which it embraced. Although the traditions on this subject are greatly dispersed and incomplete, still, the Old Testament texts permit us to reconstruct matters well enough to make clear that Israel's kingship was of the same sacral character as that of the surrounding civilized states. Thus, we are able to reconstruct the enthronement ritual in some detail. We encounter the king performing his cultic functions on different occasions, especially in the Annual Festival. We also find that the general ancient Near Eastern royal ideology was applied to him: he is the son of God, Ps. 2:7; as a matter of fact, he is divine, Ps. 45:7. Since the Spirit takes up his abode in him when he is anointed, he is the perfect lawgiver and judge. Everything is dependent on the king, who embodies *within himself* the whole people collectively. He is responsible for victory, prosperity, and well-being, for fertility and rain, and for preserving the cosmos against the repeated attacks of the powers of chaos. He discharges his responsibility first and foremost through his role in the Annual Festival, in which he appears in two aspects. On the one hand, he is Ebed Yahweh, "the suffering servant of the Lord," who by his vicarious "suffering" and "death"—reflected, for example, in the group of "Psalms of the Suffering of the King," Psalms 18, 22, 49, 88, 116, 118—expiates the sin of the whole people, for which the king is considered to be responsible.[10] The ritual on the great Day of Atonement in chapter 16 of Leviticus is a direct reflection and continuation of this royal expiation ceremony. But positively speaking, the king is also the conqueror. In a cultic conflict, which originally seems to have been performed mimically and dramatically, he gains the victory over the powers of chaos, which are represented at one and the same time by mythical powers and actual enemies of all sorts, national and personal, external and internal, all described in magical and demonic categories. This was followed by the culmination of the ritual of the Annual Festival, which consisted of the en-

10. See A. R. Johnson, "The rôle of the King in the Jerusalem cultus," in *The Labyrinth*, edited by S. H. Hooke (New York: The Macmillan Co., 1935), p. 100; Ringgren, *The Messiah in the Old Testament* (Chicago: A. R. Allenson, 1956), pp. 54 ff.

thronement with its attendant processions, hymns, and joyous songs of triumph, as well as the "fixing of destiny."[11]

As the ideas connected with the sacral king developed, there resulted an ideology firmly connected with the king as savior (Heb. *môshîaʿ*)[12] and messiah (Heb. *māshîaḥ*, "anointed"). Due to the fact that the prophets took over and expanded this Old Testament belief in the Messiah, it came to be the most important and unique phase of Old Testament religion. The future expectation, a feature which was inherent from the very beginning, was developed more and more in this process, so that the belief in the Messiah gradually attained a purely eschatological character. Therefore, all attempts to make a sharp distinction between the figure of the cultic Messiah and the purely eschatological figure of the Messiah are extremely hazardous. The unique thing about the Old Testament belief in the Messiah— which is also found in similar forms in surrounding cultures, although nowhere in such a pronounced form[13]—is the extremely dominant rôle it plays in the life of the Israelite people, and its strong national association, its inseparable connection with the Davidic dynasty.

As far as we can tell from the available information, from the historical point of view, the sacral kingship maintained its central position in Israel's life throughout the whole pre-Exilic period. But it became even more important when the prophets took over this messianic ideology. The hope of the kingdom of bliss, the kingdom of God ushered in by the Messiah, runs parallel to the belief in the Messiah in the prophets. Thus, this hope originated as a faith concept within Israel. Gradually, the idea of the kingdom of God became more and more transcendent until, finally, it came to be thought of as a heavenly kingdom of bliss which shall become a reality at the end of the times. But ultimately the idea of suffering, included in the concept of the Messiah from the beginning, becomes the most important idea of all, for it is the figure of the suffering Messiah, manifest in the Ebed Yahweh, "the Servant of the Lord," in "Deutero-Isaiah," which is taken up, perfected by, and, indeed, triumphs in Jesus.[14]

11. See further chap. 7, "New Year Festivals."
12. The term "is used of the Judges, 3:9, 15, Neh. 9:27, of Saul (the verb), 1 Samuel 9:16, cf. 11:3 ff., of David, 2 Samuel 3:18. Originally, it undoubtedly came from the royal ideology; cf. also 2 Kings 13:5, 14:27." Engnell, *s.v.* "*Frälsare*" in *Svenskt Bibliskt Uppslagsverk*, 2d ed. (hereinafter cited as *SBU*[2]).
13. "Messiah" here is simply "the anointed king," not an eschatological figure.
14. See chap. 11, "The Messiah in the Old Testament and Judaism."

When we add to this the inescapable fact that the roots of the belief in the resurrection are also to be sought in the concepts associated with the sacral king, it must be admitted that the importance of syncretism in the period of the monarchy can hardly be exaggerated.

However, opposition to this syncretism is by no means lacking. On the contrary, it is clear that from the very beginning there was a Yahwistic reaction to Canaanization, although at first it was less conscious of itself and of its purposes and was restricted to minority groups among the people. We encounter reflections of this reaction for the first time in the Song of Deborah in chapter 5 of Judges, and in the story of Gideon in Judg. 6:25 f. Such occurrences cannot possibly be later inventions, even if at first they are only episodes which confirm the general rule of peaceful assimilation.

The most important representatives of a developed and radical Yahwistic opposition were the Rechabites. To be sure, they are not mentioned until the time of Jehu, but the roots of this movement are certainly much older. The Rechabites completely repudiated Canaanization in all areas of life. They even went so far as to denounce permanent homes. The "men of God" (Heb. sing. *'ish ha' ^{a}elôhîm*) represent another Yahwistic reaction. They appear unexpectedly, announcing a radical judgment, only to disappear just as quickly, I Sam. 2:27 ff. Yahwistic visionaries, seers (Heb. *hôzîm, rô'îm*), and prophets, or nabis (Heb. *n^{e}bhî'îm*) should also be included here.

In the nabis, we are brought face to face with one of the most difficult problems in Old Testament religion: that of the relationship between the so-called *nebiim* and the literary prophets.[15] We encounter the institution of cultic prophetism everywhere in the ancient Near East. It is represented in pre-Israelite Canaan in the nebiim, with their different prophetic classes and guilds or schools, all of which are connected more or less entirely with the local sanctuaries. Also, in pre-Canaanite nomadic Israel, we must assume a phenomenon which, broadly speaking, is similar. It is from these two branches of cultic prophetism that literary or reactionary prophetism sprang up through individuals who appeared as bearers of criticism and opposition. The most striking example of this is the story of Micaiah, the son of Imlah, in chapter 22 of I Kings. Obviously, little by little, this reaction-movement spreads through the ranks of the nabis. The beginnings of such

15. For a more detailed discussion, see chap. 6, "Prophets and Prophetism in the Old Testament." Here, only a few things will be mentioned.

a development are reflected in Ahijah of Shiloh, I Kgs. 11:29 ff., and in the circles of Elijah and Elisha, even if we admit that the circumstances here are not yet representative. In any case, to some extent, the so-called reforms under kings Asa, Hezekiah, and Josiah must have been motivated by the influence of such strict Yahwistic prophetic circles. Finally, in principle, this line of opposition is also represented by the so-called doom, literary, or reactionary prophets. Without a doubt, these prophets consciously stand on the foundation of the Mosaic religion, and their preaching points back to the ideal state of things that they considered to have prevailed in the wilderness period. Conscious of their individual calls and deeply moved by their own personal religious conscience, they oppose all evil and wrong in their own day in cultural, social, and cultic-religious matters. However, one mistake which is often made is that of overemphasizing their attitude of opposition and their connection with the wilderness line. In reality, this connection is very loose and amounts to nothing more than rather stereotyped phrases and terms which the prophets used. As a matter of fact, the prophets assimilated more from the syncretistic religious process in whose midst they stood than they themselves perceived. This is the case, for example, with regard to the idea of God: the God of the prophets is the Jerusalemite El-Yahweh, the God of the Davidic dynasty and of the official royal cult—of course, as the prophets understood him. In principle, they also accepted the form of the cult which was connected with the Davidic dynasty along the lines of the sacral kingship and the messianic concepts associated with it, which (as has been said) they expanded and deepened. But the fact that the prophets are essentially messianists in no way hinders them from opposing individual kings who, in their opinion, do not fulfil the messianic ideal.

One must have this fundamental positive outlook in mind when he evaluates the anti-cultic statements that occur in some of the prophets, for, upon closer examination, these statements appear to be greatly exaggerated. At the same time, they always seem to be directed against certain forms of cult. First and foremost, they are directed against all popular bāmāh cults. From the Yahwistic point of view, these cults were considered to be foreign in character and were always repudiated. But they are also and primarily directed against all North Israelite cults. For example, this is the case as early as Amos and Hosea. These cults were regarded as the sum and substance of the apostasy from Yahweh, the only true Yahweh, the God of Zion and Jerusalem. The dissolution of the union of North and South Israel was seen from the same perspective, namely, as the apostasy of the northern tribes and as the greatest calamity which had come upon the people (compare Isa. 7:17). Furthermore, the prophets repudiate the substitution of any cult for righteousness; but they do not demand righteousness (Heb. ṣᵉdhāqāh), that is, ethical action, instead of the cult. On the contrary, they demand the cult, the true cult, *and* righteousness. Moreover, the position taken differs from prophet to prophet, and even in the same prophet, from time to time—in most cases, depending on changes in the political and religious situation, not the least of which was a change in the person who occupied the throne. And yet, contrary to the general scholarly opinion, due to the very nature and composition of the prophetic books (collections of traditions), it is impossible to reconstruct the growth of a prophet—except on the basis of dated oracles.

If we take the traditio-historical view seriously, then we must ascribe the same originality to the positive and messianic oracles as we do to the negative. In doing this, we abolish or at least greatly diminish the distinction between "pre-Exilic doom prophecy" and "post-Exilic salvation prophecy" which was maintained by the representatives of the literary-critical school. The main themes of prophetic preaching may be summarized in the following way. Yahweh chose Israel to be his peculiar people when he made his covenant with them. But the people broke this covenant and consequently brought judgment upon themselves. This judgment will be more severe in North Israel. Since the apostasy in North Israel was complete, it called down a greater degree of punishment. However, the announcement of judgment is always conditional. The possibility of conversion through Yahweh's covenant, faithfulness, and love (Heb. ḥesedh) is always open. The prophets believed that some of the people would take advantage of this possibility of conversion: a remnant (Heb. shᵉʾērîth) of righteous ones will be left after the purifying judgment. This remnant idea is a fundamental prophetic concept from the time of Amos on and is expanded particularly by Isaiah and his circle. Little by little, it inclines toward a strong national exclusivism, which is one feature that unites prophetism with later Judaism. Also, the coming messianic future, the messianic kingdom of bliss, is associated with this righteous remnant. Its material foundation is the reunited kingdom of David. It shall be governed in justice and righteousness by the ideal messianic king of the family of David. Although (as has already been suggested) the emphasis gradually shifted toward a much stronger future perspective and although the messianic figure himself came to be of a more transcendental type, still, this later eschatologized form of messianism is based on the earlier form altogether. It emanates from the cult and from the ideology of the sacral kingship, where the aspect of suffering is also an integral part.

Therefore, the dividing lines between the monarchic period, on the one hand, and the Exilic and post-Exilic periods, on the other, are very flexible. But even if the Exile is not such a decisive and creative period of transition as was maintained earlier, still, it is clear that in this period, to a great extent, the emphases are different. However, as far as the idea of God is concerned, the terrible blows which were inflicted upon the people of Yahweh only led to Yahweh's being considered more powerful and exalted than ever, for it was Yahweh and none other who was behind everything that happened. It was he who had used the world power Assyria as the rod of his anger to execute the judgment which he had decreed. But while Yahweh is becoming universal in his sphere of activity, at the same time, essentially, he is becoming attached to his people and their future more than ever. The idea of God is becoming more and more exclusive and, as a result, is also becoming a genuine expression of that which is characteristic in the new understanding. Israel's most important task is to keep alive her national spirit and to preserve her individuality in the midst of a strange and hostile world which threatens to annihilate her. The necessary means for achieving this task were worked out and cultivated in the Exile, where the ancient characteristic Israelite expressions of the soul and life of the people were actualized: circumcision, the Sabbath, and the observance of the Law. Ezekiel, the priest-prophet, is the important initial figure, the first great founder of Judaism.

The strong position which the traditional cult still retains in Ezekiel is typical. It is also significant that the ancient cultic religion blazes up again after the return and experiences a new culmination when the second temple is erected and consecrated in 515 B.C. It is certainly true that, in this new situation, the sacrificial cult is more strongly marked by the one aspect of atonement than before and that, on the whole, the cult changes character more and more. But at the same time, the general tendency is toward emancipation from the substratum of nature religion, and the Jewish religion comes to be dominated by the timeless and transcendental view, which points toward eschatology. Out of this gradually changing cultic form, a new cult emerges which will prove revolutionary for all future time, even for the Christian age. This changed cult is also put into the service of exclusivism as an expression of Israel's absolute individuality and unique position. Its new form is conditioned by the removal from the Holy Land and its center, Yahweh's temple on Zion, which was brought about by the Exile. It is the synagogue, whose most important feature is that it can provide the one thing needful to create the new people of God, the holy people, without elaborate external furnishings. The contribution of Ezra and Nehemiah is of vital importance in this development. They represent the beginning of Pharisaism, since they lay the foundations for a new, pure and "holy" people built upon the law. Here, legalism is triumphant. In scholarly circles, a persevering, detailed study of the law leads to the production of casuistic rules which, at first, were handed down orally and which were brought together gradually in the post-biblical literature of the *Mishna* and the *Talmud*.

As to its type, the earliest Israelite religion was decidedly collectivistic. As in all other ancient cultural milieux, the psychological, religious, and social views were completely dominated by the whole: the family, the tribe, the people, the cultic community. However, this does not mean that there is no room for individual difference and experience within the framework of the community. Certainly there was room for an individual, personal experience in the ancient cultic religion which was centered in the group. But ancient times knew nothing of the antithesis between individualism and collectivism. Earlier works on the history of religion in the Old Testament field lay great stress on the so-called emergence of individualism. Of course, it was inevitable that the point of view would gradually become different from that which it had been at an earlier time. But the issue does not concern two different world-views which changed places at a certain period in history. Actually, collectivism is not impaired when the individual becomes prominent in a way that he had never been before. The first real signs of the beginning of a new era appear in Jeremiah and Ezekiel. In a later period, a certain individualistic breakthrough takes place along the legalistic line just mentioned. This happens in conjunction with the legalistic piety, with its emphasis on works-righteousness, as well as in conjunction with the rôle of conversion as a creative factor in the personality. However, it is typical that, as a more purely individual, personal view emerges, it is closely associated with a dogma which has made such an indelible impression on Judaism: the dogma of retribution, with its provisory and cursory solution to the problem of suffering.

Here, we encounter another basic religious concept of the Old Testament. From very early times, after this problem had come to the forefront, the elementary idea that punishment follows crime is dominant and that, consequently, suffering is the punishment of crime, while prosperity is the reward for good conduct in the presence of Yahweh. Thus, the only possible solution to the problem of the prosperity of those who are guilty of flagrant injustices is that, in spite of the way things look, sooner or later, the wicked will be punished and, conversely, that, sooner or later, the righteous sufferer will receive his reward. This view is reflected, to a large extent, in the Psalms and in the Book of Job. It is noteworthy that, in spite of the widespread acceptance which the dogma of retribution enjoyed, it took such a long time for the comfortable solution which is implied in the eternal, heavenly perspective to be combined with it in any serious way. But there is still a third solution to this problem, and it is the most profound. As a matter of fact, it is the only tenable solution. And it can be traced to a very early period in the history of Old Testament religion. It is the idea of voluntary, vicarious suffering and is a contribution of the ancient royal ideology. Throughout the ancient Near East, the very heart of the thought-world of sacral kingship is the idea that the king expiates the sin of the entire people through his symbolic suffering and "death." As is indicated by the group of so-called Royal Passion Psalms mentioned above, this concept was also of utmost importance in Israel. The ideological consequences of this concept were further developed in the Ebed Yahweh figure in "Deutero-Isaiah." These were handed down in certain Jewish circles and reached their final form in Jesus, through whom messianism won its final great victory.

The phenomenon which we have chosen to call Old Testament religion is highly diversified—so highly diversified, in fact, that really we ought to speak of Old Testament religions. It contains widely differing types, such as remnants of the old Canaanite popular religion, the nomadic religion of Israel, sacral kingship, genuine Yahwism, and legalism, extending over a period of nearly two thousand years. But from among its many components, something must be said about Israelite skepticism as it appears in the Wisdom Literature, and especially in Ecclesiastes. Like so many other phenomena in Old Testament religion, it was ascribed by earlier research to foreign influence—in this case, Hellenistic. However, more recent research has called attention to the extent to which the historical situation affected the Israelites' own presuppositions. The starting point of the development process, as is often the case, is to be found in the idea of God. It is Yahweh's omnipotence that has come to be emphasized so strongly that he assumes the character of a powerful despot, much like Islam's Allah. This is more than a mere coincidence. It is the original ambiguous nature of Yahweh, the sky god and god of fate, which is coming to light here, once again. And such an idea of God is necessarily accompanied by a more or less pronounced skepticism, which, however, has specific Israelite features.

4

❦

The Pentateuch

THE Pentateuch is the oldest part of the Old Testament canon. Most scholars think that it was definitely considered to be canonical shortly after the time of Ezra and, in Palestinian Judaism, perhaps much earlier. Traditionally, the Pentateuch occupied a unique position in all Judaism as the basis for Jewish beliefs and customs. However, we cannot be sure whether the so-called Lawbook of Ezra is identical with the Pentateuch in its present form. According to Jewish tradition, in an indirect way, Ezra is considered to be the author of the whole canonical Old Testament. In 557 B.C., within a forty-day period, he is said to have dictated by inspiration the contents of all the Scriptures which had been lost as a result of the Babylonian Captivity (II Esdras 14).

The Pentateuch is commonly called the Books of Moses, because ancient tradition says that these books were written by Moses. But it should be carefully noted that these books themselves nowhere claim that Moses is their author, not even as regards individual sections, allegations to the contrary notwithstanding. To be sure, Moses is said to have been commissioned to write down certain divine words (compare Exod. 17:14; 24:4; 34:27 f.; Numb. 33:2), but these can-

As "Moseböckerna," this essay was published in *Svenskt Bibliskt Uppslagsverk,* 2d ed., Vol. II, cols. 152–165.

not be identified with actual portions of the Pentateuch (yet, Deut. 31:9, 24 may well be different). Furthermore, the assertion that the "Chronicler" considered Moses to be the author of the Pentateuch (on the basis of II Chron. 23:18) is very dubious. But Philo and Josephus make it clear that Jewish tradition regarded the Mosaic authorship of the Pentateuch as an established fact. Earliest Christianity (as well as Jesus himself: compare Mark 12:26) and the Church Fathers shared this belief. The most serious objection to this simple and naive view was—and to a certain extent, still is—the fact that chapter 34 of Deuteronomy relates Moses' death. If Moses wrote this chapter, we must assume that he foresaw his death and described the circumstances surrounding it while he was still alive! But as a matter of fact, internal evidence shows conclusively that the Pentateuch, both in general and in details, is written with a Canaanite orientation in time and space, which in some cases is very late. This being the case, the Mosaic authorship is completely out of the question. But at the same time, the theory that one man wrote Genesis-Numbers and Deuteronomy-II Kings, respectively, cannot be dismissed quite so easily, in spite of the fact that there are many arguments against this theory.

In the days of the primitive church, certain objections were already being raised against the homogeneity of the Pentateuch and its Mosaic authorship. But these objections did not grow out of a scientific, critical spirit, but out of a purely religious one. It was not until the emergence of humanism—especially the philosophies of Hobbes and Spinoza—that the "human" aspect of the Old Testament came to be emphasized. Then, scholars had to deal with the problem of the historical origin and authorship of the books of the Old Testament and of the history of its canon and text. The Pentateuch, in particular, aroused the interest of critics because of the special problems which it presented. Very early, scholars began to notice that it contained numerous doublets, discrepancies in linguistic usages and religious ideas, contradictions and anachronisms. Jean Astruc (d. 1766) detected a seemingly constant alternation of divine names in the Pentateuch. As time went on, his alternation idea was extended to include other words and phrases. Once these phenomena had been noticed, they gave rise to a number of so-called source hypotheses which were intended to explain their existence. Finally, a climax was reached in Julius Wellhausen's four-document hypothesis. According to this theory, generally speaking, the Pentateuch is a compilation of four different written sources: "J(ahwist)," "E(lohist)," "D(euteronomy)," and "P(riestly Code)," each with its own peculiar characteristics. "J" (which, after a time, scholars generally divided into "J¹" and "J²") uses the divine name J(Y)ahweh and is of Judean origin. It is the oldest of the written sources, dating from about 900 B.C., as may be deduced from its national self-consciousness and its more primitive anthropomorphic ideas. "E" (whose existence as an independent document has been contested in recent literary-critical research) uses the divine name Elohim, "God," and is of North Israelite origin. It dates from about 800 B.C. or, at least, from the period before 722 B.C., when Samaria and the northern kingdom fell. "E" exhibits a modified anthropomorphic view and represents a higher theological stage characterized by a certain prophetic influence. Later, "J" and "E" were combined by a "redactor" designated as "R^JE" and "Yehowist." Chronologically and theologically, this redactor is closer to "D." In the first place, "D" embraces Deuteronomy. It has a more religious tone than "J" and "E." It originated from prophetically influenced priestly circles in Jerusalem, and the primary concern of its theological programme is the requirement of the centralization of the cult in Jerusalem. Whether we use "D" to designate the whole book of Deuteronomy or, as is more often done, the "original Deuteronomy," that is, chapters 12–26 of Deuteronomy, it is usually considered to be identical with King Josiah's Law Book, which, according to chapter 22 of II Kings, was found in the Jerusalem temple and which he made the basis of his reform. During the Exile, a new "redaction" was made, combining "JE" and "D": "R^D" is its usual designation. In addition to combining these sources, the redactor of this material, "who lives in the atmosphere of D," has "taken the liberty to make major and minor changes" (Bertholet)[1] in "JE," especially in Exodus and Numbers. "P," for the most part, is to be found in Leviticus and Numbers, but also in numerous interpolations in Genesis and Exodus. It originates in a clearly priestly circle, and its interest is centered primarily on ritual laws, matters of worship. "P" uses the divine name El Shaddai, but also Elohim. It assumes that the centralization of the cult has already been completed. This is the main reason that it is considered to

---

1. A. Bertholet, "Mosebücher" in *Die Religion in Geschichte und Gegenwart*, 2. Aufl., IV, col. 243.

be the youngest of the written sources. But "P" is not homogeneous. It consists of two different strata: one called "P^G," that is, "the basic document (*Grundschrift*) of P," and the other "P^H," the so-called Holiness Code, Lev. 17:1–26:46. But both of these strata alike are characterized by "a cold, dry, learned and often pedantic tone, a legal and systematic construction and a formulaic type of schematization."[2] The fictitious creation of the author's mind which is called the tabernacle is one illustration of the obvious cultical emphasis in "P." It represents a retrojection of the Jerusalem temple into the Wilderness Period. Many scholars date "P" in 445 B.C., identifying it with the law of Ezra and Nehemiah, which was promulgated in that year. Finally, another redactor, "R^P," combined JED with "P," thus creating the present Pentateuch. In all probability, this compilation was made about 400 B.C.—in any case, before the Samaritan schism, because the Samaritans adopted the entire Pentateuch as their Scripture.

In reality, the development of the literary-critical approach in the period following Wellhausen's classical formulation, briefly outlined above, amounts to a complete dissolution of the entire system by the very scholars who defend it. Various factors have brought chaos to the systematic (but thoroughly unrealistic and anachronistic) reconstruction of the Wellhausenian school.

It is not necessary for a person to have a very profound understanding of the similarities between the various cultures of the ancient Near East to be able to see that the whole literary-critical system is based upon a complete misunderstanding of the actual situation. It reflects a modern, anachronistic *book view,* and attempts to interpret ancient biblical literature in modern categories, an *interpretatio europaeica moderna.* A modified or moderate literary-critical approach is not sufficient to evaluate this problem properly. What is needed is a radical departure from this whole system.[3] No parallel, continuous, written sources of the Pentateuch like those which literary critics presuppose have ever existed. The fact that some of the material in the Pentateuch may have been in a fixed written form from the first, or in a very early stage, is a different thing altogether. But it is even more important to appreciate better the function, extensiveness, and significance of the oral tradition stage. It is only when we assume

2. *Ibid.*
3. See chap. 1, "The Traditio-Historical Method in Old Testament Research."

that much of the material now in the Pentateuch was handed down orally at an early stage that we can explain the problem of variants in the Pentateuch, because such variants are particularly typical of literature which has been transmitted orally. In the oral stage, the material comes together according to what may be called the epic law of iteration,[4] and is arranged according to the principle of association. Obviously, obscurities and discrepancies are to be expected at the cultural and linguistic level of the Old Testament. But, in reality, they are greatly exaggerated because, in innumerable instances, our western desk logic fails to appreciate the Semitic way of thinking.[5] Too often, our judgments are based on an inadequate understanding of Hebrew mentality or, even worse, on an inadequate knowledge of the Hebrew language, especially its syntax.[6] The elementary rules of Hebrew are often disregarded by western scholars. Now that scholars think they have discovered the universal tool of source division and textual emendations, it looks almost as if they no longer consider a knowledge of the language to be necessary. And yet, this is the alpha and the omega of exegetical research.

But the only really relevant evidence in favor of the existence of continuous documents in the Pentateuch would be that each writer maintains his own unique style throughout. Spokesmen for the literary-historical approach assert that such is actually the case both the-

4. This seems to imply that what is usually regarded as doublets is, in reality, the result of stylistic repetition characteristic of oral transmission. Cf. A. Olrik, "Epische Gesetze der Volksdichtung," *Zeitschrift für deutsches Altertum,* 51 (1909), pp. 1–12 esp. pp. 3 f. For later works on oral literature, see R. C. Culley, *Oral Formulaic Language in the Biblical Psalms* (Toronto: University of Toronto Press, 1967)

5. In *Gamla Testamentet* I (Stockholm: Svenska Kyrkans Diakonistyrelses Bokförlag, 1945), pp. 192 f., Engnell himself exemplifies this statement by referring to the contradiction between Gen. 18:11 and 25:11. The contradiction exists only if Abraham is taken to be an individual and disappears when the primitive oscillation between individual and group is understood; in the first passage, Abraham is an individual; in the latter, he represents a collective group. In addition, as an ancestor, Abraham is described in the categories of the royal ideology.

6. For instance, there is no source division between Gen. 14:17 and 14:18; the alternation of verbal clause and composite nominal clause shows that the two verses belong together, which is also confirmed by the use of the same verb (*yāṣā'*) in both verses. Another example is in Gen. 27:23 ff., where the contradiction disappears if *wayᵉbhārᵉkhêhū* in v. 23 is correctly translated: "he was about to bless him" (but then he asked [once more] . . .). *Gamla Testamentet* I, pp. 268 ff.

ologically and linguistically. They call the recurring words and expressions in this material "isoglosses" (word constants), and the evidence for written sources based on the occurrence of these words and expressions, "the isogloss argument." However, refutations of the purely linguistic isogloss argument have been made several times, most recently by the Danish scholar P. V. Rubow.[7] If it is to have any validity whatsoever, the words and expressions which are given to support it must really be mutually exclusive. They *must not* occur in more than one document. A closer examination readily shows that such is not the case. What usually happens is that a critic begins his work with presuppositions as to what a given source ought to say and rejects or emends the text so that the result is unambiguous. The whole procedure turns out to be an argument in a circle, and consequently carries no weight. Of the many linguistic constants or isoglosses, the most important for the theory of written sources is still the occurrence of different divine names. This particular linguistic isogloss is on the verge of being theological.

Several things indicate that the isogloss argument is not valid. In the different supposed documents, the Hebrew manuscripts differ among themselves, and the Greek LXX differs from the Hebrew text. As a matter of fact, the LXX shows clearly that the alternation of divine names in the Hebrew text to a large degree is due to a later attempt at unification, that the alternation is not original.[8] Just as serious, if not more so, is the fact that the different documents are not consistent in their use of the divine names. And yet this is alleged to be the mark of their uniqueness! The fact that in such cases zealous advocates of the documentary hypothesis change the divine name in order to achieve complete consistency is the best argument against the soundness of this theory. Such manipulation does not make the dream come true. To some extent, there is actually a certain constant alternation of divine names, but a closer examination shows that this is not due to an alternation of documents, but to an intentional stylistic use by those who handed down the tradition. This alternation is intimately connected with the idea that different divine names have different ideological overtones and, consequently, different effects.

7. Cf. *Dansk teologisk tidsskrift*, 3 (1940), pp. 101 ff. Rubow's field is history of literature.

8. Cf. J. Dahse, *Textkritische materialen zur Hexateuchfrage* (Giessen: A. Töpelmann, 1912). This was pointed out by Dahse as early as 1903.

Thus, the name *Yahweh* is used in contexts which distinguish Israel's national god from foreign gods, relate the history of the ancestors, etc., while the name *Elohim*, "God," expresses a more theological, abstract, cosmic idea of God, and therefore is used in a broader, more comprehensive way.[9] Consequently, it is the very ones who handed down the tradition that are responsible for the alternation of divine names, and not the documents. And as far as the theological constants are concerned, it can be stated quite simply that they do not support the written source theory any more than the obscurities, differences, and discrepancies do. For example, the national self-consciousness which is supposed to be characteristic of "J," in particular, is just as characteristic of the Pentateuch as a whole and, in fact, of the entire Old Testament. And if it is argued that cruder anthropomorphism indicates an earlier date, we must object (as some scholars, among them, Pedersen, already have) that, if this is a valid criterion for determining the age of respective sources, then the Talmud is older than any book in the Old Testament. In reality, these criteria are based on nothing but an a priori, evolutionistic concept, which is inseparable from the documentary hypothesis and dictates to it. As we shall see below, the real theological differences which undoubtedly exist in the Pentateuch emanate from different theological perspectives reflected in two great historical works, which were completely different, from the beginning. A typical literary-critical approach may be seen in the treatment of "P." It is alleged that, generally speaking, this document is not concerned with ethical laws, but with ritual laws alone. So, when a large block of ethical laws appears in "P," critics argue that originally it must have been a separate document, the "Holiness Code." But it should be obvious that this conclusion is based on an a priori idea of the fundamental character of "P." It should be pointed out, further, that to the extent that we are justified in speaking of "P" as a reality (lying behind the present Pentateuch), the "P" material is, for the most part, very old, so that it is impossible to date "P" as the latest document.[10]

9. Generally speaking, F. Baumgärtel, *Elohim ausserhalb des Pentateuch* (Leipzig: J. C. Hinrichs, 1914), and U. Cassuto, *La questione della Genesi* (Firenze: F. Le Monnier, 1934), *The Documentary Hypothesis and the Composition of the Pentateuch* (Jerusalem: Magnes Press, 1961), i. a., established this point quite satisfactorily. In reality, this explanation was offered by the Rabbis as early as the second century A.D.

10. Cf. the similar argument of Y. Kaufmann, *The Religion of Israel* (London: George Allen and Unwin, 1961), passim.

This leads us into a discussion of the major criterion used to determine the chronological relationship of the different sources to each other. It consists of evaluating the extent to which a certain source emphasizes the centralization of the cult in Jerusalem. According to the usual view, which is inseparably connected with the category of time and of strait-laced evolutionism, the absence of any demand for centralization in "JE" is proof of the early date of these sources. "D" strongly emphasizes this demand and so is later than "JE." "P" rests on the assumption that the centralization of the cult has already been accomplished, making it the latest document. But the presence or absence of the demand for centralization is not a valid criterion for dating the respective documents. It proves nothing more than the existence of different interests and points of view, and these very easily can be simultaneous. After having determined the chronological relationship of the different sources to each other, scholars attempt to determine an absolute date for each of the documents. The starting-point and basis for this endeavor is the interpretation of "D" and its identification with Josiah's Law Book. If this identity is accepted, the narrative in II Kgs. 22 f. implies that "D" is to be dated in the year 622 B.C., the usually accepted year of the so-called reform of Josiah. It is true that the identification of "D" with Josiah's Law Book has become more and more disputed, even among the advocates of literary-criticism; but the majority of them still regard this as axiomatic. But the description in II Kings actually excludes the possibility that "D"—that is, Deuteronomy as a whole, or certain parts of it—can be identified with Josiah's Law Book. First of all, according to the words of Huldah the prophetess, II Kgs. 22:16, 19 f., the law book which was found in the temple had a general prophetic character, but this by no means can be said of Deuteronomy. In the second place, this law book must have contained oracles of doom against Jerusalem, its inhabitants, and its king ("this place and this people"). To be sure, some scholars try to find these oracles of doom in chapter 28 of Deuteronomy,[11] but this proves to be impossible when we analyze the context in which this chapter occurs. The section, Deut. 27:1–30:20, which deals with the ritual on Ebal and Gerizim, is a purely North Israelite tradition complex and is, in fact, in flagrant conflict with the programme of centralizing the cult in Deuteronomy. It does not con-

11. So recently, A. F. Puukko, *Teologinen Aikakauskirja* (Helsinki: n.p., 1947), and H. H. Rowley, *Men of God* (London: Thomas Nelson and Sons, 1963).

tain a single word about Jerusalem or its inhabitants. On the whole, the pronounced North Israelite provenance of Deuteronomy makes it hardly likely that it would have been found in the Jerusalem temple and, if it had, that it would have been made the basis for a reform in Judah. Third, on the basis of the measures which Josiah took in his reform, we must also assume that the law book which was found contained detailed cultic commandments, especially concerning the Passover.[12] The attempt to find these commandments in the short paragraph in Deut. 16:1–17 is hardly convincing. These arguments show that Deuteronomy cannot be identified with Josiah's Law Book. But if this is true, then the only real external criterion for determining the relative dates of the different sources, on which the absolute chronology is based, disappears. In other words, we are forced to restrict ourselves to internal criteria, and it must be admitted that, with regard to dating, in particular, such criteria are very difficult to evaluate.

With this in mind, we can now turn to the positive solution to the literary problem of the Pentateuch. We believe that the correct approach is traditio-historical, which must be supplemented by both form-critical and ideological and religio-historical insights. The realization that the vast and multifarious traditional material of the Pentateuch belongs to two different collections which originally existed independently of each other is very basic to this approach. The first of these collections includes Genesis-Numbers.[13] In an attempt to maintain a certain connection with the terminology of literary-criticism, it can be called the "P work," not because it is to be thought of as a document "P," but because it received its final form, and consequently its ideological tendency, in a traditionist circle which (with certain modifications) presents many of the features which literary-criticism attributed to the "document P" or "R^P." Another term often applied to this material is the Tetrateuch, the "four scrolls."[14] Originally, the "P circle" and the "P work" had no connection—at least, no direct material connection—with the other great collection, the Deu-

---

12. See chap. 8, "The Passover."

13. A similar view is represented by M. Noth, *Überlieferungsgeschichtliche Studien* I (Halle: M. Niemeyer, 1942), a work that was not known to Engnell when he first presented his thesis in *Gamla Testamentet* I, p. 210, note 3.

14. Both of these designations have now been adopted by a group of Scandinavian and international scholars.

teronomic history, which includes Deuteronomy-II Kings. An entirely different traditionist circle is responsible for the final form of this second collection. It can be called the "D circle." Like the "P circle," it also left its very clear, distinctive mark on the traditional material which it handed down.[15] "P," in the new sense of a traditionist circle— or, possibly, although less probably, of one bearer of tradition—is responsible for handing down to posterity the "P work" or the Tetrateuch. This circle is also responsible for a portion of the unique tradition material which, so to speak, is its own contribution, since this circle handed it down from antiquity and combined it with a large amount of other material handed down in both oral and written form. If a method resembling the documentary hypothesis is to be carried out and can be carried out in the Tetrateuch with any hope of success, it would mean that this special "P" material is separated from the "non-P" material. Without a doubt, literary criticism's "P(riestly Code)" to a rather large extent corresponds to this material, although often the classification is by no means as clear and reliable as was previously thought. The "P" material cannot be determined, verse by verse. But unlike "P," "J" and "E" can no longer be distinguished, even as strata within the tradition. Undoubtedly, such strata originally existed in the Tetrateuchal material. But in the stage of oral transmission, they were fused to such an extent that it is now impossible to distinguish between them. Instead, we must look at the Tetrateuch in its present form from an entirely different point of view: we must concern ourselves with the present organization of the material and with form-critical matters. We will have more to say about this below. There can be no doubt that the "P circle" in its final form is to be located in Jerusalem. But its roots appear to extend to Hebron and Kadesh-barnea. Therefore, it represents a southern tradition. The "P circle" is not a priori critical toward the kingship in general or toward the Davidic dynasty in particular. One of its distinguishing marks is its pronounced antiquarian interest, which is il-

15. This matter might be expressed in the following way for those who prefer to believe in written sources: "J," "E," and "P" do not extend beyond Numbers, while "D" or "R^D" is not found in Genesis–Numbers. In reality, very recent literary-critical research has tended toward this view, as is demonstrated by M.-J. Lagrange in *Revue Biblique*, 9 (1912), pp. 621 ff.; A. Bentzen, *Introduction to the Old Testament*, seventh edition, II (Copenhagen: G. E. C. Gad, 1967), p. 71; and Noth, *Überlieferungsgeschichtliche Studien.*

lustrated by the very ancient oral "history-telling" which it preserved in the form of genealogies. Another is its strong cultic and religious interests: the sacral institutions and the temple always stand in the center. But in spite of this, it is hard to believe that this circle was thoroughly priestly. Instead, it has something of the official character of the royal custodian of antiquities about it.[16] The attitude toward the inherited traditional material is conservative and positive. This material is transmitted faithfully and with little revision. For the most part, its bias is generally visible only in the actual selection of the tradition units from the enormous amount of available material. But the attitude of this circle is also expressed in its own material, and it is highly didactic and biased: the history of Israel is the history of the chosen people, particularly of its forefathers; of the glorious future of this people as the ultimate goal of God's providential guidance; and of the right way for this people to serve its God by being faithful to the everlasting covenant with him and by keeping its commandments as they were given in the law—not the least of which are the cultic and ritual commandments. At the very center of this material is the Feast of Passover (the first event and all subsequent Passovers), and at its center stands Moses. He is described in royal categories throughout.[17] But we nowhere encounter the centralization of the cult in Jerusalem, which according to literary-criticism is obviously assumed in "P." Actually, "P" seems to have no interest in centralization of the cult. This is one of the many arguments for the great antiquity of this material. Others include the genealogies, the many archaisms (which, to be sure, are not necessarily artificial), and precepts related to the festival calendar. The tabernacle tradition undoubtedly goes back to the pre-Jerusalemite period, although in many particulars it has been colored by Jerusalemite concepts. Much of the legal material in the "P work" is also of great antiquity and is solidly anchored in a concrete, actual life situation. But there is a large amount of material mixed in with this which has an exclusive Yahwistic character and

16. However, this does not mean that this circle must have been particularly favorably disposed toward the royal house.

17. Royal birth legend; he is Yahweh's *shaliach*, "the sent one"; he is king, priest, and prophet; he is "the Servant of Yahweh" (Exod. 14:31; Numb. 12:7; Deut. 34:5); he is filled with the Spirit (Numb. 27:18 f.; Deut. 34:9), works miracles, and provides life through the brazen serpent (Numb. 21:4 ff.); he promulgates law; he intercedes for the people, and his staff is the tree of life.

reflects a clear anti-Canaanite tendency. Here we are brought face to face with the extremely difficult question of the time of the "P circle's" activity. In spite of the fact that some of the tradition material in "P" is very old, in its present form, this corpus must be dated comparatively late, in the Exilic or post-Exilic period, in all probability in the time of Ezra and Nehemiah. In other words, as we shall see below, the "P work" in its final form is almost contemporary with the Deuteronomic work.

There can be no doubt that the core of the "D work" is the legal material in Deut. 4:44–30:20. Here, old and new stand side by side: statutes based on very ancient case laws alternate with laws which were constructed along purely abstract, ideological lines, reflecting an arrogant anti-Canaanite attitude. This material emanates, no doubt, from widely differing localities, and part of it is clearly of North Israelite origin. To a much greater extent, the same is true of the narrative material of the "D work." Nevertheless, in its final form, the totality is completely dominated by an intense Jerusalemite tendency: on the whole, Jerusalem is the only legitimate cult center, its temple the only one authorized, and its god the only true God. In order to give the legal material the greatest possible authority, the whole is ascribed to Moses. Deuteronomy has the form of an anticipatory speech by Moses, and therefore Jerusalem is not mentioned by name, but is called "the place which Yahweh chooses," Deut. 12:5. For the same reason, Israel is pictured in idealistic terms, further heightening the abstract character of Deuteronomy. In a typical way, Deuteronomy is arranged so that narrative and legal material alternate. Its style is highly parenetic, didactic, and moralistic, and the material is preferably presented in the form of speeches delivered by Moses. The Deuteronomic work includes the Books of Joshua, Judges, Samuel, and Kings, as well as Deuteronomy. Therefore, the theological tendency of these books and their way of dealing with their widely different material must also be taken into consideration when we wish to determine the character of the "D circle." In Judges, the didactic revision of the "D circle" is quite typical. It belongs to the so-called Deuteronomic framework, in which history is interpreted according to an apostasy-punishment-conversion-deliverance pattern. In Samuel, there are typical "D" traditions and passages, clearly "written" by the "D circle" itself, especially in chapters 8–12, where the anti-kingly and pro-clerical attitude of the circle is apparent. David remains the only ideal king—and even this is not always the case:[18] for when the early traditions put the great king in a much less favorable light, these traditions seem to be quoted with a certain malicious joy. However, David is the standard by which the other kings are judged and, according to this standard, they are condemned. All the North Israelite kings and all but a couple of the Judean kings are apostates and syncretists. Thus, the Deuteronomic circle sees the history of the people as the history of its apostate kings. Therefore, there can be but one result: the destruction of Jerusalem and the downfall of the kingdom of Judah, chapter 25 of II Kings. In this passage, toward the end of the "D work," we see as plainly as anyone could desire that the "Deuteronomist" or "D circle" represents a real writer or school of writers. But this does not mean that he is not faithful to the ancient transmission principle or that, on the whole, he does not use the traditional material with great reverence, particularly in the portions which have to do with early periods. In its pragmatic schematization, the theological viewpoint of the "D circle" is clearly related to that of the reactionary prophets. Undoubtedly, the "D circle's" outlook and view of life is directly—or, more probably, indirectly—dependent on that of these prophets, in spite of the fact that there are no references whatsoever to the prophetic writings in "D." To a great extent, this is explained, among other things, by the fact that the prophetic oracles were transmitted orally. However, we cannot characterize the "D circle" as especially prophetic in its actual so-called life situation. The Deuteronomist's negative, idealistic understanding of the king as a humble disciple of the priests far exceeds that of the reactionary prophets, who ultimately reflect a positive understanding of the king.[19] In reality, it is more correct to characterize the "D circle" as priestly than the "P circle." The reference to Jehoiachin's release by Evil-Merodach in II Kgs. 25:27 ff. indicates clearly that the date of the "D work" is after 562–561 B.C. And when we take into consideration all the details involved, as well as the general outlook and character of the work, we come down to a time contemporary with the "P work," or a little later.

No doubt, very soon afterward, these two works were combined

18. Cf. R. A. Carlson, *David, the Chosen King* (Stockholm: Almqvist and Wiksell, 1964).

19. See chap. 6, "Prophets and Prophetism in the Old Testament" and chap. 11, "The Messiah in the Old Testament and Judaism."

into one, in such a way that the beginning of the "D work" was built into the "P work." This was facilitated by the fact that "D" purported to be a great speech of Moses delivered before his death. The hypothesis that the "P work" originally gave an account of the death of Moses but that the original position of this tradition was at the end of Numbers, and that, when "D" and "P" were combined, it was given its present position in chapter 34 of Deuteronomy, is probably correct. But we are not able to say exactly when or by whom this combination of the "P work" and "D work" took place. It is conceivable that this was done by the "Deuteronomist" himself. And in spite of the fact that, in reality, no trace of a Deuteronomic revision is found in the "P work," this possibility seems to be both the most natural and the most probable. But when "D" and "P" were combined, the "D work" was divided up into its present individual books, and its original unity was lost.

In the traditio-historical solution to the Pentateuchal problem which we have suggested above, *form-critical* insights, as well as ideological and religio-historical considerations, have played an important rôle throughout. Here, we need to make some additional comments concerning form-criticism. In a form-critical examination, the material from which the two great tradition collections, the "P work" and the "D work," are composed, are seen to consist of the most varied types or categories. These include a few elements of poetical material—hymns in Exod. 15:1–21 and Deut. 32:1–43, songs of victory in Numb. 21:27 f., words of blessing and curse which correspond most closely to the prophetic-oracle type in Gen. 49:1–27 and Deut. 33:1–29, and the oracles of Balaam in chapter 23 f. of Numbers. For the rest, the prose material is predominant. Here also several different categories are found represented: speeches and documents, myths, different types of sagas and legends, etc. However, primarily, the material in the two works is divided into two main types: legal literature and narrative literature. The distinction between these two literary types is the starting-point and primary condition for a correct evaluation of the position and problem of the Pentateuch.

With regard to the "P work," narrative material is overwhelmingly predominant in Genesis. Genesis holds a unique position in the composition of the Tetrateuch, in that it serves as an introduction to the essential central complex, chapters 1–15 of Exodus. In this introduction, the emphasis shifts from the cosmic aspect in the myths of the creation, the fall, and the flood to the more specific aspects of the choice of the fathers and the history of the Patriarchs, with whom Yahweh made his covenant and through whom the blessing came to the chosen people. The Joseph narrative forms the immediate transition to what follows. It brings us to Egypt, the stage for the beginning of Israelite history in a strict sense, with Moses and the deliverance from Egypt, and beyond this to a universal evolution destined to culminate in Israel. Thus, by its very nature, the description is both theological and religious and pragmatic. Another type of material occurs in Exodus-Numbers: it is cultic, and is combined with the legends of the wilderness wanderings and interspersed with legal collections. It has the sealing of the covenant at Sinai as its wholly dominant central complex, Exodus, chapters 1–15. This complex must be characterized as the primitive Passover legend,[20] the ritual text of the Passover.[21] However, in saying this, we do not refer to its primitive ritual form, but to its disintegrated or secondary form, which was "deculticized" and historicized. It is not possible, by means of the traditio-historical or form-critical methods, or even less by means of the literary-critical method, to get behind the present form and to reconstruct some sort of primitive form, any more than it is possible to reconstruct in detail the historical events lying behind it. But even though this is true, it should be pointed out that this cultic, formal evaluation of the tradition complex in chapters 1–15 of Exodus in no way excludes the possibility of actual events lying behind this material. The attempt of literary criticism to divide the Sinai complex into a cycle of Kadesh legends (Exodus, chapters 17–18; Numbers, chapters 10–14) and a cycle of Sinai legends (Exodus, chapters 19–24, 32–34), making the former cycle primary (as held by Wellhausen, Gressmann, and Mowinckel), has completely failed. Later, the entire historical, narrative traditional material, with Genesis as its beginning and the narratives of the wilderness wanderings in Exod. 15:22 ff. as its sequel, was arranged around the cultic complex nucleus in chapters 1–15 of Exodus. Also, it is clear that the form of the wandering legends indicates that they may have had an original cultic connection, although in their

20. "Legend" here is to be understood in the sense of "reading," and is not to be interpreted as a value-judgment denying the reality of an event.
21. J. Pedersen, "Passahfest und Passahlegende," *Zeitschrift für die alttestamentliche Wissenschaft,* 52 (1934), pp. 161–175, and *Israel, Its Life and Culture,* III–IV (London: Oxford University Press, 1964).

present form they have become literature in an entirely different way. After the legal material in Exod. 20:23–23:33, the "Book of the Covenant," and further laws and particular traditions, in chapters 10–11 of Numbers, the narrative material is resumed once again, but it is interspersed with further legal material and particular traditions.

Form-criticism deals with the material in the "D work" in a way similar to that in which it deals with the material in the "P work." It divides "D" into several different types, especially into the two main groups already mentioned: narrative material and legal material. In Deuteronomy, the legal material dominates, to a great extent. As scholars have thought for a long time, the legal material in Deut. 4:44–30:20 is actually the core of "D." However, "D" also contains narrative material, which alternates with the legal material. In fact, it is prominent in Deut. 1:1–4:43, Moses' introductory and recapitulating speech. Furthermore, parenetic, didactic passages characteristic of the "Deuteronomist" are interspersed throughout the legal material. Finally, Deuteronomy ends with a narrative speech of Moses, 31:1 ff., where this thread is resumed. In the rest of the "D work," the narrative material dominates completely. From the form-critical point of view, it is to be observed especially that the "Deuteronomist," particularly in Kings, also made use of documentary material, the form of which had already been fixed in writing: royal annals, chronicles, etc.

Something also needs to be said about the way in which the material in the two collections was handed down, although we admit that this is a very complicated problem and cannot be dealt with adequately here. However, the following main points may be mentioned. First of all, it should be observed that the two possible ways of handing down the material, by oral or written transmission, should not be understood as antitheses which mutually exclude one another. On the contrary, they should be thought of as running parallel and as complementing each other.[22] Second, it should be emphasized that the process of writing down the material does not imply the creation of something absolutely new, but only a writing down of those things that had already attained a permanent form in the tradition units, tradition complexes, and tradition collections in the oral stage. While some prominent traditionist circles which stand behind the different types of literature in the Old Testament handed down the material

22. See chap. 1, "The Traditio-Historical Method in Old Testament Research."

exclusively either in oral or in written form, most circles handed it down in both forms, side by side. Third, it should be emphasized that the oral transmission of a sacral literature of such a unique sort as the Old Testament does not occasion greater risks of corruption than does the written. Just the reverse is true, in many cases. Still, the concept of oral transmission does imply a certain living transformation. In harmony with what has already been pointed out, we must realize that the material which the "P" and "D" circles had at their disposal had been handed down in different ways in many different types by different kinds of traditionist circles before it was taken over and fixed in its final form by the "P" and "D" circles. Priestly circles or scribes who were associated with the temple and other sanctuaries, who primarily are responsible for the legal material, and the story tellers, who are responsible for the Patriarchal narratives and the stories of the Judges, are the most important groups in this earlier stage of transmission. In this stage, by and large, the material in the Pentateuch may probably best be attributed to oral or written transmission as follows. Predominantly, we may assume that the narrative material of the "P work" in Genesis (the Patriarchal narratives), and in Exodus-Numbers (the traditions concerning Moses and the legends of the wilderness wanderings, as well as particular traditions, such as the golden calf in Exodus, chapter 32, Korah's rebellion in Numbers, chapter 16, and Zelophehad's daughters in Numbers, chapter 27), was transmitted orally. And although it may seem surprising, it is also very probable that the genealogies of the "P work" are to be attributed to oral transmission (Genesis, chapters 5, 10, etc.). On the other hand, the legal material must have been written down early.[23] Of course, this is especially true of the material which is obviously secondary and was never applied in real life, but came into being more or less entirely in connection with the final revision of the whole work. In a similar manner, for the most part, the narrative material in the "D work" was originally handed down orally. This is especially true of that which is North Israelite in origin: chapters 27–30, 33 of Deuteronomy. The speech of Moses in Deut. 1:1–4:43 is an exception, because it comes directly from the Deuteronomic circle itself. On the

---

23. This is not to deny that oral transmission took place side by side with the written transmission. After all, in their daily work, various priestly groups had to know and be able to apply the *tôrāh,* the law, in both cultic and legal situations.

other hand, a large part of the legal material in the central section, Deut. 4:44–30:20, was originally written down.[24] The rest of the "D work" was also transmitted in both oral and written form. The greatest part of this material was transmitted orally. This includes the narrative material in Joshua, especially the so-called Book of the Conquest in chapters 1–11; the narrative material in Judges, especially the North Israelite traditions of the Judges, in chapters 4–5, 10–12, 13–16; and most of Samuel, with the exception of such archival material as that found in II Sam. 3:2–5; 8, and the fictitious "Succession History" in II Samuel, chapters 9–20; I Kings, chapters 1–2. In Kings, the alternation of oral and written transmission is even more obvious. The legendary cycles of Elijah (I Kings, chapter 17–II Kings, chapter 1) and Elisha (II Kings, chapters 2–13) belong to the material which was handed down orally, and annals (some of which are cultic, and some of which are official-profane) belong to the material which was handed down in written form. The "P" and "D" circles were faced with a complicated task in editing the highly diversified source material available to them. The extent to which they were faithful to the Israelite tradition is amazing. And they accomplished this task in such a splendid way that they produced two of the foremost masterpieces of world literature, if not the very foremost. However, it should be pointed out that these two works represent only a limited selection from the large amount of material at their disposal.

24. We say this with the same reservations which were mentioned above with regard to the "P work."

5

⚜

The Book of Psalms

Name and Place in Canon; the Number and Division of the Psalms.—
The Hebrew name for the Book of Psalms is *t⁽ᵉ⁾hillîm*, which means
"Songs of Praise." As far as the content of this book is concerned, therefore, to some extent, this name is misleading; but, at the same time, it
does indicate the cultic mooring of the Psalms. The name "Psalter"
comes from the Greek *psaltērion*, a translation of the Hebrew *nēbhel*,
and the name of a stringed instrument often used in the cult. In the
Greek Septuagint (apart from the Codex Alexandrinus, which has
psaltērion), the usual name for the book is *biblos psalmōn*, "the book
of psalms" (compare Lk. 20:42). The Greek *psalmos*, which, through
Latin, has become our "psalm," is a literal rendering of the Hebrew
mizmôr, from the verb *zāmar*, which (like the Greek *psallein*) properly
means "to pluck with the fingertips" on a stringed instrument. In a
more general sense, both *mizmôr* and *psalmos* mean "song, psalm."
The term *mizmôr* occurs no less than fifty-seven times in the titles of
the Book of Psalms. In conjunction with the old tradition that David
was the author of the Book of Psalms, which is found in Maccabees
and the Latin Vulgate, in modern terminology, we often speak of the
"Psalter of David" or the "Psalms of David."

This essay appears in *Svenskt Bibliskt Uppslagsverk*, 2d ed., Vol. II, cols.
618–656, under the title "Psaltaren."

The Book of Psalms belongs to the third main division of the Hebrew canon, the k^{e}thûbhîm, the "Writings" (the Hagiographa), where, almost without exception, it stands as the first book. In the Alexandrian canon, it belongs to the major division called the "Poetic Books," and again it is usually the first book. But in most modern translations, the Book of Job precedes the Book of Psalms.

Many things indicate that the canonization of the Book of Psalms did not take place extremely late. One of these is the fact that the differences between the form and content of the Book of Psalms and the so-called Psalms of Solomon are so pronounced. It seems clear that the latter are deliberately modeled after the former. The same may be said with regard to the psalms which were recently discovered at Qumran, which belong to the cultic community there and probably date from the second or first century B.C.[1] It is generally assumed that the Book of Psalms was first canonized about the year 100 B.C.; but, to a great extent, this is based on the assumption that it contains several psalms from the Maccabean period, which, in reality, is by no means the case. On the contrary, I Chron. 16:36 quotes the doxology which stands at the end of the so-called Fourth Book in the Book of Psalms. The obvious conclusion that we must draw from this is that the Book of Psalms was known to the "Chronicler." But the Chronicler's work can hardly be dated later than 300 B.C. Therefore, the Book of Psalms must have been in existence at that time. But many scholars try to escape this conclusion by arguing that I Chron. 16:36 is a later interpolation. Yet, the arguments which are advanced to support this are not convincing. About 200 B.C., the Apocryphal Book of Ben Sira mentions the existence of a collection of the Psalms of David (Ecclus. 47:8 ff.). But, actually, we have no right to assume that this collection is identical with the present Book of Psalms or, for that matter, with any part of it. At the same time, the fact that there are post-Exilic psalms[2] in the Book of Psalms does not give us any more right to exclude the possibility that this book was canonized about 300 B.C. or earlier. As a matter of fact, this question must remain open. But this much is certain: the criteria based on the contents of the psalms themselves, which are advanced to prove that the Book of Psalms was not canonized until about 100 B.C., are not valid.

1. This statement may now have to be modified in the light of the discovery of the psalms scroll from Qumran.
2. Psalm 137 is the only psalm which is unquestionably post-Exilic.

In reality, we make a mistake if we think of the problem of canonization in a mechanical way, as if only written material could be considered canonical, although most scholars think of it in this way. Instead, we must realize that the tradition was living and growing. Those psalms which originated at the temple in Jerusalem, or were associated with it as ritual texts in the pre-Exilic period, must have been the first to gain canonical status. In the Exilic and post-Exilic period, a new collection and rearrangement of this psalm treasure was made in connection with the second temple and the organization of its cult. But we must also realize that, during and after this period, some psalms may have been associated with the synagogue, which had come into existence during the Exile as a complement to the temple cult and its worship. And, of course, after the temple cult came to an end, the synagogue was the only *Sitz im Leben,* "situation in life," of the psalms. Then, after the psalms had gradually gained a certain degree of canonicity by virtue of their connection with the cult, the final canonization of the Book of Psalms in its present form probably took place about 300 B.C., or perhaps even earlier. There can be no doubt that the leitmotiv and norm governing this formation of the canon is to be sought in the use of these psalms in the cult. But as has already been stated, here we must think not only of the temple cult, but also, to some extent, of the synagogue worship. However, the distinction between the two should not be exaggerated. On the other hand, we are not to think that the Book of Psalms is a "religious book" created for pious lay circles, although many scholars still try to defend this position. The arrangement of the material contained in the Book of Psalms, to some extent, appears to have followed the same principles as those which governed the arrangement, for example, of the prophetic literature: the so-called alternating pattern and the technique of association. However, it should be observed that most hymns are at the end of the Psalter, while the laments are in the first half of it.

According to the Massoretic text, the Book of Psalms contains 150 psalms; according to the Greek LXX, 151. In the LXX, Psalms 9 and 10, as well as 114 and 115, each constitute one psalm, while, conversely, Psalms 116 and 147 are each divided into two. Thus, the *Textus Massoreticus* and the LXX do not fully agree in their numbering of the psalms. In its present form, the Hebrew Book of Psalms is divided into five books, constituting, respectively, Psalms 1–41, 42–72,

73–89, 90–106, and 107–150, each ending with a doxology (praise), namely, Pss. 41:14; 72:18–19; 89:53; 106:48; and 150:6, or possibly the entire 150th Psalm. However, according to the general opinion, which is certainly correct, this five-fold division is secondary and late. It originated as an attempt to imitate the division of the so-called Pentateuch (Genesis–Deuteronomy) into five books.[3]

But this five-fold division is artificial. Actually, it is obvious that different collections of psalms lie behind the present Book of Psalms. This is usually considered to be apparent from the fact that there are duplicates in the Book of Psalms: for example, Psalms 14 and 53, 40:14–18 and 108. However, there is another explanation for this phenomenon: that such material is drawn from a large body of cultic-literary material which had been used in more than one connection. Another argument which supports the idea that different collections lie behind the present Book of Psalms is the statement made in the subscription at the end of Psalm 72 (v. 20): "The end of the Psalms of David, the son of Jesse." This statement clearly points to the existence of a separate collection of the "Psalms of David," which at one time ended with Psalm 72. The occurrence of "Psalms of David" in the Book of Psalms after Psalm 72 is another matter. Nor is this "Davidic collection" identical with the present collection in Psalms 1–72, because undoubtedly smaller collections of psalms lie behind this collection. The titles which mention authors, such as "Asaph" and the "sons of Korah," which can be interpreted only as an indication of collections that were transmitted by or emanated from groups of priests or singers which had these names, also favor the notion that different collections lie behind the present Book of Psalms. This is further supported by the collection of "The Songs of Ascents" in Psalms 120–134, by the so-called Hallel Psalms (Psalms 111 ff.), and by the doxologies at the end of Psalms 41 and 72.

The predominant (although by no means exclusive) use of the divine name *ʾᵉlōhîm*, "God," in Psalms 42–83[4] has led many scholars to assume that this is a separate collection, the so-called Elohim Psalter, in which the recurrence of the divine name *ʾᵉlōhîm*, is due to an attempt on the part of a "redactor" to make this material uni-

3. Cf. now A. Arens, *Die Psalmen in Gottesdienst des alten Bundes* (Trier: Paulinus–Verlag, 1961).
4. In Psalms 42–83, *ʾᵉlōhîm* occurs 200 times, and Yahweh 43 times. Cf. Psalms 1–41, where Yahweh cccurs 272 times, and *ʾᵉlōhîm* 15 times.

form. However, this assumption is not very likely. For one thing, this alleged Elohim Psalter is obviously composed of smaller collections; for example, it includes the group of Davidic Psalms which originally ended with Psalm 72 (as the statement in Ps. 72:20 shows), as well as the Psalms of Korah and the Psalms of Asaph. For another thing, the predominant occurrence of Elohim as the divine name is not necessarily due to a later attempt by a redactor to make this material uniform. It can just as easily be original, for it may reflect the first home and "situation in life" of these psalms.

Often, the growth of the present Book of Psalms is outlined in approximately the following way: The starting-point was a collection of "Psalms of David" which included Psalms 3–41. Later, another collection of "Psalms of David," including Psalms 51–72 (with some exceptions), a group of Asaph Psalms, and a group of Korah Psalms, were added. Still later, a redactor compiled a separate "Elohim Psalter" out of these four collections by changing original "Yahweh Psalms" into "Elohim Psalms." In time, this collection was enlarged by adding Psalms 84–89. Finally, a collection of "Songs of Ascents" was added. However, it should be observed that all such attempts to reconstruct this course of development, even in broad outline, can only be hypothetical. The available objective evidence permits only the general statement that the present Book of Psalms grew up by the gradual combination of smaller collections of psalms which originated in different milieux and are of different types. Furthermore, we must not forget that the present Book of Psalms by no means exhausts the entire Israelite store, but only represents a few psalms selected out of this store. Although these psalms reflect different points of view, they were collected in the same book primarily because they had already attained canonical status as a result of being recited in the cult at the temple in Jerusalem, irrespective of their original "situation in life." Of course, there are also psalms outside the Book of Psalms—in Judges, chapter 5 (the Song of Deborah); Exod. 15:1–18 ("The Exodus Hymn"); I Sam. 2:1–10 (Hannah's Song of Praise); II Samuel, chapter 22 (a variation of Psalm 18); Isa. 38:10–20 (The Psalm of Hezekiah); Jonah 2:3–9. All of these undoubtedly originated in the cult.

History of Tradition. Textual Criticism.—The idea that the Book of Psalms is a collection of songs or poems of the type called "spiritual songs," which were written down immediately by their authors, is still the dominant view. But this understanding, whether it be applied to the psalms or to other types of Old Testament literature—narrative, prophetic, legal, sapiential—must be greatly revised in light of the traditio-historical point of view. The traditio-historical method *must* deal not only with questions concerning oral and written transmission and fixation and literary forms, but also with problems such as the "situation in life" of the psalms and of the Book of Psalms and the origin and use of the psalms. In order to solve these problems, we must use all available criteria and disciplines, including contents, language, history of ideas, and comparison with extrabiblical materials. Therefore, to a certain extent, a traditio-historical evaluation, based on a variety of criteria, must anticipate the interpretation of the text. Its basic principle has to be the assumption that the psalms have a cultic *Sitz im Leben*. Both the comparison with extrabiblical literary and religious phenomena and the results which have already been attained by applying the traditio-historical method show that this approach is the only adequate one.[5] This is especially true with regard to the *Sitz im Leben* of the psalms, which are essentially cultic poetry. For the most part, they originated within official priestly or prophetic classes[6] at different sanctuaries in the land of Canaan, particularly at the temple in Jerusalem. The psalms which did not emanate directly from the Jerusalem temple were taken over in the cult there and—perhaps after censorship and revision—gained a respectable standing and were canonized.

In their capacity as cultic poetry, the psalms occupy a unique position, as far as the transmission of their text is concerned, because it is possible that they were fixed in writing at a very early stage, perhaps from the very beginning. It may be assumed that their original form, *Vorlage*, was preserved as a normative ritual and sacral text in order to guarantee the correctness of the textual tradition. On the other hand, the use of the psalms as cultic songs was based on oral tradition. They were known by heart and no doubt were memorized very meticulously, for the recitation of central cultic texts is always regarded as a very important complement to the sacred acts and so has to be carried out absolutely free from discrepancy in every detail. This is because it was felt that the preservation of the whole na-

---

5. See chap. 1, "The Traditio-Historical Method in Old Testament Research."
6. The distinctions between these two official classes are quite flexible.

tion and ultimately of the cosmos itself depended on the perfect execution of the cultic rites. The traditionist circles associated with the Book of Psalms are identical with the guilds of singers and groups of temple prophets mentioned above. Several passages in Chronicles (I Chron. 6:39; 9:16; 15:17 ff.; 25:1 ff.; II Chron. 5:12 ff.) connect them with the names Asaph, Jeduthun, Ethan, and Korah. The same passages make these groups contemporary with David, while in the post-Exilic period they have merged with the Levites. Whether this tradition is correct or not in every detail, there can be no doubt that it reflects the true historical situation. Allowing for differences in time, place, and *Sitz im Leben*, we may also use the circumstances surrounding the transmission of the Mishnah, which belongs to a later period, in order to gain a better understanding of the transmission of the text of the Old Testament. Written records of the Mishnah were used for private reading as an aid to the memory. But in teaching, it was required that this material be delivered orally, and therefore it had to be memorized perfectly. Actually, the way in which the Mishnah was transmitted in the Jewish period must be regarded as more important to a correct understanding of the transmission of the Old Testament text than comparisons of the Old Testament with ancient Near Eastern sources.[7]

The material from Ras Shamra occupies a unique position within the comparative material which we may legitimately use to help us solve the problem of the transmission of the Old Testament text. In some circles (especially Widengren),[8] this literature has been used to justify *ex analogia* far-reaching conclusions supporting the theory of written transmission at the expense of the oral, including even the Israelite psalm material. However, it is obvious that Ugarit-Ras Shamra occupied a particularly unique position in ancient Canaan-Syria because of the invention and use of its consonantal alphabet. The great Ugaritic cultic mythological texts were fixed in writing sometime between 1500 B.C. and 1400 B.C. As a matter of fact, they are exercises used in scribal schools. But actually they are centuries

7. This passage was added in the second edition of *SBU* as an answer to criticism and seems to be based on B. Gerhardsson, *Memory and Manuscript* (Uppsala: C. W. K. Gleerup, 1961).

8. G. Widengren, "Oral Tradition and Written Literature in the Light of Arabic Evidence, with special regard to Prose Narratives," *Acta Orientalia,* 23 (1959), pp. 214, 222.

older, and in this earlier period they must have been transmitted orally. Furthermore, it is not correct to speak of "cultic lyrical poetry from Ras Shamra" as though this material were comparable with the psalms in the Old Testament. For, in spite of all the linguistic, literary, ideological, and religious similarities between the two, the differences between Ugaritic and Israelite literature are striking—as a matter of fact, more striking than the similarities. There are no real psalm texts in the Ras Shamra material; nevertheless, hymns and songs, psalms for special occasions, and ritual psalms were used in the temple at Ugarit as certainly as they were used in Israel. Thus, the absence of written psalm texts forces us to conclude that this material was transmitted orally and not in written form. And so, when all the alternatives have been examined,[9] it must be admitted that the Ras Shamra material supports the thesis that oral transmission played an important role in Israel.[10] By way of summary, we may say that the psalms offer a typical example of how written and oral transmission went hand in hand and complemented each other. This may be said in spite of the fact that oral transmission was dominant for a long time.[11]

A survey of the actual condition and form of the text of the psalms and of the methods which the Massoretes used in interpreting and transmitting these texts (for example, by reinterpreting the headings), should also make it clear that the oral transmission of the original tradition in the cult was broken rather significantly in one way or another. Of course, this should not be exaggerated. Still, to a certain extent, we must assume that the psalms were "deculticized," or, rather, that they were "re-applied" to a different kind of cult. In other words, they originally belonged to the cult at the Jerusalem temple, and were later transferred to the synagogue worship. It is now generally thought that the psalms in the Book of Psalms were revised for the purpose of making them edifying literature. Some scholars think that this may be explained by assuming that the final redaction of the Book of Psalms as a body of literature was partly accomplished in scribal circles, and

9. Of course, this statement is made with great reservation, because at any time new texts may be discovered which would cast things in an entirely different light.

10. I.e., to the extent that comparative material can ever be considered valuable as circumstantial evidence.

11. A closer investigation shows that it is erroneous to think that oral transmission was ever completely or exclusively dominant.

not in priestly circles connected with the cult. However, this point of view should not be overemphasized, partly because it clearly rests on the assumption that the Book of Psalms contains several so-called Wisdom Psalms, which is by no means true. The peculiar contribution of the Massoretes was undoubtedly of greater importance in this process of revision. The prophets also probably played some rôle in this reinterpretation, although only indirectly, since no prophetic revision or prophetic influences can be traced in the Book of Psalms. But since they took over the literary forms of the psalms and, in general, drew from the traditional cultic language,[12] their interpretation of the psalms may have influenced later interpretations, because to a great extent they must have given the traditional forms a new meaning and used them in new connections. In any case, it is evident that the tradition, as it was in its original cultic situation, was more or less completely lost. Therefore, the fact that only implications, indirect references, or allusions of a cultic type occur in the psalms is not as significant as one might think, for comparative material—for example, from Sumer and Akkad—contains the same kind of phenomena; but we cannot doubt for a moment that we are dealing with ritual texts here. It is significant that, in the Book of Psalms, the Massoretes had no living cultic tradition on which to depend. They were often perplexed by the traditional consonantal text, and sometimes were completely unable to determine its meaning. As a result, they were clearly guilty of wrong word divisions. The Rabbinic tradition in the Mishnah is also very uncertain about the cultic *Sitz im Leben* of the psalms and confuses old and new, correct and incorrect statements. Actually, the modern exegete stands at a better vantage point, primarily because of the rich comparative material which he has at his disposal.

However, everything indicates that the tradition of the consonantal text itself is stable and, on the whole, unbroken. Because of this, and because of the nature of the Massoretes' work in interpreting the psalms, we must have a higher respect than ever for the *kᵉthîbh*, the consonantal text. At the same time, we must look upon the *qᵉrê'*—the reading of the Massoretes indicated by the vowel points—as less conclusive and less valuable than it is in other books. The fact that the old translations, especially the Peshitta and the Septuagint, in most cases leave us completely in the lurch in text-critical work emphasizes the

---

12. Cf. chap. 6, "Prophets and Prophetism in the Old Testament."

importance of depending on the tradition of the Hebrew consonantal text even more.

This indicates that text-critical work in the Book of Psalms demands greater care and discretion than anywhere else. Emendations or textual corrections must be kept at an absolute minimum. This is especially true of emendations *metri causa*—those supported by rhythmical or metrical arguments—which were so characteristic of the previous scholarly generation and are still in vogue. Hebrew metrics or prosody is so irregular and inconsistent that we are not justified in making it the basis for text-critical work. On the other hand, philological interpretation plays a much more important role in textual criticism. In fact, it is completely decisive in this area. Admittedly, it presents serious difficulties. But it also presents exceptional possibilities, especially when it is combined with a study of comparative religions and ideas. In addition to this, the so-called *parallelismus membrorum* (the mutual correspondence of the different parts into which the Hebrew stich is always divided) is very important in determining the correct text. In the areas of textual criticism and philology, the Book of Psalms presents greater difficulties than perhaps any other book in the Old Testament. But it also opens up perspectives of great importance to our general understanding of Old Testament and Israelite culture, religion, and manner of life.

The Headings of the Psalms. The Technical Terms.—The partially insoluble problem presented by different statements and technical terms in the headings of the psalms is an excellent example of the degree of difficulty encountered in psalm research. These headings may be divided into two different groups: headings or parts of headings which are obviously secondary, and headings or parts of headings which are—or, in any case, may be—primary. The latter may be further divided into several types: genuine statements concerning authorship, terms which indicate the cultic situation or the literary-cultic category, and musical terms.

The group composed of headings which are obviously secondary consists principally of historical interpretations obviously extrapolated from the contents and words of the respective psalms: for example, the statement in Ps. 3:1, "When he (David) fled from Absalom, his son," belongs here. It is based on an association of Psalm 3 with II Samuel, chapter 15 ff., especially Ps. 3:6 f. with II Sam. 17:22. Of course, this statement also assumes that the original "situation in life" of Psalm

3 was historical and that David was the author of this psalm. A similar point of view lies behind Ps. 7:1, "which he (David) sang to the Lord concerning Cush a Benjaminite." This represents a later attempt to make a historical connection between this Psalm and I Kgs. 2:36 ff.[13] Ps. 18:1, "(David), who addressed the words of this song to the Lord on the day when the Lord delivered him from the hand of all his enemies, and from the hand of Saul," may be explained in a similar way. The later attempt to give this psalm a historical background is based on the assumption that David wrote this psalm, that the psalms are to be interpreted against a historical background, and probably also on a superficial association of *shā'ûl*, "Saul," in the heading and *she'ôl*, "Sheol," in v. 6. The historical background in Ps. 34:1, "when he (David) feigned madness [literally, "changed his taste"] before Abimelech, so that he drove him out, and he went away," is also due to a superficial connection of the word *ta'am*, "taste, understanding," in the heading with *ta'am*, "to taste," in v. 9. The historical background in Ps. 51:1 is also the result of a later association, especially of Ps. 51:6 and II Sam. 12:1 ff., the Bathsheba story. These and analogous cases are without exception only scribal comments or midrashim, which are based on an erroneous conception of the real "situation in life" of the psalms.

However, there are many terms that occur in the headings of the psalms which are not scribal comments at all. They must be discussed individually. The headings pertaining to authorship are a good place to begin. We provide a list of these here in order to get an over-all view:

1. Psalms 1–2 have no such headings.

2. In Psalms 3–41, all the headings have *le dhāwidh* ("of David") except Psalm 10, which is considered to be a direct continuation of Psalm 9, and Psalm 33, which is either a continuation of Psalm 32 or perhaps a later addition to it. In addition to this, Psalm 39 has the heading *lîdhûthûn* ("to Jeduthun"). Cf. Psalms 62 and 77: *'al ye dhûthûn* (also rendered "to Jeduthun" in English translation).

3. Psalms 42–49 have the heading *libhnê qōrah*, "of the sons of Korah," except 43, which is either a continuation of Psalm 42 or perhaps a later addition to it.

---

13. Cf. especially Ps. 7:17 and I Kgs. 2:44. It seems that, later, Shimei, the son of Gera, was confused with Shimei, the son of Kish, in Esth. 2:5. Psalm 7 is used in the ritual of the Purim Festival.

4. Psalm 50 has the heading *l'āsāph*, "of Asaph."

5. In Psalms 51–71, all the headings have *l'dhāwidh* except 66–67 and 71, which undoubtedly is a direct continuation of Psalm 70.

6. Psalm 72 has the heading *lishlōmōh*, "of Solomon."

7. Psalms 73–83 have, without exception, the heading *l'āsāph*.

8. Psalms 84–85 and 87–88 have the heading *libhnê qōrah*. In addition, Psalm 88 also has *l'hêmān*, "of Heman."

9. Psalm 86 has *l'dhāwidh*.

10. Psalm 89 has *l''êthān*, "of Ethan."

11. Psalm 90 has *l'mōsheh*, "of Moses."

12. Psalms 91–100, 102, 104–107, 111–121 have no headings pertaining to authorship.

13. Psalms 101, 103, 108–110, 122, 124, 131, 133 have *l'dhāwidh*.

14. Psalms 123, 125–126, 128–130, 132, 134–137 have no headings pertaining to authorship.

15. Psalms 138–145 have *l'dhāwidh*.

16. Psalms 146–150 have no headings pertaining to authorship.

17. In addition to this, the heading *lamnaṣṣēaḥ*, "to the choirmaster," stands over Psalms 4–6, 8–9, 11–14, 18–22, 31, 36, 39–40, all of which also have *l'dhāwidh*; 42, 44–47, 49, all of which also have *libhnê qōrah*; 51–62, 64–65 (also *l'dhāwidh*); 66–67, 68–70 (also *l'dhāwidh*); 75–77, 80–81 (also *l'āsāph*); 84–85, 88 (also *libhnê qōrah*); 109, 139–140 (also *l'dhāwidh*).

In the twelve psalms which are ascribed to Asaph—Psalms 50 and 73–83—the Hebrew *l'* of the heading would certainly seem to have been intended (or, in any case, *may* have been intended) from the very beginning to provide real information concerning authorship. In this case, *l'* means "of," even though its real meaning may be "belonging to (the Asaph collection)." As has already been pointed out, it is impossible to determine whether the tradition of the Chronicler concerning Asaph[14] is original. However, all the Asaph Psalms bear a certain similarity. Based on the criteria of language and contents, such as the names of Jacob or Joseph, it is most natural to conclude that they originated in North Israel, although it is obvious that they have been re-interpreted in a Jerusalemite spirit, especially Psalms 50 and 76. The idea of God is also quite typical: Yahweh is

14. In addition to the passages mentioned above, cf. also Ezra 2:41; Neh. 11:22.

the creator and god of fate but is also inseparably connected with Israel's history. The tone of these psalms has something of a prophetic ring about it. It is emotional—almost passionate, at times—and the author seems to betray a deep personal involvement. The Asaph Psalms are predominantly National Psalms of Lamentation. The idea of the covenant is quite prominent in them. All these things indicate that the Asaph Psalms form a homogeneous group, and that the heading *lᵉ'āsāph* is original.

It is even more likely that *lᵉhêmān* in Psalm 88 and *lᵉ'êthān* in Psalm 89 are intended to provide information concerning authorship. Heman and Ethan are mentioned in I Kgs. 4:31 (Heb. 5:11) as renowned wise men of the time of Solomon. In Chronicles, they are portrayed as ancestors of later Levitical guilds of singers. The tradition concerning these psalms is just as reliable as that concerning the Asaph Psalms. In fact, these two psalms remind us of the Asaph Psalms in type, language, and contents. Thus, even though Psalm 89 originated in North Israel,[15] still, in its present form, it is strongly oriented to Jerusalem and David.

It is clear that the primary purpose of *libhnê qōrah* in the heading of some psalms is not to give authorship information, but to indicate that these psalms belong to the guild of temple singers called "Korahites," the "Korah guild," or the guild of "the baldheaded" (tonsured), as the name signifies. Thus, in the heading of Psalm 88, which has both *lᵉhêmān* and *libhnê qōrah*, the former may refer to the traditional "author" in a strict sense, while the latter may refer to a guild of singers in whose circle this psalm belongs. Based on the criteria of language and contents, there can be no doubt that the psalms of the sons of Korah had their origin in North Israel. The evidence for this is even stronger than it is for the North Israelite provenance of the Psalms of Asaph, Heman, and Ethan. At the same time, the contents of Psalms 48, 84, and 87 (this psalm appears to be relatively late) in particular indicate that they were transferred to Jerusalem and adapted to the cult there.[16]

Psalms 72 and 127, which are ascribed to Solomon, and Psalm 90, which is ascribed to Moses, are in a class by themselves. It is obvious

15. G. Ahlström, *Psalm 89* (Lund: Ohlssons, 1959), pp. 182 f., cf. p. 13.
16. See now G. Wanke, *Die Zionstheologie der Korachiten. Beihefte zur Zeitschrift für die alttestamentliche Wissenschaft,* 97 (Berlin: A. Töpelmann, 1966), with somewhat different conclusions.

that the headings of these psalms refer directly to authorship, and that they are secondary. They clearly come from a circle which assumed that the psalms must be interpreted historically.[17] Thus, they are of the same type as the first group dealt with above, in which the headings are secondary and depend primarily on a historical exegesis of the psalms.

However, *leedhāwidh* is the most important term in the headings of the psalms, because the way in which it is interpreted has far-reaching implications for the understanding of the entire Book of Psalms. With the help of recent discoveries (Ras Shamra, Mari), some contemporary scholars have attempted to put this term in new relief and to shed new light on its meaning and original "situation in life."[18] The Old Testament itself contains an ancient tradition that King David was a singer and poet. The songs of lament over Saul and Jonathan (II Sam. 1:19–27) and Abner (II Sam. 3:33–34) are specifically ascribed to him. But even if the Davidic authorship of these two dirges be called into question, there is no reason to deny the originality of the tradition that David was a singer and poet. Thus, it is not necessary to think that this tradition originated from a misinterpretation of the heading *leedhāwidh* over several psalms, and is therefore secondary, as Mowinckel argues.[19] In fact, the opposite is probably true. The original tradition that David was a poet and singer increased because of David's importance as the founder of the Jerusalem cult, and so his name came to be associated with the Book of Psalms as the foremost author of this collection of songs. The fact that the LXX has fourteen more Davidic psalms than the MT (including Psalm 137, which is clearly post-Exilic!) is an indication of an increasing tendency to ascribe psalms to David. Furthermore, the very presence of the term *leedhāwidh* in the headings of several psalms, which was clearly interpreted to mean "of David" in the tradition, is best explained by assuming that the tradition of Davidic authorship was gradually extended to include more psalms. However, recently discovered com-

---

17. Cf. "the king's son" in Ps. 72:1 and the tribute from Seba in Ps. 72:10. Ps. 127:1 is interpreted so as to refer to the building of Solomon's temple. Ps. 90:9–10, 15 is interpreted as having to do with the generation of the "wilderness wanderings."

18. See I. Engnell, *Studies in Divine Kingship in the Ancient Near East*, 2d ed. (Oxford: Basil Blackwell, 1967), pp. 175 f. with notes.

19. S. Mowinckel, *Psalmenstudien* VI (Oslo: J. Dybwad, 1924), pp. 72 ff.; *The Psalms in Israel's Worship*, I (New York: Abingdon Press, 1962), pp. 77 f.

parative material offers strong evidence that originally *lᵉdhāwidh*
meant something quite different from that which it came to mean in
the tradition.

We have already seen that, in reality, the term *libhnê qōraḥ* can
have a flexible meaning and can be interpreted, not as a direct designation of authorship, but as "belonging to the Korah collection." In
light of the discoveries at Ras Shamra, we must conclude that by far
the most probable meaning of *lᵉdhāwidh* is "belonging to the Davidic
collection," for there are expressions in the colophons of the great
mythical and dramatic ritual texts found at Ras Shamra which are
wholly analogous to *lᵉdhāwidh*. These include *lbʻl* (*libaʻli,* corresponding to the Hebrew *lᵉbhaʻal*), which means "belonging to the *Baʻal*
[-series]"; *lʼaqhat* [*liʼaqhat*], "belonging to the Aqhat [-series]"; *lkrt*
[*likārit*], "belonging to the Keret [-series]." By analogy, the most exact
meaning of *lᵉdhāwidh* is "belonging to the David [-series]," "David
Psalms." At the same time, many exegetes think that originally David,
dāwidh, was not a proper name, but a title, a royal term (whether
the primary meaning is "ruler, prince," or "darling"), and that King
David adopted this title when he took Jerusalem. It was part of the
ideological complex associated with the cult forms which David took
over when he subdued the whole Amoritic Jebusite kingdom.[20] When
the term *dawidūm,* which was thought to mean "prince," turned up
also in the Amoritic Mari, it led some scholars to think that the history
of this term could be traced from Mari to Jerusalem by way of the Amoritic Jebusites. In more recent years, however, it has been admitted
that this word may have a different meaning.[21] For the present, therefore, we must leave open the question of whether the meaning of this
term can be illuminated by the Mari texts. On the other hand, the fact
that the psalm literature is intimately connected with the figure of
the sacral king and his cultic functions in its origin, type, and entire
use, as the latest psalm research has shown, is of utmost importance.
For this reason, it is impossible to escape the conclusion that the real
significance of the term *lᵉdhāwidh* is "for the king," that is, that this
term indicates that we are dealing with a Royal Psalm. The fact that,
in some passages in the Old Testament, "David" does not mean the

20. See Engnell, *op. cit.* p. 176.

21. H. Tadmor, "Historical Implications of the Correct Rendering of Akkadian
dâku," *Journal of Near Eastern Studies,* 17 (1958), pp. 129 ff.; cf. Ahlström,
op. cit., p. 168.

first David, but the reigning descendant of David,[22] lends some support to this view. It should be clear from this that *l^edhāwidh* in the headings of the psalms may also have this meaning. Of course, the occurrence of this term in the heading of a psalm does not *prove* that it is a Royal Psalm, but only indicates that it *may* be. We must not exclude the possibility that *l^edhāwidh* in the heading of a psalm may be secondary. At the same time, however, the tendency of the LXX to increase the number of "Davidic" headings in the psalms is no particular proof that the same thing took place in the MT. Furthermore, the fact that this term does not occur in *all* Royal Psalms is not a valid objection to the interpretation suggested here. For it should be observed that *l^edhāwidh* indicates a *Jerusalemitic* Royal Psalm. But, of course, the Book of Psalms contains Royal Psalms of North Israelite origin (i.a., Psalms 66, 74, 84) which do *not* have or have not been given the designation *l^edhāwidh*.[23] Another clue as to the meaning of the term *dāwidh* is that it is probably related to *dōd* in some way or other.[24] *Dōd* is a Canaanite word for the deity which is usually called "the god of vegetation." Its literal meaning is "darling." Basically, the sacral king is associated with this type of god in a special way, and the same is true in Israel. It is also significant that the name *David* is always written *defectively* in the Book of Psalms, that is, as *dwd*, and not *dwyd*.[25] On the other hand, it seems wholly unlikely that the historical King David could ever have been called anything other than simply David (*Dāwidh*)—for example, he was never called Dod (*Dōd*). However this may be, and however we may conceive of the formation of the cultic and ideological facts in ancient Jerusalem, it is still true that the term *l^edhāwidh* in the heading of a psalm is an indication that it is a Royal Psalm—an indication, but in itself not a proof. There are other criteria which must be used to determine whether a psalm is to be regarded as a Royal Psalm—that is, language and content. These can be adduced only by an objective examination of the actual material itself, an examination which requires great and deep insights, not least into the comparative material, especially the

22. Cf., e.g., I Kgs. 12:16, where *dāwidh* refers to Rehoboam, and Pss. 18:51; 144:10, where it refers to the reigning king.
23. Bentzen has drawn both of the erroneous conclusions mentioned here.
24. G. Ahlström, *op. cit.*, pp. 163 ff., cf. Engnell, *op. cit.*, p. 176, with note 7.
25. With but two exceptions, the same is true in I and II Samuel and I and II Kings. The *plene* writing on a large scale appears first in the Chronicler's work.

Sumerian and the Akkadian. At the same time, this examination must be very comprehensive and take all conceivable criteria into consideration, including typological and form-critical considerations, the nature of the description of adversity or the enemies, indications of the cultic situation, special terminological expressions, and the occurrence of specific elements of the royal ideology. We do not make any progress by using the criteria "it follows the pattern of Psalm 2," or "it unites collective and individual features,"[26] or the enemies are national in character,[27] alone, although these criteria can be legitimately applied. This examination must begin with those psalms which are incontrovertibly Royal Psalms, that is, psalms which are filled with "royal" content in situation and type, in terminology and ideology. First, we must work out carefully the peculiar characteristics of these psalms, their forms of expression, ideas, linguistic details; and then, on the basis of these, we will be in a position to make judgments concerning less pronounced "royal" psalms. To be sure, we can obtain nothing more than circumstantial evidence in this way; but such an approach, by its very nature, demands that we content ourselves with a greater or lesser degree of probability. It now appears that such a careful examination yields the following results: of the 73 "Psalms of David" in the Book of Psalms, about 30 are incontrovertibly Royal Psalms; about 30 others are, with a high degree of probability, Royal Psalms, while nothing specific can be said about the rest. In evaluating these results, it should be kept in mind that, unfortunately, our knowledge of the different aspects of the royal cult and of the functions of the sacral king in the cult is rather imperfect. Therefore, the fact that a "Psalm of David" cannot be definitely placed among the Royal Psalms is hardly a strong argument against this thesis. Thus, it may be said that the evidence clearly favors the interpretation of *l^edhāwidh* suggested above.

Two other matters related to this problem should also be considered. First, it cannot be emphasized too strongly that when we speak of "Royal Psalms," we have in mind the *original* "situation in life" and literary context of the psalms: that is, their formal character as Royal Psalms. The *actual* use, application, and interpretation of a

26. Probably A. Bentzen, *Det sakrale Kongedømme* (Copenhagen: B. Lunos, 1945); cf., e.g., p. 41.

27. H. Birkeland, *The Evildoers in the Book of Psalms* (Oslo: J. Dybwad, 1955).

psalm is another matter, and the scholar always has the responsibility of dealing with the question of the "disintegration"[28] and "democratization" of the psalms, with their further application to individuals other than the king. Second, it should be pointed out that the designation "Royal Psalm" could also be given a more general meaning: it might be used to include not only psalms in which the king himself appears as the liturgical subject, or psalms in which he is the immediate subject of the sacral acts—for example, in the form of intercession or blessing—but also psalms which, on the whole, had a place in the royal cult. The adoption of this more general sense of the concept "Royal Psalm"—which we reject because it is clearly less suitable than the interpretation suggested above[29]—would harmonize best with still another interpretation of the term *leḏhāwidh*: "belonging to (the Psalms of) David," that is, belonging to the Jerusalemite, royal corpus of temple songs. In a way, this interpretation of *leḏhāwidh* would perhaps seem to be the most likely, irrespective of the meaning assigned to the term "Royal Psalm" and in view of parallels from Ras Shamra. This would imply that there is no reason to assume that the term *leḏhāwidh* is simply to be regarded as secondary in cases where a certain psalm does not immediately appear to be a distinctly Royal Psalm in the limited sense suggested above. Of course, this is not to deny that sometimes the term *leḏhāwidh* can actually be secondary. However, if we adopt this interpretation of *leḏhāwidh*, then we are faced with the problem of explaining why not all, or practically all, of the psalms in the Book of Psalms have the heading *leḏhāwidh*. And the only logical explanation would be to assume that the other psalms were inserted into the canon from other quarters which were not associated with the temple cult—at any rate, not during the monarchical period. But this forces us into such a conflict with the internal criteria of these psalms that the problem is only further complicated. Thus, the interpretation of the *leḏhāwidh* psalms as Royal Psalms in a specific and limited sense is still the most probable.

It should be obvious that this interpretation of the term *leḏhāwidh* by no means settles the question of whether there are psalms in the Book of Psalms written by King David himself. It should not be de-

---

28. The term comes from S. H. Hooke, editor, *Myth and Ritual* (London: Oxford University Press, 1933), p. 6.
29. We are not aware of anyone who has used the term in this sense.

nied a priori that there is a theoretical possibility of Davidic authorship. Indeed, some of the more conservative scholars still want to assume that individual psalms were written or could have been written
by King David. However, it must be admitted that the probability of
this is minimal. Thus, it can be said that there are indeed "Psalms of
David" in the Book of Psalms, but hardly any psalm "by David."

A term whose meaning is intimately connected with this interpretation of *l^edhāwidh* is *lamnaṣṣēaḥ*, the English translation of which is
"to the choirmaster" (RSV), a term which occurs no less than a total
of 55 times in the headings of the psalms. It also occurs in the last
verse of the psalm which is found in Hab. 3:1–19 and which is a
typical Royal Psalm. Formally, *lamnaṣṣēaḥ* is a *pi'el* participle from
the Hebrew verb *nāṣaḥ*, which sometimes means "to shine, beam,"
and sometimes, in the same stem form, also "to lead, direct." It is
probable that both meanings are particularly associated with the figure of a leader or conductor. The translation, "to the choirmaster"
(leader of music, conductor), is due to the association of this term
with I Chron. 15:21. But this association is secondary, as is the association with *'alāmôth* and *sh^emînîth* in the same passage; and this
translation does not occur in the old *Versiones*, the Greek LXX, the
Syriac Peshitta, or the Aramaic Targum. Aquila and Jerome render it
"for the victor," a translation also adopted by some modern exegetes,
usually with a Messianic interpretation. According to one theory,
held by Mowinckel,[30] the verb means "to make radiant," viz.,
Yahweh's countenance, that is, to implore his mercy. This would
imply that the term indicated a "psalm of expiation," or the like.
But this interpretation is linguistically impossible. The only natural
way to find a suitable meaning for this term is to begin with the
primary sense of *nāṣaḥ*, "to lead, direct," and, on the basis of this,
to conclude that *lamnaṣṣēaḥ* means "for the leader." But the leader
is the king! In other words, the term *lamnaṣṣēaḥ* is parallel to
l^edhāwidh. But an examination of the psalms in whose headings
lamnaṣṣēaḥ occurs seems to indicate that they are North Israelite
in origin.[31] Therefore, *lamnaṣṣēaḥ* must be the northern counterpart
to the Jerusalemite *l^edhāwidh*. It is admittedly very difficult to prove
this thesis, partly because of the Jerusalemite revision to which the

30. Mowinckel, *Psalmenstudien* IV, p. 17 ff.
31. No such investigation has been made known; Engnell never published
his.

psalms have been subjected throughout, and partly because so much still remains to be done in the area of philology with regard to differences in dialect between North and South. But in spite of this, occurrences of names such as Jacob, Joseph, Bashan, Zalmon, Gilead, Manasseh, Ephraim, Zebulun, and Naphtali in some of the *lamnaṣṣēaḥ* psalms are important indications of northern origin. Sometimes, northern origin is reflected by philological considerations (for example, in Psalms 55, 139)—not by merely purely linguistic criteria, but also by a characteristic poetic style which often has numerous parallels in Ras Shamra. Furthermore, it has already been pointed out that the Asaph and Korah Psalms are of North Israelite origin. In any case, this much is certain: no better hypothesis for the interpretation of *lamnaṣṣēaḥ* than the one proposed here has been suggested.

It has been generally assumed that most of the other terms found in the headings of the psalms are musical terms. However, recent studies have reduced the probable number of these considerably. Now, only *binghînôth, 'el hannᵉḥîlôth,* and *higgāyôn* are usually declared to be musical terms with a greater or lesser degree of hesitation. *Binghînôth* ("with stringed instruments") occurs in the headings of Psalms 4, 6, 54, 55, 67, and 76. The meaning of *'el hannᵉḥîlôth,* which occurs in the heading of Psalm 5 and is usually translated "for the flutes," is extremely uncertain. The meaning of *higgāyôn,* which appears in Pss. 9:17 and 92:4 (note that this term occurs in the body of the psalm rather than in the heading; in the RSV, it is not translated), is in reality also dubious. The verb *hāghāh* means "to mumble, meditate," which may indicate that *higgāyôn* is a term indicating the type of the psalm, rather than a musical term. Originally, perhaps, it meant "Psalm of Lament," or the like. It is also possible to find a musical term in *'al shōshannîm* in Pss. 45:1 and 69:1, translated, in English, "according to lilies," and in *'el shōshannîm* (*'ēdhûth*) in Ps. 80:1 ("according to lilies; a testimony"—in this case, it would mean "on the six-stringed" [instrument]). Some scholars have suggested that these are cultic terms referring to the delivering of oracles with the help of flowers. But this hypothesis is also uncertain. It is tempting to associate these expressions with the Accadian *susāpînu,* "bridal knight," a title of Tammuz, the god of vegetation.

Most exegetes still agree that the oft-recurring term *Selah,* occurring seventy-one times in the Book of Psalms and three times in Habakkuk, should be regarded as a musical term. *Selah* does not appear in the headings of the psalms, but functions as a kind of dividing word at the end of a section within them. In reality, the precise meaning of *selāh* is unknown. The LXX renders it by *diápsalma,* "interlude." It is usually derived from the verb *sālal,* "to lift up, elevate," and so could indicate either a crescendo by the accompanying music or a cultic cry raised by the cultic community. The Sumerian psalm terms *bar-sudam,* which is very close to "crescendo," and *sag-ba tugam,* "diminuendo," may offer some support to the former interpretation.

With approximately the same degree of probability, the expressions *mizmôr,* which occurs fifty-seven times in the headings of the psalms, and *shîr,* which occurs fifteen times in the headings of the psalms, not counting the "Psalms of Ascents," can be included in the category of musical terms or of terms indicating the type of the psalm. We can assume that *mizmôr* indicates that the psalm is to be accompanied by musical instruments of one type or other, while *shîr* seems to be a more general designation for a psalm indicating that it is intended for vocal recitation. Both terms have exact counterparts in Accadian: *zamāru,* "song, psalm," and *šēru,* the common designation for a part of a cultic song. The terms *mizmôr* and *shîr* are combined in Pss. 67:1, 68:1, 87:1 and 92:1.

There are also other terms whose meanings are uncertain: *'al hashsheᵐînîth, 'al ᵃlāmôth,* and *'al haggittîth. 'al hashsheᵐînîth,* "according to the Sheminith," occurs in the headings of Psalms 6 and 12. It means either "on the eight-stringed" [instrument] or "at the eighth," that is, at the eighth [royal] rite of purification. *'al ᵃlāmôth,* "according to Alamoth," occurs in Ps. 46:1. Some scholars interpret this expression to mean "in the Elamite [key]," which is wholly untenable, and others, "with female voices." Literally, *ᵃlāmôth* means "virgins," and this term would seem to refer to the rôle which female cultic servants undoubtedly played, even in Israel.[32] *'al haggittîth,* "according to the Gittith," occurs in Pss. 8:1, 81:1, and 84:1. It has often been interpreted to mean "on the Gittite

32. In the article "Virgin," in *SBU²,* Engnell says: "Among both Eastern and Western Semites the virgin-goddess Ishtar-Anat and her virgins, i.e. her female cult-servants, have played a significant part, of which there are clear reflections in the O.T., e.g. Judg. 11:30 ff. (Jephthah's daughter); Ps. 45:15; Song of Songs 2:2; I Kgs. 1:2; Joel 1:8 (where it appears that even a 'virgin' may have a hus-

[instrument]." However, in all probability, this term also has a thoroughly cultic character. Perhaps it has something to do with the "Gittite" Obed-edom, who plays a special rôle in David's bringing of the ark to Jerusalem, II Samuel, chapter 6. On the basis of the LXX, some scholars emend the text to *gittôth*, "winepresses." From a cultic point of view, this reading might suggest that these psalms were connected with the Vintage Festival, but this theory has little to commend it.

Some of the difficult headings in the Book of Psalms obviously refer to the literary genre of the respective psalms and also, to some extent, to their cultic situation. This kind of heading is well known from Sumero-Accadian literature. Not only *tᵉhillāh*, "hymn" (in English, "a song of praise"), Psalm 145, and *tᵉphillāh*, "prayer," Psalms 90, 102, 142, but also, no doubt, *shiggāyôn*, *mikhtām*, and *maśkîl* belong to this category. *Shiggāyôn*, which is found only in Ps. 7:1 and in Hab. 3:1, is undoubtedly related to the Accadian *šigū*, a kind of lament, corresponding to the Sumerian *ir-ša-khun-ga*, "a song which comforts the heart" [viz., of the deity], and is associated, it would seem, partly with the god Hadad, and partly with the person of the sacral king.[33] *Mikhtām*, Psalms 16, 56–60, RSV "Miktam," also indicates a kind of lament, probably connected with expiation.[34] *Maśkîl*, Psalms 32, 42, 44–45, 52–55,[35] 74, 78, 88–89, and 142, is undoubtedly the technical term for a particular kind of "Enthronement Psalm" belonging to the central part of the ritual of the annual festival which describes the act of atonement of the king [catchwords *ransom* and *covenant*] both in its negative and especially in its positive aspects, and refers to the result of the atonement and the hymnic motif associated with it.[36]

---

band, or 'lord,' *baʻal*, at her side); Isa. 7:14 (sg. *ʻalmāh*); Pss. 46:1; 68:26 (pl. *ᵉlāmôth*); etc."

33. See now C. R. Dalglish, *Psalm Fifty-one* (Leiden: E. J. Brill, 1962), pp. 21 ff.

34. Cf. the Accadian *irrēti ša kitme*, "sorceries for expiation," literally "covering," which is also the primary meaning of the Hebrew stem *kātham*. Acc. to W. Von Soden, *Akkadisches Handwörterbuch* (Wiesbaden: Otto Harrassowitz, 1959), *irtu* is a kind of song or lament; *kitmu* means "covering" in some cases, but in this combination it is taken as "a kind of flute (?)." The argument, thus, is inconclusive.

35. *Maśkîl* is probably secondary in the heading of Psalm 53, where it is due to v. 3.

36. Cf. the use of the same stem in Isa. 52:13 referring to "the Servant of the Lord." See the discussion in Ahlström, *op. cit.*, pp. 21 ff.

Lᵉthôdhāh, lᵉhazkîr, ʾal maḥᵃlath, and *lᵉʿannôth* are more distinctly cultic terms. *Lᵉthôdhāh*—RSV, "a psalm for the thank offering"—occurs in the heading of Psalm 100, and no doubt indicates that this psalm is connected with the giving of a thank- or praise-offering. *Lᵉhazkîr*—RSV, "for the memorial offering"—is found in the headings of Psalms 38 and 70, and connects these psalms with *ʾazkārāh,* the "memorial offering." The heading *ʿal māḥᵃlath*—RSV, "according to Mahalath"—occurs in Psalms 53 and 88. In the heading of Psalm 88, it is followed by *lᵉʿannôth;* both terms are transliterated, not translated, into English. Both terms seem to indicate that these psalms belong to the suffering phase of the ritual of the annual Royal Festival.³⁷ The term *lᵉʿannôth* means "for humility," "with humility," and *maḥᵃlāh* is cognate with *ḥālāh,* "to be weak, sick," or with *ḥālal,* "to pierce" (cf. Isa. 53:5), or—which is most likely—with *ḥālal,* "to profane," but certainly not with *ḥālil,* "flute." Thus, the meaning "with flute-playing," which scholars sometimes assume, is incorrect, in spite of the Sumero-Accadian parallels *er-šem-ma* or *takkaltu* (or *takribtu*) *chalchallati,* "[public] lament on the flute."³⁸

The meaning of the expression *lidhûthûn*—RSV, "to Jeduthun"—in the heading of Psalm 39, or *ʿal yᵉdhûthûn*—RSV, "according to Jeduthun"—in the headings of Psalm 62 and 77, is also difficult to determine. The Chronicler (I Chron. 25:1 ff.; II Chron. 5:12) understood this term to refer to authorship. Recent research has suggested the hypothesis that it is to be understood as cognate with the verb *yādhāh* in its special sense of "confess."³⁹ If this were correct, these psalms would most logicially be understood as Penitential Psalms, an interpretation which agrees rather well with their contents and tone. But this theory is hardly likely, and the expression remains an enigma. To a certain extent, the same is also true of *lᵉlammēdh*—RSV, "for instruction"— in Ps. 60:1, although an approximate solu-

---

37. At the same time, *maśkîl* occurs in the headings of both psalms, and their contents show clearly that they are related to the Annual Festival. Psalm 88 is, in the final analysis, a characteristic "Ebed-Yahweh" psalm, a Royal Passion Psalm. Engnell has hinted at this subject in *Studies in Divine Kingship* (see Index, *s.v.* "Passion"); cf. Engnell, "The Ebed Yahweh Songs and the Suffering Messiah in 'Deutero-Isaiah,'" *Bulletin of the John Rylands Library,* 31 (1948), pp. 54 ff.
38. W. von Soden, *op. cit.,* takes *ḥalḥallatu* as "drum."
39. But this is the meaning of the *hithpaʿel* form of the verb.

tion can perhaps be seen here, for everything seems to indicate that this term, which also occurs in the heading of David's lament over Saul and Jonathan, II Sam. 1:18, refers to a [royal] oracular procedure in connection with which this psalm was used.

The term *'al 'ayyéleth hashsháhar*—RSV, "according to the Hind of the Dawn"—in the heading of Psalm 22 is very special. It is usually interpreted to refer to a certain melody bearing this name, to which the psalm was sung. However, it has also been suggested, by Mowinckel,[40] that this expression refers to a sacrifice of a hind with which this psalm was connected. It is certainly possible that the red deer was considered to be a legitimate sacrificial animal in ancient Israel, although this was not the case later: cf. Deut. 12:15—to understand the form *'ayyéleth* as the feminine of *'áyil*, "ram," is linguistically impossible. It is also true that sacrifices were offered especially in the morning, but the same can also be said of other central cultic acts. Furthermore, there is an Accadian parallel to this, not cited by Mowinckel, which tells of the king's offering a special sacrifice of a white gazelle to the moon god Sin.[41] However, we suggest a completely different interpretation of this heading, which seems to be more plausible. The expression may be connected with the prayer in v. 20, *'aeyālûthî leezrāthî hûshāh* (cf. Ps. 88:5), "O thou my help [on the basis of Aramaic etymology], hasten to my aid." There is now a parallel to this in a Ras Shamra text. If this is correct, the meaning of the heading would be "at the help which comes at dawn," which may be an allusion to the point in the ritual of the Annual Festival at which the "suffering" of the king is changed to victory.[42] Psalm 22 is one of the most advanced "Ebed Yahweh Psalms" in the Book of Psalms, and the interpretation of the heading of this psalm suggested here harmonizes very well with its entire structure and contents.[43]

The heading of Psalm 56 is also hard to interpret, viz., *'al yônath 'elîm*[44] *rehōqîm* (in Swedish, "according to 'the speechless dove afar

40. Mowinckel, *Psalmenstudien*, IV, pp. 26 ff.
41. We have not been able to locate this quotation.
42. Cf. A. R. Johnson, *Sacral Kingship in Ancient Israel* (Cardiff: University of Wales Press, 1955), *passim* (see Index, *s.v.* "Dawn"), H. Ringgren, *Israelite Religion* (Philadelphia: Fortress Press, 1966), p. 236 with references.
43. Cf. Isaiah 53.
44. Scholars usually accept this reading following the LXX, instead of *'elem*, "silence."

off,'") which means, literally, "at the dove of the distant gods," provided that the reading suggested here is accepted. The rôle which the dove played in the Israelite cult is well known, particularly as an expiatory- or a trespass-offering [cf. Lev. 1:14 ff.; 5:6 ff.; 14:2 ff.]. The exact meaning of the expression under discussion admittedly remains obscure, but the concept of "the distant god" which lies behind it is well known from other sources, and this expression has parallels, i.e., in Accadian Tammuz liturgies.[45] The heading '*al tashhēth*—RSV, "according to Do Not Destroy" (which is a literal translation of the Hebrew phrase)—in Psalms 57–59 and 75 is also rather obscure. The most common interpretation is that this is a musical term having to do with the tune to be used when these psalms are recited. But it has also been suggested, by Mowinckel, that this term indicates that these psalms belong to a particular group named after the catchword '*al tashhēth*. This method of designating literary pieces has many parallels in Sumero-Accadian literature. This expression has also been associated with the rite connected with a cluster of grapes mentioned in Isa. 65:8. If this is the case, it might refer to the cultic situation in a fertility- or harvest-festival with which it was originally connected. Finally, a few remarks need to be made with regard to the expression '*al mûth labbēn*—RSV, "according to Muth Labben"—in Ps. 9:1. Some scholars connect this term with '*ªlāmôth*, "virgins." Others interpret it as an instruction concerning the tune to be used when the psalm is recited. We might also connect this term with the god *Môt* in the Ras Shamra texts, and with his epithet *bin ilîma*, "son of god," which is based on the Tammuz pattern. However, it is also possible that the most literal translation, "at the death of the son," comes closer to the original idea, as some scholars have suggested. This could be interpreted in light of the rôle of the sacral king as "the son of God." If this is correct, this psalm would be a Royal Psalm belonging to the suffering or "death" section (cf. v. 14) in the ritual of the Annual Festival. But after all is said and done, these possibilities remain only conjectures.

Finally, let us notice the headings of the so-called Songs of Ascents, Psalms 120–134, *shîr hamma'ªlôth* (Psalm 121, *shîr lamma*

---

45. E.g., the text quoted by T. Jacobsen, *Proceedings of the American Philological Society,* 107 (1963), p. 477.

ᶜᵃlôth). The old Danish translation of these headings, "a song on the stairs"—the older Swedish translation read "a song in the higher chancel"—certainly pointed in the right direction. The proper and original meaning of the Hebrew *maᶜᵃlāh*, singular of the plural *ma ᶜᵃlôth*, is "step," and the distinct cultic and ideological rôle which steps played in the temple (there are parallels to this, i.a., from Egypt)[46] is in harmony with this meaning.[47] Thus, we may suppose that the steps of the temple were the stage for several acts in the cultic drama, and that the entire concept of the temple was concentrated and symbolized in them as *pars pro toto*, the part for the whole, representing the temple as a whole, and this precisely in its special function as the symbol for the mythological and ideological concept of "the cosmic mound," the cosmic mountain, the first to be created or to rise up out of chaos—the place where the holy and edifying powers are concentrated, the permanent center, "the navel of the earth."[48] But on the basis of type or content, it is very difficult —and hardly necessary—to reduce the "Psalms of Ascents" to a specific formula or to assign them to a definite cultic situation or to a particular festival, for example, by interpreting them as Psalms of Procession belonging to the so-called Enthronement Festival (a hypothesis which in itself is logical) and by understanding *ma ᶜᵃlôth* in a broad sense as a title for the collection, as Mowinckel suggests. Thus, in reality, nothing more exact can be said. The only reason that these psalms were put together in a separate group is that they all had the same term, *ma ᶜᵃlôth*, in their headings.

This investigation of the headings of the psalms in the Book of Psalms may appear to yield rather meagre results. We have shown that the technical terms involved are quite incidental, and that often it is impossible to know their exact meaning because we have no basis for interpreting them in a specific tradition. However, this should not come as too much of a surprise, since—as scholars know well—sim-

46. E.g., W. B. Kristensen, *Het leven uit de dood,* 2d ed. (Haarlem: n.p., 1949), pp. 89 ff.

47. Cf. also the so-called altar with steps in the Old Testament.

48. For the primordial hill in Egyptian belief, see, e.g., J. Černy, *Ancient Egyptian Religion* (New York: Hutchinson's University Library, 1952), pp. 44 ff.; S. G. F. Brandon, *Creation Legends of the Ancient Near East* (London: Hodder and Stoughton, Ltd., 1963), pp. 18 f., etc. (see Index, *s.v.* "Primaeval Hill"). For the cosmic mountain, see S. N. Kramer, *History Begins at Sumer* (Garden City, N. Y.: Doubleday, 1959), pp. 82 ff.; Brandon, *op. cit.,* p. 71.

ilar circumstances exist in other ancient literature, particularly in the Sumero-Accadian incantation and psalm literature. In this material, there are groups of technical terms, coming, for the most part, from the Sumerian period and written in the Sumerian language, many of which the Accadian traditionists were completely unable to understand. It is not incredible to assume that when the pre-Israelite, Canaanite literature, and more precisely the psalmic literature, was taken over into Hebrew, in many cases the technical terminology was not understood. A fresh, thorough investigation of the headings of the psalms, based on a systematic study of the Sumero-Accadian material, would undoubtedly be a great contribution to our understanding.[49] But even without this, the present study has made it clear that the different, often obscure, technical terms in the Book of Psalms are of utmost importance in that they point toward the same conclusions with regard to our understanding of the Book of Psalms as a whole and of the *Sitz im Leben* of the psalms. They indicate unmistakably that the psalms were connected with the cult, that they are ritual texts, and that they are the product of the official Israelite religion, the temple cult. This provides an important supplementary corrective to the usual understanding of the Israelite cult, in that it helps us to see that the official cult was not concerned exclusively with sacrificial worship, but also with more profound matters.

The Psalms As Poetry. Form-Critical Considerations.—This is no place to engage in a detailed discussion of the poetic problems connected with the psalms, such as rhythm and meter, strophic structure, different types of *parallelismus membrorum* (mutual symmetry of verse members—a phenomenon the importance of which has hardly been fully realized).[50] Only a few basic observations can be made here.

There are several ways in which the psalms can be classified. They can be divided according to liturgical subject: that is, the "I" who speaks in the psalm. A psalm may be collective or national, in-

---

49. Of course, it is impossible to undertake such an investigation here. Very little of this kind of material is found in Dalglish, *op. cit.*, pp. 233 ff.

50. In the article "Poetry" in SBU[2], Engnell argues in favor of the Sievers' system of Hebrew metrics, stressing the fact that there is no regularity in the use of meter so that no emendations *metri causa* are advisable. He also admits the existence of strophic structure, although this does not play the same significant rôle as in modern literature.

dividual, or liturgical, depending on whether the subject is plural or singular, or alternates between the two. The formal structure of the psalm is: introduction, body, conclusion. Form-criticism divides the psalms into several so-called categories or types (called, in German, "Gattungen"): there are hymns—including hymns of the annual festival, also called "Enthronement Psalms," and "Hymns of Zion" as special types—psalms of thanksgiving, and psalms of lament, including Penitential Psalms and Psalms of Innocence, which were originally Royal Psalms belonging to the annual festival, as special types. The so-called Royal Protective Psalms—Psalm 20 is a typical example—may very well be added to these types. These psalms often take the form of a liturgy (with alternating subjects), and a blessing for or a wish for the prosperity of the king is their central element. The purpose of this blessing is to "create," cultically, good fortune or victory for the king, especially when he engages in military campaigns and wars. These Royal Protective Psalms typically include a prophetic oracle delivered by a cult prophet or a priest. Such oracles occur in other compositions, too.

Here it should be emphasized that the so-called literary types can hardly be regarded as conscious literary patterns or developed models, as is still often done, to which new compositions necessarily had to conform. Even if the external form is strongly dependent on the tradition, as is always true of cultic data, the cultic situation itself is a far more important factor than the literary types as such. After all, the classification of the psalms according to types is nothing more than a means of arranging the literature in an orderly fashion in order to enable us to engage in a scholarly investigation of the material. Therefore, the attempt to write a literary history of the psalm types (corresponding to the work of Gunkel and others) was doomed to failure from the very first. As a matter of fact, it is simply one expression of an evolutionistic, wishful dream and is based on a preconceived idea of how the development *must* have taken place and on a strongly subjective theory as to the age of the psalm material—a theory which is now undergoing thorough revision. Thus, in view of the limitations of type analysis, if we are to use this criterion as an aid to the literary-historical investigation of the psalms, we must use it cautiously. Most important of all, we must not interpret the different types as empirical quantities or as detailed and normative models— we must not use them as fixed patterns by which to emend, delete from, add to, or in other ways manipulate the Hebrew text so as to transform it into what, at times, appears to be nothing less than a new edition of the massoretic text, as Gunkel, Mowinckel, and others have emphasized. This use of type analysis has led to offenses as serious as those resulting from the attempt to emend the text purely on the basis of meter.

We have already tried to emphasize strongly that the Royal Psalms play an important rôle in the general analysis of the Book of Psalms as a whole and of individual psalms. But here we must call attention to the fact that the term "royal psalm" is not a form-critical classification, but an analysis of the *contents*. Thus, theoretically, "royal psalms" can include hymns and psalms of thanksgiving as well as laments and protective psalms. These remarks are also applicable to the term "enthronement psalms" or "psalms of the annual festival," the latter designation being preferable. It should also be observed that, according to the ways of classifying the psalms suggested above, different psalms belonging to each of the types—hymns, psalms of thanksgiving, laments, and protective psalms—may be collective or national, individual, or liturgical, depending on whether the subject in a psalm is "we," "I," or both, alternating between "we" and "I." Finally, it should be pointed out that it is impossible to classify the psalms according to form-critical categories alone. We must always take into consideration the contents of a psalm and other criteria when we attempt to classify it.[51]

Principles of Interpretation. Different Possibilities and Variations.— The cultic understanding of the Book of Psalms, which is the most recent principle of interpretation, may seem to be dominant and self-evident. However, this understanding is not very old and has yet to gain general acceptance in scholarly circles. In other words, the "situation in life" of the psalms has been and still is understood in very different ways.

Here, we offer a survey of the leading methods which have been used in interpreting the Book of Psalms, beginning with the historical approach, which is undoubtedly the oldest. As a matter of fact, this approach is already represented by the headings discussed earlier, referring to "historical events" found in the canonical Book of Psalms itself. But this basic conception of the original *Sitz im Leben* of the

---

51. Cf. Mowinckel's remarks in *The Psalms in Israel's Worship*, pp. 31 ff.

psalms is also encountered elsewhere in the Old Testament, in the many passages where a psalm is placed in a definite "historical" (more or less profane) situation, as in "the Song of Deborah" and "the Psalm of Hezekiah." The LXX, New Testament, and particularly the Church interpreted the psalms in this way, and some Old Testament exegetes have adopted this approach more or less uncritically. Its conclusions are based on supposed historical allusions in a psalm, on a modern, anachronistic understanding of its "situation in life," and on the unspoken assumption that all events—at least, all essential events—in the history of Israel have always been handed down to us somewhere in the Old Testament. Using these criteria, the psalm is given a historical situation. The fact that scholars adopting this approach have generally arrived at widely divergent conclusions is the strongest proof of its weakness and subjectivity. Psalm 68, for example, has been assigned to approximately thirty different dates, ranging from a very early period down to the Maccabean Age, and each date has been defended in great detail. And yet, one scholar who has analyzed and criticized these positions very recently—W. W. Cannon[52]—has concluded by suggesting his own "historical" exegesis. The thoroughly erroneous idea that the principal forms of the Hebrew verb, especially the perfect,[53] are real tenses has proved to be an important argument used in favor of this approach. By and large, the Swedish translation of the Book of Psalms is based on just such a historical principle of interpretation and thus, for all practical purposes, not least by its translation of the tenses, has succeeded throughout in transforming the psalms from the cultically timeless character and life setting which they actually possess into texts which depict pious scenes from Israel's religious history. Indeed, this erroneous principle of interpretation is still widely adopted in scholarly circles, Protestant as well as Catholic, and Jewish in addition: e.g., Pfeiffer, Buttenwieser, Torczyner—Tur-Sinai).[54] The "geographic" type of interpretation is a

---

52. W. W. Cannon, *The 68th Psalm* (New York: The Macmillan Co., 1922). Later works include S. Mowinckel, *Der Achtundsechzigste Psalm* (Oslo: J. Dybwad, 1953), with a cultic interpretation.

53. Engnell's opinions concerning Hebrew "tenses" are laid down in his *Studies in Divine Kingship*, pp. 207–209 and in his *Grammatik i gammaltestamentlig hebreiska* (Stockholm: Norstedt, 1960). Cf. also Ahlström, *op. cit.*, pp. 189–192.

54. R. H. Pfeiffer, *Introduction to the Old Testament* (New York: Harper and Brothers, 1941), pp. 619 ff.; M. Buttenwieser, *The Psalms, Chronologically*

variant of the historical. An example of this is T. H. Robinson's interpretation of the description of chaos in Psalms 42–43 as the words of a Jew in Exile who had almost drowned in a brook at the foot of Mount Hermon.[55]

We may regard what might be called the *spiritualistic* interpretation as a distinctly separate approach, although it is often intimately connected with the historical understanding of the psalms. This interpretation regards the Book of Psalms as a collection of "spiritual ballads" or songs written for the purpose of edification or originating as subjective expressions of spiritual experiences, as "deep religious sighs." Advocates of this approach also occasionally seem to think that some psalms were designed for a more collective religious use of one type or other, such as the edification of laymen in a "conventicle," or the like. It is not difficult to see what recent development in Christendom is responsible for this interpretation, which reads into the Book of Psalms its own idealistic sort of piety in an anachronistic *interpretatio europaeica moderna*. This approach interprets all genuine cultic realities reflected in the psalms directly or by implication as only symbols or figures of spiritual realities. It is true that the LXX had already taken the first and important step in this direction and consequently inaugurated an exposition of the psalms based on a misunderstanding of the most elementary facts concerning the *Sitz im Leben* of the Book of Psalms in ancient Israel. The *aestheticizing* approach, which has been applied especially to the so-called nature hymns, represents a special form of the spiritualistic interpretation. But this understanding is also untenable, because it introduces ideas into the psalms which were unheard-of in ancient Israel, where, always, even in late times, attention is focused on realities—on attaining positive objectives and benefits, not the least of which was the face-to-face encounter with Yahweh in the cult.

The *didactic* interpretation of the psalms may also be regarded as a special form of the spiritualistic interpretation, or if one prefers, it may be considered an entirely distinct approach. We have already

---

Treated with a New Translation (Chicago: University of Chicago Press, 1938). The reference to Torczyner (Tur-Sinai) is probably to his article, "The literary character of the Book of Psalms," *Oudtestamentische Studiën*, 8 (1950), pp. 265 ff.

55. T. H. Robinson, *The Poetry of the Old Testament* (London: Duckworth Press, 1947), p. 121.

mentioned this understanding in connection with the traditio-historical and canonical problems of the Book of Psalms, and have seen that
it is certainly possible that so-called scribal circles had a part in re-
arranging the psalm material—probably in the early part of the post-
Exilic age. In this process, a certain amount of reinterpretation may
have taken place in the direction of making the psalms didactic literature. From this point of view, one could even go so far as to say
that it is actually erroneous to assert that the Book of Psalms in its
present final form arose exclusively as "the Hymnbook of the Second
Temple." However, that the psalms may have been understood and
interpreted didactically by the final collectors and editors, especially
in the post-canonical tradition and also by the Massoretes, is one
thing; but what the individual psalms really were, originally, is an
entirely different matter. And from this latter perspective, it is impossible to assert that the psalms inherently are expressions of a "lay
piety" which had been set free from the cult and was even partly
anti-cultic, or that they arose predominantly for the specific purpose
of promoting any such thing.[56] Furthermore, the tendency to put
psalms interpreted as didactic poems or as wisdom psalms in the
same category as apocryphal poems, such as the Psalms of Solomon,
the Prayer of Manasseh, and relevant passages in the Book of Ben
Sira and the Book of Baruch, is very misleading. Experts should be
able to see that the latter represent a later poetry of a wholly secondary type, and—as the real absence of the kind of poetry found in the
psalms in a later time shows—how firmly the ancient psalm literature
must have been connected to the temple and its cult.

However, the rather widely accepted notion—often overemphasized—that the Book of Psalms contains numerous so-called Wisdom
Psalms is the essential point in this connection. But this idea is based
on the erroneous belief that the wisdom literature, as such, is of late
date. The truth of the matter is that the Book of Psalms does not contain any "wisdom poems," at all. Often, several psalms are interpreted
in this way, and especially Psalms 1, 112, and 127. But these psalms
are to be understood differently. It is true that Psalm 1 can be said to
function as a kind of introduction to the entire Book of Psalms. Nevertheless, a detailed analysis of this psalm shows that it belongs to an
entirely different situation—that undoubtedly it was originally con-

56. Thus, e.g., Pfeiffer, *op. cit.*, p. 265, still in 1941.

nected with the cult. This is indicated by some of its peculiar phrases and expressions, as well as its ideas. Psalm 1 belongs to the so-called Torah-liturgy type originally connected with the king. The description of the way of the righteous or the way of life, in contrast to the way of the unrighteous, indicates a definite cultic situation in which the so-called ethical requirements were cultivated. This psalm is a kind of "word of blessing" connected with a so-called *ṣᵉdhāqāh*-table, a "mirror for kings,"[57] and therefore is one of those psalms which in reality are the basis for the parenetic style, which both prophetic and "sapiential" circles adopted from the cult.[58] Much the same can be said of Psalm 112, in spite of the fact that its type is more "disintegrated" than that of Psalm 1, thus indicating that it has deviated further from its original "situation in life" than Psalm 1. Psalm 127 is different, for it appears to have retained its original "situation in life," that is, the cult. These three psalms are no more "didactic" in the sense of being songs independent of the cult, or "profane" songs, than are any of the other psalms. Thus, it is incorrect to maintain as does A. Bentzen, that the Book of Psalms is "not only a ritual song book, but also a 'Wisdom Book.' "[59]

The problem of the so-called alphabetic psalms is closely connected with the question of the didactic character of certain psalms and of their relationship to the wisdom poetry. Alphabetic psalms, or acrostics, are psalms arranged in such a way that each succeeding verse or group of verses begins with the following consonant in the Hebrew alphabet.[60] We may immediately dispense with the theory that such an arrangement points to a predominantly "magical" significance. Instead, the usual explanation of this phenomenon as an artistic production is undoubtedly correct. And yet, almost without exception, those who take this position interpret it as evidence of a di-

---

57. Engnell has set forth his interpretation of Psalm 1 in his article " 'Planted by the Streams of Water,' Some Remarks on the Problem of the Interpretation of the Psalms as illustrated by a detail in Ps. 1," *Studia Orientalia Ioanni Pedersen* (Hauniae: E. Munksgaard, 1953), pp. 85–96.

58. As far as this is concerned, there can be no doubt that Jer. 17:5–8 is a secondary prophetic paraphrase similar to Psalm 1, if not dependent on or based on this very psalm.

59. A. Bentzen, *Introduction to the Old Testament*, 7th ed., II (Copenhagen: G. E. C. Gad, 1967), 170 (the reference is to the *later use* of the book).

60. Only Psalms 25, 34, 37, 111, 112, and 145 can be certainly listed as acrostics.

rect influence of the wisdom literature on the psalms, since the same phenomenon is characteristic of both. This leads to the inescapable conclusion that such psalms are "colorless," "written by epigones," and, above all, that they are late works.[61] But the fact that a psalm is alphabetic does not prove that it is late, even if most of the acrostic psalms do not appear to be very old. In contrast to the usual approach, the correct method is to begin with the psalms themselves, which originally had a cultic *Sitz im Leben,* and are predominantly of a hymnic-parenetic type—especially with regard to the theme of "the two ways." This indicates that it is the alphabetic arrangement of the psalms which has influenced the analogous phenomenon in the wisdom poetry, and not the alphabetic arrangement of the wisdom literature which has influenced that of the psalms.

However, most modern exegetes no longer adhere to a purely didactic line of interpretation, but generally defend *a mixed type of interpretation containing both didactic and cultic elements.* These scholars assign a greater or lesser number of psalms to the non-cultic type and occasionally even to the anti-cultic type, admitting at the same time that there are cultic psalms. This generally accepted view seems to have originated with the eminent German exegete H. Gunkel (d. 1932), who was the first to apply form-criticism to the literature of the Old Testament in a definitive way.

According to Gunkel, the psalms belong to two main groups: the cultic, and the non-cultic or "spiritual." The cultic psalms may be divided into several major *Gattungen* or types: hymns, national laments, individual laments, and individual thanksgivings, as well as lesser types, such as *Tôrāh* Psalms, "psalms of entrance," and "psalms of blessing and curse." The non-cultic psalms include essentially the same types. It is in this group that the eschatological "Enthronement Psalms" are to be placed among the hymns. Gunkel also finds some "mixed types" in the Book of Psalms, especially the so-called liturgies, as well as *Weiterführungen*—further development of types and motifs— and the "reflective lyrics."[62] He considers the Royal Psalms to be a distinct type lying between the two main groups, because they are not

---

61. In light of the prevalent scholarly opinion, it is important to keep in mind that only a relatively few psalms of this type are to be found in the Book of Psalms.

62. H. Gunkel, "Psalmen," *Die Religion in Geschichte und Gegenwart,* 2. Aufl., IV (1930), col. 1626.

genuine cult lyrics, in spite of the fact that they are related to the cultic poetry. The interpretation and division of the psalms which originated with Gunkel is full of discrepancies and is unsatisfactory, especially in its understanding of the non-cultic, spiritual poetry. According to this view, it was prophetic influence which gave rise to non-cultic poetry in the psalms. When the psalms which are said to be non-cultic actually contain direct allusions to the cult, it is argued that these were added later, when the non-cultic poetry—which at one time itself grew out of the cultic poetry, which even Gunkel himself considers to be earlier—was connected with the temple and its cult "in the very same way that songs from hymn-books of sects have been included in the hymn-book of the church in our day."[63] Even though this cycle with its intermediate stage of non-cultic "religious songs" is nothing but pure fiction and impossible to maintain, nevertheless, as has already been mentioned, most scholars hold the same position as Gunkel, or a similar position, and thus assume the existence of both cultic and non-cultic categories of psalms in the Book of Psalms. As a matter of fact, Kittel, Hempel, Eissfeldt, and Pfeiffer often speak of cultic psalms rather reluctantly. In defense of a non-cultic interpretation of certain psalms, Gunkel argued that their contents are so profound and seem to reflect such personal religious experiences that they cannot possibly be cultic songs. But this argument clearly pronounces judgment upon itself and reflects the inherited inability of Protestantism to understand the nature of the cult. There is simply no reason to assume a profane situation in life for "non-cultic" psalms—to the extent that they do occur at all—until the late Jewish period.

The Norwegian scholar, S. Mowinckel, whose abiding contribution to Old Testament research lies precisely in his consistently worked out *cultic* interpretation of the psalms, deserves credit for subverting this compromise solution. To be sure, more or less groping attempts in the direction of a cultic interpretation had been made before Mowinckel, by B. Jacob, J. P. Peters, St. John Thackeray, and, to some extent, also J. G. Herder;[64] and since Mowinckel's work has been published, other scholars have adopted his basic understand-

63. *Ibid.*, col. 1622.

64. B. Jacob, "Beiträge zu einer Einleitung in die Psalmen," *Zeitschrift für die alttestamentliche Wissenschaft,* 16 (1896), pp. 129 ff., and 17 (1897), pp. 48 ff.; 263 ff. J. P. Peters, *The Psalms as Liturgies* (New York: Putnam, 1922). H. St. John Thackeray and J. G. Herder, references not identified.

ing, including A. C. Welch, Oesterley, Wensinck, Calès, Bentzen, and Weiser.[65] However, no one has worked out this interpretation as consistently as has Mowinckel himself. Ever since the publication of his *Psalmenstudien*, it has been clear that, *in principle*, any understanding of the psalms other than the cultic is out of the question.

We have already pointed out that in the Book of Psalms there are inescapable allusions to the cult, even if they may be sparse to some extent, and that the language of the psalms is frequently saturated with cultic expressions. The technical terms in the headings of the psalms and comparative material in the world around Israel offer convincing proofs of this cultic emphasis. Our growing knowledge of the ancient Near Eastern material through new archaeological discoveries is confirming this view more and more. But the most conclusive proof of the cultic *Sitz im Leben* of the psalms is that this is the only satisfactory explanation for all the problems with which we are confronted in the content, form, and language of the psalms—with regard to the descriptions of adversity, the enemies, the I, etc.

On the other hand, an essentially cultic interpretation does not mean that a priori we are to regard every psalm in the Book of Psalms as a cultic text. Instead, it means that we are obligated *first* to investigate the possibility of interpreting a psalm cultically and that, only if this interpretation is found to be inconsistent with the contents and over-all attitude of the psalm, its ideology and language, then another interpretation may and must be sought. But in reality, the careful analysis of the psalms in recent years has yielded many arguments which show that, by and large, they are cultic or ritual texts and that, on the whole, this can be doubted only in a few cases. In fact, it is ultimately very debatable as to whether a cultic interpretation is impossible in any single instance. If it is, it is most likely in Psalm 137, a psalm which is in a class by itself.

One would hardly have suspected, two decades ago, what signifi-

65. A. C. Welch, *The Psalter in Life, Worship and History* (Oxford: Clarendon Press, 1926); W. O. E. Oesterley, *A Fresh Approach to the Psalms* (New York: Charles Scribner's Sons, 1937); A. J. Wensinck, "The Semitic New Year and the Origin of Eschatology," *Acta Orientalia*, 1 (1922), pp. 158 ff.; J. Calès, *Le livre des Psaumes* I–II (Paris: Beauchesne, 1936); A. Bentzen, *Indledning til de Gammeltestamentlige Salmer* (Copenhagen: G. E. C. Gad, 1932), *Fortolkning til de Gammeltestamentlige Salmer* (Copenhagen: G. E. C. Gad, 1939), and *Det sakrale Kongedømme* (Copenhagen: G. E. C. Gad, 1945); A. Weiser, "The Psalms" in *The Old Testament Library* (Philadelphia: The Westminster Press, 1962).

cant results would be reached by a variation of the consistently cultic interpretation, which might be called *Royal-Sacral*. This is a natural correlate of the view that sacral kingship played a central rôle also in Israel—a fact which recent research has made inescapably clear. The texts which are most relevant to this interpretation are to be found precisely in the psalms, especially in the Royal Psalms. Analogies from other ancient Near Eastern religions, such as Egyptian and Meso-potamian,[66] also show clearly that originally the psalm material had its center altogether in the royal cult and in the peculiar rôle of the sacral king in this cult. The origin of the psalm literature, on the whole, is to be sought in the royal cult. In a very real sense, the psalms in the beginning were "royal" literature. However, it is true that this exclu-sively "royal stage" itself represents a hypothetical construction. We know that this kind of literature, both in Israel and in other ancient Near Eastern countries, exists only in "disintegrated" and "democra-tized" form.[67] Of course, at first, the psalm ritual was actually used by the king himself; but as a rule, in the cult, the psalms became the responsibility of his sacral representatives, the priests and other cultic officials. Moreover, also from the very beginning, because of their deep emotional involvement in the performance of the cultic drama, the individual cult attendants, both high and low, undoubtedly trans-ferred and applied to themselves the living contents and purpose of the ritual. Therefore, the recent recognition that "the most important 'reinterpretation' is the 'democratization' of Psalms originally belong-ing to the *royal* ritual"[68] is fully justified.

Now, in light of this, one might perhaps ask whether it makes sense at all to ascertain the "royal" character of a psalm or to ask for its "royal" affinities in general. However, in the interest of scholarly in-vestigation, it is both proper and necessary to do so; and, furthermore, this problem is of utmost importance to an understanding of history as well as the history of religion. Just because it is often impossible to

66. Cf. G. Widengren, *The Accadian and Hebrew Psalms of Lamentation* (Stockholm: Thule, 1937), pp. 77, 217-230.

67. I.e., what originally applied only to the king was transferred to ordinary people. For the term *democratization*—a term that was probably introduced into religious history by J. H. Breasted, *Development of Religion and Thought in Ancient Egypt* (New York: Charles Scribner's Sons, 1912), p. 257, cf. p. 280—see Engnell, *Studies in Divine Kingship*, Index, *s.v.* "Democratization." See also S. Mowinckel, *The Psalms in Israel's Worship*, chap. III, section 7.

68. Bentzen, *Introduction to the Old Testament*, II, p. 169.

give a definite answer to a question is no justification for failing to consider it. Nevertheless, it is clear, when we study specific cases, that it is very difficult to determine where the "line of disintegration" is, where a royal "I" is speaking and where another "I"—a priest or a member of the cult—has taken its place. As always, the whole issue must be decided on the basis of circumstantial evidence: naturally, the more a psalm is filled with royal-ideological and royal-sacral motifs, the more likely it is that this psalm is a genuine Royal Psalm. At the same time, however, there is an inherent possibility that this terminology merely indicates a certain style and metaphorical language, that even in the Royal Psalms we encounter what has been called a royal "court style," and therefore that the hyperbolic language does not reflect a real situation. But so much is now known about the rôle that sacral kingship played, both in Israel and throughout the ancient Near East, that this explanation must be rejected. Also, to understand the Royal Psalms as relating to the eschatological Messiah, the Savior of the End Time,[69] or to date them in the Maccabean Age, are interpretations which do not merit acceptance. Against the former view is the fact that an eschatological messianism in a strict sense had not had time to develop in the Prophets, much less, in the Book of Psalms. The latter is inadmissible because the Book of Psalms in its present form had certainly gained canonical status much earlier, before what can really be called a Maccabean kingdom came into existence,[70] and because this kingdom never attained the position of importance in the eyes of the people as the one described so vividly in the psalms. Therefore, there can be no doubt that, in the Royal Psalms, we encounter the genuine, historical, living Messiah whose righteous acts in the cult, especially in the Annual Festival, give the worshippers victory and prosperity, good, blessing, and fertility for the people and the kingdom, whether they have to do with the positive or the negative aspect of the ritual, whether the king is victorious and exalted or is humiliated and suffers as atonement for his own sins and the sins of the people, in the rôle of the "suffering servant of the Lord."

Finally, we must emphasize very strongly that it is impossible to interpret the so-called Enthronement Psalms as referring to *Yahweh's* enthronement in the Annual Festival without any co-operation whatso-

69. Thus Gunkel and many others, especially in their interpretation of the so-called Enthronement Psalms.

70. This took place first with the Hasmoneans, 105 B.C.

ever from his Messiah, or as reflecting an antithesis between Yahweh's kingdom and the earthly-sacral kingdom. In doing so, we readily admit that the theocratic concept does exist in the Old Testament and that it is contrasted with the royalistic concept in Old Testament literature, especially by the Deuteronomic circle which is responsible for Deuteronomy–II Kings.[71] But in this form, this concept is obviously secondary and reflects the religious struggle between the priesthood and the royalty which runs throughout the literary fabric of the history of ideas in the Old Testament as a red thread. This anti-royalistic idea has no place in the psalms, which, properly speaking, are the most important texts of the royal-official religion, nor is it found in them. The conventional argument that it always says *Yahweh mālakh,* "*Yahweh* is (now) king," and never "So-and-so is now king," will not bear critical scrutiny. Analogies from Accadian literature show conclusively that this is not the case, because in the ritual of the Annual Festival (in the Assyrian form), *Aššur šar,* "Assur (the god) is king," always occurs, even though it is quite clear that the reference is to the enthronement of the currently reigning king.[72] Of course, this is not to deny that the king is regarded as the antitype and incarnation of the god, in conformity with the concept of identity which characterizes their relationship.[73] Such a unity between Yahweh and his Messiah exists in Israel's religion from the first and continues unimpaired as her religion develops. It is best expressed in the renewal of the "covenant" and its re-creation of the cosmos in the Annual Festival.[74]

The Question of Dating. "Universalism" in the Psalms. Prophetic Influence? "Anti-Cultic" Psalms?—Scholarly opinion as to the original date of the psalms has varied widely throughout the history of research. This problem is closely connected, particularly, with the question of the relationship of the Book of Psalms to the literary prophets. The critics who thought that the Book of Psalms was not canonized until the post-Exilic period were predisposed to assume that the

71. Cf. chap. 4, "The Pentateuch."

72. K. F. Müller, *Das assyrische Ritual* (Leipzig: J. C. Hinrichs Verlag, 1937), p. 8 (= KAR), 216, 27 ff., Engnell, *Studies in Divine Kingship,* p. 17, note 5; cf. now also R. Frankena, *Tākultu* (Leiden: E. J. Brill, 1954), pp. 64, 133.

73. This idea is stressed by Engnell several times in *Studies in Divine Kingship:* see Index, *s.v.,* "Identity king-god"; the theory is defended against J. de Fraine in a review of the latter's book *L'aspect religieux de la royaute israelite* in the *Svensk Exegetisk Årsbok,* 18–19 (1955), pp. 204 ff.

74. Cf. chap. 11, "The Messiah in the Old Testament and Judaism."

psalms which it contains were also post-Exilic in origin. On the basis of this a priori inclination, they read into the psalms details of the historical situation of the Exilic and post-Exilic period according to the way in which they were generally understood.

One important argument which scholars used to make in defense of the Exilic and post-Exilic date of the Book of Psalms was the outlook of "universalism" in the psalms, which they considered to be a legacy from the Prophets. Looking at the psalms from the perspective of the historical development of ideas inherited from the system of Wellhausen, scholars concluded that the piety of the Prophets lay behind the "law," the "wisdom literature," and the psalms. Just as the poetry of the Psalms of Lament in the Book of Psalms went back to Jeremiah, and just as the poetry of the hymns went back to "Deutero-Isaiah," so the "psalms of law," such as 78, 81, 95, were dependent on the sources of the Pentateuch, which were dated late, and Ezekiel. Psalms like 84, 87, 106, and 122 were thought to be connected with pilgrimages of Diaspora Jews to Jerusalem, while others—15, 127, 128, 133, and 144—were believed to reflect the initial period of happiness of the post-Exilic age. R. H. Pfeiffer, in his *Introduction to the Old Testament* (p. 630), even thought that psalms like 89 and 132 went back to "the late midrash of II Sam. 7," and that Psalm 89 was originally a so-called hymn of nature which a pious Jew rewrote. He also contended that these two psalms alluded to the fact that the Davidic dynasty had already fallen. As the doctrine of the post-Exilic origin of the Book of Psalms was developed—by the German-Swiss B. Duhm, for example—it was concluded that nearly half of the psalms were Maccabean. Two criteria other than universalism and alleged historical data were advanced in support of this position. One was linguistic: the occurrence of so-called Aramaisms here and there throughout the Hebrew language of the psalms. The other was the interpretation of the enemies and the part which they played in the psalms.

However, there has been what is comparable to a revolution in the understanding of all these points, particularly in the last ten years or so. This complete revaluation is already clear in the cultic interpretation of Old Testament literature. But it has penetrated more or less remarkably into psalm research, which, in a strict sense, does not represent the cultic interpretation.

Thus, more and more scholars have opened their eyes to the fact that the Israelite piety which is represented in the Book of Psalms must be older than the "prophetic." They have also become much more hesitant about speaking of any prophetic (i.e., literary prophetic) influence on the Book of Psalms. Leading exegetes, persuaded, obviously correctly, that the cultic interpretation of the psalms essentially points in the right direction, have reversed the understanding of the relationship of the Book of Psalms and the Prophets. The psalms as cult poetry represent an older and more original type of piety and *Sitz im Leben,* which the Prophets presuppose and upon which they depend to a large extent. The Prophets draw from the cultic piety and develop specific ideas, such as justice and the judgment connected with the "day of Yahweh," the day of the Annual Festival, not least its positive side—the saved "remnant," the future kingdom of blessedness created by the Messiah, the savior king. The Prophets are also the ones who receive, and not the ones who give, as far as language, form, and style are concerned: they draw from the ancient sacral language which is to be found, in part, in the psalms with their fixed liturgical terms and phrases, their forms and figures.[75]

This is not so strange, because in the cult, the official cult, to which, in the majority of cases, expression is given in the poetry of the Book of Psalms, undoubtedly *prophets* played a very prominent role. "Cult prophets" were part of the temple personnel and figured prominently in prescribed liturgical contexts, especially by mediating and proclaiming the oracle. The oracle occupied a central place in the cult, and there are numerous traces of it in the psalms, for example, in the form of the word of blessing concerning the king.[76]

The question of universalism is also to be considered in light of these facts. In reality, in the modern sense, there is no universalism in the Book of Psalms or in the Prophets. It can be said that the mental horizon has been enlarged to include the whole world, the whole cosmos,[77] and that Yahweh has come to be considered exclusively the God of the whole world in the Book of Psalms and in the Prophets. But actually, this universalism is closely connected with the most

75. J. H. Patton, *Canaanite Parallels in the Book of Psalms* (Baltimore: Johns Hopkins Press, 1944); M. Tsevat, *A Study of the Language of the Biblical Psalms, JBL Monograph Series* IX (Philadelphia: The Society of Biblical Literature, 1955)

76. On this cultic nebiism and the problem of its relationship to the so-called literary prophetism, see chap. 6, "Prophets and Prophetism in the Old Testament."

77. However, this meant something entirely different in ancient Israel from its meaning for modern man.

highly developed nationalism. Yahweh's Anointed, the king of Israel, and his people with him, claim to have world dominion.[78] The other nations participate in the coming "kingdom of peace" only through Israel's triumph over her enemies. The expected peace is a *pax israeli-tica,* through and through. Nowhere in the Old Testament is this nationalism more developed than in the Book of Psalms. This form of nationalism already exists in the peculiar nature of the sacral kingship and its ideology. Basically, Israel's kings share this, not only with the monarchs of the great powers, but also with the smallest minor rulers of Canaan. As a matter of fact, Israel took over the sacral kingship and all that pertains to it from Canaan. In process of time, the typical traditional Yahwistic exclusivism has only further strengthened the trend which it set.[79] We may conclude from what has just been said that "prophetic religion," in the sense of literary prophetic religion, was not an influence on the type of piety reflected in the Book of Psalms. In fact, it does not even occur in the Book of Psalms. Therefore, there are no "prophetic" psalms in the usual sense of the word, but only psalms which contain cult prophetic elements, such as oracular pronouncements. Thus, "prophetic influence" and "universalism" are not valid arguments for dating certain psalms in the post-Exilic period.

Two psalms in particular that are usually dated in the post-Exilic period are worthy of a little more careful consideration: Psalms 74 and 106. Actually, the date of Psalm 74 is wholly uncertain. It cannot be dated definitely—as has been attempted—either in the year 586 B.C., the year Jerusalem fell, or in 168 B.C., during the reign of Antiochus Epiphanes. To be sure, it is said in v. 9 that prophecy is dead, but this can very well be understood *pro tempore* and so can mean "for the time being, in the immediate situation of the psalm." By no means does it *have* to refer to the later doctrine of the death of prophecy after Malachi. Even if the psalm refers to the "myth of the flood" in the "P" form—the primary written source, "the Priestly Code"—this still does not necessitate a post-Exilic date. Furthermore, the term

78. Cf. especially Psalm 2. Certainly this is not a feature which presupposes the post-Exilic age.

79. Actually, in principle, the "universalism" in "Deutero-Isaiah" is of the same type. Engnell used to deny vigorously the existence of any kind of universalistic outlook in Deutero-Isaiah; on the contrary, Deutero-Isaiah was "nationalistic," looking forward to a future when Israel was to rule the nations.

môᶜªdhê-'ēl, "meeting places of God" (RSV), does not prove that the synagogue was already in existence when this psalm was written (v. 8). This is an unwarranted assumption. The reference is simply to different cult places and cult communities, concerning which nothing more specific can be said. Verses 12–17, where the king can be thought of as the liturgical subject, may suggest the general situation of the Annual Festival. It is impossible to determine whether the ravages of the enemy are to be interpreted as real historical events or, more generally, as "cult mythological" ones. In any case, it is impossible to make an identification with a specific historical pillage of the temple.[80] In fact, there is much to indicate that Psalm 74 was originally North Israelite.[81] Thus, there is really no compelling reason to date it in the fifth or fourth centuries B.C.[82] The situation of Psalm 106 is more complicated. This psalm is a psalm of national lament, a psalm of penitence with a "positive confession," but in collective form. It almost seems to be a kind of historical legend, in the sense of a text for ritual recitation, in the Passover Festival. Psalm 106 is the last psalm in the Fourth Book and can be of post-Exilic origin. However, this is not intrinsically necessary by any means.

In recent years, there has also been a distinct change in the alleged linguistic argument. In more and more quarters, scholars have ceased to conclude mechanically that so-called Aramaisms are a clear proof of a late version, because they have come to realize that Hebrew itself contains a stratum of ancient Aramaisms which have roots as far back as the period of the Conquest. It is an open question as to whether these so-called Aramaisms[83] in reality may not simply be forms of the North Israelite dialect. This possibility is derived from the fact that the origins of the psalm literature of the Old Testament are to be sought particularly in North Israel—a conclusion based on general cultural and historical considerations, which has been emphasized by foremost contemporary authorities. Israel was a more culturally pro-

80. Cf. F. Willesen, "The Cultic Situation of Ps. LXXIV," *Vetus Testamentum,* 2 (1952), pp. 289 ff. Willesen argues in favor of a purely cultic interpretation of this psalm.

81. Also, it is a Psalm of Asaph.

82. The same is true of Psalm 79, the character of which is very similar to that of Psalm 74. Psalm 79 is even more vague and more general in tone, expressions, and the like, than Psalm 74.

83. For this question, see, e.g., G. R. Driver, "Hebrew Poetic Diction," *Supplements to Vetus Testamentum,* 1 (1953), pp. 26–39.

gressive country than was Judah, and was responsible for mediating the Canaanite literary traditions to Judah. Psalm literature undoubtedly occupied a very prominent place in these traditions, as is clear from the Canaanite psalm fragments in the Tell el-Amarna tablets.[84] Furthermore, it is a truism that even if the final form of a tradition is late (assuming, for argument's sake, that so-called Aramaisms indicate a late date), this does not have anything to say about the original date of the tradition itself. All these facts make it clear that the linguistic criteria for dating the psalms are inconclusive and that they have not yet been sufficiently investigated. They can be considered as only of little importance or, rather, as no proof worthy of consideration at all, in defense of the late origin of the psalms.

Finally, it may be pointed out that a historical interpretation of the psalms which involves dating them in the post-Exilic period is usually characterized by circular reasoning. Scholars know that the last three or four centuries B.C. are "obscure." Very little historical information is available because of the scarcity of primary sources. With this in mind, scholars use the psalm material—which in and of itself actually cannot be dated—to fill in the historical gaps. Thus, in a trice, the psalms are transformed into the most important historical source for the otherwise relatively little-known post-Exilic period. M. Buttenwieser is a typical representative of this type of reasoning.[85] He throws an unexpected light on history by assigning a group of psalms (6, 22, 30, 31, 38, 71, and 88—by one and the same author) to the year 344 B.C., the year that the general of Artaxerxes III, Ochus Orofernes (Holofernes), attacked Judah. He argues that this event was of utmost importance and served as the historical background for the Book of Judith.

By way of summary, these illustrations pertaining to the problem of dating are sufficient to show that it is no longer proper to ask: "Are there any pre-Exilic psalms in the Book of Psalms?" But one may ask, "On the whole, are there any post-Exilic psalms there?" In answering, we should not go to the opposite extreme and deny a priori the presence of post-Exilic psalms. On the contrary, Psalm 137 is a *memento* of

---

84. The fact that distinctive psalm literature is not to be found in the Ras Shamra material can be taken as an indication of the oral transmission of this kind of "literature," because it certainly cannot have been absent from the service in the Phoenician temple.

85. Buttenwieser, *op. cit.*

psalm literature from the post-Exilic period. And yet, it is difficult to escape the impression that the type, form, and contents of this psalm put it in a class by itself. In reality, it is *possible* that certain psalms in the Book of Psalms come from the post-Exilic period in only a limited number of cases, and *probably* in only a very few.

The alleged existence of so-called anti-cultic psalms in the Book of Psalms is an important argument for a spiritualizing interpretation of this material, as well as for the theory of prophetic influence upon it and the late dating of the psalms. Assuming that anti-cultic psalms are to be found in the Book of Psalms, it is clear from what has already been said that they must be explained in some way other than by prophetic influence. As a matter of fact, in reality, the prophets did not display a piety which can be described as independent of the cult, or anti-cultic. This would be a *contradictio in adjecto,* a self-contradiction, in the world of the Old Testament.[86] Therefore, we must be careful not to look at this problem in the traditional evolutionistic and time-bound way. The Exile did not change the character of Israel's religion with a single blow by doing away with the cult and introducing an individual religion. Even if the emphasis shifted, to some extent, the continuity is far more impressive. The Exile tended to strengthen Jewish exclusivism and, in part, to create new forms, especially by the emergence of the synagogue as a complement to the temple cult. But the temple continues to be predominant as long as it endures. The sacrificial cult reaches a peak after the return from exile and the rebuilding of the temple.

But this notion of a historical development has also been adopted by some representatives of an essentially cultic interpretation of the Book of Psalms in order to explain the existence of so-called anti-cultic psalms. Thus, Mowinckel has invented a development within the cult itself, away from bloody sacrifices, in the direction of other cult forms in their place, especially psalms of thanksgiving. He argues that this movement was supported by classes of singers at the temple as a conscious polemic against the sacrificial priesthood.[87] But even though antagonisms and severe conflicts between groups of cultic personnel are natural and well-attested, Mowinckel's hypothesis is still unsatisfactory. If scholars could only free themselves from the traditional nar-

---

86. See chap. 6, "Prophets and Prophetism in the Old Testament."
87. Mowinckel, *The Psalms in Israel's Worship,* II, pp. 109 ff., 141 ff.

row, wooden picture of the temple cult and envision the richly diversified condition which no doubt actually existed, it would not be very difficult to find situations within the cult in which most "anticultic" psalms can be placed. The psalms most often cited as anticultic are 40 (vv. 7 f.), 50 (vv. 8 ff.), 51 (vv. 18 f.), and 69 (vv. 31 f.). And yet, all four of these psalms are, without doubt, genuine and original cult psalms. Psalms 40, 51, and 69 are Royal Psalms of lament. Psalms 51 and 69 are also psalms of penitence with "positive confession." Psalm 50 is more specialized: it is a kind of cult prophetic parenetic psalm connected with the annual or Covenant Festival. At any rate, in these psalms, we encounter hyperbolic (consciously exaggerated) phrases which, in accordance with typical Hebrew thought and linguistic usage, are analogous to modern abstractions, of which the Israelite was not capable. A cultic situation in which statements of this sort are quite conceivable is the official function of the king in the Annual Festival, especially in connection with the transition from the negative "aspect of death" to the positive aspect of creation through victory and return to life.[88] This seems plausible because a so-called royal—in any case, originally royal—"$\text{\d{s}}^e dh\bar{a}q\bar{a}h$-table," a "mirror for kings" with its "promise of righteousness," is a part of this moment of transition. It insists on ethical and social virtues with less regard for the cultic motifs.[89] This is often connected with the "inducement-" or "interference-motive" and the formulae or phrases of humility such as we encounter, for example, in Pss. 40:18 and 69:30 ff. Closely associated with this is an emphasis on the fact that Yahweh, the absolute ruler, creator, and possessor of all things, does not need different kinds of sacrifices. On the contrary, he demands "righteousness," "a pure heart," "a preserving of the law in the heart," "a holy spirit," and not merely a profession of these qualities with the mouth, praise, and (*zebhaḥ*) *tôdhāh,* which undoubtedly simply means "thank-offering" (in

---

88. Engnell here refers to a paragraph in his article "Conversion," in *SBU²,* where he deals with the expression *shûbh sh^ebhûth,* which he interprets as "turning the destiny" with reference to a ceremony in the New Year Festival, comparable with the determination of destinies in the Babylonian *akitu* festival, through which fertility, prosperity, and blessing were created. "A typical example," he writes, "is Ps. 126, where vs. 1 should be translated: 'When Yahweh turns (changes) the fate of Zion, then we *are* like dreaming,' i.e., the Hebrew perfect forms have consistently a cultic-present significance. Vss. 5–6 allude to a rite of vegetation characteristic of the New Year Festival."

89. Engnell, in *Studia Orientalia Ioanni Pedersen,* p. 91.

English, "sacrifice of thanksgiving," Ps. 50:14, "thanksgiving," Pss. 50: 23; 69:31) whether *zebhaḥ*, "sacrifice," occurs or not. It is only by forcing a modern anachronistic concept of a cultless religion into such passages as these and, thus, by actually misinterpreting them, that scholars have been able to propagate the thesis that there are "anti-cultic" psalms in the Book of Psalms. This thesis found acceptance because it suits the modern ethos. But it corresponds poorly with the Israelite culture and religious milieu which is reflected in the prophetic literature and much more in the Book of Psalms.

The "I" of the Psalms. The "Description of Adversity" and the "Enemies." The "Godly."—The question of the identity of the first person singular and plural subjects "I" and "we" in the psalms has been hotly debated in recent research. Starting with psalms like 129, which designates "Israel" as the speaker in v. 1, and yet has Israel speaking in the first person singular in the psalm, and with the collective interpretation which appears already, for example, in the heading of Psalm 30 and in the transition from an individual to a collective subject, as in Pss. 51:19–21 and 69:33–37, scholars in the Wellhausenian school (J. Olshausen, 1853, and especially R. Smend, 1888) began to adopt the collective interpretation of the "I" in the Book of Psalms.[90] E. Balla (1912) reacted strongly to this view, as did Gunkel, and brought about a return to the individual interpretation, especially in the literary-critical camp. This was due to the fact that such a view agreed with the late dating of the psalms and with the evolutionistic understanding of Israel's religion as a constant development toward individualism. R. Pfeiffer's position clearly shows how an individual interpretation of the "I" may be championed as the only interpretation which corresponds with the idea that the Book of Psalms is a poetic product of individual pious laymen.[91] Scholars of this school—including R. Kittel and S. Mowinckel—explain the transition to a collective view in such psalms as 51 and 69 as a later addition which reflects a secondary reinterpretation of these psalms.[92]

Later research showed, among other things, that, in the psychology

90. Actually, this interpretation is to be found in isolated cases in the LXX, as well as in older Jewish commentators and in the Church Fathers.

91. Pfeiffer, *op. cit.*, pp. 625, 634.

92. R. Kittel, *Die Psalmen* (Leipzig: Deichert, 1929), pp. 194, 232 f.; as for Mowinckel, the statement in the text seems to contradict what he says in *The Psalms in Israel's Worship*, II, pp. 13 f., 17, 20 ff.

of primitive peoples, there is a typical lack of differentiation between individual and collective and that a collectivism characterized ancient Oriental civilizations. To some extent, this gave impetus to the collective interpretation of the "I" in the Book of Psalms, with special emphasis on the rôle of the king as mediator.[93] If we will only refrain from psychologizing the idea to an extreme, it can be said that the rôle which the king plays in the cult puts the whole problem in a new light, thus making the earlier controversy seem rather superfluous. When the king appears as liturgical subject, he represents his people— not always, of course, but in most cases—and, in this situation, the distinction between individual and collective is virtually obliterated. The typical alteration between "I" and "we" in many psalms also indicates that this distinction should not be made.[94] Thus, in their advanced dogmatic forms, the extreme individual and collective interpretations are both erroneous. Instead, each psalm must be interpreted as individual or collective separately, after all relevant criteria have been taken into consideration.

An even more important question is that of the identity of "the enemies" and "the evil" in the psalms. This is a much more difficult question than the one just considered, and has caused a lively and incessant debate. Scholars are so far away from reaching any agreement on this problem that it must be admitted that the various interpretations differ more drastically than ever, especially since the evidence seems to compel us to concur that a more and more consistent cultic interpretation of the psalms is basically the correct one. It has been and still is most natural that in the greatest degree one's understanding of "the enemies" and "the evil" should be dictated by the prevalent general impression which he has of the Book of Psalms, the date of the psalms, the *Sitz im Leben,* and various other factors. Since we have dealt with this problem elsewhere,[95] we may limit our statements to a few summary observations in the following paragraphs.

---

93. Mowinckel, *The Psalms in Israel's Worship,* Chap. III.

94. The presence of liturgies is also important here, and thus there are psalms in which a formal and real alternation between individual and collective subject occurs within the framework of the actual cultic situation.

95. The reference is to other articles in *SBU*[2], in which the following ideas are expounded. History is conceived as a drama of cosmic proportions implying a struggle between chaos and cosmos, or good and evil. As the representative of Yahweh, the anointed king of Israel has to defend cosmos and the good against all evil forces, mythical or real. From one aspect, this struggle is also fought be-

In many types of psalms—especially in individual psalms of lament but also in other types—more or less detailed descriptions of adversity are to be found. In these descriptions, the psalmist relates his unfortunate situation: he is consumed by disease, his soul and body (the two are one) pine away, he is bound and in captivity, he is already in Sheol, he is exposed to conspiracies and evil designs, to attacks from enemies and to curses from the wicked (in Hebrew, usually *rᵉshā'îm*) and evil-doers (*pō'ᵃlê 'āwen*). Sometimes these evil-doers are depicted as demonic figures, as wicked spirits, or in the guise of different animals, such as dogs, lions, or wild beasts. These instances suggest the possibility of two main interpretations: the literal and the figurative or spiritualistic. Advocates of the literal interpretation envision different types of situations of adversity, such as illness, in the majority of cases, or captivity, or persecutions of various kinds. Those who espouse the figurative interpretation believe that these descriptions are figures of spiritual suffering. The decision as to which interpretation is correct is complicated partly by the intensity of the metaphorical language and partly by Israelite psychology, which makes no distinction between corporeal and spiritual.[96]

There are several variations of the literal interpretation. One of these goes hand in hand with the literary-critical school's late dating of the psalms and individual interpretation of the "I." It is the interpretation of the enemies as personal opponents and enviers. Such is said to belong to a milieu in which there were sharp class antagonisms and contentions between different social strata and religious factions: it was the poor, the humble, the pious, and those who were faithful to the law who were oppressed and persecuted by the rich, the arrogant, and the worldly-minded. In time, this understanding of the psalms grew to such an extent that scholars began to interpret them as reflecting the antagonism between the Ḥasidim (the predecessors of the Pharisees) and the Sadducees.[97] This view is untenable because it

---

tween Israel, the chosen people, and her enemies. It is concentrated in the cultic sham fight of the New Year Festival, in which the king, as Yahweh's representative, defeats chaos and restores cosmic order. Here, "myth and history, cosmology, cultic experience and eschatology [the final victory of the good] merge into one totality."

96. This statement is based on the view expressed in J. Pedersen, *Israel, its Life and Culture* I–II (London: Oxford University Press, 1964).

97. The typical representative of this view is R. Kittel in his commentary on the psalms. Cf. note 92.

assumes an indefensible date for the psalms, as well as social and religious conditions which did not come into existence until a very late period.

Another variation of the literal interpretation can be called the "magical." This view apparently corresponds better with the earlier dating of the psalms. Its advocates—especially S. Mowinckel—understand the adversity described in the psalms predominantly as illness caused by wicked men, sorcerers or wizards, who resort to the black arts of magic in order to inflict injury.[98] However, this view is open to grave misgivings. Even if parallels from so-called primitive peoples and societies have a great degree of relevance, the analogies with Israelite society must not be carried so far as to exaggerate the primitive nature of the religion, culture, and social status of ancient Israel. We must also give due consideration to what has been said above concerning the use of hyperbole in the metaphorical language of the psalms and the indefinite line of distinction between corporeal and spiritual, as well as to the strongly tradition-bound and conservative nature of the language and terminology. To be sure, there may be isolated cases of genuine psalms of illness in the Book of Psalms: for example, Psalms 6 and 30; but their number has been greatly exaggerated, especially by Mowinckel.[99] With these reservations, it must be admitted that the theory of magic contains a certain degree of truth, and there is no reason to try to evade this interpretation entirely, for example, in the way in which Mowinckel now seems to want to do by returning to the "party interpretation" with its accompanying late dating of the psalms.[100]

Finally, a third variation of the literal interpretation of the enemies in the Book of Psalms goes back to the oldest view of the "I" in the psalms, the ancient collective interpretation. Since the "I" is Israel, the enemies are different national adversaries of Israel. The conditions caused by the wicked consist of visitations upon the people of Israel,

98. Mowinckel, *Psalmenstudien I.*

99. The existence of some so-called Prayers of the Accused, Imprisonment Psalms, presumably recited by accused persons being kept in custody in the temple while waiting for an ordeal, etc., is also dubious, to say the least. The theory was propounded by H. Schmidt, *Das Gebet des Angeklagten im Alten Testament* (Giessen: A. Töpelmann, 1928), and accepted by A. Bentzen in his *Indledning til de Gammeltestamentlige Salmer.*

100. In *The Psalms in Israel's Worship,* I, p. 207, Mowinckel considers the possibility of such an interpretation for a few *late* psalms, e.g., Psalms 1, 37, 73.

their conquest and subjugation by other nations, by the heathen. In more modern times, this "national" interpretation was adopted first by W. M. L. De Wette, and has been championed quite recently in an energetic but unilateral way by H. Birkeland,[101] primarily as an argument for the interpretation of the individual psalms of lament as Royal Psalms.

If we wish to carry out a consistent cultic interpretation of the psalms, it seems necessary to understand the enemies in the psalms in a figurative sense.[102] The cult reflects as its fundamental motif the ever-continuing, ever-repeated conflict between good and evil, cosmos and chaos, blessing and curse, between Yahweh, his people, and his Messiah on the one hand, and all hostile powers on the other. Because of this, the distinction between spiritual and temporal powers and between enemy nations and native insurrectionists or enemies of the nation and enemies of the king, are entirely obscured. It is simply assumed that all enemies use all sorts of black magic, and conversely that all sorts of "white" magic should be employed as instruments of retaliation. The enemies are described throughout in demonic categories. The figure who completely dominates this cultic drama and who stands at the center of the conflict (which is personal, national, and cosmic, all at the same time) is the king-Messiah. It is his victory and, consequently, his people's victory and Yahweh's victory, which is "created" in the cult and achieved in an anticipatory but thoroughly efficient way. There could be no doubt about this, because it was Yahweh himself, the God of Israel, the only powerful one among the gods, who intervened and promised victory and salvation. However, this is "created" not only in actual conditions of adversity, such as war or another type of visitation,[103] but also and, as a matter of fact, primarily, in the regularly recurring ritual drama of the Annual Festival. The so-called ritual combat or sham fight must have been an important part of this drama[104] and, in one way or another, the enemy powers must have been represented figuratively, that is, mimetically

101. H. Birkeland, *The Evildoers in the Psalms.*

102. By using the term *figurative,* we do not mean to imply a *spiritualistic* interpretation. On the contrary, the reality of the *figurative* interpretation must be emphasized.

103. Psalms which originated in such circumstances are called Psalms for Special Occasions and were used in connection with the special occasion under consideration.

104. Cf. chap. 7, "New Year Festivals."

or dramatically, by a cultic group equipped with weapons, masks, and other paraphernalia. It is very difficult to determine those elements in the description of the enemies which reflect a cultic reality and those elements which are only formal, figurative reminiscences of this reality. But a number of the most important psalms which refer to enemies of the king must be seen against this background. Thus, these psalms do not necessarily presuppose a real situation of adversity with real enemies.[105] The attack of these "enemies" must have been very closely connected with that phase of the Annual Festival in which the king "suffered" and figuratively descended into "Sheol." Therefore, the so-called "Royal Passion Psalms" or "Ebed Yahweh Psalms"[106] are also typical "psalms concerning enemies." The prominent rôle of the enemies in the psalms clearly indicates that the combat motif was central in Israel's Annual Festival. It is closely connected with the strongly dynamic and dramatic national character of Israel's religion. Some scholars have argued that the emphasis on this element in the Annual Festival to the neglect of the fertility motif is to be regarded as an *interpretatio israelitica,* a specific Israelite reinterpretation of clearly pre-Israelite material.[107] However, in opposition to this, it should be pointed out that a proper evaluation of the Old Testament material shows that the fertility motif is present. Here, we must also keep in mind the historicizing tendency suggested above.[108] Finally, perhaps it should be pointed out that this cultic, symbolic, timeless interpretation of the "psalms concerning enemies," viewed from a religious standpoint, is just as valuable as a historical interpretation of these psalms as more or less personal psalms for special occasions containing hatred and vengeance, which belong to a relatively late Israelite or later Jewish social milieu.

The term *the godly*[109] must also be understood in light of the interpretations of the "I" and of the "enemies and the evil" of the psalms

---

105. Of course, this should not be taken to mean that therefore the cultic event itself was not energetic and real.

106. See Engnell, *Studies in Divine Kingship,* p. 176, note 4; and cf. H. Ringgren, *The Messiah in the Old Testament* (London: SCM Press, 1956).

107. The reference is not clear.

108. Cf. note 95; the cosmic struggle is manifest in the opposition between Israel and her enemies.

109. Hebrew *ḥᵃsîdhîm* and synonymous expressions. Cf., in English translation, the "poor," "oppressed," "needy," "those who fear God," "humble," "righteous," "meek," "lowly," etc.

which have just been discussed. Thus, *the godly* are not to be identified with the Hasidim, the forerunners of the Pharisees, any more than *the enemies* are to be identified with the Sadducees or their predecessors. *The godly* (the Hebrew *ḥāsîdh*, "godly," means primarily "devoted, faithful") in the Book of Psalms is simply a designation for the members of the cultic community, the cultic congregation, which in turn ideologically represents the people (cf. Pss. 30:5; 31: 24; 32:26; 37:28), as is now coming to be recognized generally.[110] Therefore, the tendency is clearly to extend the idea to include all Israel, cf. Ps. 50:5. On the other hand, in harmony with the typical Israelite concept of corporate personality, "the godly"—hence, the cultic congregation and, indirectly, the whole people—are embodied in "the godly *one*" in a special sense, that is, in the king. The king is called "the godly one" in Pss. 4:4 and 16:10. This actual meaning of the term *the godly* is easy to demonstrate from the psalm material itself, and it fits perfectly into the picture of the psalms drawn from the unavoidable fundamental cultic interpretation.[111] It is only when we recognize the cultic background and realize the alternation between individual and collective that the most profound meaning of *the godly* as the most common and genuine "I" of the psalms as it stands in contrast to *the enemies* and functions in various situations of affliction stands out clearly. And Yahweh, the mighty God of Israel, the Lord of the covenant, the giver of salvation and blessing, always stands behind *the godly* as they participate in the activities of "the godly *one*," the king, in his righteousness, suffering, victory, and blessing.[112]

Conclusions. The Method of Psalm Exegesis. The Place of the Book of Psalms in Religious Life.—In this essay, it is not possible to deal with the type, contents, and specific problems of each of the 150 psalms. However, it is necessary to point out that a thorough scholarly exegesis of any psalm must include the following items: a traditio-historical and text-critical investigation; a philological interpretation, internal and comparative; a poetic, rhythmic, metrical analysis; a

110. Cf. H. Ringgren, *The Faith of the Psalmists* (Philadelphia: Fortress Press, 1963).

111. It goes without saying that the meaning and scope of the term *the godly* can vary somewhat from passage to passage.

112. Accordingly, the prophetic idea of the "remnant" grew out of the notion of these "godly ones," the cultic congregation. In turn, the idea of the "remnant" was gradually transformed into that of the faithful and loyal who shall stand in the judgment and inherit the land and the coming messianic kingdom.

form-critical analysis; an interpretation of the history of ideas and religion; and a discussion of the problem of the "real" situation and application of the psalm: its reinterpretation, "disintegration," and "democratization," its original, historical, and final *Sitz im Leben*. We have already called attention to the fact that, in reality, these different facets of psalm exegesis can only be separated from one another theoretically. When we include the extensive textual difficulties found in the psalms, in language as well as in form and content, there can be no doubt that the exegesis of the psalms has a unique position among the various branches of Old Testament exegesis. But at the same time, the study of the psalms constitutes a field of research which completely captures the interest and opens up the most far-reaching prospects within Israel's religious history, particularly in its cultic, sociological, and psychological aspects. With its specific piety, the Book of Psalms exhibits a weaving together of religious fibers which were most central in Israel. And the first thing necessary to a correct understanding of the religious history of the people in its entirety is a correct understanding of the world of the psalms. It is obvious that the ultimate goal of psalm exegesis—the deepest possible understanding of the Book of Psalms—still lies far away. But we have already travelled a good part of the way, and there is good reason to believe that it is possible to reach this farther down the road.

It is not possible in this essay to discuss in detail the fact that the Book of Psalms was of immeasurable importance, not only to Israel, the people which produced this absolutely unique cult lyrical poetry,[113] but also to Jesus and the New Testament, as well as to the various branches of the Christian Church. The Book of Psalms was of special importance to Luther and Calvin, as well as to later Protestantism. From a religious point of view, it would not be an exaggeration to say that, in this respect, the Book of Psalms occupies a unique position among the Old Testament scriptures, and this is true, to some extent, even in the secularized world of the present. It is obvious that the reason for this is the liturgical use of the Book of Psalms: in the Christian Church, the Book of Psalms has regained something of its original *Sitz im Leben*, although the circumstances are quite different.

The unique position of the Book of Psalms already stands out in

---

113. Without going into detail, this statement finds justification in a comparison of the Book of Psalms with Egyptian and Sumero-Accadian literature of the same type.

the New Testament. A very interesting and illuminating example of this, one which demonstrates the extraordinary tenacity of the tradition, appears in those psalms which the recent "royal-sacral" interpretation has shown to be originally messianic, which the New Testament with its messianic-eschatological interpretation applied to Jesus, his person, and work. One example may suffice: Jesus' last saying on the cross, "My God, my God, why hast thou forsaken me?", is a quotation, in Aramaic, from the "Royal Passion Psalm" or "Ebed-Yahweh Psalm," Psalm 22 (v. 2), which is one of the most representative Royal Psalms in the entire Book of Psalms, with its almost model reproduction of motifs which characterize this type of Royal Psalm of Lament. Finally, for purposes of illustration, we offer a brief analysis of this psalm, which is completely woven around the theme of death-life, *descensus-ascensus* (descent into Sheol-resurrection). Psalm 22 begins with an invocation in the form of a plaintive cry, vv. 2–3; this is followed by the motif of trust, vv. 4–6; a formula of humility and a description of adversity, vv. 7–9; and, again, the motif of trust, based on the fact of election, and ending with a plea for help, vv. 10–12. Then, in vv. 13–19, there is a very characteristic "magical-demonic" description of the enemies and a renewed description of adversity, in which the psalmist's destitute situation reaches its climax in a death sentence (v. 16). This section ends with a renewed plea for help, and is followed by a further description of the enemies and the affliction, vv. 20–22. Then comes a description of salvation with collective participation introduced by hymnic motifs: the cultic congregation—indeed, all Israel—shares in the salvation and participates in the anticipatory praise, vv. 23–27. The same theme is repeated in vv. 28–32, but now it takes on universal, cosmic proportions and has as its center the assurance of victory over death, of the resurrection from Sheol for the "Servant of the Lord" and for his people, the future messianic people.[114] The Massoretes have not understood, or have not wanted to understand this Psalm; neither has any modern translation.

114. Vss. 30 ff. may be translated: "Yea, to him (the messiah-king) all those wrapped in the earth prostrate themselves, before him kneel all those who go down to the dust, for he (God) certainly brings his soul to life. Posterity serves him; the generation which is to come is told concerning our Lord, and his righteousness (i. e., salvation, resurrection) is proclaimed to the people who are to be born, for he has performed (his work)." Cf. this with Isaiah 53. Of the two passages, Psalm 22 is primary.

6

⚜

Prophets and Prophetism
in the Old Testament

Introductory Considerations and Terminology.—"Prophet" is an extremely multifarious concept. One of the main reasons for this is that it occurs in several different cultures and religions, both in the highly developed cultures of antiquity and in different primitive peoples of our day, with very diverse meanings and in widely different contexts. However, broadly speaking, "prophet" can essentially be understood in two different ways: institutionally and inspirationally. Institutionally, the prophets are understood as more "official" in their activities, as professional cultic servants with specific tasks, frequently of a mantic (divinatory) type. Here the distinctions between the prophetic and priestly offices become very blurred. As a matter of fact, in Egypt and Rome, "prophet" was simply a title for certain priestly classes.[1] In-

Part of this essay summarizes two articles by Ivan Engnell published in Swedish: "Profetia och tradition," *Svensk exegetisk årsbok,* 12 (1947) pp. 110–139; and "Profetismens ursprung och uppkomst," *Religion och Bibel,* 8 (1949) pp. 1–18. These papers have been utilized in preparing the notes. The complete essay, entitled "Profeter, profetism," appears in *Svenskt Bibliskt Uppslagsverk,* 2d ed., Vol. II, cols. 562–602.

1. This remark is obscure. The Egyptian *ḥm-nṯr* is traditionally rendered as "prophet", but it is not commonly argued that this kind of priest was a prophet in the Old Testament sense. If the reference to Rome aims at the *vates,* it cannot be argued that he was a priest, nor is the *augur* or the *haruspex* really a prophet.

spirationally, emphasis is placed on the psychological characteristics of prophetism. The inspirational or ecstatic element in the nature of prophetism and in the activities of the prophets is regarded as typical and decisive. Then, the "consciousness of having been called," that sense of compulsion which drives the prophets to deliver more or less publicly that which they have experienced in ecstasy,[2] is also included among the psychological characteristics.

But even though these two aspects of prophetism are often very clearly distinct and well-developed, in reality, they must not be played off against each other as mutually exclusive alternatives. On the contrary, they both represent attributes and characteristics inherent in and indispensable to the idea of "prophet." It is certainly true that the personal inspirational element can have a very prominent place within the framework of the institutional. But recent research in Israelite prophetism has been characterized by a strong emphasis on the institutional aspect.[3] The result is that the terms *prophet* and *priest* have come to be understood as more or less equivalent, which conflicts sharply with the earlier idea that they are diametrically opposed to each other.

Another axiom for a modern and undogmatic study of the Old Testament is that Israelite prophetism cannot be studied as a completely isolated and thoroughly unique phenomenon. Instead, it must be evaluated in conjunction with and against the background of prophetism in general. But at the same time, it should be obvious that the comparative material must be handled with caution: to illuminate and to stimulate thought; and that it must be used for the genetic reconstruction of Old Testament phenomena only exceptionally and in obvious cases. The Israelite material must be analyzed on the basis of its own presuppositions and always with the purpose of determining the uniqueness of Old Testament prophetism.

The primary meaning of the word *prophet* (Greek *prophētēs*, from *prophēmi*, "to speak," "to foretell"),[4] is also very intimately connected with the dual character of prophetism. In agreement with clas-

2. J. Lindblom, *Prophecy in Ancient Israel* (Oxford: Basil Blackwell, 1962), pp. 182 ff., 194 ff

3. See, e.g., A. R. Johnson, *The Cultic Prophet in Ancient Israel* (Cardiff: University of Wales Press, 1944); A. Haldar, *Associations of Cult Prophets among the Ancient Semites* (Uppsala: Almqvist and Wiksell, 1945).

4. E. Fascher, *Prophētēs* (Giessen: A. Töpelmann, 1927), pp. 4 ff.

sical tradition, in an earlier period of investigation, the term *prophet* was considered to mean "foreteller." Emphasis was placed on the idea that prophets were diviners, men who, by divine inspiration, had the gift to see into the future and to foretell coming events. However, modern research has clearly tended to adopt the more neutral meaning of "forth-teller": proclaimer of the divine message in general. Thus, to a great extent, the aspect of divination in the word *prophet* has been shoved into the background. But in reality, this term contains both the idea of "foreteller" and the idea of "forthteller."

But more important than the question of the meaning of the Greek word *prophētēs* is the problem of the etymology of the Hebrew noun lying behind it, *nābhî'*, "prophet," with its cognate verbal stems *hinnābhē'* (niph'al) and *hithnabbē'* (hithpa'el), both of which mean "to act like a prophet," "to appear as a prophet," "to prophesy," in most cases with particular emphasis on the ecstatic aspect of prophecy (compare Numb. 11:25 ff.; I Sam. 10:5 ff.; I Kgs. 18:29). The prevalent attempt to define *nābhî'* and its cognates in light of the Arabic *naba'a*, "to gush forth," is hardly convincing. It is much more likely that *nābhî'* should be connected with the Accadian *nabū*, "to announce, proclaim" (compare the Arabic *naba'a*, "to proclaim"). If so, we find a priori further support for the neutral meaning, "forth-teller, proclaimer," for the Hebrew term. This definition, "mouthpiece, proclaimer," is also made probable by such passages as Exod. 4:16; 7:1 f. (Aaron) and by the fact that the prophet can be characterized as "Yahweh's mouth," Jer. 15:19 (compare Amos 3:8 and Hos. 6:5). We may also call attention to the regular introductory formula of prophetic oracles, "thus says Yahweh" (*kōh 'āmar Yahweh*), and similar phrases, in support of this meaning. But in spite of the fact that these evidences all point in a specific direction, when all is said and done, it must be admitted that the etymology is so uncertain that the question of the meaning of the term *nābhî'* cannot be absolutely determined by this method. In fact, it can only finally be determined by investigating the contents of the pertinent material which has been handed down.

The Earliest Prophetism in the Canaanite-Israelite Region; Its Origin and Type.—A so-called primitive prophetism, the general type of prophetism mentioned above, is known to have existed in the ancient land of Canaan from an early period—through the Amarna Letters, the Ras Shamra texts, and the description of Wenamun's journey

in an Egyptian papyrus[5]—but especially through the narrative concerning the prophets of Baal, Asherah, and Yahweh in the time of Elijah in
I Kings, chapter 18. According to a common widespread interpretation, two different groups or types can be discerned in this early
prophetism: the so-called seers (Hebrew singulars *rō'eh* or *hōzeh*;
plural, *ro'îm*, *hōzîm*); and the prophets (singular, *nābhî'*; plural,
n^ebhî'îm). The "seers" are often thought to be of "genuine Israelite"
(pre-Canaanite) origin,[6] whereas the "prophets" are considered to be
Canaanite in origin. Sometimes the "seers" are said to have been more
of the institutional type mentioned above and, thus, the more techni-
cally oriented mantics or diviners, while the "prophets" are supposed
to represent the ecstatic, free, spirit-inspired type.[7] Some critics have
even thought that they detected a difference in degree between
"seers," *rō'îm*, and "visionaries," *hōzîm*, where the latter are regarded as
a higher, more spiritual type.[8] But as far as we are able to judge from
the meagre references in the Old Testament and relevant comparative material, all of these distinctions are artificial and cannot be supported by an objective interpretation of the pertinent texts. On the
whole, there is no foundation for making any distinctions (least of
all, distinctions of the type represented by the time-bound approach
based on the assumption of an evolution of ideas) between the ancient "seer" and the ancient "prophet." Both were ecstatics, even if
there was some degree of difference between the intensity of their
ecstatic experiences, between an emotional or "excited" experience
including violent bodily movements and a quietistic or tranquil, subdued type.[9] Also, both seer and prophet were professional men who
were "organized," i.e., who lived together in guilds under the leadership of a sheik or master; it is clear that they were predominantly associated with the cult and thus were connected to or active in the
different sanctuaries, including the central royal sanctuary. And be-

5. Haldar, *op. cit.*, pp. 47 ff.; for the Egyptian Golénischeff papyrus, see J. B.
Pritchard, editor, *Ancient Near Eastern Texts* (Princeton: Princeton University
Press, 1955), pp. 25–29. Cf. Lindblom, *op. cit.*, pp. 29 ff.

6. Some scholars have attempted to show that *rō'eh* and *hōzeh* are to be
traced back to an Arabic and an Aramaic root, respectively.

7. S. Mowinckel, *Psalmenstudien*, III (Oslo: J. Dybwad, 1923), pp. 9 ff.

8. J. Lindblom in an unidentified earlier work; in *Prophecy in Ancient Israel*,
p. 90, he regards the two terms as synonyms.

9. See chap. 2, "The Science of Religion." Lindblom, in *Prophecy in Ancient
Israel*, pp. 4 f., 48, uses the terms *orgiastic* and *passive (lethargic)* ecstasy.

cause of the close proximity of the royal palace and the temple, it is possible to speak of "court prophets."[10] There is no sufficient evidence in the pertinent texts to justify the view that the nabis were men connected with the cult, and that the seers and "ḥōzîm" were "free" diviners.[11] Furthermore, it is impossible to differentiate between the origins of these two groups. The only thing that can be said is that this more primitive prophetism (including seers and "ḥōzîm") undoubtedly has a twofold background: an Israelite or pre-Canaanite, and a Canaanite.[12]

On the whole, it needs to be pointed out that an evolutionistic view combined with various kinds of presuppositions was carried much too far when it was applied to all the problems of prophetism. The theories which have been suggested on the basis of this evolutionistic presupposition pertaining to the present discussion are the idea that two offshoots emerged from the oldest surviving branch of prophetism, and the notion that the main offshoot of nebiism was gradually transformed and evolved into the higher, spiritualized form represented by later "Yahwistic" prophetism, "doom-" and "reaction-prophetism." The former theory means that so-called primitive prophetism (without being Israelitized and surviving as Canaanite) gradually branched off into two offshoots: a "cult prophetism at the sanctuaries," and a "free vulgar prophetism."[13] Literary products of this prophetism must have been preserved, especially in a number of prophecies of salvation in our existing prophetic books. These prophecies are considered to be secondary and, on the basis of the usual criteria employed by literary criticism, are set apart from their surrounding contexts, which are regarded as authentic. However, this whole point of view is nothing more than an evolutionistic invention. The truth of the matter is that even if it were possible to demonstrate

10. Cf. Haldar, *op. cit.*, pp. 137 ff., 148 ff.

11. Probably an allusion to R. Kraetzschmar, *Prophet und Seher im Alten Israel* (Tübingen: n.p., 1901).

12. The idea that the so-called pure Semitic race—here represented by the pre-Canaanite Hebrews—lacked the psycho-physical presuppositions necessary for an ecstatic prophetism is nothing more than the manifestation of an untenable racial dogma.

13. The reference is to an earlier Swedish work by Lindblom, *Profetismen i Israel* n.p.: n.p., 1934), pp. 172 ff. In *Prophecy in Ancient Israel*, he seems to have modified his views. Engnell also refers to Sellin here, but we are unable to locate the reference.

from the sources that such a distinction was made between a "free" prophetism and a prophetism connected with the cult, this distinction existed from the very first—it did not gradually emerge. But in reality, this distinction is only imaginary. All pre-Yahwistic prophetism was closely connected with the cult: it was cult prophetism. Furthermore, Yahwistic or "reaction" prophetism continued to be connected with the cult to a much higher degree than was formerly thought, as modern prophetic research has abundantly shown.[14] Indeed, generally speaking, prophetism is too complex to divide neatly into cultic and anti-cultic categories.

Thus, throughout Israel's religious history—certainly from the time Israel entered into the land of Canaan and apparently up to the time just preceding the Exile and perhaps even later—we encounter prophets assembled in guilds of "sons of the prophets" (Hebrew singular, *ben nābhî*, "the individual member"; plural *b^enê hann^ebhî'îm*), cf. I Sam. 10:5 ff., 19 f.; I Kgs. 20: 35 ff.; 22:6 ff.; II Kgs. 2:3 ff.; 4:1, 38; 5:22; 6:1; 9:1 ff. The circle had a leader who was called master or father: I Sam. 19:20; I Kgs. 22:11 f.; II Kgs. 4:1, 38; 6:1, 5, 21; 8:9; 13: 14, around whom the disciples were gathered, living together, unmarried or married (compare II Kgs. 4:1). As a rule, they seem to have lived on the remuneration which they received from their practice of the art of divination, a practice for which they were often censured: I Sam. 10:2; 28:6; II Sam. 7:1 ff.; I Kgs. 14:1 ff.; 22:5 ff.; II Kgs. 6:21 f.; 8:7 ff.; 22:14 ff.; or simply on alms: II Kgs. 4:8, 42; 5:22. The Yahwistic prophets Amos (7:14) and Micah (3:8) clearly repudiate the practice of accepting pay for their prophetic activities. Evidently, the prophets were also recognized by their appearance: they might wear a special hairy mantle and a leather girdle, Zech. 13:4 (compare Matt. 3:4 with parallels), or be marked by a "class symbol" on the forehead (I Kgs. 20:35 ff.), or by scars left by wounds inflicted during prophetic ecstasy (I Kgs. 18:28; Zech. 13:6) during religious exercises undoubtedly led by the prophetic master.[15] For the most part, the prophets lived at the sanctuaries of the cults with which they were more or less permanently connected: "Gibeah of God," I Sam. 10:5 ff.; Ramah, I Sam. 19:18 ff.; Bethel, II Kgs. 2:3; Gilgal, II Kgs. 2:1; Sa-

---

14. Cf. Mowinckel, *op. cit.*; Johnson, *op cit.*; J. Pedersen, *Israel, Its Life and Culture*, III–IV (London: Oxford University Press, 1964), pp. 107–149.

15. Haldar, *op. cit.*, p. 144.

maria, I Kgs. 22:10 ff.[16] We are not justified in assuming that because they were "professional prophets," they could not experience "calls" or receive special divine commissions or appear with oracular messages on their own initiative: compare II Sam. 7:1 ff.; 12:1 ff.; 24:11 ff.; I Kgs. 11:29 ff.; 13:1 ff.; 14:1 ff.; 16:1 ff.; 20:13 ff. Such prophets are mentioned as a collective or group within society: Hos. 4:4 f.; Isa. 3:2 f.; 28:7; Mic. 3:11; Zeph. 3:4; Jer. 6:13; 8:1; 14:18; 18:18; Ezek. 13:9.

The royal prophets or court prophets seem to have had a somewhat different status, although the distinctions between them and the types of prophets mentioned above are very obscure. The court prophets were connected with the royal sanctuaries in a more "stationary" way: they appeared there as intermediaries of the divine word and as proclaimers of the divine response in connection with petitions, sacrifices, and auguries. Naturally, most of the time, their pronouncements were positive and included promises of victory, prosperity, and blessing. These prophets functioned within the framework of the daily cult and also in cultic festivals, as on days of penitence, before an army marched out to battle, etc. In campaigns, they accompanied the king and performed similar functions. We know of such "royal" prophets from the early period of the monarchy under Saul down through the centuries: compare I Sam. 28:6 (during Saul's reign); II Sam. 7:1 ff. (Nathan, as David's servant); 24:11 (Gad, also as David's servant); II Kgs. 3:11 ff. (Jehoshaphat's reign).

The prophets used various means to induce ecstasy, such as singing and music (cf. Exod. 15:20; I Sam. 10:5; II Kgs. 3:15), incessant cultic cries (I Kgs. 22:10 ff.; 18:26 ff.), rhythmic movements and dancing (Exod. 15:20; I Kgs. 18:26; compare II Sam. 6:5, 14; I Sam. 18:6 f., etc.), or even cutting their own bodies (I Kgs. 18:28; 20:41; Zech. 13:6). During the ecstasy, they might even tear off their clothes (I Sam. 19:24; compare Isa. 20:2; Mic. 1:8) or fall into rapture (I Sam. 19:24; compare Dan. 8:18, 27; 10:8 f.).[17] On the other hand, Elijah seems to have experienced a quietistic ecstasy, at least according to I Kgs. 18:42 ff. (however, compare v. 46). It was most natural that the ecstasy of the prophets was a spectacle which was attractive and unattractive at the same time (compare I Sam. 10:9 f.; 19:20 ff.;

16. *Ibid.*, pp. 118 f.
17. J. Wellhausen, *Die israelitisch-jüdische Religion*, 2. Aufl. (Berlin: B. G. Teubner, 1909), p. 20; R. Kittel, *Die Religion des Volkes Israel* (Leipzig: Quelle and Meyer, 1921), pp. 103 ff.

I Kgs. 22:10 ff.). But when we consider all the variations in time and place, it is possible that the ecstatic element of prophetism in some century at one time or other developed in a way which had something of a psychic contagion about it.

The Origin of "Genuine Yahwistic" Prophetism. "The Transitional Figures."—In the preceding section, we have described prophetism as a phenomenon in the Israelite period and in the land of Canaan. Now we are faced with the major question of how this primitive (or, better, "common") prophetism, nebiism, is related to prophetism in the usual restricted sense: to "reaction prophetism," "literary prophetism," or whatever one prefers to call it. It has already been pointed out that the usual explanation of this relationship is clearly founded on evolutionistic assumptions: a branch of the "lower" prophetism was transformed, "Yahwicized," spiritualized, and ethicized until it attained the "higher," "spiritual," ethical, monotheistic form represented by "reaction prophetism." Advocates of this view claim that this development is clearly attested in a series of so-called transitional figures. It was pointed out above that, in reality, this is an invention of the imagination which cannot be supported by the evidence which is to be found in the texts themselves. An unprejudiced examination shows that the things which we are told about these transitional figures are so particular and varied that they cannot be forced into this sort of developmental pattern.

Samuel is usually considered to be the first of these figures, and his contribution is often regarded as fundamental. It is thought that Samuel stood at the head of the nabi movement and consciously tried to transform these crowds of ecstatic enthusiasts into ardent Yahwists and bearers of a higher, spiritualized form of religion.[18] However, I Samuel, chapter 10, does not adequately support this reconstruction,[19] and Samuel's own attitude is somewhat ambiguous from a "genuine Yahwistic" point of view.[20]

18. This hypothesis goes back to A. Kuenen and J. Wellhausen, and has recently been energetically defended by R. Kittel, evidently in accordance with a liberal, personalistic view of history.

19. In the article "Samuel" in *SBU*[2], Engnell argues that Samuel, whose "conversion to Yahwism" (not prophetic call) is described in I Samuel, chapter 3, was not really opposed to the syncretism of El and Yahweh and was actively involved in the cult of the high places (I Sam. 10:5 ff., 19:19 ff.) and in the "royal cult" (10:1 f., 17 ff.).

20. Cf. G. Ahlström, "Der Prophet Nathan und der Tempelbau," *Vetus Testamentum*, 11 (1961), pp. 113–127.

David's court prophets, Gad and Nathan, are included in the transitional figures. But the fact that Gad advised David to build the altar at the "threshing floor of Araunah" (II Sam. 24:18 ff.), which evidently means that he was encouraging him to adopt the old Jebusite cult traditions directly,[21] is compelling evidence that this prophet's attitude was syncretistic. The reactionary characteristics which—at least, to some extent—are found in Nathan seem to be due to a Deuteronomistic reinterpretation of the facts, and the same may be said of Samuel. In reality, he seems to have had a syncretistic attitude. We are unable to tell what the attitude of the "man of God"[22] Shemaiah (I Kgs. 12:22 ff.) was, in this respect. Ahijah of Shiloh (I Kgs. 11:29 ff.) seems to represent a clearer Yahwistic position, but the circumstances are somewhat obscure in his case, also. And we cannot ignore the Deuteronomistic stamp which has been left on the traditional material concerning him, either.

Scholars usually attach great importance to the narrative concerning Micaiah, the son of Imlah, in I Kings, chapter 22. But to make this prophet an individualist, a pure Yahwistic proclaimer of doom, a prophet different from the other four hundred who were gathered around the kings, Ahab and Jehoshaphat, is pure eisegesis. Like these prophets, Micaiah was, to be sure, a "Yahwistic" court prophet. His late appearance on the scene is only a stylistic device, a so-called retarding feature, designed to increase the suspense of the narrative. His opposition to the other prophets is not based on principle or ideology but, as the text expressly says, is limited to this specific situation, and perhaps has a personal, constitutional basis. Actually, the narrative specifically says that *in this situation* Yahweh puts a lie in the mouth of the other prophets. In any case, critics have greatly exaggerated Micaiah's importance as a type of transitional figure between early prophetism and reaction prophetism.

But there may be some justification for regarding the prophet Elijah as a borderline figure between nebiism and reaction-prophetism, because he was concerned with defending Yahweh worship and with preserving traditional principles of justice. And yet he was not involved in a fundamental conflict between Yahweh and Baal, but in a very special and immediate conflict with the Tyrian Baal-Melkart, who

---

21. See the discussion by H. Ringgren, *Israelite Religion* (Philadelphia: Fortress Press, 1966), p. 262.

22. Hebrew *'ish hā'ᵃᵉlōhîm*, a term which is used for "visionary," "seer," and "prophet," but has a more general meaning.

was just as exclusivistic as Yahweh. Furthermore, there is no indication that Elijah opposed image cult or cultic forms in general. And
there is no evidence that he combined a proclamation of doom with
messianic prophecies in his oracles. It is also a mistake to make Elijah
one of the great individualists. He was undoubtedly an extraordinary
person, but he was also associated with guilds of nabis (II Kgs. 2:1
ff.). Again, it is much less reasonable to think that Elisha belonged to
the series of transitional figures than Elijah. Elisha is a typical ecstatic
nabi-sheik with guilds of disciples in Bethel, Jericho, and Gilgal. He is
ultra-nationalistic and pro-monarchic, a prophet deeply involved in
politics. But nothing is said about cultic tensions which, along with
his chauvinistic attitude, might have determined his activity. Besides,
he differs rather radically from the generally accepted model of a reaction prophet.

But even though a careful scrutiny of the alleged evidence indicates that the idea of a development from early prophetism to reaction
prophetism through a transitional period with its Yahwistic predecessors is erroneous, we still have not solved the problem of when Yahwistic prophetism originated. Furthermore, we have not determined
whether this was due to a division or differentiation within prophetism
in general. Did Yahwistic prophetism arise suddenly and unexpectedly
with the first of the "prophets of doom," Amos?—i.e., was Amos a
different kind of prophet from the others of his day, one of an entirely
new type, perhaps even with an antagonistic attitude toward the
nabis with whom he and his hearers were familiar? Did he flatly denounce any connection with the nabis, as the generally accepted interpretation of Amos 7:14 would suggest? In answer to these questions, it
should be pointed out, first, that the problems involved are very complicated. The statements of Amos in 7:14 are so ambiguous that we
must interpret them in light of Amos's attitude toward the prophets
expressed elsewhere in the book which bears his name. The pertinent
passages (2:11 f. and 3:7) indicate clearly that his estimation of the
nabis was very positive. And it should be emphasized strongly that the
context makes it quite clear that these passages refer to Yahwistic
prophets of the same type as Amos and with whom he felt himself to
be intimately associated. In light of this evidence, it is clear that Amos
was not the originator of something absolutely new and distinctive in
the development of prophetism. This is further substantiated by the
fact that in 7:12, Amaziah, the high priest in Bethel, addressed Amos as

ḥōzeh, "seer," and in the same verse describes his work with the verb nibbāʾ, "to act as a prophet." What is more, in 7:15, Amos uses the same word in speaking of himself. The statement that Amos was among the herdsmen of Tekoa (1:1) is also of great interest. Non-Israelite parallels (most recently from Ras Shamra) show unmistakably that the word used here, nōqēdh, has a clear, technical, sacral meaning:[23] it probably refers to a local group of temple herdsmen at Tekoa which, in turn, no doubt belonged to the Jerusalem temple as a kind of branch to it.[24] However, it is of utmost importance that, linguistically, the correct interpretation of 7:14–15 is that Amos does not say that he *is* not a nabi,[25] but rather that he *was* not a nabi or member of a nabi-guild, since it was Yahweh's call which caused him to leave his flock. Indeed, if we look at this passage purely from a linguistic standpoint, the most plausible meaning is that, after his call, Amos actually was a "prophet's son," that is, a member of a prophetic guild, even if this interpretation is not absolutely mandatory in and of itself. Be this as it may, there is no foundation for the view that Amos completely dissociated himself from the nabis and nebiism, as is often asserted. The context of Amos 7:14–15 and Amaziah's ironic words show that what Amos was trying to emphasize was that he did not prophesy to gain bread or money, but because of Yahweh's personal call. It should also be noted that Amos was not the first prophet to refuse remuneration for his services. Elisha did the same thing, according to II Kgs. 5:15 f. So, in itself, Amos's position here is no argument against his being a nabi.

But if Amos's contemporaries actually considered him, the first of the (literary) prophets, to be a nabi, "prophet," in the usual sense of the term, then we are still faced with the question of when and how the new prophetism of doom originated. And, in reality, this question cannot be answered. The differentiation and division within prophetism did not "originate," at all—at any rate, not in such a way that it can be traced. It was there from the very beginning, conditioned by per-

23. Cf. H. H. Rowley, "Was Amos a Nabi?", *Von Ugarit nach Qumran. Festschrift O. Eissfeldt* (Halle: M. Niemeyer, 1947), pp. 191 ff.

24. Indeed, most scholars want to read nōqēdh instead of bōqēr in Amos 7:14 also. It is true that the context renders the meaning "herdsman of cattle, breeder of cattle," impossible, but it may be that bōqēr means "observer, seer," and so is a synonym of ḥōzeh and rōʾeh.

25. Cf. Rowley, *op. cit.*

sonal qualities and actualized in specific situations. Thus, we must
think of it in this way: individual rebels appeared spontaneously in
both Yahwistic and non-Yahwistic circles, at both non-Yahwistic or
syncretistic sanctuaries and cult centers and at the royal court. This is
supported by the fact that we know of rebels of the same type from
other areas in the ancient Near Eastern world.[26] Of these rebels in
Israel, we know the Yahwistic best—or, rather, we know them alone,
simply because it is their words and the traditions concerning them
which have been handed down to us, in a Jerusalemite edition.

Also, it seems clear that, to some extent, these Yahwistic rebels are
actually connected with an ancient line of reactionaries whose existence
is attested by such figures as Deborah, Gideon, and the man of God
who condemned the house of Eli at Shiloh, I Sam. 2:27 ff. But it is
very misleading to interpret the literary prophets exclusively according
to this "wilderness line" on the basis of this connection.

The Problem of the "Wilderness Line" in Yahwistic Prophetism.—
In spite of everything which Old Testament "reaction prophetism"
has in common with earlier prophetism, we cannot escape the fact that
it has its own distinctive character. But it is a very difficult task to ascertain this character, to find the "genuine Yahwistic" criteria. The
most convincing proof of this is the widely different scholarly interpretations of the nature of Yahwistic prophetism. The idea of a homogeneous movement which can be called Old Testament prophetism
turns out to be largely imaginary and the result of a view founded on
evolutionistic presuppositions. Be this as it may, each scholar must
strive as far as possible to free himself from preconceived ideas and
keep his eye open for other possibilities. As one of these possibilities,
we suggest in particular that one must take the concept of "prophetic
circle" under consideration rather than to try to determine when Yahwistic prophetism originated and how it developed.[27] In other words,
we must always keep in mind that prophetism as a phenomenon is
very heterogeneous and rich in variations.

As one of the answers to the question of what it is that makes
Yahwistic prophetism unique, we may notice first an explanation to
which we have already alluded and which is often given: the "Bed-

---

26. It is not clear to whom this statement refers.

27. Variations within Old Testament prophecy should be explained as the
result of differing opinions in different circles of prophets and their disciples,
rather than as a chronological development along one line.

ouin character" of prophetism, emphasized at an early stage of the modern historico-critical prophetic research and continued with great tenacity as a leading explanation in scholarly circles. A very high appreciation for Moses (which in itself is completely correct) as the first prophet and founder of the prophetic religion lies behind this interpretation. As a result of the work of W. Vatke and A. Kuenen,[28] the emphasis placed on the "Bedouin line" in the development of prophetism (characteristic of all the literary-critical exegetes dependent on J. Wellhausen) was transformed into an axiom and a master key to Israelite religious history on the whole. This view has been espoused in particular by a group of Arabists (MacDonald, Montgomery, and Margoliouth) and by French exegetes (Dhorme, Lods, and Toussaint; there are also the Swiss scholar Humbert and the Swedish scholars Nyberg and Nyström).[29] According to this theory, the rôle of the prophets in the religious development of Israel is that of advocates of the ideal Bedouin ethic of the Days of the Fathers.[30] They purified the popular Israelite religion, which resulted from the influence of the Canaanite paganism on the Israelites when they settled in the land, by opposing the cult. Gradually, this wilderness ideal was elevated to an ethical monotheism which reached perfection in "Deutero-Isaiah." However, this view has two major weaknesses: it is obviously characterized by an evolutionistic concept of Israel's religion, and it involves an exaggerated interpretation of the Bedouin element itself. The romantic view of the desert which this hypothesis presupposes is clearly out of touch with reality: the more positive the appreciation for the wilderness period is, in the Old Testament, the farther removed the writer is from that period. In most cases, people who live near the desert usually reach an opposite conclusion. An unprejudiced investigation indicates that in the prophets also (although, of

28. W. Vatke, *Die Religion des Alten Testaments* (Berlin: G. Bethge, 1835); A. Kuenen, *De profeten en de profetie onder Israël* (Leiden: P. Engels, 1875).

29. MacDonald (unidentified); Montgomery (unidentified); D. S. Margoliouth, *The Relations between Arabs and Israelites* (London: Oxford University Press, 1924); A. Lods, *Les prophètes d'Israël et les débuts du Judaïsme* (Paris: La Renaissance du livre, 1935), pp. 70 ff.; C. Toussaint, *Les Origines de la religion d'Israël* (Paris: P. Geuthner, 1931), passim; P. Humbert (unidentified); H. S. Nyberg (refers rather to his general attitude than to any particular book or passage); S. Nyström, *Beduinentum und Jahvismus* (Lund: C. W. K. Gleerup, 1946), pp. 122 ff.

30. This opinion is ascribed to H. Winckler by Engnell in the *Svensk Exegetisk Årsbok*, 12 (1947), p. 112.

course, with considerable variations) the desert is seen from the perspective of the period after the settlement in Canaan: the desert itself and the "Bedouin period" are by no means something ideal in Israel's history. On the contrary, the desert represents evil; it is the land of darkness, terrors, and death, the incarnate *she'ôl*, Hades,[31] while Canaan (that is, Israelite, Yahwistic Canaan) is the Promised Land, the land of the messianic future. Therefore, the character of the wilderness wandering is that of a *rite de passage*, a rite of passage from death to life, which could be accomplished and survived only by Yahweh's merciful guidance. After all, the prophets looked upon the "period of the Fathers" in the desert as an apostate age, from the very first: Israel had already sinned with the golden calf and Baal-Peor, with Sakkuth and Kaiwan (Amos 5:26).[32] A correct exegesis of the Book of Hosea, which takes the context into consideration, shows that this prophet also (who, according to the usual interpretation, is the clearest exponent of the Bedouin ideal among the prophets) looks at the desert period in the same way.[33] To be sure, according to Hos. 2:16 ff., it is Yahweh's purpose that Israel go out into the wilderness, but one must not overlook the fact that the reason for this is that Israel might spend a period of quarantine there (compare the symbolic description in 3:3 ff.) and afterwards enter into the Promised Land, where the messianic future would come. In other respects, also, it is evident that the prophetic attachment to the desert is quite loose, consisting for the most part in inherited stereotyped expressions and phrases without any real positive content. The prophets share in the Canaanite peasant ideal in its advanced form, which is succinctly summarized in Mic. 4:4 (RSV): "But they shall sit every man under his vine and under his fig tree: and none shall make them afraid."

It has also been maintained that the prophets realized the Bedouin ideal toward which earlier prophets halfway tended, as is apparent in the Rechabites.[34] But we must ask whether even this modest judgment

31. Cf. J. Pedersen, *Israel,* I–II, pp. 454 ff.; A. Haldar, *The Notion of the Desert in Sumero-Accadian and West-Semitic Religions* (Uppsala: Lundequist, 1950), pp. 43 ff.

32. Based on the exegesis of this passage advocated by G. A. Danell, *Studies in the Name of Israel in the Old Testament* (Uppsala: Appelberg, 1946), p. 123.

33. Lindblom, *Prophecy in Ancient Israel,* p. 344, has modified his earlier view; cf. also H. W. Wolff, "Hosea" in *Biblischer Kommentar Altes Testament* (Neukirchen-Vluyn: Neukirchener Verlag, 1965), 2:16 ff.

34. Pedersen, *Israel,* III–IV, p. 522.

says too much. By the way, the ideal of the Rechabites, as well, is far from being consistent. In any case, the notion that the red thread of "genuine" prophetism consists of the Bedouin ideal is wholly misleading. This understanding is the result of a modern anachronistic view and is actually an invention based on a preconceived and idealistic interpretation of the entire religious history of Israel. Furthermore, this whole wilderness concept is contrary to a well-established conclusion of modern research in the fields of archaeology, anthropology, philology, and the history of religion, namely, that *Canaan* played a very important rôle in the history of Israel. In this respect, prophetism cannot a priori be assigned any exceptional position. Its opposition to the extremes, corruption, and decay of "Canaanized" Israelite religion is another matter.

The "Anti-Cultic" Problem. The Relationship between Cult and Ethics.—Ethics is intimately connected with the idea of the rôle of the desert in "genuine" prophetism. Exegetes have unanimously placed strong emphasis on ethics as perhaps the most important factor which distinguishes "genuine" prophetism from "false" prophetism, which very indiscriminately is regarded as lacking ethical character and is characterized by its association with the cult. In other words, the literary prophets are conceived of as representatives and cultivators of the persisting ideal Bedouin ethic, which was practiced in the time of the fathers before the Canaanite era of degeneration set in with its materialistic and sensualistic religion. According to this view, the prophets return to this Bedouin ethic and thus come forth with an essentially anti-cultic proclamation. Their message is that righteousness should supplant the cult. As a result, the prophets create a new "spiritual" form of religion which is "without cult." This understanding, which is still predominant (at any rate, in popular expositions and text-books), is undoubtedly prompted by a Protestant tenet that cultic piety is of inferior power, a view inherited from the Age of the Enlightenment and Rationalism. Advocates of this position operate on a purely anachronistic assumption that the prophets propagated a "spiritual" religion which was independent of the cult. But, in reality, this is completely foreign to ancient Israel, including her prophets. Due especially to contributions by Scandinavian scholarship, which has energetically emphasized the positive, central rôle of the cult in Israel, it is true that in recent years considerable modification of the time-honored interpretation has been effected. However, even when it has been conceded that the prophets did not propagate an essentially cult-free religion, still, in most cases, the basic outlook itself has not been changed.

In reality, the problem of the relationship between the cult and ethics in prophetic preaching is very complicated. But here we may mention some ideas that are fundamental. First of all, we must not treat all the "literary prophets" alike or assume that all the prophets had the same attitude toward the cult. On the contrary, this varies from prophet to prophet, and often from situation to situation, in the attitude of one and the same prophet. As he is influenced by religio-political factors (especially by the conduct of the king), a prophet can change his view from one time to another. The prophet Jeremiah is a good case in point. Again, we should keep in mind that, in general, the so-called anti-cultic sayings are greatly overemphasized, for emotional reasons. Furthermore, it is very important to realize that the idea of righteousness (*ṣeḏhāqāh* or *ṣedheq*) in the prophets actually has a meaning entirely different from that which modern views would lead a person to conclude. It does not have a narrow ethical, social hue. Its meaning is much broader than this; righteousness also has a cosmic dimension and at the same time reflects a cultic orientation.[35] In reality, the demand for righteousness is a demand involving cultic responsibilities. In fact, it includes a demand for cult, for a *right* cult, of Yahweh, a genuine Yahwistic cult, unmixed with foreign elements and combined with ethical and social blamelessness. This sort of cult is, in a real sense, a sustaining power, essential to the preservation of the equilibrium in the community and among the people, for its welfare and prosperity, and for the preservation of the cosmos in the never-ending war against the power of chaos.[36] Sometimes the idea of righteousness is even clearly synonymous with "worship," "cult"; compare, for example, Isa. 56:1, Ezek. 18:5. Therefore, it is completely incorrect to think of the prophetic demand for righteousness as an alternative excluding the cult. The prophets do not demand righteousness *instead of* the cult, but righteousness *and* cult, right cult, to the right god and at the right place, that is, Jerusalem.[37]

35. Cf. Ringgren, *op. cit.*, pp. 83 f., 132 f.

36. Cf. S. Mowinckel's conception of the cult, *The Psalms in Israel's Worship* (New York: Abingdon Press, 1962), pp. 112 ff., and A. R. Johnson, *Sacral Kingship in Ancient Israel* (Cardiff: University of Wales Press, 1955), esp. pp. 92 f.

37. Cf. H. H. Rowley, *From Moses to Qumran* (New York: Association Press, 1963), pp. 87 f., 116 f.

This righteousness is related to the Jerusalemite high god in a very special way. It is by no means exclusively or even primarily a legacy of the desert. Therefore, the prophets are not founders of an ethical Israelite religion. Such a religion had already originated, long before their time. But they did deepen and sharpen the ethical demand as far as its application to personal experience was concerned, and they insisted on it even in spite of the lives of their own people. Naturally, in most cases, in the actual situation, their most important and urgent task was to emphasize the ethical and social side of man's relationship to God, of the "covenant" requirements. The idea of an ethical, spiritual, relationship to God, that is, a relationship not involving any cult, is certainly a modern anachronism (in fact, even a self-contradiction), which suggests a completely wrong picture of the real attitude of the prophets.

No fundamental declarations of anti-cultic principles are to be found in the prophets, no matter how diligently scholars persist in their attempts to find them. In an unprejudiced, true exegesis, which takes the context of the sayings into consideration, it is evident that, in reality, these so-called anti-cultic sayings refer to special cases: they are directed either against certain definite forms of the cult (foreign types, or types which claim to be Yahwistic but are not acknowledged as such by the prophet in question—which first of all is true of all North Israelite cults without exception), or against a cult whose advocates are incriminated in one way or other, especially in their inferior ethical and social practices. The polemical sayings which have been interpreted as essentially anti-cultic (for example, Amos 5:21 ff.; Hos. 6:6; Isa. 1:11 ff.; Jer. 7:21 ff.) fall into one of these categories.

This is the case with Amos 5:21 ff., as with all of chap. 5. This saying is directed against North Israel and North Israelite cults, especially the one practiced in Bethel. When the text of vv. 25 f. is interpreted correctly in its context—and the interpretation suggested here is unavoidable from a linguistic point of view—it is clear that it does not say anything about a non-cultic ideal period during "the forty years." Rather, it declares that, at that time, Israel had already apostatized from Yahweh by worshipping the foreign gods Sakkuth and Kaiwan.[38] The same is true of Jer. 7:21 ff., which does not denounce right sacrifices. On the contrary, this passage assumes that they belong even to the pre-Mosaic period. The fact that it emphasizes the so-

38. Cf. Danell, *op. cit.*, p. 123.

called ethical aspect of a right covenant relationship with Yahweh is another matter. Hos. 6:6 is directed against murderers and criminals. It is *their* cult which Yahweh will not acknowledge, and this is the meaning, whether this passage denounces both North Israelite and Judean cults or (as is more likely) the North Israelite cult in Gilead. In a similar way, in Isa. 1:11 ff., it is a false cult which Yahweh repudiates, a cult which is "vain" (Heb. *shāw'*), which is an "abomination" (*tō'ēbhāh*) to Yahweh *because it is associated with evil* (*'āwen*) in the lives of the worshippers, who approach him with blood-stained hands and thus completely set aside the ethical aspect of religion, vv. 13 f. If this passage were fundamentally anti-cultic, then Yahweh would have to be understood as denouncing prayer also (v. 15).[39]

Thus, an interpretation which overemphasizes the anti-cultic nature of oracles such as these is misleading. At the same time, we must also avoid exaggerating the effect of the proclamations of the prophets on the people of their own day. There can be no doubt that, in general, the people did not respond favorably to their proclamations, even long after they were delivered. The fact that they obviously became very important to a later generation is an entirely different thing.

Something further needs to be said about the Jerusalem orientation of the prophetic demand for righteousness. Righteousness, in its cosmic dimension, as the sustaining principle in the world, corresponds entirely with the picture of the Jerusalemite ethically superior sky god and god of destiny, Yahweh-El Elyon, "God Most High", who is also called *Ṣedheq*, "Righteousness" (Isa. 1:21, 26; Jer. 31:23).[40] Thus, here is another point where the Canaanite element has made an important contribution to Israel's religion, even in its prophetic form.

The fact that the prophets connect righteousness with the Messiah, the savior figure who emanated from the person of the sacral king and the complex of ideas associated with him, is also intimately related to this. This Jerusalemite righteousness[41] plays a central rôle in the picture which Isaiah, Jeremiah, and "Deutero-Isaiah" paint of the Messiah

39. Cf. Rowley, *From Moses to Qumran*, p. 117.
40. This thesis is briefly alluded to in Engnell's *Studies in Divine Kingship in the Ancient Near East*, second edition (Oxford: Basil Blackwell, 1967), p. 177; cf. G. Widengren, *The Accadian and Hebrew Psalms of Lamentation* (Stockholm: Thule, 1937), pp. 70 ff.; A. R. Johnson, *Sacral Kingship in Ancient Israel*, p. 46.
41. Cf. A. R. Johnson, *Sacral Kingship in Ancient Israel*, pp. 31 f., 46, etc.

and the future messianic kingdom.[42] This is another thing which shows how misleading the anti-cultic interpretation of prophetic preaching is. Here, again, it is important to avoid a modern anachronistic view and to adopt an organic and realistic one.

In turn, this implies an impartial evaluation of the inescapable fact that, in reality, the so-called literary prophets were connected with the cult, in one way or another, directly or indirectly, to a much greater extent than scholars usually want to believe or observe. The close relationship of Amos to nebiism that we have established above applies to other so-called literary prophets, in spite of certain differences between them. Joel, Nahum, Habakkuk, Haggai, and Zechariah, the individual prophetic figures who must be assumed behind the "books" which bear their names, can distinctly be characterized as cult prophets. There are also points at which Hosea, Isaiah, Jeremiah, and Ezekiel are positively connected with cultic milieux of some kind or other.

Thus, Hosea is a nabi in the same sense as Amos. He manifests a positive attitude toward the prophets (cf. Hos. 12:11; 4:4 ff.; 9:8), and demonstrates the same positive attitude toward a right cult, that is, a Yahwistic Jerusalemite cult, a cult which advocates high ethical ideals. These presuppositions are necessary to explain all of his actions: compare, for example, 3:4 f. and 9:3 f.[43] Isaiah has the official title of nabi (*yeshaʿyāhû bhen 'āmôṣ hannābhîʾ*, Isa. 37:2; 38:1). The king consults him both on public problems pertaining to government and on private matters. Isaiah receives his call in the temple. He has a circle of disciples around him. These factors, together with many others, have led more than one scholar to see him as a cult nabi in a strict sense.[44] His wife also seems to have been a professional prophetess (Isa. 8:3). Directly or indirectly, he always supports a true Jerusalemite cult. Jeremiah belonged to a priestly family (Jer. 1:1) and has the title of nabi. He appeared publicly in priestly and prophetic

---

42. See chap. 11, "The Messiah in the Old Testament and Judaism."

43. In his article on "Hosea" in *SBU*[2], Engnell argues that Hosea was a Judaean who was active as a prophet in the northern kingdom and condemned the *northern* cult in favor of Jerusalemite praxis (of the pro-Judaean passages 1:7; 2:2; 3:5; 4:15; 6:11). That he was a *nabi* is clear from 12:10 and the positive evaluation of prophets which is reflected in 4:4 ff., 9:8, as well as from his use of symbolic action (marriage with Gomer). Hos. 3:4 f. and 9:3 f. show that Hosea did not envisage religion without cultic activities as ideal religion.

44. Cf. I. Hylander in *Le Monde Oriental*, 25 (1931), pp. 62 f.

functions (28:5 ff.; 42:2). He also clearly felt that he was amenable to priestly obedience and jurisdiction (Jer. 20:1 ff.). Behind his severe oracles of doom against the actual cultic conditions of his day lies a strong zeal for the cult, for the right Yahwistic cult. Ezekiel also calls himself a nabi (Ezek. 2:5) and is a professional priest (1:3). His distinct and strongly positive interest in the cult is clear from his outline of the organization of the cult in Jerusalem in chapters 40 ff. of the book which bears his name.

It is necessary to emphasize strongly all of these positive factors of the relationship of the prophets to the cult in reaction to the traditional one-sided picture. But now we must point out that this insight should not be allowed to obscure the fact that "prophetic preaching," to use a much too general expression, to a certain extent actually did contribute to the undermining of the existing official cult and to shaping future conditions. But this is to be understood in light of what has been said above; that is, we must guard against exaggerating the prophets' contribution to and influence on their own times. As long as we keep this in mind, there can be no doubt that, over a long period of time, there was a shift in the main emphasis in Israelite religion, a shift which may be due especially to the prophetic opposition to the idea that the cult functions *ex opere operato*, that is, in a purely mechanical way, without regard for inner qualities. This shift involved a change of emphasis from the offering of bloody sacrifices to other elements in the worship. But the movement away from bloody sacrifices was a relatively late development and was not the result of prophetic propaganda, but of external factors. We emphasize that this recognition of the influence of the prophetic proclamation on Israelite religion is something quite different from adopting the one-sided evolutionistic view which was the object of our polemic above. This view consciously regards the prophets as essentially anti-cultic propagandists, an interpretation which does violence to the prophetic texts and understands the historical reality anachronistically. Against this, we must evaluate the prophets according to the standards of their time, not according to modern standards. This is a prerequisite which any realistic interpretation of the Bible must inevitably come to accept.

The Problem of Prophetic "Monotheism."—This same principle of interpretation is also true in a study of the prophets' attitude toward and influence on the development of so-called monotheism in Israel's religion. We have already mentioned, incidentally, that an earlier generation of scholars, whose thinking was dominated by the evolutionistic approach, naively oversimplified this problem. They traced Old Testament religion from polytheism in the Patriarchal Period through the stage of "monolatry" in the Mosaic Age to a monotheistic form of religion which was advocated for the first time by the prophets and attained its fullest expression in "Deutero-Isaiah," the supposed author of Isaiah, chapters 40–55.[45] According to this scheme, the prophets were deliberate monotheistic propagandists and educators of the people, who led their contemporaries by the hand through the jungle of popular religion or "natural religion" to enlightened, ethical monotheistic faith, a faith which they themselves created. This reconstruction of the history of Old Testament religion, based on a preconceived idea of historical development throughout, will not stand the test of more recent scholarly investigations into the historical and phenomenological aspects of the history of Israel's religion. On the whole, the old terminology used to describe Israel's religion needs to be re-examined. The term *monotheism* itself is ambiguous.[46] In some cases, it may refer to an affective monotheism, but, in others, to a rational and theoretical philosophical monotheism. Affective monotheism means that the god who stands in the center, the one to whom the worshipper is praying and offering sacrifice and to whom he is turning, is also *de facto* considered to be the only god.[47] This type of monotheism is characteristic not only of the Mosaic religion, but also of the patriarchal religion; in other words, it is not limited to any particular time period nor is it the result of historical evolution. An objective evaluation of this problem has been complicated to a certain extent by the introduction of the term *Ur-monotheism*, which can be misleading and thus should be avoided. It is better to use the phrase *belief in a high god*,[48] and to interpret it purely phenomenologically,

45. The expression seems to imply that Isaiah, chapters 40–55, is not the work of one person but the result of the activity of a "circle" of disciples. This seems to militate against the classification of Deutero-Isaiah as a book of the "liturgy" type, which is more likely to have been written down from the very beginning. In chap. 13, "The Figurative Language of the Old Testament," Engnell expresses himself a little more explicitly: "the man or the circle" responsible for the book.

46. Cf. chap. 2, "The Science of Religion."

47. Cf. Widengren, *op. cit.*, pp. 54 ff. The term *affective monotheism, ibid.*, p. 54, with reference to J. Hehn, *Die biblische und babylonische Gottesidee* (Leipzig: Hinrichs, 1913), p. 99.

48. See chap. 2, "The Science of Religion."

without a priori injecting a value concept into it. If we look at it in this way, Yahweh, the Mosaic form of "El of the fathers," is a high god or a sky god, from the very first. To be more specific, he is a high god of the atmospheric type, and in his Jerusalem form, is distinguished by his ethical qualities. In the land of Canaan, then, the Mosaic high god is transformed from the god of the amphictyony into the god of the Israelite people and nation. This is reflected especially in the dynamic, dramatic cultic acts of the Annual Festival, with their reactivation of the ideas of creation and salvation, couched in the framework of covenant categories. But actually, this concept already contains all the elements which characterize the prophetic picture of God. The prophetic view cannot be regarded as a new creation but possibly can be characterized as a development of the exclusivistic attitude which is such a strong element in the traditional picture of God in Israel. The fact that the prophets elevate Yahweh to such an extent that he can even punish his own people does not weaken this point in any way, for this concept was undoubtedly a part of the ideology of the Annual Festival.[49] What actually happened was that, as Yahweh's exclusivism came to be emphasized more and more, his sphere of influence was gradually extended; and in this process, he tended to become not only the only powerful god, but the one and only God.

This empirical monotheism is not exactly the same thing as a thought-out, well-reasoned, rationalistic, philosophical monotheism. Actually, this kind of thinking did not come within the purview of prophetic thought. Rather, their monotheism was the result of their own affective experience with God. "Deutero-Isaiah's" vigorous declaration of Yahweh's superiority over all other gods also reflects this type of monotheism, and there are parallels to his oft-recurring monotheistic formulae and phrases in other ancient Near Eastern literature, for example, in Assyrian and Babylonian prayer literature.[50] The background of his biting irony against the makers of gods and their images, in Isa. 44:9 ff., is undoubtedly twofold: real apostasy among his fellow countrymen in the Babylonian diaspora, and the rôle which the manufacture and preparation of idols played in the Babylonian

49. This obviously has reference to the theory that Yahweh's judgment of the peoples and of Israel was part of the New Year Festival; cf. the judgment motif as part of Mowinckel's Enthronement Festival.

50. See now C. J. Labuschagne, *The Incomparability of Yahweh in the Old Testament* (Leiden: E. J. Brill, 1966), pp. 33 ff.

cult.[51] Finally, it is particularly important to remember that ultimately the polemic of the prophets against idolatry undoubtedly has its origin in analogous phenomena in the cultic context of the Annual Festival, where such polemic was thought to "create" the victory over the enemies.[52]

The Problem of Ecstasy.—We have already pointed out that ecstasy played a very important rôle, both in earlier nebiism and in the work of the so-called transitional figures, such as Elisha. A survey of the ways in which the ecstatic possession of "the spirit" (*rûaḥ*) manifests itself in this period shows that there are important general similarities between these earlier prophets in the Canaanite-Israelite region and the medicine men, thaumaturges, and charismatic leaders whom we encounter elsewhere in the world of religion. Thus, the spirit-filled leader can transfer his "supernatural" (parapsychic) power to his disciples, especially to the prophet who is to succeed him as leader (compare II Kgs. 2:9 ff.).[53] The prophets have power over thunder, lightning, and rain (I Sam. 7:7 ff.; I Kgs. 17:1; 18:36 ff.). They can cause and cure illnesses (I Kgs. 13:4 ff.; II Kgs. 5:9 ff.—here is a typical situation in which the prophet is set over against the king, and an originally royal prerogative is tendentiously transferred to the prophet—5:25 ff.; Isa. 38:21 f.). According to popular belief, they can cause death and raise from the dead (I Kgs. 17:17 ff.; 20:35 f.; II Kgs. 1:1 ff.; 2:3 ff.; 4:32 ff.; Jer. 28:15 ff.). But in speaking of all these prophetic capacities, it should be pointed out that there is an important nuance which the Old Testament emphasizes throughout in describing this earlier period: that it is Yahweh himself who acts, and the prophets are his instruments. Other kinds of miracles are also ascribed to these earlier prophets, among them the ability to walk through water dry-shod and to multiply food and drink. But the ability which seems to be most characteristic of these prophets is that of seeing and hearing, irrespective of time or place: their clairvoyance, the ecstatic state, in which they receive their revelations (or psycho-

---

51. See the ritual for the Babylonian New Year Festival in Pritchard, *op. cit.*, pp. 331–334, 11. 190 ff.

52. Cf. A. Bentzen, "The Ritual Background of Amos i, 2–ii, 16," *Oudtestamentische Studiën*, 8 (1950), pp. 85–99; Haldar, *Associations of Cult Prophets*, pp. 152 ff.

53. In one case, I Kgs. 19:16, anointment with oil is practiced, obviously a democratization of a royal ritual (cf. Isa. 61: 1), which probably refers to the Messiah, not to the prophet. (From *SBU²* II, cols. 383, 1032).

logically speaking, their visions and auditions), is the most typical thing about them. Before we examine the ecstatic element in the so-called literary prophets, however, we must emphasize once more that the prevalent scholarly understanding of the relationship of the literary prophets to ecstasy is clearly just as dependent on the general evolutionistic view as are the general interpretations of the problems already discussed. Scholars have usually subscribed to the position maintained by A. Kuenen and J. Wellhausen, that the ecstatic element in the prophetic movement was suppressed more and more until it was spiritualized and rationalized. Many scholars, including W. R. Smith and, in modern times, K. Cramer, A. Weiser, N. Micklem, and A. Heschel,[54] have come to the more or less radical position of denying that Old Testament prophetism on the whole has an ecstatic character. Consequently, they transform the prophets into religious preachers and thinkers who declare divine truths with intellectual clarity and force. Under the influence of modern religious trends, some scholars have even emphasized the divine "word" (Heb. *dābhār*) as "the rational element" in prophetic religion[55] and as the true expression of its uniqueness in contrast to seizure by the "spirit." But an unprejudiced investigation makes it clear that the phrases "to be seized by Yahweh's spirit" or "hand" are completely identical with the phrase "Yahweh's word comes to" the prophet, and that all of these expressions reflect the ecstatic experience.[56] Furthermore, there can be no doubt that the attempts to eliminate the importance of ecstasy in the great prophets are due to a modern negative evaluation of ecstasy, which is foreign to ancient Israelite thought. According to the traditional Israelite view, ecstasy does not imply infirmity or insanity, but suggests hyperactivity and concentration of power. Literally, it means to be filled with the divine spirit. The fact that the ecstatic phenomenon itself could make an ambiguous impression is another matter.

One of the most radical methods which scholars have used to dis-

---

54. W. Robertson Smith (unidentified); K. Cramer, *Amos. Versuch einer theologischen Interpretation* (Stuttgart: W. Kohlhammer, 1930), especially p. 20; A. Weiser, *Die Prophetie des Amos. Beihefte zur Zeitschrift für die alttestamentliche Wissenschaft,* 53 (Giessen: A. Töpelmann, 1929); N. Micklem, *Prophecy and Eschatology* (London: G. Allen and Unwin, Ltd., 1926); A. Heschel, *Die Prophetie* (Berlin: Erich Reiss, 1936).

55. S. Mowinckel, "'The Spirit' and the 'Word' in the Pre-Exilic Reforming Prophets," *Journal of Biblical Literature,* 53 (1934), pp. 199–227; and see Mowinckel's article in *Revue d'Histoire et de Philosophie Religieuses,* 22 (1942), pp. 69 ff.

56. A. Haldar, *Associations of Cult Prophets,* pp. 115 f.

sociate the prophets from ecstatic experiences is that of distinguishing between genuine vision and literary form. Some scholars maintain that much of what appears to be an expression of ecstatic seizure is actually only metaphorical language or traditional literary forms adopted by the prophets. In and of itself, there is no reason why this cannot be true. It is always difficult to make a decision on this point because, very often, no conclusive objective criteria are available. We cannot emphasize too strongly that the prophets used traditional literary forms very extensively. However, in the literary prophets, in most cases, we are also dealing predominantly with real or genuine visions and auditions, experienced in varying degrees of hypnagogic states, from purely nocturnal dream-visions to visions of a more moderate diurnal hypnotic type, which sometimes are accompanied by special phenomena such as sensations of taste (Ezek. 3:3), photisms (phenomena having to do with light: Ezek. 8:3), or levitations (sensations of being transported from one place to another: Ezek. 11:1).[57]

We cannot discuss the psychological aspects of ecstasy to any great extent in this essay, but can make only a few observations.[58] Usually, a distinction is made between two types of ecstatic gifts. One is eidetic or visionary, having to do predominantly with the faculty of seeing; and the other is auditory, pertaining to the faculty of hearing. Both types are represented among the literary prophets, but the auditory is obviously much more common than the visionary. However, the type which occurs most frequently is a mixture of the two, and this is the the type which we encounter most of the time in Israel and in the Old Testament. There is a much stronger emphasis on visions in Amos than there is in Hosea, where we find auditory revelations almost exclusively. Further, scholars often make a distinction between two different types of visions:[59] one is said to be plastic, clear and simple, concrete and compact, and to have sharp outlines, while the other is described as abstruse, fantastic, circumstantial, without outline, and sometimes absolutely grotesque. The former is much more common among the great prophets (compare Isaiah, chapter 6), but the latter does occur, for example, in Ezekiel.

We cannot discuss the much debated question of the relationship

---

57. Cf. G. Widengren, *Literary and Psychological Aspects of the Hebrew Prophets* (Uppsala: Lundequist, 1948), pp. 94 ff.; Lindblom, *Prophecy in Ancient Israel*, pp. 195 ff.

58. See chap. 2, "The Science of Religion."

59. Lindblom, *Prophecy in Ancient Israel*, pp. 122 ff., only distinguishes between "pictorial" and "dramatic" visions.

between ecstasy and inspiration here. We must content ourselves with pointing out that, from a psychological point of view, the difference between inspiration and ecstasy is not a difference in type, but in degree. Many scholars consider the term *inspiration* to be too weak —to be sure, it is often associated with the psychic state of the poet or writer—and the term *ecstasy* to be too tainted or entangled with primitive ideas for either of these alone to describe adequately the prophetic state. Therefore, in an attempt to bring out the characteristic element in prophecy, J. Lindblom has coined, instead, the term *revelatory state*[60] (a "sub-ecstatic" hybrid lying somewhere between ecstasy and inspiration), to describe the prophetic rapture, and the term *revelation,* to describe that which is seen or heard. At the same time, great emphasis is placed on the similarities between the prophetic literature of the Old Testament and so-called revelation literature in the Middle Ages. But even if we were to adopt the terms *revelatory state* and *revelation,* we would not be characterizing a new psychological state, something absolutely *sui generis,* wholly unique and distinct from *ecstasy* and *inspiration,* nor should we ascribe greater value to them. From a psychological point of view, these terms express nothing new. Furthermore, it is clear that Old Testament prophecy and prophetic literature had a direct psychological and literary influence on the mystics of the Middle Ages and on medieval revelation literature. Therefore, we must examine the latter in light of the former, and not vice versa. It is true that the similarities between medieval revelation literature and Ezekiel and Zechariah are especially impressive; but generally speaking, it may be said that there is more emphasis on auditory revelations in the prophets and on visionary revelations in the mystics.[61]

At this point, we are ready to examine the ecstatic element in the literary prophets. There can be no doubt that ecstasy played an important rôle in these prophets. Both the actual occurrence and their own accounts of spiritual experiences, visions, auditions, and the very form in which their oracles or sayings appear, indicate that this is the case. Thus, evidence for the ecstatic state is offered by stylistic features such as abrupt expressions, heaping up of questions, exclamations, imperatives, the full use of all kinds of metaphorical figures.

60. Lindblom, *Prophecy in Ancient Israel,* pp. 173 ff.
61. T. Andrae, *Mystikens psykologi* (n.p.: n.p., 1926), pp. 301 ff.

Also, the change of subject, where the prophet, identifying himself with Yahweh in declaring an oracle, suddenly changes from Yahweh in the third person to "I" in the first person, has a place among the psychological characteristics (compare Amos 3:1). However, it is obvious that this identity between Yahweh and the prophet as his mouthpiece or "mouth" does not have the same nuance as the *unio* of the mystic, the mystic's "unity" with God. Another thing which indicates the spiritual excitement of the prophets is chiaroscuro, the mysterious half-darkness which characterizes the prophetic oracles. Thus, the presence of allusive circumlocutions and the avoidance of giving direct information concerning dates, for instance, is an original characteristic of prophecy, a part of its very nature. It is not the result of secondary corruptions of originally crystal-clear prophetic words, any more than the linguistic irregularities which we have just mentioned. This observation is a *memento* to the text-critical treatment of the prophetic literature which hitherto has almost completely been overlooked.

We have already pointed out that it is a very difficult task to ascertain the relationship of the form of a prophetic passage to its content—of determining whether a passage merely reflects a particular style or whether it describes a genuine spiritual experience. Actually, there is no peremptory solution to this problem in most cases, even if it is possible to demonstrate a pure imitation by detailed analysis. However, it should be emphasized that spiritual experience and style must not be played off against each other as if they were mutually exclusive alternatives. On the contrary, they are to be regarded as complements of each other. Thus, there is no compulsory reason to regard Amos 8:1 f. merely as a formal expression of a paronomasia: *qāyiṣ*, "summer(fruit)"-*qeṣ*, "end." It is more likely that what we have here is a genuine visionary experience caused by a previous more or less conscious combination of ideas.

Another characteristic of the psychical state of the prophet is the extremely strong feeling of compulsion, that inescapable inner urgency to declare the divine message, even though at times this seemed to be heavy and bitter to the prophet himself and in spite of the fact that sometimes he sought zealously to avoid it. Closely connected with this is a strong feeling of self-consciousness, an experience of participation in the divine which fills the prophet with assurance and gives him a superior and independent attitude in relationship to his fellowmen. Both this compulsion and this self-consciousness may be traced back to the experience of a special divine call, an initial and fundamental psychical experience of an ecstatic nature, often in visionary form, by which a man is authorized to be a prophet (compare especially Isa. 6:1 ff.; Jer. 1:4 ff.; Ezek. 1:1 ff.).[62] From the time of this call, the dominant factor in the prophet's life is the strongly subjective consciousness of the importance and dignity of the prophetic office. As far as the literary prophets are concerned, their call establishes their identity as genuine Yahwistic prophets and, thus, they repudiate the legitimacy of the call of the so-called false prophets (compare especially Micah and Jeremiah). So, it is clear that consciousness of having been called is an important subjective criterion for distinguishing between "genuine" and "false" prophetism. But at the same time, it is also clear that this criterion is not the kind which we may use as an objective criterion for making this distinction. And yet, in saying this, we must not exclude the possibility that the characteristic call visions, for example, in Isaiah and Ezekiel, have also to a certain extent a more durable, abiding, and conscious didactic purpose.[63] Indeed, in this connection, it should be pointed out that, to a great extent, the prophetic call, by the process of what modern religio-historical research calls "disintegration," borrows both its formal categories and its ideological elements from the complex associated with the sacral king, who combines three offices in his own person: the royal, the priestly, and the prophetic. This can be seen especially in the calls of Isaiah (in Isaiah, chapter 6)[64] and Jeremiah.

The so-called symbolic acts of the prophets are also intimately connected with the ecstatic feature of prophecy, especially when it comes to the communicating of oracles. Symbolic acts are attention-getting actions which formerly were called magic. Their purpose is not merely to illustrate the event which is announced, but also to influence directly this event in the channel intended. The prophetic word by its very nature is a creative potency: filled with divine power, it molds that which takes place according to the will of Yahweh. Thus, in reality, the word is *the act*, and therefore the distinction between the word and the symbolic act is flexible. This is most apparent in the use

62. Lindblom, *Prophecy in Ancient Israel*, pp. 182 ff.
63. This statement is not perfectly clear. Does it mean that these visions are, to some extent, literary products with a didactic purpose?
64. I. Engnell, *The Call of Isaiah* (Leipzig: Otto Harrassowitz, 1949).

of symbolic names to strengthen the prophetic proclamation: compare, for example, Hosea's "Jezreel," "Lo-Ruhamah," and "Lo-Ammi," and Isaiah's "Shear-Jashub," "Maher-shalal-hash-baz," and "Immanuel." But as the nebiim did before them (compare, for example, Zedekiah, according to I Kgs. 22:10 ff., and Elisha, according to II Kgs. 13: 14 ff.) and kept on doing, so, to a large extent, the "reaction prophets" also made use of symbolic acts in a literal sense. Hosea illustrates and thereby "creates" his people's relationship to Yahweh by his "symbolic marriages"—which were undoubtedly real (Hosea, chapters 1, 3). Isaiah goes "naked and barefooted" for three years, as a foretoken of his people's calamity (Isa. 20:2 ff.). Jeremiah's "girdle magic," Jer. 13:1 ff., and "pitcher magic," surely to be associated with ancient cultic traditions[65] (Jer. 19:1 ff.), are well-known symbolic acts. Jeremiah also puts "band and yoke" around his neck on one occasion (Jer. 27:1 ff.). Ezekiel makes a graphic model depicting the siege of Jerusalem and symbolizes this event by performing certain activities which are both physically and psychically very trying (Ezek. 4:1 ff.). On another occasion, he symbolically foretokens the Exile by digging his way through a wall (12:3 ff.). But in evaluating these acts, we should not forget that they were actually consciously sensational, and thus extraordinary, and were not confined to the ecstatic features of prophecy alone.

Although the ideas which have been suggested here are necessarily summary in nature, they are sufficient to warrant our drawing some conclusions. It is clear from what has been said that the great prophets were involved in ecstasy more than most scholars have wanted to admit. In light of this, we have felt compelled to reject the thesis that prophetism gradually lost its ecstatic character and developed in the direction of spiritualization and rationalization—at least, as this thesis is usually explained. But even if we do not completely deny the possibility that there is a kernel of truth in this interpretation, it is obvious that the degree of ecstasy and the way it was expressed, like the prophetic appearance and attitude in general, differed greatly. They were different in different circles of prophets, as in the early and the late periods; they are different in nebiism and literary prophetism, in different individuals, and even in one and the same

65. The reference is possibly to the Egyptian custom of breaking a jar with the enemies' names written upon it; cf. Bentzen, *op. cit.*, p. 85, note 3.

prophet as he appeared on different occasions and under different circumstances. Therefore, we must guard against making sweeping generalizations, even when certain features can be shown to be characteristic. Thus, we cannot speak of a uniform prophetic movement in either the earlier or the later period, as far as the rôle of the ecstatic phenomenon in this movement is concerned. Therefore, the ecstatic element is not conclusive in determining the essence of "genuine" prophetism.

Individualism and Collectivism in Prophetic Preaching.—As heirs of the period of enlightenment and liberalism and, to some extent, also the heirs of a persistent doctrine of verbal inspiration, contemporary scholars still exaggerate the idea that the great prophets were solitary figures—inspired, great individuals who stood outside the community and, for this very reason, represented the high point of Old Testament religion. Thus, critics still refer to Amos as "the shepherd from Tekoa," to Hosea as "the foreigner among his own people," to Isaiah as the perceptive but misunderstood politician, to Jeremiah as the individualistic sentimentalist among the prophets, to Ezekiel as the individualist and the seer. Only quite recently, this aspect has been carried so far that it has been maintained that the one thing which makes the great prophets unique is their asocial individualistic character.[66] In connection with an evolutionistic view of Israelite religion, even in our day, scholars often interpret these prophets as the conscious champions of individualistic religion in contrast to the collective piety connected with the cult. Thus, the prophets are thought to have contributed more than any other group to the elevation of Israel's religion from the earlier and more primitive stage of collectivism to the higher plane of individualism. Frequently, this development is thought to have reached its climax in the psalms.

For a system of exegesis based on modern religio-historical and religio-sociological research, this interpretation must be looked upon as a veritable caricature. Generally speaking, individualism is not an evolutionistic stage which supersedes an earlier and more primitive collectivism. The concept of collectivism is one of the most distinctive features of Old Testament religion and, on the whole, it remains unimpaired and dominant throughout Israelite history. This is true,

66. H. Birkeland, *Jeremia, profet og dikter* (Oslo: Gyldendal Norsk Forlag, 1950), p. 5.

in spite of the fact that it undergoes certain transformations in the post-Exilic period.[67] At the same time, even in the earlier period, individual religious experience finds genuine expression; and in reality, personal piety reaches perfection only in the framework of the collective.[68]

There can be no doubt that this applies also to the great prophets in the most profound sense. They themselves belong to an organic social structure, first of all, to the prophetic group. As we have already seen, to a great extent, the traditional picture of an Amos, Hosea, or Isaiah is wrong. The texts themselves tell a quite different story. The idea that Hosea is a "foreigner" is based on Hos. 4:5 and 9:8. But in reality, these verses depict the *Judean* Hosea, in contrast to apostate North Israel, and this immediately puts things in an entirely different light. The great prophets were strong, powerful, and stimulating personalities. The most compelling proof of this is the presence of the "books" which bear their names. In almost every case, the existence of these books can be said to presuppose circles of disciples who were responsible for preserving and handing down the traditional material, and upon whom the respective prophetic masters made their impression throughout. But this is one thing, and the doctrine of individualism is another.

Another illuminating fact important to a study of this problem is that, in their preaching, the prophets usually did not address individuals—and when they did, most of the time they were speaking to the kings. On the contrary, they ordinarily directed their oracles to groups, such as a certain group of people or social class, a cultic group at a sanctuary, a certain city or its inhabitants; but even more often, they addressed the entire people—Judah or Israel—and, in their oracles of doom, especially Israel. Furthermore, the prophetic view of history shows how collectivistic their thinking was. Everything they say revolves around Israel, Yahweh's chosen people with whom he had made his covenant, around Israel's sin and apostasy, her breaking

---

67. In the essay "Omvändelse" (Conversion, Repentance) in the *SBU*[2], Engnell develops this idea a little further: because of the prophets' strong, personal experience of God, it is natural that the call to repentance takes on a more individual character in prophetic preaching. On the other hand it should not be forgotten that most of their preaching is addressed to the people, not to individuals.

68. Cf. chap. 3, "Old Testament Religion."

of the covenant, and Yahweh's imminent punishment which this apostasy necessitated, and around the remnant, which shall be converted and remain, and which consequently constitutes the kernel of the restored people in the coming messianic kingdom. It would be difficult to find parallels to the prophets' dedication to their people. They suffer with them, they contend for them as their intercessors even before Yahweh and, in periods of crisis, they are in complete solidarity with them. In an earlier period, scholars greatly exaggerated the notion that the prophets represent social ideals in the deepest sense. But if we were to go to the opposite extreme and describe them as social individualists, this would certainly be just as misleading, and we would be guilty of turning the problem topsy-turvy. It is true that the prophetic plea for ethico-social and religio-cultic transformation enjoyed only very minimal response and that, in the pessimism of the moment, the prophets sometimes seem to look upon their people as a *massa perditionis*. But this is irrelevant to the issue under consideration here.

However, in and of itself, this view of the great prophets as individual men, as exclusivists, constrained by Yahweh's call to go forth in sovereign indifference in his way without fear of man, without regard for king or people, proclaiming the divine (condemnatory) message, may contain a portion of truth. But when this is exaggerated, it presents a wrong picture. This is especially clear when we examine the closely related question of the form and style of prophetic preaching. We have already mentioned this problem in our discussion of the perpetual tension between form and content and of the ecstasy reflected in the prophetic oracles. Scholars who defend the idea that the prophets were great individuals (whether they consider the prophets to be predominantly "foretellers" or "preachers," or their oracles to be originally in oral or written form) have also concurrently regarded them as creative personalities who are responsible for the entirely new forms in which their messages are couched. They assume that, along with the immediate divine inspiration, the prophet also receives directly the credentials for the public proclamation of the divine message, including appropriate style, meter, strophe, linguistic expressions, and metaphors. The prophets are regarded as individual creative artists, as original and unique poetic personalities—an idea characteristic of a Romanticist like J. G. Herder, but one which also often appears in more recent times under the influence of the doctrine of verbal inspiration. When the form-critical school began to examine the prophetic texts of the Old Testament from a literary point of view, it soon became clear that this interpretation was erroneous. It was discovered that the prophets used the literary forms current in their day. Recent studies and discoveries have made it clear that these literary forms are a link in a long chain of tradition. The first link in this chain was Canaanite cult-prophetic poetry, with its ancient style forms. This was handed down to the "reaction prophets" or "literary prophets" through nebiism. Therefore, we must look for the root of the characteristic prophetic language of the Old Testament in the old traditional forms of sacral speech in the ancient Near East, with their characteristic phrases and terms, their stereotyped expressions and metaphors, their introductory and concluding formulae. The evidence for these forms in comparative literature (such as Sumerian and Accadian texts or the Amarna letters) has been definitely corroborated by the Ras Shamra discoveries.[69] Thus, it is now clear that the idea that the prophets were artists and poets is anachronistic. It is characteristic of the modern view to maintain that poets are original, creative individualists and pioneers, who often deliberately make a break with earlier traditions. But in the thinking of ancient man, the proof of a person's artistic ability was his sovereign mastery of traditional forms.[70] If we keep this in mind, then it is correct to think of the prophets as artists, even in Israel. In view of these insights, based on a growing body of literature form the ancient Near East, we have to correct the earlier overemphasis on the individual uniqueness of the great prophets of Israel. At the same time, of course, we must continue to appreciate fully the fact that the personalities of the prophets, their peculiar talents and dispositions, are also typically expressed in their writings. But this aspect of the question is a *memento*, when we have to do with the problem of prophetic individualism in its entirety. And thus the question of the uniqueness of Yahwistic prophetism is not so simple that it can be solved in terms of individualism versus nebiistic collectivism.

Doom and Salvation. Messianism.—For a long time, it has been

---

69. In the *Svensk Exegetisk Årsbok*, 12 (1947), p. 182, Engnell refers to such authorities as Dussaud, Harris, Gordon, Albright, Patton and Baumgartner (without being more specific as to works or pages) to substantiate this statement.

70. Cf. chap. 13, "The Figurative Language of the Old Testament."

naively assumed that there is a conclusive criterion whereby "genuine" Yahwistic prophetism can be distinguished from "false" prophecy, namely, that genuine prophets always delivered oracles of doom, while false prophets delivered oracles of salvation. Literary-critical scholars have allowed themselves to be guided by a one-sided and narrow understanding of a prophetic polemic, such as that found in Jer. 6:14; 8:11, and by an a priori doctrinaire psychological notion that the great prophets were absolute negativists and monomaniacal preachers of doom; and on the basis of this, with very few exceptions, they have considered it axiomatic that all, or almost all, of the so-called messianic oracles in the prophetic books are secondary insertions from the post-Exilic period. Indeed, they have gone so far as to maintain that, by and large, the prophets of doom, as Amos and his successors so often are characteristically called, had no positive outlook. But a number of different arguments can be given against this position.[71]

First of all, it is rash and incorrect to argue that since the literary prophets condemned the so-called false prophets because they *always* preached salvation (especially in direct proportion to the amount of money they were paid for their services), they themselves could *never* have preached salvation. As an example, we may notice Jer. 28:1 ff., especially vv. 8 f., where Jeremiah, it is true, in light of the testimony of history, takes a skeptical attitude toward an exaggerated nationalistic type of salvation preaching; but in principle, he still leaves the possibilities for salvation open. It is true that there is a difference in degree between the amount of preaching salvation or doom done by the two groups of prophets; but it is clear that this must not be interpreted in a doctrinaire manner as a difference in essence. Thus, the major premise itself—the evaluation of the literary prophets themselves—must be modified.

Again, we must object to the basic psychological view which considers the prophets to be consistent preachers of doom. As a matter of fact, the psychology of religion demands a priori that prophetic preaching include two aspects: for, even if we accept the prevalent idea that the prophetic "books" were "written" by *one* man, still it does not follow that the actual existence of oracles of salvation and oracles

---

71. Cf. chap. 11, "The Messiah in the Old Testament and Judaism" and chap. 1, "The Traditio-Historical Method in Old Testament Research."

of doom, side by side, and in typical, almost stereotyped alternation, "makes a psychological understanding of the personalities of the prophets impossible," as held by O. Eissfeldt and A. Bentzen.[72] On the contrary, this violates a fundamental religio-psychological principle: that the religious experience contains two elements, human sin and divine forgiveness. Man by necessity postulates that God operates in a twofold way: with wrath and with love. This was previously pointed out, correctly, but with different nuances, by J. G. Herder, W. Staerk, and L. Dürr.[73] But the doctrinaire, one-sided emphasis on the doom aspect of prophetic preaching transforms the prophets—often characterized as religious geniuses—into religious monomaniacs.

On the other hand, even literary-critical scholars sometimes reckon with the reality which is called the prophet's circle of disciples. But they do this for the express purpose of explaining the origin of the positive messianic elements in the prophetic "books." These messianic elements are said to have originated in the circle of disciples under the influence of external literary impulses, or else the two types of oracles in the prophetic books, oracles of doom and oracles of salvation, are explained as representing "a broad human tendency": the psychological law of emotional ambivalence, the twofold nature of the religious experience.[74] But in doing this, they are obviously guilty of a glaring inconsistency: they apply a general psychological law to the disciples but not to the prophet-master himself, and thus they divest him of these human reactions. It is clear that this position rests on a tendentious and a priori evaluation of the prophets, which no doubt ultimately goes back to the old doctrine of verbal inspiration.

But at the same time, it is easy to see how the idea that the prophets preached doom exclusively, or almost exclusively, is connected with an evolutionistic approach to the Old Testament, whether it pertains

72. The reference to Bentzen is to his Danish work, *Indledning til det gamle Testamente* (Copenhagen: G. E. C. Gad, 1941), p. 120 (cf. p. 344); in the English edition, *Introduction to the Old Testament*, 7th ed., II (Copenhagen: G. E. C. Gad, 1967), p. 146, this section is entirely reworked. Cf. O. Eissfeldt, *Einleitung in das Alte Testament* (Tübingen: J. C. B. Mohr, 1934), p. 166.

73. This is partly in accordance with R. Otto, *Das Heilige* (Breslau: Trewendt und Gramer, 1922); J. G. Herder, *Vom Geiste der ebräischen Poesie* (Wien: C. Haas, 1819), p. 60; W. Staerk [quotation not specified in *Svensk Exegetisk Arsbok*, 12 (1947), p. 125, note 1]; L. Dürr, *Wollen und Wirken der alttestamentlische Propheten* (Dusseldorf: L. Schwann, 1926), p. 22.

74. Bentzen, *Introduction to the Old Testament* I, p. 258 f.

to the prophets themselves or to the work of collectors or "redactors"—
the people who, using what has been described as the scissors-and-
paste method, put together the prophetic oracles which had been written down from the beginning with all the secondary material to make
our so-called prophetic books—or to the prophetic movement, taken
as a homogeneous entity. For even though it is sometimes admitted
that, at first, a certain prophet may have cherished some sort of hope
of conversion and salvation, it is still maintained that, sooner or later,
he discounts this uncompromisingly and thus finally, always, becomes
a pessimist and a preacher of doom. In order to demonstrate this development, critics apply the literary-critical method to the texts of the
prophetic books; and on very subjective grounds, they take out the
positive passages and assign them to a different date and place. According to this method, in the circles of disciples (if their existence is
admitted) and even more in prophetism in general, there is a constant and uniform evolution from prophecies of doom, said to belong
to the pre-Exilic period, to prophecies of hope, which are assigned
predominantly to the post-Exilic period. Consequently, pre-Exilic
prophetism is often characterized simply as "doom prophecy," and
post-Exilic prophetism as "hope prophecy," or the like. But in opposition to this one-sided and schematic approach, whose exponents
think in terms of time and evolution, we suggest that it is more accurate
to assume that there is a differentiation between different prophetic
circles which, on the whole, is independent of temporal factors.

But the real decisive argument in defense of the early date of positive oracles is a formal one and can be demonstrated by a correct form-
critical and traditio-historical approach. Since we will deal with this
aspect of the matter in the next section, here we call attention only to
those things which are relevant to the present discussion. To a certain
degree, one proof of the originality of positive oracles is the way in
which the smaller tradition units within the larger complexes are usually combined, according to the so-called catchword- or association-
principle. This principle of arrangement involves not only formal and
linguistic considerations, such as recurring words or expressions, but
also positive connections in the content. But an even more important
argument—and, in reality, one which is entirely conclusive—for the
early date of hope oracles in the prophets is the so-called alternation
scheme. This is a very old and fixed principle of arrangement, consisting of recurring alternation between a time of adversity and a time of

salvation, between prophecies of doom and prophecies of salvation. Its literary form originated in the cult to which the prophets were heirs and was adopted by the literary prophets. This type of arrangement occurs in related literature, both in the Sumero-Accadian and in the Egyptian religions.[75] Although he did not deal with the subject exhaustively, H. Gressmann[76] realized long ago the importance of this phenomenon, which obviously had its roots in the cultic event, especially as it was expressed in the rites and ideology of the Annual Festival, with its dramatic struggle between chaos and cosmos, darkness and light, death and life, as S. Mowinckel pointed out earlier.[77]

More recently, Mowinckel has assumed that this alternating scheme originated in a late period in the circles of prophetic disciples or in the editing of the prophetic writings as a manifestation of the specific Jewish hope of rehabilitation in the future. But this cannot be the case, because this scheme is just as basic in the tradition collections and tradition complexes which, even in the forms we inherited, indisputably belong to a much earlier period (for example, Isa. 6:1–9:6) as Mowinckel himself has shown.[78] The contention that this alternating scheme was adopted in circles of disciples who preserved the tradition, often even in the first generation, but was neither available to nor used by the prophet-master himself, is untenable. Whenever scholars deny the existence or validity of this alternating scheme to the great prophets, they do so on the basis of obvious a priori considerations. They think that this scheme *must* be secondary because of their preconceived idea that the prophets were inspired personalities and therefore enjoyed distinct absolute independent status. In other words,

75. Cf. M. R. Weill in *Journal Asiatique*, 11 (1913), pp. 535 ff.; L. Dürr, *Ursprung und Ausbau der israelitisch-jüdischen Heilandserwartung* (Berlin: C. A. Schwetschke & Sohn, 1925), pp. 1 ff.; T. E. Peet, *A Comparative Study of the Literatures of Egypt, Palestine and Mesopotamia* (London: Oxford University Press, 1931), pp. 120 f.; H. G. Güterbock, "Die historische Tradition und ihre literarische Gestaltung bei Babyloniern und Hethitern bis 1200," *Zeitschrift für Assyriologie*, 42 (1934), pp. 1–91.

76. H. Gressmann, *Der Messias* (Göttingen: Vandenhoeck und Ruprecht, 1929), pp. 69 ff.

77. S. Mowinckel, *Psalmenstudien*, II (1922), pp. 77 f. Cf. also Haldar, *Associations of Cult Prophets*, pp. 128 f. The implication is that the cult drama of the Annual Festival represents the temporary victory of the powers of chaos followed by the triumph of Yahweh (or the king) and the restoration of normal conditions.

78. S. Mowinckel "Komposisjonen av Jesajaboken kap. i–xxxix," *Norsk Teologisk Tidsskrift*, 43 (1942), pp. 65 ff.; 44 (1943), pp. 159 ff.

the denial of hope oracles to the great prophets is based ultimately on a dogmatic, unhistorical, and unscientific approach.

Thus, the picture which literary-critical scholarship has given of the great prophets as preachers of doom exclusively must be revised to a great extent. Here, it should be pointed out that the motif of doom as such is pre-prophetic and originally belongs to the ideology of the Annual Festival.[79] The prophets adopted this motif from the Annual Festival, sharpened it on the basis of their deep personal experiences of God's demands, and proclaimed it—often in very harsh form—to a people who had fallen away from their election and the duties of the covenant. But behind this, there is always the consciousness of election and although, at times, the prophet may seem to have given up completely, in reality, he never entirely loses hope. The judgment upon Israel is not a condemnation or a judgment of annihilation, but a judgment of purification, and the preaching of the prophets is a *preaching of conversion.*[80] They do not grow weary of warning; they threaten; but in spite of everything, they hope, they believe in the remnant which shall be left and to which the Messiah shall bring the future kingdom of salvation.[81] Therefore, the Rabbinic idea that a genuine prophet is one who preaches conversion is a fundamental part of the true picture, even if it is not the whole picture.

Thus, no matter how central the idea of doom is in the thinking and preaching of the prophets, it is only one of several elements. As a matter of fact, in reality, it is subordinated to and put in the service of the belief in the Messiah and the messianic expectations, which ultimately is the vital nerve of prophetic preaching. The *Messiah* and the messianic future is the positive focus of prophetic ideology, and this alone explains why the prophetic books in the Old Testament were pre-

79. Mowinckel, *Psalmenstudien*, II, pp. 65 ff.
80. In the article "Kvarleva" (Remnant), in *SBU²*, Engnell maintains that, in the Annual Festival, Yahweh judged all enemies; the remnant then was Israel as a whole. But from the very beginning this involved the demand that Israel be "righteous", i.e., the ethical aspect was there. The reactionary prophets continue and develop this line of thought. Yahweh's judgment is going to strike Israel, too, because she has broken the covenant. But a remnant of those who have repented, or "turned" (*shûbh*) to Yahweh will survive. This element is present already in Amos and has a central position in the preaching of Isaiah. It is not to be ascribed to disciples who add positive statements to the original oracles of doom.
81. The originality of some messianic oracles is defended by Mowinckel, *Psalmenstudien*, II, pp. 304 f.; cf. Engnell, *Studies in Divine Kingship*, p. 176, note 1.

served in the living tradition and were mediated to us. In other words, messianism is the leitmotiv of the prophetic literature.

In another essay, we have described the emergence of the figure of the Messiah.[82] Therefore, in this essay, we will deal only with the question of whether messianism is a proper criterion for distinguishing between "genuine" and "false" prophets. We believe that this is not a valid criterion, because it is most logical that if a situation was ever ripe for the development of a messianic faith and preaching, it would have been among the royal court nabis and, generally speaking, among the nabis who were involved in the official cult. And we must assume that messianism existed in these circles and occupied a central place there.[83] It is crucial to the question of the origin of Yahwistic prophetism that messianism is a leading characteristic in the preaching of its representatives, the "reaction prophets," and that it plays a dominant rôle in all of them. But at the same time, it should be observed that the royal messianic concept which the nabis espoused must have been predominantly contemporary in character, because they looked on the reigning king as Messiah, which is different from the reaction prophets. To be sure, the literary prophets took over the messianic lines as the main line in their preaching. But it is essential that, as their thought develops, they gradually set the messianic complex of ideas free from its immediate cultic and historical moorings and gave it a futuristic content which gradually led to its eschatologization.

Thus, the great prophets were all messianists, although in varying degrees. But as their own understanding of the messianic royal ideal developed, and they realized that the reigning king did not fulfil its expectations, they emerged as his bitterest critics. But even so, they could not set themselves free from *one* historical mooring: the Davidic. Their adherence to the Davidic dynasty is never broken. The Messiah is to come from the lineage of David. He is to be *David redivivus*, who will return in order to reunite the divided kingdom. The reason that the great prophets are able to hold this view is that they share the typical Israelite concept of corporate personality and collectivism which is

82. See chap. 11, "The Messiah in the Old Testament and Judaism."
83. Cf. the definition of the term given by Engnell himself: "By 'messianism' I mean elaborate king ideology, not 'eschatological' messianism." *Studies in Divine Kingship*, p. 43, note 3. In principle, this agrees with G. von Rad, *Old Testament Theology*, I (New York: Harper, 1962), p. 316, note 13.

connected with the king and the patriarchs in a special way.[84] Therefore, in spite of the tendency toward eschatologization, in the prophets,
the messianic kingdom has a manifest realistic character. Its coming
is described in particular as a time of victory and temporal salvation,
of blessing and fruitfulness in abundance. It also has a clear nationalistic aspect. The prophets are Judean nationalists, and this includes
Hosea. None of them attains to a true universalism in the strict sense.
Amos seems to have been the most advanced in this direction.[85] The
fact that they thought of God as omnipotent and of Yahweh, the most
powerful of the gods or even the only true God, as the ruler of the
whole world, is another matter. Therefore, the alleged contrast between nationalism and universalism is not a convincing criterion for
distinguishing between "false" and "genuine" prophets.

But just as there are valid reasons for warning against an exaggerated eschatologization in the literary prophets of the Old Testament, there are also strong objections to an exaggerated spiritualization of their description of the Messiah and the messianic kingdom.
But there are even greater reasons for warning against an all-too-
human interpretation of messianism. The Davidic Messiah is "the son
of God,"[86] and it is only through Yahweh's wonderful intervention that
the messianic kingdom is to be brought into existence and not through
an evolutionary process in this world or through human effort and
achievement. Such an evolutionary concept is completely foreign to
the prophets and wholly incompatible with their understanding of
God and man.

By comparing Isaiah, Joel, Jeremiah, "Deutero-Isaiah," and Ezekiel, one can see that messianic preaching and the idea of the Messiah
in these different prophets is rich and varied. But in spite of this, messianism as such has a clear-cut profile in the Old Testament. It is unlike any other ancient Near Eastern belief in a "Savior," and at the
same time, it is the crucial thing which unites the great prophets.
Therefore, messianism is a very important criterion for determining
"genuine" prophetism. At the same time, it is an element which holds a
dominant and critical place in the main ideological line of Israel's
religion and history.

84. The king or the ancestor "embodies" the people in a certain way.
85. This statement is probably based on the fact that chapters 1 and 2 are
directed against foreign peoples, implying that Yahweh makes ethical demands
on them, and on passages like 9:7.
86. Pss. 2:7; 110:3 (LXX); II Sam. 7:14.

Oral Preaching and Written Fixation. The Problem of Transmission. Literary Typology.—One of the many arguments which have been advanced to distinguish between the great prophets and the nabis is that the former are "writing" prophets (compare the commonly used term, "literary prophets"), whereas the nabis and transitional figures, such as Elijah and Elisha, are not. In reality, the absence of "books" bearing the names of Elijah and Elisha is not due to the fact that they spoke orally, while the great prophets wrote down their oracles, but to the fact that the traditional material in which they occur belongs to a different *Sitz im Leben* and has a different character from that which we find in Amos or Hosea. Above all, the leitmotiv of the great prophets—messianic preaching and Jerusalemite ideology— does not appear in their thought. It has often been maintained that one of the main reasons that the work of the prophets, on the whole, from Amos on, was preserved, is that the great prophets wrote down their prophecies, more or less completely, with their own hands. In fact, sometimes it is said that a major contributing factor to the success of genuine prophetism was the literary fixation of the prophetic oracles. Scholars who defend this position also connect the transition to the stage of written prophecy with the theory of "the general cultural progress,"[87] a view obviously associated with an evolutionary concept. However, as we have pointed out above, this whole outlook is erroneous. It represents a modern anachronism which reads a modern bookview back into the ancient Near Eastern world, Israel's world, but no such thing existed in that world. Although it is true that the circumstances surrounding the individual prophets were very different, we are not justified in thinking of them in general as professional scribes or writers, as authors of books or central cores of books which can be reconstructed by means of literary-critical analytical methods. On the basis of the available evidence, we must conclude that the great preachers among the prophets did not themselves commit their prophecies to writing, except in very rare instances and on very rare occasions. Instead, they preached orally, and at first their oracles were preserved primarily by oral transmission. This continued until, for one reason or another, these oracles were fixed in written form; but even

87. E. Sellin, *Israelitisch-jüdische Religionsgeschichte* (Leipzig: n.p., 1933), p. 69; G. Widengren, *Literary and Psychological Aspects of the Hebrew Prophets,* chap. III; and "Oral Tradition and Written Literature," *Acta Orientalia,* 23 (1944), pp. 201 ff.

then, the oral transmission continued alongside the written in all sub-sequent periods.[88]

It is clear from their type that the "books" of Amos, Hosea, and Micah are based on oral preaching and subsequent oral transmission throughout. The same is true of Isaiah (i.e., "Proto-Isaiah"). On the basis of indirect but sufficiently clear evidence, we may be sure that Isaiah himself wrote down only seven words altogether, as symbolic acts: the four words, *lᵉmahēr shālāl ḥāsh baz* (RSV note, "The spoil speeds, the prey hastes") in Isa. 8:1; and the three words, *rahabh hēm shābheth* (RSV, "Rahab who sits still") in Isa. 30:7. Furthermore, the idea that Jeremiah was a writing prophet and the theory that Baruch's written original scroll was expanded into the present book of Jeremiah are based primarily on a widely held but nevertheless com-pletely erroneous interpretation of Jeremiah, chapter 36. This chap-ter makes it quite clear that the reason that Jeremiah had to send his disciple Baruch was because he was prevented from appearing in per-son in the temple, and that the reasons Baruch made a written docu-ment containing oracles of judgment by Jeremiah were to demonstrate that he was authorized to speak for Jeremiah and to present a symbol that would create reality. It should be observed that Jeremiah did not receive the commission to make this special writing until he had worked orally as a prophet for twenty-three years. It is also significant that, after the king destroyed the scroll to counteract its magic, Jere-miah was immediately able to dictate his words again, wholly from memory. It is also clear, from its formal style and composition tech-nique, that the rest of the book of Jeremiah is based on oral tradition. This is not inconsistent with a correct interpretation of Jer. 36:32 f., which must follow along the general lines suggested by E. Nielsen.[89] To judge from Jer. 51:60, it is possible, if not absolutely certain, that Jeremiah himself was able to write, although M. Buttenwieser, for ex-ample, has denied this.[90] But even so, the symbolic act mentioned in this passage along with a collection of oracles of doom against Baby-

---

88. Cf. Widengren, *Literary and Psychological Aspects of the Hebrew Prophets,* chap. III; and for the most recent discussion, Lindblom, *Prophecy in Ancient Israel,* chap. IV.

89. E. Nielsen, *Oral Tradition* (Chicago: Alec R. Allenson, Inc., 1954), pp. 64 ff.

90. M. Buttenwieser, *The Prophets of Israel* (New York: The MacMillan Co., 1914), pp. 133 ff.

lon in no way militates against the view that the Book of Jeremiah was transmitted orally. Again, the presence of the concept of the heavenly book in Ezekiel (Ezek. 2:9 f.) does not prove at all that Ezekiel himself wrote down his prophecies—as has been maintained by G. Widengren, who also completely misunderstands the situation in Jeremiah[91]—any more than the symbolic act related in Ezek. 43:11 f. This "book" also has undoubtedly arisen from material which was transmitted orally and compiled in the traditionist circle.

The comparison of the prophetic literature of the Old Testament with ancient Near Eastern parallels, such as Arabic or Phoenician, to the extent that scholars usually take it always involves great risks. Arabic specialists hold very divergent views of the rôle of oral and written transmission in Arabic literature.[92] Furthermore, the great differences in time and place, in the religious and cultic involvement between Old Testament prophetic literature and Arabic literature must be taken into consideration. Again, a number of scholars deduce, from their understanding of Israel's cultural development, that her traditions were transmitted orally only in the desert period—although they seldom or never make it clear what they mean by the desert period—and thus were transmitted in written form after the settlement in Canaan.[93] However, Israelite traditions were certainly transmitted orally in the period after the entrance into Canaan, and Israel never became so completely Canaanized in a few centuries, especially not in prophetic circles, that they abandoned their inherited forms of tradition in such a way as to become slaves of the written word. In fact, in the ancient Near East, the practice of writing was predominantly restricted to different kinds of official transactions. In spite of the danger of building an argument *e silentio*, on the absence of material, one must admit that it is remarkable that there have been no discoveries in Palestine of written texts of the character, for example,

91. Widengren, *Literary and Psychological Aspects of the Hebrew Prophets,* pp. 71 ff.

92. H. Ringgren, "Oral and Written Transmission in the Old Testament," *Studia Theologica,* 3 (1950), pp. 34–59; Widengren, *Literary and Psychological Aspects of the Hebrew Prophets,* pp. 11 ff.; *Acta Orientalia, op. cit.,* pp. 201 ff.

93. J. Hempel, *Die althebräische Literatur und ihr hellenistisch-jüdisches Nachleben* (Wildpark-Potsdam: Akademische verlagsgesellschaft Athenaion, 1930), p. 11; J. van der Ploeg, "Le rôle de la tradition orale dans la transmission du texte de l'AT," *Revue Biblique,* 54 (1947), pp. 5–41; Widengren, *Literary and Psychological Aspects of the Hebrew Prophets.*

of the literature from the Phoenician Ras Shamra, in spite of the fact that archaeological investigation in this country has been extremely thorough. This is true in particular of the psalm literature.

In any comparative study, the absolute, specific "setting in life" of the Old Testament—the fact that it is made up of sacral and holy literature throughout—must also be carefully considered. Therefore, it is absolutely essential that our evaluation of the traditio-historical problem be based on an internal examination of the Old Testament material itself. Such an examination of the prophetic literature arose from oral tradition, because this is the only way we can explain the typology which we encounter in most of the prophetic "books" or in large portions of them. In other types of Old Testament literature, something quite different would have to be said.

But this is not to imply that *all* the prophetic books or that the individual prophetic "books" *throughout* are based on oral preaching and oral transmission.[94] On the contrary, the situation differs with the separate "books" and with different portions of the same "book." Although we run a risk whenever we make generalizations, it seems necessary to point out that, *broadly speaking*, the prophetic literature may be divided into two main types, which may be called the liturgy type and the *dīwān* type. Both these terms have their shortcomings, but it is difficult to find better expressions. The terminology adopted here is derived from this writer and is accepted, i.a., by A. Bentzen (in *Introduction to the Old Testament*, I, 257). It should be noted that we are using *liturgy* here purely as a form-critical term, and that, in itself, it does not suggest any cultic connection of a "book" or portion of a book and, thus, has no implications as to whether a passage is a direct cultic text or a prophetic imitation of a cultic text. In order to determine this often very difficult question, we must bring other criteria into our study. This prophetic "liturgy literature" has a more consistent poetic form. It is an artistic work in a sense different from the *dīwān* type. In this case, one cannot simply postulate an oral presentation or a traditionist circle behind the work because, while this *can* be true in some cases, it is also possible that the work in question may actually come from an individual master who may well be called a poet. As a rule, only uncertain solutions can be given to this problem.

94. S. Mowinckel, *Prophecy and Tradition* (Oslo: J. Dybwad, 1946); H. S. Nyberg, *Studien zum Hoseabuche* (Uppsala: Lundequist, 1935), p. 8.

However, we do not mean to imply by this that the liturgy type, as such, exhibits a well-worked-out unity in its motif and content. Instead, different motifs and units are brought together, often according to the so-called principle of association (which, first of all, is certainly to be regarded as a mnemonic expedient) but, at the same time, often with a certain definite alternation which is undoubtedly of cultic or cult-mythological origin: for example, the so-called Tammuz-liturgy, with its alternating motifs: lament-*descensus-ascensus*-hymnic conclusion.[95] The Books of Joel, Habakkuk, Nahum, and the so-called Deutero-Isaiah belong to the liturgy type. But at the same time, Joel and Habakkuk are probably actually cult poetry, while the book of Nahum, probably, and Deutero-Isaiah certainly are prophetic imitations of cult poetry. In addition to these books, there are also larger or smaller sections in other prophetic "books" of the *dīwān* type which clearly represent the liturgy type: for example, Amos, chapters 1–2, Hosea, chapters 5, 6, and 9, and "Proto-Isaiah," chapters 3–4, 5, and 10. This is simply due to the fact that these prophets used the liturgy as a stylistic form. The result is that the lines of distinction between the liturgy type and the *dīwān* type are somewhat obscured. But this must not be allowed to influence the classification of the different prophetic books in their entirety according to the liturgy type or the *dīwān* type.

The *dīwān* type gets its name from the Persian-Arabic word *dīwān*, which means, literally, "a piece of furniture" but which has come to mean the collected works of a poet. It should be noted that the term *dīwān* in no way implies that the literature of the Old Testament is dependent on Arabic literature.[96] Within every particular Arabic *dīwān*, the material is arranged predominantly according to rhymes while, in the Arabic anthologies, it is arranged according to the topics of association. Therefore, the application of this term to the prophetic literature is inconsistent and yet it is very useful in placing emphasis on the fact that the prophetic literature is made up of the whole collection of words and sayings attributed to a certain prophet and also of the

95. Engnell refers to Tammuz religion and Tammuz liturgy in a broad sense, implying the cultic celebration of the death and resurrection of the fertility god. As a literary form-category, Tammuz liturgy refers to a composition consisting of lament containing a description of death and chaos, followed by restoration and triumph. Examples include Isa. 5:8–30; 10:28–33; 32; and the major part of Joel.

96. Nyberg, *op. cit.*, pp. 18 f., was the first to use the term "the *dīwān* of Hosea."

available traditions concerning him, his person, and his deeds. Generally speaking, the formal compilation of the material is not very uniform and the composition is loose, although sometimes a certain principle seems to be predominant, as, for example, the combination of sayings whose introductory formulae or beginning words are similar in form, or of sayings directed toward the same or related situations or groups of people, or of sayings whose contents are similar. The prophetic books are not arranged according to chronological order, although sometimes smaller collections of tradition complexes may have been put together because they contain oracles which came from the same general time period. Instead, the prophetic books of the *dīwān* type are generally consistently arranged according to the so-called alternating scheme mentioned above. At the same time, the principle completely dominating the method by which the tradition units are put together is the principle of association. The alternation between poetic and prose complexes is also typical. On the whole, there is great freedom and there are numerous variations within the prophetic *dīwān* literature.

As a rule, there is undoubtedly a circle of disciples (which at first consisted of the prophet-master's own disciples) immediately behind a *dīwān*. The fact that these circles of disciples are seldom mentioned is another matter (compare, however, Isa. 8:16). Sometimes one of the disciples seems to have occupied the position of private secretary to the prophet-master and to have served as his main traditionist, as in the case of Jeremiah and Baruch, where Baruch is clearly analogous to the Arabic traditionist figure called *mustamli*.[97] In this circle of disciples and traditionists, the *dīwān* received its form and was then handed down by continued oral transmission. It is very difficult, if not impossible, to determine when the form of a prophetic piece goes back to the prophet-master himself and when it goes back to his disciples. But it is clear that, both in form and in the whole ideological or theological outlook, the prophet-master himself has left his mark on the whole work throughout.

Essentially, this oral transmission does not endanger the stability and "intactness" of the tradition. On the whole, in the ancient Near East, oral tradition is not an inferior form of tradition involving great

---

97. Cf. M. Weisweiler, "Das Amt des Mustamli in der arabischer Wissenschaft," *Oriens*, 4 (1951), pp. 27 ff.

risks for the tradition material. Actually, the situation is just the opposite. And this is true *very especially of the literature of the Old Testament,* as far as both the poetic and the prose material are concerned, because it was firmly moored in a definite ideological attitude and religious "situation in life." However, that a certain living transformation of the tradition took place is inescapable and self-evident. But we must assume that this transformation did not affect fundamental matters and that it was not of any radical nature whatsoever, although, during the period of transmission, the material may have been gradually expanded in different contexts. As in other types of literature in the Old Testament, we may assume that any censorship of the prophetic literature took place as the prophet-master or the prophetic circle of disciples selected the tradition material. However, it is basically incorrect to play the traditionist circle off against the master; instead, the two are one. Therefore, it is also fundamentally incorrect to make the systematic separation of the *ipsissima verba* of the prophet—the words from the master's own mouth—from the secondary material *the basis of the critical scientific approach,* or to evaluate the material according to this standard. This is not to say that, on the whole, it would be illegitimate to raise the question of whether a saying or a tradition may have come from the prophet himself. In accordance with the essentially positive attitude of the traditio-historical method toward the tradition, we believe that there is every reason to have confidence in the tradition when it explicitly ascribes a saying to the prophet himself, especially when this saying is connected with a definite historical situation. But of course, in examining such passages, we must make use of all available criteria. And yet, it is apparent continually that these criteria are inadequate, which should admonish us to develop a healthy skepticism about the possibilities of obtaining conclusive results. The modern anachronistic book-view, coupled with a doctrinaire evolutionistic outlook, and the literary analytical method, with its essentially negative attitude toward and distrust of the tradition, have left forbidding marks. We know the great prophets through their traditionist-circles, but the fact that the Old Testament tradition was transmitted faithfully in oral forms is the best guarantee that, through the traditions, we can also really know the prophets themselves.

The Criterion of Fulfilment of Prophecy.—Another criterion that is often used to determine genuine prophecy—which, upon superficial consideration, seems to be within reach and which the layman certainly often applies—is that what was predicted is fulfilled. A mere glance at the prophetic material in the Old Testament shows that the prophets in no small way prophesied about the future and actually predicted coming events, happy events, but especially calamities and visitations, even of a personal nature: compare, for example, Amos 7:17; 9:10; Isa. 8:1 ff.; Jer. 20:4 ff.; 29:32. It is just as obvious that, for the prophets themselves and their contemporaries, the fulfilment of a prophecy was of decisive importance, since this was considered to be the thing which demonstrated the difference between "false" and "genuine" prophetism. This is already clear, indirectly, in the very fact that the prophets, considering themselves to be true prophets, made predictions; it is actually asserted, in Jer. 28:15 ff. and Ezek. 12: 21 ff. "Deutero-Isaiah," especially, refers continually to the fulfilment of earlier prophecy as a proof that more recent prophecies will be fulfilled and thus should be believed: compare Isa. 41:21 ff.; 42:9 ff.; 44: 25 ff. But the fervent way in which "Deutero-Isaiah" argues this point shows clearly that he was having to contend with the skepticism and apostasy of his fellow countrymen: compare also Ezek. 12:21 ff.

The "Deuteronomist" also accepts the fulfilment of prophecy as a standard for true prophetism (Deut. 18:22), although not as an entirely decisive standard (13:1 ff.). The same is true of Rabbinic Judaism: according to Rabbinic thought, the fulfilment of prophecy is a criterion which assures the genuineness of the message, but only one criterion among others. For the Rabbis, the decisive criterion is the character of the preaching as conversion preaching.

In a modern attempt to determine whether a prophecy is genuine or not, either by scholarly research or on the basis of a faith judgment, the criterion of fulfilment cannot be considered valid, because the predictions of false prophets were sometimes fulfilled and because, to a great extent, the predictions of genuine prophets were not fulfilled. On this point, we must concur with the judgment expressed in Deut. 18:19 ff. On the whole, this aspect of the problem has seldom even come up for discussion among professional exegetes. Wholly different and internal criteria would have to be used to produce a decision in this matter.

The Standardization of "Genuine Yahwistic" Prophetism: The "Deuteronomistic" Line.—If none of the criteria discussed in the preceding survey are conclusive (even though several of them individually contain some truth), then what is the criterion for determining what genuine prophetism is or, on the whole, is there no such criterion? Must the distinctions between genuine and false prophetism be completely abandoned? It is obvious that the only type of criterion which can be valid in determining this is internal. We have already touched on this lightly in our discussion of the messianic preaching of the prophets. It is also obvious that, from a scientific point of view, a criterion which consists of a religious value judgment cannot be accepted as conclusive, as, for example, this kind of definition, given by Rowley: a genuine prophet is one "whose word at bottom is a revelation of the nature of God."[98] But if we change this to a judgment founded on history, by speaking of the prophets as proclaimers of *Israel's* God, then in reality we have said the essential thing. Genuine prophetism must mean "genuine Yahwistic" prophetism and, thus, if we are to determine what genuine prophetism is, we must plainly establish historically what "genuine Yahwistic" religion is and especially the nature of the idea of God in this religion. There can hardly be any doubt on this point. The "genuine Yahwistic" line, the main line in Israel's religious history, is the Jerusalemite-"Deuteronomistic" line with its idea of God as the Jerusalemite, ethically differentiated high god who chose Israel to be his people and made his covenant with them, made his will and his demands known in the law, and promised to save and to restore his people through his Messiah, when they have been converted and reformed. So genuine prophetism is prophetism which proclaims this Yahweh on Zion. Amos is certainly not the first of these prophets, but he is the first whom we know with certainty.

The Characteristics of Prophetic Religion.—The characterization of genuine Yahwistic prophetism which has just been given warrants a somewhat closer examination of its specific religious character. This task is very difficult, because the prophets are so different from each other, both in their personal endowments and disposition and in their "situation in life" (which, of course, is strongly affected by the fact that they lived at different times) and preaching, that any attempt at an over-all view involves the great risk of creating a false uniformity and schematization.

98. H. H. Rowley, "The Nature of Old Testament Prophecy in the Light of Recent Study," *The Servant of the Lord* (Oxford: Basil Blackwell, 1965), pp. 95–134, especially p. 128.

First of all, then, we must emphasize again that, in reality, we are not justified in speaking of "Israelite prophetism" as if it were a homogeneous movement with internal continuity and common development. A significant proof that this is not the case is the fact that the prophets in the Old Testament do not refer to each other in their oracles, which must imply, from a traditio-historical point of view, that the points of mutual contact between the prophets and the prophetic circles were not essential, if indeed they existed at all. In spite of this, it is obvious that the prophets and their circles shared certain fundamental ideals, as their idea of God, allowing for personal variations, is the same. If we ask the legitimate question about a possible common origin of their ideals and idea of God, the traditional answer is that they came from Moses and the formation of the primitive Israelite religious concepts in the Mosaic Age. And it can hardly be denied that this answer contains a great deal of truth. But as we have seen, the Jerusalemite traditions are of greatest importance—indeed, perhaps they are conclusive.

Here, it is important to emphasize once again that the prophets should not be regarded as founders of a new era in Israelite religion, much less as founders of a new religion, a characterization which has been propagated for a long time. Actually, to a great extent, the great prophets were bound to earlier forms and inherited traditions.[99] They adopted and developed ideas and complexes which had already originated in the Israelite religion, especially in the forms which were associated with the cult. There is no need to question the fact that an actual development took place, but we should avoid a one-sided anachronistic view of this development and should think, instead, in terms of the circle. Of course, in a religion like Israel's, whose history extends over such a long period of time and whose nature is so highly complex, we encounter such circles (or, if one prefers, "currents") with very different "situations in life," functions, and ideals outside the prophetic movement. And it is precisely by confronting the form of religion in these other circles and by comparing them with the form of religion which we find in prophetic circles that we may see the uniqueness in the religion of the prophets most clearly. This means that we must compare the form of prophetic religion with that of the

99. See now R. E. Clements, *Prophecy and Covenant* (Naperville, Ill.: Alec R. Allenson, Inc., 1965).

popular Baalistic religion, the royal-official religion, and the Rechabite religion, as well as with the peculiar ideologies that characterized the circles which stand behind the "P work" (Genesis-Numbers) and the "D work" (Deuteronomy-II Kings, the "Deuteronomistic" circle).[100]

It is easy to see how strongly the great prophets oppose popular Baalism, the variegated and very syncretistic Yahweh cult. Sometimes the only thing which this religion has in common with that represented by the prophets is the name. Here we can see clearly both the Mosaic and the Jerusalemite influences on the prophets. On the one hand, the prophets were committed to Mosaic legal principles and social ideals founded on the Mosaic law; it is because of this, primarily, that they deserve the name "reaction prophets." At the same time, they were also devoted to Jerusalemite ideals, as is clear through their absolute condemnation of all local cults and their extremely energetic zeal for Yahweh on Zion, the only true, powerful, and righteous God. As we have already seen, the relationship of the prophets to the royal official religion has been greatly misunderstood. The prophets by no means have as negative an attitude toward this religion as has been supposed; in principle, they are not anti-royalistic, but have a positive attitude toward the nation and the king. The best evidence of this fact is that they adopt and develop the figure of the Messiah and the messianic ideology. But at the same time, using the Messiah as their standard, sometimes they have become the sharpest critics of existing conditions and contemporary rulers in both the cult and the ideology.

It is also profitable to compare the prophets with the Rechabites. Here, it becomes clear that, in spite of their harsh criticisms, the prophets do not represent such a radical anti-Canaanite attitude as often seems to be the case and as scholars have often thought to be true. The prophets' resolute zeal for the ideals given in the law and the tradition does not produce a distinctly anti-cultural or antisocial attitude, as is the case with the Rechabites. The prophets are reactionaries, but moderate reactionaries. They manifest realism and social solidarity.

However, a comparison of the prophets with the representatives of the "Deuteronomic" line, the man or men responsible for the "Deu-

100. Some hints on this question are given by R. A. Carlson, *David, the Chosen King* (Uppsala: Almqvist & Wiksell, 1964), pp. 20 ff.

teronomic History"[101] and its peculiar ideology, is of the greatest
interest. These two groups have much in common: dependence on the
law of Moses, agreement on social and ethical ideals, the centralization
of the cult in Jerusalem and the adoption of the general nationalistic
Judean point of view, the typical Jerusalemite idea of God, and the
whole "Deuteronomistic" view of history and theology based on
the pattern of election-covenant-apostasy-judgment-restoration—the
prophets share all this with the "Deuteronomist." But they also differ
from each other in some of their distinctive characteristics. First of
all, the Deuteronomists are clearly anti-royalistic and correspond-
ingly pro-priestly. Also, the Deuteronomistic view of history is nationalistic in a different way from that typical of the prophets, who
may be nationalistic in their own way. The Deuteronomic concept of
the future has a more limited horizon than that of the "kingdom of
God" in the prophets, which is unique principally by its being brought
to reality through Yahweh's Messiah, the savior-king of the Davidic
dynasty. Although there are differences between the various prophets,
the similarities (even in form-critical matters such as parenesis and
"sermon style") between them (mostly in the case of Jeremiah) and
the Deuteronomic material are great enough to necessitate the question of the genetic relationship between the prophets and the Deuteronomists. The forms of their respective ideologies—especially their
attitude toward the king—style, local color, and linguistic peculiarities make it certain that the "Deuteronomist" is secondary to the prophets and that the collections of the prophetic traditions, to some
extent, at least, must have been known in the Deuteronomistic circle,
undoubtedly in oral form. Using an extreme expression, we may possibly venture to say that not only are the great prophets predecessors
of the "Deuteronomist," but that they can even be characterized as
"Deuteronomistic" or, perhaps better, "pre-Deuteronomistic propagandists."

It is also rewarding to compare the prophets with the tradition circle of the "P work." The "P circle," it is true, has the same idea and
scheme of history as the prophets and the "Deuteronomist." But while
the "P circle" characteristically has a strong positive interest in the
time and work of the Patriarchs, the prophets take a much more negative attitude toward them, especially toward the patriarch Jacob, the

101. See also chap. 4, "The Pentateuch."

special ancestor of North Israel. The "P circle" is "unionistic" in attitude and focuses on the common historical past of all Israel. The prophets are also "unionists," but they focus on the future—on the messianic kingdom. They have a decidedly, if not completely, negative attitude toward North Israel and its liability. A comparison of the prophets with "wisdom" and "legal" piety would also be interesting, but it is not relevant in this study in the same way that these other comparisons are. The idea of mystical elements in the religion of the prophets has already been mentioned and cannot be taken up here.

We trust that enough has been said to establish the legitimacy of ascribing to the great prophets a unique position in Israel's religious history. This does not mean that we can force them into a rigid pattern to such an extent that we can work out a prophetic theology. When we speak of the great prophets, we must mean principally Amos, Hosea, Micah, Isaiah, Jeremiah, and Ezekiel. The other prophets belong in a different category, especially since most of them are of the liturgy type. The personalities of the prophets which may have stood behind these books are very difficult to apprehend. As a matter of fact, this is also true of the great prophets, to a much greater extent than is usually thought. Actually, it is impossible to write a biography of any of the prophets because the information in the available material is too meagre. Biographies of the prophets written with the help of the imagination and a hypothetical development are very subjective. Other prophetic books, such as Jonah and Daniel, occupy a completely unique position. Because of these conditions, it is best not to attempt a survey of the great prophets here.

However, even though we do recognize the differences between the great prophets, still we may demonstrate their unique position in Israel's religious history by briefly calling attention to two factors which they all have in common. One is the ethical attitude which characterizes their preaching in a unique way, and the other is their messianism. As Sellin has put it: "Ultimately all the prophets strive for one and the same goal, the kingdom of the one holy God on earth."[102] With regard to these two factors, we do not exaggerate when we assert that, on the whole, prophetism in Israel is a *unicum* in the world of religion.

---

102. E. Sellin, "Propheten", *Die Religion in Geschichte und Gegenwart*, 2 Aufl., IV (1927–1931), col. 1559.

The fact that some kind of change, which must be called a development, took place in the idea-content of prophetism is inescapable. To a certain extent, this development involves a liberation from cultic and materialistic connections and consequently (if one wishes), a so-called spiritualization. A tendency toward a continuing eschatologization is also fully perceptible.[103] In some cases, this eschatologization even develops further into apocalypticism, for example, in Joel, Zechariah, and Daniel. On the other hand, the universalistic tendency, which undoubtedly is already present in Amos, is never fully developed. It is certainly not possible or permissible to isolate so-called national prophecies of hope from our present prophetic books and to re-create a development of prophetic thought along the lines of the literary-critical approach. According to one theory,[104] this development began with the prophecies of Isaiah and was cultivated within the so-called Isaianic circle of disciples, which may be responsible for the Books of Obadiah, Nahum, Habakkuk, and Zephaniah, books which actually represent so-called false prophetism. In reply to this, we must point out that nationalism, viewed from a historical perspective, emerged victorious. To the extent that we can speak of a development, it must be admitted that prophetism results in the exclusive religious world of Judaism and not in the New Testament and Christianity. The conclusion that prophetism (again to make a value judgment) reached its zenith early—at least as early as Amos—is inescapable. For a consistent evolutionistic historian, this would surely be evidence of a long history. And it is just as certain that the decline of prophetism came relatively early.

Chronological Stages in Israelite Prophetism. The Dying Out of Prophetic Writings.—Finally, this last statement raises a couple of difficult questions. The first is the problem of determining the chronological stages through which Israelite prophetism passed—a problem which an over-all view of Old Testament prophetism seems to present. Literary critics usually answer this in the following way. The initial stage extends from the earliest time to the time of Samuel. Sometimes this is called the period of primitive prophetism. (The use of the term *prophet* for figures like Abraham, Moses, and Aaron is generally considered to be secondary and is attributed to late source strata.) The

---

103. See chap. 11, "The Messiah in the Old Testament and Judaism."
104. Proposed by S. Mowinckel in *Jesaja-Disiplene* (Oslo: J. Dybwad, 1926).

next period embraces the time from Samuel to Amos. During this period, primarily through Samuel, the "restraining" of certain circles of nabis takes place. This results in the emergence of Yahwistic prophetism by way of the transitional figures which have already been discussed. The following period dates from 800 B.C. to 500 B.C. This is the age of "doom prophetism" ("reform prophetism" or "reaction prophetism"), from Amos to the Exile—often reckoned exactly to the time that Ezekiel changed to preaching salvation in the year 587 B.C. It is during this period that the great prophets, the radical preachers of doom, appear. According to this reconstruction, then, the Exile or the Babylonian captivity denotes a radical turning-point in the history of prophetism. After this event, prophecy is purely a proclamation of salvation, and it remains just that until it dies out with Malachi.

It is clear that there must be *some* truth in such a chronological reconstruction, since prophetism as a historical phenomenon is dependent on external conditions and events. But this reconstruction is based on a fundamentally evolutionistic concept and is carried out by means of the harsh methods of the literary-critical handling of the text and a historistic interpretation based entirely on the principle of dating.[105] And as far as the development of the history of ideas is concerned, this view greatly exaggerates the impact of the Exile on prophetism. The whole reconstruction outlined above shows the erroneousness of such a schematization, which in reality must be entirely misleading. Therefore, it is undoubtedly best to abandon all attempts to reconstruct chronological stages in prophetism and to be content with a typological approach, all the while giving due attention to questions of historical background.

But even if we adopt this approach, we are still faced with the problem of terminology. What should we call the prophetism which the great prophets represent? Actually, all the terms commonly used are loaded in one way or another and, thus, are not very suitable. The term *doom prophetism* reflects and calls attention to the element of doom, admittedly common in the great prophets; but, as we have already seen, it is by no means the only element or even the most important one. The term *literary prophetism* is also one-sided, because it

---

105. I.e., on the attempts to date exactly each prophetical saying and place it in a well-defined historical context. Engnell denies the possibility of doing so in the majority of cases.

suggests that the great prophets were unique in that they wrote down their oracles, a view whose difficulties have already been pointed out above. *Reform prophetism* is a frequently used term, but it should be used as a synonym to the other terms and not, as is sometimes done, be restricted to post-Exilic prophetism.[106] But this designation is also weak, because it tends to exaggerate the rôle of the prophets as social and ethical reformers and to overlook the even more important religious and ideological aspect of their work. Relatively speaking, the best term is *"reactionary prophetism.*[107] But in expressing preference for this term, we must warn against reading into it too much emphasis on the "Bedouin line" and the anti-Canaanite element, which, to be sure, are to be found in the prophets, but much less extensively than is usually assumed. We do not recommend that any of the terms mentioned here be used invariably. Rather, the terminology must be suited to the exposition of a given context.

It is also very difficult to answer the question of how and why prophetism died out. Of course, for a faith judgment, it is clear that this was due to the fact that the spirit of Yahweh had ceased to work. This is also the Old Testament's own explanation: thus, in Zech. 13:2 ff., the complete decay of prophetism is assumed and only false prophets now remain. Neh. 6:6 ff. still shows that there were prophets and prophetesses who took part in the political disputes. Many consider John the Baptist to be the last prophet. It should be observed that John the Baptist's preaching is by no means exclusively negative: the judgment he announces is a judgment of purification and includes admonitions to conversion and the proclamation of the coming of the Messiah and the messianic kingdom. Jesus is also considered to be a prophet, by his contemporaries, by Jewish scholars of later times, and by an advanced liberal Christian theology.

But when we approach this problem from a historical-critical point of view, naturally, we must look for both external and internal psychological factors to explain the dying out of prophetism. The historical circumstances of a later age were so radically different from the age of the great prophets that the idea of doom, which had been a cornerstone in the preaching of the great prophets, no longer possessed the same reality. The tensions in Israel during the last few

106. See Lindblom's earlier book, *Profetismen i Israel;* in *Prophecy in Ancient Israel,* he uses only the term "post-Exilic prophecy."

107. J. Pedersen, *Israel,* III–IV, pp. 131 ff.

centuries B.C. were not less pronounced than before, but they were of a different kind. Also, it is natural for a phenomenon like prophetism gradually to weaken. The later age simply no longer produced the great personalities needed to sustain a prophetism of the depth represented by the great prophets. But the most important element in the preaching of the great prophets was not lost in the later age: the belief in the Messiah was kept alive and was taken over by Christianity, where it was carried further.

Finally, we point out only a few things very briefly with regard to the canonization of the prophetic writings. First, it is important to keep in mind that even an oral tradition can certainly have canonical status, and this was obviously the case quite early in the prophetic circles which stand behind the books of the great prophets. The fixation of the prophetic canon (*n*ᵉ*bhî'îm 'a*ʰᵃ*rōnîm, Prophetae posteriores*) itself was undoubtedly completed, at the latest, about 300 B.C. The idea that the prophets were inspired certainly played some rôle as a leitmotiv in determining the formation of the canon, but it was not the principal criterion. Rather, the fundamental motif was the content of the prophetic books: the prophetic books which were canonized were those which expressed the central salvation event in Israel's religious history and reflected the idea of God, the ideology and view of history, the dramatic idea of the world, and the concept of man which may be called typically Israelite: that is to say, "Deuteronomic." There can be no doubt that the final conscious choice of canonical prophetic books was made in circles or a circle identical with or very close to the "Deuteronomic"—which is not the same thing as saying that all the prophetic books were subjected to a Deuteronomic redaction. Another underlying presupposition which had a part in determining the "books" that would be canonized was that they were connected with the cult, either with the temple cult (so, at least, were some belonging to the liturgy type) or with the synagogue, where they were read as *haphtārôth* (readings from the prophets) alongside the *sidrā'* (the reading from the law).

7

❦

New Year Festivals

THE New Year is a crucial and important time for mankind and all nature—and this may be said of humanity in general, since it is reflected in the most divergent cultures. At this time, the cosmos itself (the right order of nature, its "righteousness") is in jeopardy, and victory over the powers of evil and destruction can be guaranteed only by the intervention of the gods and especially by their worshippers—people who, through their cultic activities, contribute to the victory and "determine destinies"[1]—"create" order, fertility, and blessing for the time to come. In Israel, this "creation of destiny" is accomplished by the central rite of "making the covenant" between Yahweh and his people, who are represented by the king.[2] This dramatic concept of the New Year is expressed in the New Year festivals, which exhibit certain fundamental and recurring characteristics and rites in various places around the world. These rites both depict and affect the process by which nature is born again in the victory of life and order over the powers of death and chaos. To some extent,

---

This essay appears in *Svenskt Bibliskt Uppslagsverk,* 2d ed., Vol. II, cols. 336–340, under the title "Nyårsfester."

1. The term is derived from an element in the Babylonian *akītu* festival.

2. Cf. H. Ringgren, *Israelite Religion* (Philadelphia: Fortress Press, 1966), pp. 192 f.

we can reconstruct the contents and ideology of the New Year festivals from the ceremony of the festival ritual, which was presented mimetically and dramatically. Since the New Year and the New Year festivals are almost always connected with the solstices and the return of the sun,[3] there are often two New Year festivals every year. This is true, to a great extent, in the Semitic world, both in the East, in the cities of Uruk and Ur and in the West, as in Israel. Because of this special connection with the sun and light, fire rituals often play a prominent rôle in these festivals as, in the Semitic world, in the Accadian *akītu* festival, in the autumn festival at Ras Shamra, and in the Israelite *sukkôth,* the Feast of Booths.

The intensely dramatic character of the New Year festivals is reflected in particular in a sham fight[4] between groups of cultic actors who represent the powers of chaos and the powers of cosmos. In this battle, the king (or the ruler) is the central figure, as head of those who represent the powers of order and life. But the dramatic presentation also characteristically includes a portrayal of the state of chaos which precedes the victory of cosmos. The destructive powers enjoy a temporary victory. Chaos reigns, either in the form of an unbridled frenzy, often of an ecstatic sexual type—a "Witches' Sabbath" —or in the form of a "Death Sabbath." The "Witches' Sabbath" depicts a condition in which everything is turned upside down:[5] law and order are abolished, the weak are exalted and the mighty are subdued, the slave becomes a lord and the lord becomes a slave. Where there is a sacral kingship, we often find a transitory regency of the so-called mock king.[6] The "Death Sabbath" is so called because all life in the world of nature and men stops and death reigns completely: the temple lies in ruins, priests and cultic servants are eradicated, and

3. The expression is somewhat obscure. New Year festivals often fall at the equinoxes, too. Cf. T. H. Gaster, *Thespis,* second edition (Garden City, N. Y. Doubleday, 1961), pp. 47 f.

4. Sham fight or "ritual combat" is a fight or battle enacted in a ritual in order to illustrate a battle told of in a myth; the result of this battle is the destruction of the enemies of the cosmic order or of the life of the community. Cf. I. Engnell, *Studies in Divine Kingship in the Ancient Near East,* second edition (Oxford: Basil Blackwell, 1967), Index, *s.v.* "Sham fight." See also Gaster, *op. cit.,* pp. 37 ff.

5. J. G. Frazer and T. H. Gaster, *The New Golden Bough* (New York: Criterion Books, 1959), pp. 559 ff.

6. *Ibid.,* pp. 231 ff., 559 ff.

"the youthful god" himself descends into Sheol.[7] In most cases, these two blocks of ideas are found together. But finally, the victory of life is assured by sacrifices and other rites; and so, next come joyful processions, such as rites of enthronement, the sacred marriage, rites of harvest and fertility. Throughout the ancient Near East, which is characterized by a more or less homogeneous cultural level dominated by the institution and ideology of the sacral kingship, the unique characteristic of the New Year festivals above all is the central rôle which the king plays in them. He leads the fight against the power of chaos, is temporarily defeated, "dies," and "descends into Sheol," but "rises" again and brings home the victory, ascends the throne, celebrates his *hieros gamos,* and "determines the destinies"—creates fertility and blessing, prosperity and good years—by certain symbolic rites; and he does all this in his capacity as the incarnate "youthful god."[8] Since this renewal of the cosmos has the character of a renewal of the first creation, it is only natural for the creation epic to occupy a prominent place in the New Year festivals. It is the cultic text recited in these festivals. This is best known from Babylon, where the *Enūma eliš,* the Accadian creation epic, has this central rôle in the *akītu,* the New Year Festival. Texts like Genesis, chapter 1, and Pss. 74:12 ff., 89:9 ff. allow us to suppose that there was an analogous situation in Israel. As far as this is concerned, it is no exaggeration to speak of a common pattern in the ancient Near Eastern New Year festivals,[9] although everyone admits that this pattern in its complete form is a synthetic construction and therefore that, in every reconstruction of these different forms, we must allow for local variations which depend on different factors including national and religious peculiarities. There are great differences between the New Year festivals in the important Eastern Semitic centers, themselves; and these differ even more from their counterparts in western Semitic royal cities and peasant society. But now, thanks to the Ras Shamra material, we know what an extraordinary rôle the New Year Festival

---

7. The reference is primarily to the Tammuz ritual, especially as described by M. Witzel, *Tammuz-liturgien und Verwandtes* (Roma: Pontificio istituto biblico, 1935).

8. This is more or less the fundamental thesis of Engnell's *Studies in Divine Kingship;* see, especially, pp. 33 ff.

9. See S. H. Hooke, editor, *Myth and Ritual* (London: Oxford University Press, 1933), especially the introductory essay.

(especially the Autumn Festival) played in the West.[10] Because of the central position which the enthronement of the divine king occupies in the ancient Near Eastern New Year festivals, they are usually called *Enthronement Festivals*, but this is not a very happy term. It is better to speak simply of the New Year Festival and of its double form as a Spring Festival and an Autumn Festival. Further, it should be observed that the ideas of sin, judgment, and atonement were closely associated with the above-mentioned ideas and rites[11] and that the New Year festivals were also characterized by strong social relations, by communion with the dead, and by national fellowship which was renewed by the achievement of the king.

There can be no doubt whatsoever that the New Year was celebrated in the land of Canaan and Israel and that the New Year festivals were dominant throughout the country. This cannot be denied in spite of the fact that the source material is rather meagre. In the land of Canaan, Judg. 9:27 testifies to a New Year Festival (*'āsîph*) in Shechem connected with *Baʿal bᵉrîth*, "the lord of the covenant," and celebrated "in the field"[12] in conjunction with a sacrificial meal and carousal. Accordingly, the reconstruction of these New Year festivals must be based on extrabiblical material and on forms of the New Year Festival from later periods which may be used to work out the nature of these festivals at an earlier time. This approach is not only permissible, but also justified from a methodological point of view. We sometimes hear it said that no "enthronement festival" was known in Israel.[13] Not only is this hyper-skeptical, but we now know that it is clearly erroneous, insofar as the "enthronement festival" is taken to mean the same as the New Year Festival for, in its double form, this festival is as well attested in the Old Testament as one could wish: the Spring Festival in the *pesaḥ-maṣṣôth*, the Passover and the Feast of Unleavened Bread, and the Autumn

10. Engnell, *op. cit.*, pp. 97 ff.

11. E.g., the Israelite Day of Atonement, the humiliation of the king, and the purification of the temple court during the Babylonian *akîtu* festival.

12. The expression "in the field" is emphasized because part of the Babylonian festival was celebrated in the *akîtu* house "in the field" (*ina ṣēri*) outside the city.

13. The reference is probably to the criticism of Mowinckel's theory of an enthronement festival. However, this festival, as described by Mowinckel, is supposed to have been a festival of the enthronement and kingship of Yahweh, which is not exactly the same.

Festival in the *'āsîph-sukkôth,* the Feast of Harvest and Booths. The same thing applies to the three forms of the Autumn Festival in a later period: the Feast of Booths, the New Year Festival (in a lim-ited sense) or *rō'sh hashshānāh,* and the Day of Atonement. But when we see the connection between these different forms of the ancient Annual Festival and realize their connection with its earlier form, it is also erroneous to admit that there was a *Jewish* New Year Festival and still regard it as a late innovation. This conclusion is due to a complete misinterpretation of the Old Testament psalm material,[14] for the so-called Enthronement Psalms constitute perhaps the most important foundation for the reconstruction of the earlier Israelite Annual Festival.[15]

On the other hand, there can be no doubt that the uniquely Israelitic New Year festivals were influenced from without. But the question of when and how this influence took place is complicated. First of all, it is clear that we must assume that there was such influence at a very early period: Israel's New Year festivals are principally taken over from and mediated by ancient Canaan, which in turn had al-ready been influenced by Eastern religions in the pre-Israelite period. But this does not mean that we should not look first to Israel and Canaan in order to determine the independent and highly unique form of the festival within the framework of the general pattern.

14. N. H. Snaith, *The Jewish New Year Festival* (London: S.P.C.K., 1947); H. J. Kraus, *Die Königsherrschaft Gottes im Alten Testament* (Tübingen: J. C. B. Mohr [Paul Siebeck], 1951).
    15. See especially chap. 5, "The Book of Psalms."

8

The Passover

THE Passover, Hebrew *pesah*, is one of Israel's oldest festivals and, in certain periods, especially in the age of Judaism after the destruction of the temple, its most important festival. From a scholarly point of view, the Passover presents a group of problems which have been dealt with again and again. The sources themselves show the complicated nature of these problems, and a conclusive solution can hardly be given now and probably never will be given, in spite of the fact that research in recent years along myth-and-ritual lines has opened up important new insights. The Passover is also an illuminating example of the thesis that "the meaning passes away, but the rite remains."

In different contexts in the original sources, there are numerous descriptions of the Passover, or allusions to it, but never in sufficient detail. In the source materials of the "P circle,"[1] the Passover stands firmly at the center as the Israelite festival above all others (yet more *idealiter* than *realiter*), while *sukkôth*, the Feast of Booths, seems to be the main festival of the "D circle" in North Israel. The fact that

Under the title "Påsk," this essay appears in Vol. II of *Svenskt Bibliskt Uppslagsverk*, 2d ed., cols. 664–672. Part of it was published in a somewhat different form in *Orientalia Suecana*, 1 (1952), pp. 39–50.
1. See especially chap. 4, "The Pentateuch."

the "D circle" is North Israelite is illustrated by the fact that the Feast of Booths is of Canaanite origin, as is now known from the Ras Shamra texts.[2] The most important reference to the Passover in the "P material" is in Exod. 12:1 ff. It should be observed that in this passage the Passover is not "instituted" but, rather, the way in which it is to be celebrated is set forth. As a matter of fact, it is assumed to have been in existence before the Exodus, in Exod. 7:16; 8:1, 27 f.; 9:1, 14; 10:3, 7, 11. All of these passages clearly refer to the Passover, even though they do not call it by name. The Passover is also mentioned in Exod. 34:18 ff. (v. 25) and 23:15; in this passage, however, it is not called Passover, but only "the Feast of Unleavened Bread". In these passages, the Passover is called a *hagh*, a "pilgrimage festival," or—better—a "procession festival," but nothing is said about where it was celebrated. The more detailed precepts concerning the form of this festival are completely integrated with the historical context of the narrative. Again, in the "P material," we encounter the Passover in Lev. 23:4 ff., where this festival is given a specific date: the fourteenth of Nisan (Abib, approximately April) as the beginning of the Feast of Unleavened Bread, *maṣṣôth,* which begins on the fifteenth of Nisan and continues for seven days. It is obvious that, in this passage, *Passover* is a special term for the Passover sacrifice. Finally, in this same circle, the Passover is also found in Numb. 28:16 ff., where a group of special sacrifices are mentioned, together with the Passover sacrifice, including a "male goat for a sin offering" for atonement (v. 22). In reality, these different references to the Passover reflect a long history extending from the early part of the monarchical period to the Exilic and post-Exilic period, but it does not seem possible to reconstruct this history with any degree of certainty.

Another source for our knowledge of the Passover is Ezek. 45:21 ff. Here, there is still an indication of the cultic rôle of the king in the Passover, although this appears in unpretentious forms, through the person and achievement of the "prince." The strong emphasis on the atoning character of the festival in Ezekiel is also distinctive.

The Passover festival also appears in traditional material of the "D circle" ("Deuteronomy") but hardly in a prominent way. It is mentioned in Deut. 16:1–8, 16 f., where it is called alternately the

2. I. Engnell, *Studies in Divine Kingship in the Ancient Near East,* 2d ed. (Oxford: Basil Blackwell, 1967), pp. 149, 157 ff.

"Passover" and the "Feast of Unleavened Bread." One thing that is new in this material is the demand for centralization: the Passover was to be celebrated "at the place which the Lord your God will choose" (v. 6, RSV), i.e., Jerusalem. It should also be observed that the custom of living in tents during the festival is clearly assumed here (v. 7).

Finally, the Passover is also mentioned in the historical literature (although characteristically very rarely), especially in II Kgs. 23:21 ff. in connection with "Josiah's Reform." But it should be noticed that this passage does not provide any more precise information concerning the form of the festival. And yet, it does state expressly that "no such passover had been kept since the days of the judges who judged Israel, or during all the days of the kings of Israel or of the kings of Judah" (v. 22, RSV). This is an important argument against identifying "Josiah's Lawbook" with Deuteronomy,[3] and also against the oft-heard assertion that the Passover was an "Israelite backbone," a safeguard against syncretism and Canaanization throughout the entire history of Israel. This verse clearly shows Canaanization as an inescapable fact. (To interpret this statement to mean that, on the whole, the Passover was not celebrated before the time of Josiah and that, therefore, it was wholly an innovation when it was introduced at that time—as does N. Nicolsky[4]—cannot possibly be accepted.) The Passover is also mentioned in II Chron. 30:1 ff., alternately under the names "Passover" and "Feast of Unleavened Bread." This passage mentions an attempt by King Hezekiah to carry out a reform of the Passover and says repeatedly that, prior to this time, it was not celebrated in a correct manner. In II Chronicles, chapter 35, there is a description of Josiah's celebration of the Passover which is parallel to II Kings, chapter 23. It is celebrated on a very large scale, and the passage says expressly that "no passover like it had been kept in Israel since the days of Samuel the prophet" (v. 18, RSV). It is especially important to notice the extraordinarily central and prominent rôle which the king plays in all of these "historical" descriptions of the Passover. According to Chronicles, the king and the Levites are responsible for every cultic activity, and the people only share in the meal. Further, it should be observed that, in Chronicles, as in "D," the Passover, together with the Feast of Un-

---

3. See especially chap. 4, "The Pentateuch."
4. N. Nicolsky, "Pascha im Kulte des jerusalemischen Tempels," *Zeitschrift für die alttestamentliche Wissenschaft*, 45 (1927), pp. 171 ff., 241 ff.

leavened Bread, continues for seven days, as compared with the eight days in "P." A passover is also described in Ezra 6:19 ff., where it is looked on especially as a covenant which preserves the unity of "pure-blooded" Jews (compare Exod. 12:43 ff.; Jubilees 49:9). Finally, we also encounter the Passover in an important historical document of a relatively early date outside the framework of the Old Testament, in one of the papyri from Elephantine, dated 419 B.C.[5] This papyrus is a letter containing permission from the Persian king to celebrate the Passover and giving instructions as to the right way that this should be done. This shows that the Passover was celebrated in the Diaspora, evidently in opposition to or in ignorance of the demand for central-ization in Deuteronomy. In connection with this, it should be pointed out that, according to Exod. 8:22, (Eng. 8:26), Moses fears a possible Egyptian retaliation because the Jews sacrifice "that which is abomi-nable to the Egyptians." (RSV). We know that the temple in Elephan-tine was destroyed in 410 B.C. by a pogrom caused by controversies over sacrifice—probably the sacrifice of a lamb, which was not lawful, according to the Egyptian religion. In fact, it has even been suggested that the Passover Legend in Exodus, chapters 1–15, received its final form in the Egyptian diaspora, especially in light of the detailed knowledge of Egyptian affairs reflected in the narrative. But from a traditio-historical point of view, this hypothesis hardly seems likely.

The most detailed description of the Passover given in the passages cited above is found in Exod. 12:1 ff.: on the tenth day of the first month, the heads of the families choose a lamb—or a kid—without blemish. The sacred victim or sacrificial animal is kept until the eve-ning of the fourteenth day, when it is sacrificed by the heads of the families. Then, a sprig of hyssop is dipped in its blood, and the blood is sprinkled on the doorposts and the lintels "of the houses in which they eat them." (v. 7, RSV). The animal is roasted and eaten during the night, together with unleavened bread and "bitter herbs." Nothing may be left till morning; everything which is not eaten is burned with fire. It shall be eaten "in haste" by the Israelites, who shall "gird up their loins," have shoes on their feet and staffs in their hands—all of which is to commemorate the haste associated with the "Exodus out of Egypt." The blood will serve to save the Israelites, because when Yahweh slays the first-born of the Egyptians during the night, He will

---

5. See P. Grelot, "Études sur le "papyrus pascal" d'Elephantine," *Vetus Testa-mentum*, 4 (1954), pp. 349 ff.

"pass over" (*pāsaḥ,* the same stem as *pesaḥ,* "passover," so that the aetiological etymology of this word is given in vv. 13 and 27, although it is
undoubtedly secondary) the houses of the Israelites and spare their
first-born; during the night, no one is to leave the house (v. 22). Then,
during the next seven days, the fifteenth through the twenty-first, the
Feast of Unleavened Bread is celebrated (vv. 15 ff.), and there is an
indisputable demand that anyone who violates this festival "shall be
cut off from the congregation of Israel, whether he is a sojourner or a
native of the land" (v. 19, RSV).

A major characteristic of this narrative is its "historicizing": the
whole sequence of events is alleged to have taken place in the framework of the "historical event" called the "Exodus out of Egypt." But
modern scholars unanimously agree that the first prerequisite to a
correct understanding of the true nature of the Passover is that we
virtually disregard this historicizing and realize that, essentially, we
are dealing with something of an entirely different character. The
Passover is a nature festival, a distinct type of primitive annual festival,
with various kinds of religio-historical parallels,[6] having a distinct content and distinct rites and ideas, a festival which—at any rate, until
quite recently—scholars have unanimously alleged to have had a nomadic character and to have been a "wilderness festival" belonging to
"the genuine wilderness legacy." Among other things, this Passover
Festival has been compared with the Arabic ʿatīra festival[7] and, consequently, has been considered a spring festival with the sacrifice of
firstlings for the consecration of the flocks, possibly located at a
special wilderness sanctuary. Scholars usually call attention to two
central elements in this Passover Festival. The first is a communal meal
establishing a communion of blood, a renewal of the unity within the
family and between the family and the deity. Also, the smearing of
blood on the doorposts is understood as strengthening the communion.
Second, along with this, scholars strongly emphasize the apotropaeic
(warding off of demons) character of this festival, characterized by
the rites of blood and eating of "bitter (i.e., cleansing) herbs," parallels to which are found in the Greek Anthesteria.[8] Also, it is often as-

6. Cf. T. H. Gaster, *Thespis* (New York: Schuman, 1950), chaps. 2 and 3.
7. J. Wellhausen, *Reste arabischen Heidentums* (Berlin: G. Reimer, 1897),
pp. 118, 121.
8. J. Harrison, *Prolegomena to the Study of Greek Religion* (Cambridge: The
University Press, 1903), p. 39 ("they used to chew buckthorn and anointed their
doors with pitch" [Photius]).

serted that the sacrificial meal of this type is apotropaeic. This is said
to stand out especially in the prohibition against leaving something
until morning, which is connected with the idea that the sacrificial animal is a substitute for the deity, or perhaps for an original human
sacrifice; there is no concrete evidence for the latter.

But actually, the interpretation of the Passover as primarily a nomadic festival of this type is untenable. There are a number of things
which indicate that this is erroneous, some of which may be mentioned
here, mainly in agreement with the criticisms of Wensinck and
Hooke.[9] The command to put the blood on the door-posts and lintel
does not fit a nomadic situation, because it assumes a settled community with more permanent types of houses. However, this is
to be regarded as an anachronistic mode of expression by the traditionist, based on his own sedentary *Sitz im Leben.* The fact that
the Passover was originally a lunar festival proves nothing: lunar
calendars were used in the civilized country of Canaan, and they were
used in Babylon from time immemorial. The fact that a lamb or a kid
was used in this festival is no proof that it has to be nomadic. These
sacred victims or sacrificial animals played a prominent rôle in Canaan, as well as in Ras Shamra and Babylon. The name of the festival,
pesaḥ, is of great importance. It is being recognized more and more
generally that the aetiological explanation given in Exod. 12:13, 27, is
secondary, as has already been suggested above. It is true that this
name is connected with the verb *pāsaḥ,* but this is a technical term for
a cultic dance[10] (probably belonging to the "limping dance type" [I Kgs.
18:26] and mournful in character), which celebrated the cultic death
of the deity represented by the sacrificial animal. There are several
religio-historical parallels to this cultic practice.

In addition, it is probably not insignificant that, in the modern
Jewish Passover, the dew plays a prominent rôle as a hymnic motif
(in connection with Hos. 14:5 and Isa. 26:19), centered around the

9. A. J. Wensinck, "The Semitic New Year and the Origin of Eschatology,"
Acta Orientalia, 1 (1923), pp. 159 ff.; "Arabic New Year and the Feast of
Tabernacles," *Verhandelingen der Koninklijke Akademie van Wetenschappen te
Amsterdam,* Deel 25, No. 2 (Amsterdam: Akademie van Wetenschappen, 1925);
S. H. Hooke, *The Origins of Early Semitic Ritual* (London: Oxford University
Press, 1938).

10. W. O. E. Oesterley, *The Sacred Dance* (Cambridge: The University
Press, 1923), pp. 50 f.

idea of the resurrection.[11] It is also typical in the modern festival to use the Song of Songs as a ritual text on the eighth day of the Passover; here, the motif of the *hieros gamos* appears.[12] The connection of judgment (directed against the "enemy"—Egypt) with the Passover is also a characteristic feature of the annual festival.[13] Also, scholars have called attention to the fact that, from the day of preparation on the tenth of Abib (Nisan) to its conclusion on the twenty-first, the Passover lasts eleven days, which is exactly the same as the Accadian *akītu* festival. Finally, it should be pointed out that, in "historical" sources and Ezekiel, the Passover is associated with the person of the king. The extraordinary importance of this is obvious when it once becomes clear that, in reality, the central figure in the Passover—Moses—is modelled after the figure of the sacral king throughout. This statement has no bearing on the question of whether Moses was a historical person.[14] Thus, Moses is "the one sent by Yahweh" (Exod. 3:13; 4:28), the "servant of the Lord" (Exod. 4:10; 14:31) who is preceded by the angel of God (Exod. 14:19), the one who is carried by the spirit, the possessor of the wonder-working rod (i.e., the royal sceptre, identified with the "tree of life" in Rabbinic tradition[15]), the master of the wind, the weapon with which Tehom, the Sea, is overcome (Exod. 14:16 ff.).[16] As the saving Messiah, Moses leads his people in their "exodus"

11. In Canaanite religion, the dew was connected with the idea of life and renewal of life. In another essay, Engnell asserts that the dew was led in channels into the tombs at Ras Shamra, obviously in order to ensure life to the dead person. In addition to the passages mentioned in the text, there is also Ps. 110:3 and the proper name *Abital*, "my father is the Dew."

12. H. Ringgren, *Israelite Religion* (Philadelphia: Fortress Press, 1966), pp. 188, 197 f.

13. For the judgment motif, see S. Mowinckel, *Psalmenstudien*, II (Oslo: J. Dybwad, 1922), pp. 65 ff.; *The Psalms in Israel's Worship*, I (New York: Abingdon Press, 1962), pp. 133 ff.

14. The obvious implication is that it seemed natural to the later narrators to describe Moses as a king, though kingship did not exist in Israel in his time. In addition to the examples given in the text, Engnell mentions in another article in *SBU*² that Moses mediates the spirit to Joshua (Num. 27:18 f.); restores life through the Nehushtan (Num. 21:4 ff.); leads his people to victory through the Sea of Reeds; receives the tablets of the law (cf. the Code of Hammurabi and the Babylonian "tablets of destiny," cf. G. Widengren, "King and Covenant," *Journal of Semitic Studies*, 2 (1957), pp. 5 ff.); he is also the intercessor who atones for the people's sin (Exod. 32:30 ff.).

15. See G. Widengren, *The King and the Tree of Life in Ancient Near Eastern Religion* (Uppsala: Lundequist, 1951).

16. Cf. the Babylonian Epic of Creation, Tablet IV.

to the celebration of the Passover; then the enemy, Egypt, is overcome in a series of dramatic scenes—clearly reflections of the cultic sham fight[17]—culminating in the victory over Pharaoh, the counterpart of Kingu, the Accadian form of the "rival king," who, like Kingu, certainly is not killed but, according to Rabbinic tradition, is held a prisoner in the Red Sea (Sheol) for fifty days, after which, because he is immortal, he is stationed forever at the gate of Sheol.[18] All of this shows, as clearly as anyone could wish, that it cannot be correct to consider the Passover, even in its earliest form, a nomadic festival. As far back as we can trace it, the Passover was an annual festival or, more exactly, the spring celebration of the annual festival.[19] The type of nomadic Passover Festival which many scholars portray is a pure invention. The "march out into the wilderness" which is presupposed in order to celebrate the Passover can and should be explained in another way: as a description of the cultic procession going out to participate in the central rites which take place "in the wilderness," like the Accadian *inaṣ ēri* and the Hebrew *bassādheh*, "in the field," "in the open."[20] Another factor which emphasizes that the Passover has the character of an annual festival is the impression that it makes of being a so-called *rite de passage* because of its connection with circumcision (Exod. 4:24 ff.; 12:44; Josh. 5:2 ff.).[21] It is possible to carry such a cultic interpretation so far as to deny that there is any historical nucleus behind the description of the Passover. But this is neither necessary nor correct. The cultic interpretation which has just been suggested in no way necessarily precludes a historical reality but only asserts that this is expressed in cultic categories. On the other hand, it is extremely difficult or entirely impossible to extract and reconstruct the historical reality behind the cultic presentation from the cultic presentation itself.

Apparently, from Israel's earliest existence in the settled civilized land of Palestine, this Passover Festival (which, from all indications, was of southern origin) was amalgamated with the Feast of

17. See chap. 7, "New Year Festivals." Engnell regards the plagues as elements of a kind of ritual combat aiming at the destruction of the Egyptians.

18. This is mentioned, though without source references, in Engnell's article in *Orientalia Suecana*, 1 (1952), p. 47.

19. This is strongly emphasized in chap. 7, "New Year Festivals."

20. Cf. Engnell, *Studies in Divine Kingship*, p. 156, note 4.

21. A. van Gennep, *The Rites of Passage* (London: Routledge & Paul, 1960).

Unleavened Bread, *māṣṣôth*, which was undoubtedly the special Canaanite-North Israelite form of the spring festival. This was done so completely that, actually, the two festivals cannot be distinguished from each other except theoretically. Contrary to the usual view, this amalgamation was not due only to the fact that the two festivals happened to occur at the same time. Rather, the main reason that these two festivals merged is that, in reality, they are identical; they are one and the same festival, although they have somewhat different emphases: the Passover places more emphasis on the blessing and fecundity of the flock, while the Feast of Unleavened Bread places more emphasis on the fruitfulness of the earth and field.[22]

The typical Israelite or "Mosaic" Passover emerged as a result of this amalgamation. Its final form is found in Deut. 16:1 ff. but, actually, it is much older. After this, the character of the festival gradually changed more and more. The tendency to historicize the Passover became greater and, as this happened, its original connection with nature was severed and it became a memorial festival.

However, this does not mean that the Passover ceased to be a cultic festival with a cultic event at its center. In spite of the change in ideology, the Passover continued to be a cultic drama whose ritual text is preserved in the so-called Exodus Legend (we use *legend* here in the sense of *recitation,* i.e., a ritual text) in Exodus, chapters 1–15.[23] This drama was apparently a theatrical production of the "plagues in Egypt." The Passover sacrifice is the focal point of the ritual (12:1 ff.). And the emotional pitch of this drama reaches its peak in victory and salvation (13:17 ff.). The Passover night is also a *lêl shimmurîm* (12:42), a "night of watching" (RSV), a festival night, and at dawn the victory is celebrated by the hymn found in 15:1–12—the concluding liturgy of the Passover, recited by Moses and the Israelites, i.e., the cult leader—the king—and the cult community—and the dance of victory by the women (compare I Sam. 18:6). However, it should be observed that the final form of the text does not reproduce the pure original cult legend, but a "deculticized" and "disintegrated" form of that legend. Still, as we have pointed out else-

22. See chap. 7, "New Year Festivals."

23. Cf. J. Pedersen, "Passahfest und Passahlegende," *Zeitschrift für die alttestamentliche Wissenschaft,* 52 (1934), 161 ff.; *Israel, Its Life and Culture* (London: Oxford University Press, 1964) pp. 728 ff.

where,[24] Exodus, chapters 1–15, is the nucleus of the "P work" (i.e., Gen.-Numb.) around which all the other material in this work was gathered. This makes it quite clear that the Passover occupied a central position as far as the "P circle" was concerned. Recent studies have shown that the literary-critical division of the Exodus Legend into three sources ("J," "E," and "P") has no justification.[25] This division is based on the erroneous idea that the traditional material is an ordinary narrative, while, in reality, it is a cult legend, primarily of hymnic character, glorifying the victory of Yahweh and Israel. The fact that the tradition was "revised" by a later attempt to play off Aaron, the high priest, against Moses, the king, is another matter.[26] In spite of everything which scholars have advanced, the extent to which it is possible to determine and reconstruct the different historical periods through which the Passover went (Pedersen still distinguishes the pre-Canaanite-Israelite, the Jerusalemite, and the post-Exilic eras, although not according to literary-critical presuppositions) is an open question. However, we can say this much: it was only gradually and not, finally, until the destruction of the temple that the Passover lost its dramatic character as a temple festival and—especially through the predominance of the Feast of Unleavened Bread—became a special religious festival of the home. The important connection of the Passover with Jerusalem is still clear in Josephus, the New Testament, and Philo.

Subsequently, in the Jewish-Rabbinic period, the Passover continues to be a festival of the home, but it is expanded in two ways. In the first place, its *haggādhāh*, that part of the Passover which has its center in the ritual word, while having the Exodus Legend (Exodus, chapters 1–15) as its focal point, contains different "recitations" of the traditional material and legendary material with blessings. Second, its *sēdher*, the meal ritual itself, is described in great detail, as to the breaking of the bread, the eating of the bitter herbs, etc. The four traditional cups of wine, one of which is drunk for Elijah, the representative of the Messiah, play a prominent rôle in this later festival, and there are special regulations concerning the bodily position at the meal (i.e., reclining), concerning the clothing of the father of the house

24. Particularly in chap. 4, "The Pentateuch."
25. Cf. Pedersen, *loc. cit.*
26. Pedersen, *ibid.*, pp. 731 ff.; Engnell, *Orientalia Suecana*, 1 (1952), p. 48, note 2.

(i.e., white), which he is to wear during the New Year Festival and on the Day of Atonement.

One Passover which is still celebrated today and undoubtedly preserves very old traditions deserves special attention: the Passover of the Samaritans. These Samaritans, who compose a small sect in Palestine of about two hundred members, still celebrate their Passover in the open, on their holy mountain, Gerizim, during which time they live in tents on the mountain. The Passover celebration begins on the fourteenth day of the first month with the Passover sacrifice itself and continues through the night to the fifteenth. In the course of the readings and hymns by the officiating high priest and other participants, the chosen lamb is slaughtered at an altar in the open, immediately after sundown, by specially selected representatives of the community, clothed in white. The entrails are burned on the altar, while the bodies of the animals are roasted on spits in specially built ovens, to be eaten with unleavened bread and bitter herbs later, in family groups, with the men and the women separated from each other. The leftovers are burned on the altar. The Passover Feast, a joyful festival, is concluded with prayer, two hours after sunrise the next morning.[27] There can be no doubt that this Passover has preserved much of the character and many of the ceremonies of the original Israelite Passover. It is of particular interest that this festival is a *ḥagh* (a "Pilgrimage festival") in type and is celebrated by living in tents.

There can be no doubt that the Passover is one form of the Israelite Annual Festival since, generally speaking, it contains the original elements of this festival; at the same time, it is equally clear that the spring Passover Festival is not the most important or most characteristic form of the Annual Festival. Rather, its most important form is the Autumn Festival, the *sukkôth*, the Feast of Booths and the *rō'sh hashshānāh*, the New Year Festival in a restricted sense.[28] This festival contains even more clearly representative essential elements of the Annual Festival than does the Passover, such as "death" and "resurrection," the *hieros gamos*, the central place of the king in the cult. There are two reasons for the predominance of the Autumn Festival. In the first place, the calendar was changed, so that the New Year was transferred to autumn and, thus, more and more emphasis came to be

27. J. Jeremias, *Die Passafeier der Samaritaner. Beihefte zur Zeitschrift für die alttestamentliche Wissenschaft,* 59 (Giessen: Alfred Töpelmann, 1932).
28. See chap. 7, "New Year Festivals."

placed on *sukkôth*. Second, to a very great extent, the Passover as a religious festival is an example of "disintegration," of breaking up the original cultic model or pattern which at one time was dominant in Canaan in the pre-Israelite and Israelite periods. But even though it is secondary to the Feast of Booths in the New Year Festival, the Passover presents special problems and difficulties. For this reason, it is constantly a fascinating object of research, as is indicated by the extraordinarily plentiful literature on this subject.

9

ॐ

The Exodus from Egypt

ACCORDING to the unanimous tradition of the Old Testament, the Exodus from Egypt is the fundamental historical event which establishes Israel as a people, stands at the beginning of her history, and as an act of salvation—looking at it from the standpoint of revelation—determines her future destiny. According to Gen. 15:13 ff., the story of the choice of Abraham, Yahweh foretells the four hundred years of bondage in Egypt, the victory over the Egyptians, and the Exodus from Egypt. When "Jacob" and his "sons"[1] move to Egypt (described in the Joseph traditions in Genesis, chapter 37 ff.), the stage is set for the dramatic events related in Exodus, chapter 1 ff., which lead to the Exodus. The tribes multiply so greatly that the Egyptians begin to feel that they are a threat to peace in Egypt and to the stability of the kingdom. This causes a new Pharaoh "who did not know Joseph" (Exod. 1:8, RSV) to put the Israelites to task-work, primarily in building the "store cities" of Pithom and Raamses, and to decree that all newborn Hebrew male children be killed (1:16, 22). Moses is saved from this fate in a wonderful way by the intervention of

This essay appears in *Svenskt Bibliskt Uppslagsverk*, 2d ed., Vol. II, cols. 1357–1367, under the title of "Uttåget ur Egypten."

1. The quotation marks indicate that Jacob and his sons are not understood as individuals but as tribes.

Pharaoh's daughter. After he is grown, the future leader of the people murders an Egyptian slave-driver in anger and then flees to Midian, where he sojourns with the priest Reuel-Jethro and marries his daughter Zipporah (2:21). Moved by Israel's lament over her oppression in Egypt, Yahweh remembers his covenant with the fathers, calls Moses and, by means of miracles, prevails upon him to undertake the mission of leading the people out of Egypt. With his brother, Aaron the Levite, beside him as helper and "mouth," Moses returns to Egypt, demonstrates that the power of Yahweh is with him by doing signs and wonders, and becomes Israel's leader and spokesman before Pharaoh. He asks permission from Pharaoh to let Israel go three days' journey into the wilderness to keep Yahweh's festival, *pesaḥ-maṣṣôth*, the Passover and the Feast of Unleavened Bread. When Pharaoh refuses and "hardens his heart," Yahweh sends ten severe plagues upon Egypt by Moses (Exod. 7 ff.), the last of which, the killing of all the first-born in the land, results in Pharaoh's granting the Hebrews permission to leave the land of Egypt. After celebrating the Passover in Egypt, the Israelites make their exodus from Egypt, ending their four-hundred-and-thirty-year sojourn there (12:40 f.). Apparently, their place of departure is Raamses. However, they do not take the direct route to Canaan by way of the land of the Philistines, but choose a circuitous route, "by way of the Sea of Reeds" (13:17 f.). When Pharaoh changes his mind about permitting the Hebrews to leave and begins to pursue them with an army, Yahweh, using the wind as his weapon, intervenes and thwarts this danger by the miracle at the "Sea of Reeds," which crowns the Exodus with final success and is celebrated in the songs of praise in Exod. 15:1–18 and 15:20 f.

The rest of the Old Testament tradition refers to this fundamental act of deliverance again and again. Yahweh is invoked and praised as the one who led Israel out of Egypt, the "house of bondage," and he takes pride in this event (compare Numb. 15:41, etc.). This motif occurs especially in the parenetic speeches of Israel's great leaders—Moses, Joshua, and Samuel—which give a survey of the nation's history. According to the "Deuteronomic historical work" (Deut.-II Kgs.),[2] from time to time, these figures stand up and rehearse Israel's history, giving the Exodus a prominent place (compare Deut. 29:1 ff.; Josh. 24:1 ff.; I Sam. 10:17 ff.). The Exodus is also referred to in the

2. See chap. 4, "The Pentateuch."

Book of Psalms and in the prophetic literature, Pss. 80:9; 105:23 ff.; 106:7 ff.; Amos 3:1; Hos. 11:1; Jer. 11:2 ff.; Hag. 2:6. The following discussion should make it clear that, essentially, the Exodus from Egypt is a cultic motif in ritual texts, such as Psalm 105 and Exodus 15, and that it was taken over from this cultic *Sitz im Leben,* passed on, and given a more and more basic and completely dominant significance in the prophets and even more in the "narrative" traditionist circles, and also later in the Jewish haggadah. This has nothing to do with the question of whether the Exodus from Egypt is a historical reality.

The most natural interpretation of the narrative concerning the Exodus (in the context in which it stands in the "P work") would seem to be that it is a "historical" narrative and, thus, has to do with actual historical events, even though they may be embellished with legend or exaggerated. This interpretation was more or less completely adopted by critical-scientific exegesis. As a natural correlate to this understanding (and quite typical of the times), scholars have made several rationalistic attempts to explain the different miraculous works which are a part of the Exodus narrative and especially the decisive miracle of the crossing over of the "Sea of Reeds." It is usually assumed that the "Sea of Reeds" refers to some part of the Red Sea, primarily because the LXX renders the Hebrew *yam sûph,* "the Sea of Reeds," everywhere by *thálassa eruthrá,* the "Red Sea." The most common explanations of this miracle include theories concerning the phenomenon of ebb and flow and attempts to show, among other things, that in shallow gulfs, sand-bars can rise up suddenly.

The attempt to localize the Exodus from Egypt geographically and to arrange the events connected with it in a chronological scheme (either relatively or absolutely, both from an Israelite and from an Egyptian perspective, with the help of other relevant ancient Near Eastern material) is closely connected with this interpretation. In using this source material, scholars have wholly adopted the natural traditional view and, up until the last ten years or so, have suggested a countless number of hypotheses working along these lines. All of these hypotheses have one thing in common: they agree partially with the Old Testament, partially with extrabiblical materials, and partially with neither of these.

There are several weaknesses in dealing with the Exodus story as a historical narrative. In the first place, it must be observed that the literary-critical partitioning of the narrative material into different sources has by no means solved the problem but has only complicated it.[3] This whole treatment of the text is based on an erroneous view of the nature and content of the material, and the alleged distinctions between the sources are purely fictitious.[4] Second, the opinions of scholars differ sharply as to the correct geographical locations of the places mentioned in the Exodus narrative. Critics usually base their arguments on wholly uncertain identifications of these places with modern Egyptian and Arabic place names. They also assume that the territory around the Gulf of Suez and between the Gulf of Suez and the Mediterranean Sea was considerably different in antiquity from what it is today. Most scholars still think that the Exodus from Egypt took place along the *Wâdi Tumilât,* but opinions—or, to put it more correctly, conjectures—as to the place where Israel crossed over the sea vary all the way from the Gulf of Aqabah, the northeastern branch of the Red Sea, to some gulf of the Mediterranean Sea.[5] This hypothesis, however, is clearly precluded by the Old Testament tradition, which consistently distinguishes *yam sûph,* "the Sea of Reeds," from the Mediterranean Sea, *hayyām haggādhôl,* literally "the Great Sea." Nevertheless, most scholars, including Naville and Lagrange, place the crossing over of the sea in the region near the west branch of the Red Sea—the Gulf of Suez—either at Serapeum, located between Lake Timsach and the so-called Bitter Lakes; or at the southern tip of the Bitter Lakes; or at some other place. There is only one conclusion to be drawn from this whole lengthy and somewhat confusing debate: that every geographical location which has been suggested for the crossing over of the sea remains uncertain. As a matter of fact, the basic view which this approach reflects is essentially erroneous.

With regard to the problem of dating the Exodus from Egypt, scholarship during the first decades of the twentieth century generally agreed that this event took place at the end of the thirteenth century B.C. This hypothesis seemed to be confirmed by the excavations at

3. Cf. G. Fohrer, *Überlieferung und Geschichte des Exodus. Beihefte zur Zeitschrift für die alttestamentliche Wissenschaft,* 91. (Berlin: Alfred Töpelmann, 1964).

4. J. Pedersen, "Passahfest und Passahlegende," *Zeitschrift für die alttestamentliche Wissenschaft,* 52 (1934), pp. 161 ff.

5. O. Eissfeldt, *Baal Zaphon, Zeus Kasios und der Durchzug der Israeliten durchs Meer* (Halle: M. Niemeyer, 1932).

Tell el-Mashuta, which was identified with Pithom, which was built under Ramses II (1292–1225 B.C.). The difficulty with this view is that there are already allusions in the Amarna letters to *ḥabiru* (Hebrews) living in Canaan; and there is also a specific reference to Israel in the Merneptah stele, from an earlier period, but scholars have tried to avoid this problem by the so-called Spiegelberg hypothesis, which argues that the Leah tribes, especially Judah, had penetrated into Canaan earlier, directly from the south.[6]

As a result of intensified archaeological excavations in Palestine in the 1930s, this interpretation was remarkably changed. Scholars declared that archaeology had "proved" that Jericho fell about 1400 B.C. With the support of the statement in I Kgs. 6:1, this "fixed date" was used to assign the date of the Exodus from Egypt to the middle of the fifteenth century B.C. and accepted by Garstang, T. H. Robinson, and J. Phytian-Adams. But later excavations have proved that the destruction dated by Garstang about 1400 B.C. actually took place around 1900 B.C. and that, at the time assumed for Joshua, no remains of city walls are to be found.[7] Furthermore, in more recent years, the advocates of the early date have modified their position considerably, and many scholars, including Vincent, De Vaux, and Albright, have insisted on the late date of the Exodus in the 1200s. However, for a while, Albright espoused the early date. If one deals with this problem from an unprejudiced point of view, he must admit that it is not valid to base the chronology of the Exodus on the results of excavations. At the same time, we are now in a position to affirm that the general impression which the excavations give (i.e., the general demolition at Lachish, Tell bet-Mirsim, and other places, and the excavations in south and southeastern Palestine) definitely favors dating Israel's conquest of Palestine in the 1200s, B.C. Therefore, the events lying behind the Exodus from Egypt as a so-called historical nucleus from the standpoint of Palestinian archaeology are probably to be dated in the period between 1300 and 1200 B.C.

The Old Testament also indicates that the entrance into Canaan took place during the Iron Age, not during the Bronze Age. And the excavations in Egypt have shed no light whatsoever on either the en-

6. W. Spiegelberg, *Der Aufenthalt Israels in Ägypten im lichte der ägyptischen monumente* (Strassburg: Achlesier & Schweikhardt, 1904); and cf. H. H. Rowley, *From Joseph to Joshua* (London: Oxford University Press, 1950).

7. Engnell's own statement has been replaced with this sentence.

trance into Egypt or the Exodus from Egypt. It is supposed that Raamses was the place where the Exodus began. Some scholars (Montet, Albright, and others) have identified Raamses with Avaris (and perhaps Zoan), in which case the immigration to Egypt did not take place during the Hyksos period (ca. 1730–1580 B.C.), as was once thought. In reality, the so-called Merneptah stele does not stand in the way of the "low" date of the Exodus.[8] Furthermore, it is true that the *ḥabiru* of the Amarna letters are undoubtedly identical with the *'apiru* of the Egyptian inscriptions, but they are by no means identical with the immigrants who were with Moses and Joshua; instead, they are to be connected with the immigrations of Abraham, Isaac, and Jacob.[9]

In the Old Testament traditions, the immigration to Egypt is dated in the year 1877 B.C. and the Exodus from Egypt, in 1447 B.C. (Exod. 12:40; I Kgs. 6:1). The immigration to Egypt is dated 430 years before the Exodus from Egypt and the Exodus, 480 years before the beginning of the building of the temple. If we subtract "forty years in the wilderness" from the date of the Exodus, we get the year 1407, a date which corresponds only too well with the dating of the fall of Jericho by Garstang and others on the basis of archaeological evidence. It is difficult to avoid the suspicion that the maxim, "the Bible is true," dictated this result. But the date in I Kgs. 6:1 is undoubtedly due to later speculation, and there are no fixed points at all for an Israelite chronology before the ninth century B.C. The high date of the Exodus from Egypt is in conflict with both the genealogical lists in the Pentateuch and the period of "Abraham's" immigration to Canaan. However, the tendency now is in the direction of abandoning the identification of the Amraphel of Genesis, chapter 14, with Hammurabi, king of Babylon; and besides, scholars now date Hammurabi around the year 1700 B.C. or later, and not around 2100 B.C., as was once generally done. Another detail which needs to be kept in mind is that "forty" is a round number which simply means "many." Notice that, according to the Old Testament tradition, Moses lives "forty years" in Egypt, "forty years" with Jethro in Midian, and "forty years" during the "wilderness wanderings." Thus, he attains the age of 120 years,

8. The name "Israel" originally referred to a group of tribes in Canaan, though they are not identical with the later twelve tribes, not with the so-called Leah tribes.

9. For the latest treatment of the *ḥabiru* problem, see W. F. Albright, *Yahweh and the Gods of Canaan* (London: University School of Oriental and African Studies, 1968), pp. 64 ff.

which Gen. 6:3 considers to be maximal. Just as all attempts which have been made up until now to solve the chronological problems connected with the Exodus from Egypt have turned out to be unsatisfactory, so also future attempts to solve this problem will continue to be unsuccessful, no matter what hypotheses or combinations of hypotheses scholars may defend. This is the case with H. H. Rowley's very recent attempt to solve the problem.[10] He advances the idea of a double penetration into Canaan involving the tribes of Leah and Joseph, partially from the east, and partially from the south by Judah, Simeon, Levi, and Reuben, an idea which is incompatible with the tradition. In developing this hypothesis, Rowley is much too emphatic in using the Joseph narrative as a personal historical document, relies on the unprovable so-called Kenite hypothesis of the origin of Yahweh throughout, maintains a two years' period of wandering in the wilderness instead of "forty," etc. Thus, all that we can say about the chronological problems involved is that it is most probable that the historical nucleus which lies behind the narrative concerning the Exodus from Egypt in Exodus, chapters 1–15, is to be dated in the 1300–1200s B.C.—in that case, certainly during the reign of Pharaoh Merneptah—and not in the 1400s.

However, as has been pointed out in other essays,[11] the form-critical analysis and cultic interpretation of Exod. 1:1–15:21 puts the problem of the Exodus from Egypt in an entirely new light. This interpretation considers the so-called Exodus Legend, which forms the central tradition complex around which the whole so-called Tetrateuch or "P work" (Gen.-Numb.) is built, to be a historicizing representation of an original cultic myth. In other words, Exodus, chapters 1–15, is a ritual text belonging to and dealing with the south Canaanite and Israelite annual festival, the Passover, and the Exodus, our primary concern here, is the cultic procession out to the vital rites of this festival which are celebrated "in the field" or "at the edge of the wilderness," out in the open. Only the realization that there are cultic realities lying behind the present narrative can enable us to do justice to it and to explain many of the details which it contains. In this connection, the following things should be pointed out.

The whole legend is introduced by a so-called cultic sham fight represented by dramatic scenes which describe the ten plagues that

10. Rowley, *op. cit.*
11. Cf. chap. 4, "The Pentateuch," chap. 7, "New Year Festivals," and chap. 8, "The Passover."

afflict the Egyptians (Exod. 7:14 ff.).[12] Here, the Egyptians are characteristically represented by their "magicians," while the Israelites are represented by Moses and Aaron, who were introduced in the early parts of Exodus. Moses is described in royal divine categories as the Messiah, the saving figure, and Aaron as the high priest acting at his side. After the Passover is instituted by divine decree (12:1 ff.), the Exodus from Egypt begins at Raamses, where the Passover meal is eaten (12:28, 37), and advances to Succoth (which means "booths"), where the *maṣṣôth*, the Feast of Unleavened Bread, is celebrated. According to the cultic interpretation, these place names represent the first two stations in the cultic procession, the "Exodus from Egypt." The description of this Exodus contains many marvellous details. The people go forth "equipped for battle" (13:18), but they are also carrying their kneading-bowls and their unleavened dough. Their loins are girded up, they have staffs in their hands, and they carry gold, silver, and clothing "captured" from the Egyptians. The Israelites march out "in haste," numbering "about six hundred thousand men on foot, besides women and children" (12:37, RSV—these swarming hordes of Israelites who were attended at birth by *two* midwives, Shiphrah and Puah, 1:15), and "a mixed multitude also went up with them, and very many cattle, both flocks and herds" (12:38, RSV). This "exodus" takes place during the night, which is "a night of watching by the Lord" (*lêl shimmurîm lᵉyahweh*), a "night of watching kept to the Lord by all the people of Israel throughout their generations" (12:42, RSV, i.e., "generation after generation"). This account, which has some parallels in other Old Testament passages (compare especially II Sam. 6:1 ff.), is reminiscent of an analogous cultic "exodus" in the annual festival at the ancient Phoenician Ugarit, described in the so-called Keret text from Ras Shamra.[13] From Succoth, Israel marches on to Etham, "on the edge of the wilderness" (13:20—an equivalent expression occurs in the Keret text).[14] After this, the people encounter the enemy for the last time at "Pi-ha-hiroth in front of Baal-zephon"

12. In a special article on the plagues, Engnell maintains that they cannot be regarded as historical facts but must be interpreted as elements in a cultic sham fight. He refers to a Sumerian text "belonging to the same sphere," in which the water is also changed into blood (obviously the myth of Inanna and Shukal-letuda, S. N. Kramer, *The Sumerians* [Chicago: University of Chicago Press, 1963], p. 162.)

13. I. Engnell, *Studies in Divine Kingship in the Ancient Near East*, 2d ed. (Oxford: Basil Blackwell, 1967), pp. 156 f.

14. *Ibid.*, p. 159.

(14:2, 9, RSV). The name Baal-zephon is clearly Canaanite and cultic in type. Since its counterpart occurs in the Ras Shamra texts,[15] it cannot possibly have a southern provenance. It is as impossible to locate as the other place names in the narrative. Here, "in the morning watch," Yahweh performs a miracle through Moses, destroying the "enemy army." Afterward, the victory is celebrated by "the song of praise by Moses and the Israelites" (15:1–18), a typical song of the Annual Festival which ends with the refrain "The Lord will reign for ever and ever" (v. 18, RSV) and by the dancing and singing of the prophetess Miriam and the women (15:20–21). Thus, again, the victory is won over chaos (Tehom, the primitive deep), represented by the "Sea of Reeds," and over Sheol, represented by the hereditary foe Egypt,[16] and, as a result, cosmos is preserved; blessing, prosperity, and fruitfulness are created anew through the rites of the Passover, which are accompanied by the "myth" of the Passover Festival, the cult dramatic text of the "Exodus from Egypt." Here, it should be pointed out that the original cultic *Sitz im Leben* of the narrative shines through clearly in what follows, in the description of the so-called wilderness wandering in Exod. 15:22 ff.[17]

But it is important to observe that the narrative of the Exodus from Egypt *in its present form* is not the original cultic text, but represents a later "disintegrated" form which has been set free from its original cultic connection. Nevertheless, in its historicized form as a "memorial text," the narrative also continued to be a cultic text in the sense that, in later periods, it was used as a "reading text," as was the case also in the Synagogue. Furthermore, it is impossible to reconstruct the original cult myth, the ritual text, by some text-critical method or other means. As a matter of fact, we can only surmise the large outlines of the original myth.

It is also important to point out that myth and historical reality are not mutually exclusive ideas in ancient Israel, but complement each other. Thus, the fact that categories of the cultic *form of presentation* appear in the narrative does not exclude the possibility of a real historical event.[18] As has already been suggested, it is not only possible,

---

15. Şaphon as the mountain of Baal.

16. Egypt is more or less identified with the powers of chaos, Isa. 30:7; Ps. 87:4.

17. See chap. 10, "The Wilderness Wandering."

18. Cf. H. Ringgren, *The Faith of the Psalmists* (Toronto: Ryerson Press, 1963), chap. VIII.

but also probable, that a so-called historical nucleus is hidden behind the narrative of the Exodus from Egypt. It is not very likely that we are dealing with a pure cult myth, which did not give rise to a "historical narrative" until later by means of a historicizing process. The reason for this is simply the fact that the Old Testament tradition is so unanimous and consistent in its presentation of the origin and earliest fortunes of the people of Israel and especially of their most prominent leading figure, Moses, whose historical existence and contribution cannot be called into question. But we are in no position to say in greater detail how cult myth and historical reality were combined. It is usually thought that a historical Mosaic "Exodus from Egypt" coincided with the celebration of the Passover Festival.[19] But one thing is clear: the cultic type of narrative form used in Exodus, chapters 1–15, does not permit a detailed reconstruction of historical data. From a historical point of view, the Exodus from Egypt certainly corresponds to a very complex reality; due to the actual nature of the sources, it is impossible to make a detailed reconstruction of the cultic reality lying behind the sources, but there can be no doubt that there was such a reality.

In the Jewish haggadah, the Exodus from Egypt plays a major rôle as a fundamental act of salvation for the chosen people. Here, the Exodus is embellished with several legendary features that further develop its miraculous character, which is already typical of the Old Testament narrative. At the same time, it is often used as a theological motif.[20] Elsewhere in Judaism, the tendency is to rationalize the legendary features in the Exodus narrative, especially the plagues in Egypt.

The New Testament interprets the Exodus, together with the celebration of the Passover, typologically as prototypes of Baptism and the Lord's Supper respectively, with emphasis on the character of the Exodus as a *rite de passage,* a passing from death to life or to salvation in Christ (compare especially I Cor. 10:1 ff.). In Heb. 11:29, the Exodus from Egypt is used as an exemplary event, made possible by faith.

19. F. F. Hvidberg, *Den israelitiske Religions Historie* (København: Munksgaard, 1944), p. 79.
20. E.g., in the Dura synagogue.

10

❦

The Wilderness Wandering

"WILDERNESS WANDERING" is a term with somewhat varying content, but it usually refers to Israel's wandering "in the desert" after the Exodus from Egypt, up until their entrance into Canaan from the east, across the Jordan. Sometimes, however, "wilderness wandering" refers only to the time after the sojourn at Sinai; then, the narrative of the wilderness wandering would begin with Numb. 10:11, or possibly 13:1. However, this implies a much too narrow distinction, due, to a large extent, to a misunderstanding of the word *forty* in Numb. 14:33 f. as an exact number for the years that Israel spent in the desert: actually, here, as in several other passages dealing with the wilderness wandering, *forty* is a round number meaning "many."

If we look at it objectively, we must admit that the distinction between the wilderness wandering and the Exodus from Egypt is very flexible because, actually, the wilderness wandering begins with the Exodus. In the Exodus narrative in Exod. 1:1–15:21, the first four stopping places or *stationes* of the wilderness wandering are mentioned: Raamses, the place of departure; Succoth; Etham, "on the edge of the wilderness"; and Pi-ha-hiroth, "in front of Baal-zephon."

In the essays on "The Passover" and "The Exodus from Egypt," we

As "Ökenvandringen," this essay appears in *Svenskt Bibliskt Uppslagsverk,* 2d ed., Vol. II, cols. 1501–1507.

have shown that, from the standpoint of form-criticism, composition, and content, Exodus, chapters 1–15, was originally a ritual text, a "cult myth," connected with the *pesaḥ-maṣṣôth* festival. No definite conclusions can be drawn from this type of tradition concerning the historical data lying behind it. In reality, the detailed problems of chronology and geography connected with the Exodus are unsolved and insoluble, first of all because the "Exodus from Egypt" is a ritual drama reaching its climax in the passing over of the "Sea of Reeds" and the victory over the Egyptians, celebrated by the songs of praise in Exod. 15:1–18 and 20–21. And yet, this literary and cultic interpretation of the source material, which is inescapable and obvious, may not and cannot be carried so far as to deny the possibility that historical events lie behind it. To reach such a conclusion would only show an inadequate understanding of the real meaning of the ideas of myth and history and their relationship to each other.[1] Another factor which has made scholars skeptical of understanding the Exodus narrative as fundamentally cultic is the very common notion that the connection between the Exodus narrative and the Passover was altogether secondary and was accomplished for the first time by means of a later "historicizing" of the Passover. This erroneous idea is due to a one-sided, literary-critical source analysis and a lack of traditio-historical insight into the composition of the "P work," coupled with a one-sided, negative disregard of the unity of the Old Testament tradition. As far as composition is concerned, the so-called Exodus Legend[2] is the nucleus of the "P work" or "Tetrateuch" (Genesis-Numbers), around which this whole work is built; and in its present, final form, this legend, as the central element in a historical description, is the beginning of a "historical work."[3]

This "historical account" is continued with material which is narrative in type, beginning with Exod. 15:22 and touching, in particular, on the "wilderness wandering." This strand turns up again in the "D work," the "Deuteronomic historical work" (Deuteronomy-II Kings), more specifically in Deuteronomy, where it is concluded by the description of the death of Moses in chapter 34, and is followed by the tradition of the "Conquest" beginning in the Book of Joshua.

1. Cf. H. Ringgren, *The Faith of the Psalmists* (Toronto: Ryerson Press, 1963), Chap. VIII.
2. See chap. 8, "The Passover."
3. See especially chap. 4, "The Pentateuch."

But the narrative of the wilderness wandering is not a self-contained unit; rather, it is complex and in part highly contradictory. Literary criticism has offered several penetrating attempts at analysis, but its division of the material into the different so-called Pentateuchal sources, "JE," "P," and "D," has failed to produce any clear results or to solve the discrepancies and difficulties. In conjunction with J. Wellhausen and H. Gressmann, scholars commonly divide this legend into the "Kadesh complex" (Exodus 17–18 and Numbers 10–14) and the "Sinai complex" (Exodus 19–24, 32–34). They maintain that these complexes are, themselves, composite, due to complicated intermingling of the various written sources and strata which they contain. It is clear that, to some extent, there are parallel variant traditions in this material and that the significant names in these traditions are Sinai and Horeb on the one hand, and Kadesh on the other. But it is also clear that the different tradition complexes have been combined into a unit (and, to some extent, mutually harmonized) in such a way as to defy a source-critical analysis, even of a traditio-historical type. However, this much is certain: it is obviously impossible and erroneous to consider one complex as primary in relationship to the other. After these two complexes were combined into a special and (in its present form) very artificial narrative composition (to the extent that we can speak of a unified composition at all), they were interspersed with various materials of another sort—legal materials and special traditions of different types—to such an extent that they hardly help to make the narrative as a whole any clearer. This is due partly to the fact that clarity was not a particular Israelite talent and partly—and more especially—to the very special *Sitz im Leben* which the wilderness wandering had from the very beginning as a motif and theme.

If we temporarily ignore the many discrepancies, we may reconstruct the main outline of the wilderness wandering in the following way. After departing from *yam sûph,* the "Sea of Reeds" (which, in conjunction with the LXX, is traditionally identified with the Red Sea, although this is entirely hypothetical), the Israelites, after having "encamped" at several places, go into the "wilderness of Shur" (Exod. 15:22 ff.), then to Elim (15:27), the "wilderness of Sin, which is between Elim and Sinaï" (16:1 ff.), Rephidim (17:1 ff.), and the "wilderness of Sinaï" "before the mountain" (19:1 ff.). Following this, we have the so-called Book of the Covenant in Exodus 21–23, the concluding of the covenant at Sinai, chapter 24, instructions concerning the building and use of the tabernacle, chapters 25–33, with its variant tradition in chapters 34–40. After this comes all the legal material in Leviticus and the census in the desert in Numb. 1:1–10:10. Thus, the thread of the wilderness wandering is not resumed until we come to Numb. 10:11. The wandering continues through the "wilderness of Paran" (Numb. 10:11 ff.) with "stations" at Kibroth-hattaavah (11:34) and Hazeroth (11:35). Here, the sequence is broken again by various types of material. The narrative of the wilderness wandering is resumed in Numbers, chapter 20 "in the wilderness of Zin," where the Israelites stay at Kadesh. According to what is perhaps a fictitious tradition, a distinction is made between this Zin, Heb. *ṣin*, and the Sin which is mentioned in Exod. 16:1 and Numb. 33:11 ff., Heb. *sîn*.[4] The next place that Israel "encamps" is Mount Hor "on the border of the land of Edom" (20:22 ff.). After making a circuit around Edom, Israel encamps at Oboth (21:10); Iye-abarim, "in the wilderness which is opposite Moab, toward the sunrise" (21:11); the valley of Zered (21:12); on the northern bank of the Arnon (21:13 ff.); at Beer (21:16 ff.); Mattanah (21:18); Nahaliel (21:19); Bamoth (21:19); on Mount Pisgah in Moab (21:20 ff.); and, finally, "in the plains of Moab beyond the Jordan at Jericho" (22:1 ff.). In Numb. 33:1–49, there is a variant to this material: it is simply a list of forty places where Israel "encamped." This is usually considered to be a later list; sometimes, it has been regarded as an itinerary, a travel guide for pilgrims from Palestine to Sinai.[5] Another major variant of the entire wilderness wandering is found in Deuteronomy, chapters 1 ff., in the speech of Moses, which clearly reflects a Deuteronomic hue and structure. In form, it purports to be a retrospective survey of the entire wilderness wandering, but this is not given in detail. Rather, this material has more the character of a brief resumé, intended to serve as a basis for the view of history which the "Deuteronomist" puts into the mouth of Moses. Thus, the death of Moses is not recorded until Deuteronomy, chapter 34 (we may assume that this account was the conclusion of the "P work" from the beginning, i.e., that it was the conclusion of the Book of Numbers), and this event is the formal conclusion of the

---

4. This remark seems to have been induced by the fact that both names appear in Swedish in the form *Sin*. In Hebrew, the difference between *ṣadhêh* and *samekh* should have been clear enough.

5. M. Noth, "Der Wallfahrtsweg zum Sinai," *Palästinajahrbuch*, 36 (1940), pp. 5 ff.

wilderness wandering and is followed by the Conquest of Canaan in Joshua, chapters 1 ff. Looking at the wilderness wandering in broad outline, scholars usually divide the whole narrative into three large sections: (1) from Egypt to Sinai (to Numb. 10:10), (2) from Sinai to Kadesh (Numb. 10:11–20:13), and (3) from Kadesh to Moab (Numb. 20:14–36:13 or Deut. 34:12). But because of the nature of the material, this division, which actually amounts to a historical reconstruction, is more or less fictitious.

That this is true is clear from a closer examination of the narrative from the point of view of form-criticism and motif analysis. Such an examination indicates that the wilderness wandering, which seems to be historical, in reality must have had an original *Sitz im Leben* similar to the *Exodus Legend,* and must have been given its structure under similar circumstances, because again and again characteristics appear in the account of the wilderness wandering which clearly reflect a distinct cultic background. The most important of these is the striking way in which this "wandering" legend, like the Exodus Legend, is built upon what is known as *the ritual combat.* In the wandering legend, in most cases, this combat appears in the form of the so-called verbal contest: a regularly recurring murmuring against or disputing with Moses, the cult leader, the primitive king, who, by means of various miracles, overcomes the rebellious enemies, the representatives of the power of chaos. Thus, in the "wilderness of Shur," the people are already murmuring, and this is overcome by the miracle of providing water at Marah (Exod. 15:23 ff.). The same type of "murmuring" occurs in the "wilderness of Sin" and is overridden by the miracle of quails and manna (16:22 ff.). (Notice the special miraculous character of the narrative in vv. 18, 23 ff., the connection with the show-bread manna in vv. 32 ff., and the phraseology in v. 35). The "disputing" and the "murmuring" at Massah and Meribah is connected with the sojourn at Rephidim and is overcome by the miracle in which Moses smites the rock with his rod and water comes forth (17:2 ff.). The description of the attack by Amalek and Israel's victory over this people (vv. 8 ff.) is of the same character. In a similar way, there is an account of the rebellion at Taberah during the sojourn in the "wilderness of Paran," which is overcome by the mediating intervention of Moses (Numb. 11:1 ff.). Similar events occur at Kibroth-hattaavah (11:34 f.). The rebellion of Aaron and Miriam takes place at Hazeroth and is also brought to an end by a miracle of

Moses (12:1 ff.). The special tradition concerning the rebellion of Korah, Dathan, and Abiram (Numbers, chapter 16) is another variation on the motif of the ritual combat. As the result of an ordeal, no less than 14,950 Israelite lives are lost. This account is followed by another case of "murmuring," which is overcome by the miracle of the budding of Aaron's rod (chapter 17), and by the dispute at Meribah, which is overcome by the miracle of Moses' rod (20:1 ff.).

In the other great variant complex, beginning with the dramatic event involving the "fiery serpents" and the bronze serpent (21:4 ff.), the two motifs of rebellion and miracle alternate in the same way. Here, we must keep in mind the clear cultic background of the Sinai tradition itself, where Moses appears as the central figure of the ritual and is described throughout in royal categories (see especially Exodus, chapters 19, 24, and 34). Like the special tradition concerning the spies (Numbers, chapters 13–14), the tradition in this narrative bears the strong stamp and color of a cultic drama in many of its details. The "inspection" of Israel's tribes, their order of march (Numb. 1:1 ff.; 26:1 ff.), clearly betray a cultic connection.[6] The same is true of the rôle of the pillar of cloud, as well as of many other phenomena in the narrative of the wilderness wandering.[7]

In addition to this, there is the problem of the place names mentioned in the narrative of the wilderness wandering. In a few cases, scholars have suggested identifications—hardly convincing—with modern Arabic place names; however, in most cases, no identifications have been offered. Many of the names are peculiar and are clearly secondary or artificial. To put it quite simply, we are compelled to admit that every attempt at a geographical and historical reconstruction of Israel's route during the wilderness wandering is a fiction. Also, as has already been pointed out, it is impossible to determine how long Israel was in the wilderness from the reference to the "forty" years in the narrative. Thus, we cannot escape the fact that the description of the wilderness wandering in Exodus-Numbers does not permit any direct historical conclusions, since the narrative is cultic in type and is clearly influenced by its original cultic *Sitz im Leben*.

6. In other words, the places of encampment are, in reality, stations during a cultic "Exodus."

7. The pillar of cloud and the pillar of fire naturally reflect Yahweh's character of an atmospheric high god, but they may be assumed to have been represented by some visible device in the cult.

However, on this point, several facts should be emphasized. Although the original *Sitz im Leben* of the narrative of the wilderness wandering is cultic, it is not to be concluded that the present form of the legend of the wilderness wandering represents the actual original cultic situation. We can only guess at the general type of this situation: it must be regarded as an imitative, dramatic production connected with the Passover Festival. Thus, the places where Israel "encamped" during the wilderness wandering must be understood as stations which follow the order of procession in the cultic drama; for, in its final form, the account of the wilderness wandering is a narrative which has been deculticized, "historicized," transformed, reinterpreted, and understood in an entirely different way from its original setting because it has been made a part of the large historical complex called the "P work." Also, it is to be observed that this cultic interpretation of the wilderness wandering in no way necessitates a denial that real historical data lie behind the narrative, any more than does the Exodus Legend. To some extent, the cultic narrative works with historical material which it dramatizes and tendentiously reconstructs. General considerations and direct statements found in the Old Testament make it quite clear that Israel experienced a real wilderness wandering, which was subsequently re-enacted again and again in the holy drama of the cult. But the historical reality lying behind the biblical narrative is very complicated. Perhaps we should say that Israel (i.e., the "Hebrew" fathers) experienced not one, but several wilderness wanderings. According to the unanimous tradition of the Old Testament— and thus, in all probability, historical—one of these was led by Moses, and it gained precedence over all the others. All the wilderness experiences have been concentrated in it. Therefore, it has become the *only* wilderness wandering. But on the basis of its form and the fortunes it reflects, this "historical" narrative must be taken for what it is: a cultic narrative, subsequently "historicized," which cannot be utilized according to the demands of modern historical-critical methods.

On the same point, it is not without importance that the Old Testament itself understands the wilderness wandering as a historical event. The allusions to this event in different contexts, in the prophets (compare Amos 2:10; Hos. 13:4 f.; Jer. 2:6; Ezek. 20:9 ff.), make it clear that this is the way in which the Old Testament interprets it. But it is also important to observe the ideas which these passages express. They never regard the period of the wilderness wandering as an ideal period: rather, it is a wandering through "a land of drought and deep darkness" (Jer. 2:6, RSV), a wandering through Sheol, which can be endured only by Yahweh's leadership. Indeed, it is by divine leadership alone that Israel is able to win the victory over her enemies, carry out the conquest of the promised land, the land of the messianic future, and enjoy salvation, in spite of all sin, all apostasy, and all trials and punishment.[8] In other words, the wilderness wandering is understood as a typical *rite de passage,* and there can hardly be any doubt that this interpretation is based on the original cultic connection of this narrative and on the recurring dramatic cultic event. This is also confirmed by the rôle which the wilderness wandering plays in the Book of Psalms (compare Pss. 68:8 ff.—notice especially v. 18, which states that Sinai is located "in the holy place," RSV margin—107:4 ff.)

Finally, it should be pointed out that the positive rôle which scholars so often assign to the desert period as a leitmotif in the religious history of Israel seems even less convincing when one conceives of the wilderness wandering as an actual, non-recurring historical event. Furthermore, it seems wholly unlikely that a forty-year wandering through the wilderness—which, by a literary-critical source analysis, is sometimes reduced to a shorter period, even as short as two years (compare H. H. Rowley[9])—involving such difficult external circumstances and great hardships as the account declares could have created, formed, and leavened Israel's entire manner of life and future ideal. However, as has already been pointed out, investigation of the traditions concerning the wilderness wandering from the point of view of form-criticism, content, and theme clearly indicates that the naive historical interpretation of the wilderness wandering is untenable, in spite of the fact that it is asserted in the framework of the Old Testament itself.

8. Cf. chap. 6, "The Prophets."

9. H. H. Rowley, *From Joseph to Joshua* (London: Oxford University Press, 1948), pp. 133, 164.

11

ೞ⊹ಿ

The Messiah in the Old Testament and Judaism

The Old Testament. A Historical Survey of Scholarly Views: Leading Positions.—In the Bible, both in the Old Testament and the New (with its characteristic interpretation of the Old Testament in light of messianism), and in the church and its preaching, the figure of the Messiah plays a very dominant rôle. And yet, ever since the emergence of modern critical research, and especially during the literary-critical era, Protestant scholarship has adopted a reserved attitude toward the rôle of the Messiah and messianism in the Old Testament, to say the least. There can be no doubt that in reality this attitude is the result of a specific a priori philosophy of history. This preconceived attitude toward the whole complex problem has resulted in a harsh treatment of Old Testament materials using the methods which are characteristic of literary-historical research. This is especially clear in the prophetic literature, where scholars have rejected, on wholly insufficient grounds, a large portion of the numerous central messianic sayings as unauthentic or secondary. But those who take a realistic view of the Bible and use an exegetical approach which attempts to understand the Old Testament in its historical context (i.e., its general ancient Near Eastern milieu and its particular Canaanite and Israelite

"Messias" is the title given this essay in *Svenskt Bibliskt Uppslagsverk,* 2d ed., Vol. II, where it appears on cols. 77–91.

milieu) without preconceived ideas of any sort, have an entirely different attitude toward Old Testament messianism.[1] The usual literary-critical view of the messianic problem generally follows this pattern: on the whole, the word *Messiah* as it is usually interpreted, i.e., futuristically, in the conventional sense of a coming or eschatological salvation figure, does not occur in the Old Testament until it appears in the apocalyptic literature. In the Old Testament, this term occurs only in the combination "the Messiah of Yahweh" (Heb. *mᵉshîaḥ yahweh*, "Yahweh's anointed"), and is used in the pre-Exilic period of the reigning king[2] and in the post-Exilic period of the high priest, or in a figurative sense of the patriarchs (Ps. 105:15), Cyrus (Isa. 45:1), or the people of Israel (Hab. 3:13; Pss. 28:8; 84:10; 89:39). *Messiah* is also interpreted as referring to a real historical royal figure in Pss. 2:2; 105:15, and similar passages.

The explanations for the actual occurrence of the concept of the Messiah in Old Testament materials differ greatly. The most common is the idea that all messianic oracles in the pre-Exilic prophets were inserted later in the post-Exilic period and thus belong to the "massive jungle of editorial material in which all genuine prophecies are now hidden."[3] Oracles like Isa. 2:2 ff., 9:1 ff., and 11:1 ff. are numbered among these inserted passages. The criteria which are used to justify this include such things as: "The picture in these pericopes is painted with colors which are not found elsewhere in Isaiah's genuine oracles," for "the fact that their contents are compatible with Isaiah's thought world does not prove they are authentic."[4] Similar "arguments" are made concerning the messianic oracles in Hosea, Micah, Jeremiah, Habakkuk, and Ezekiel. Sometimes we find the theological counter-argument that the royal Messiah is to be looked at in contrast to Yahweh, who himself is Israel's real Messiah, while the Davidic leader is only a human *advocatus dei*.[5] This opinion certainly is very old. To

1. For the different arguments favoring the originality of the messianic oracles in the prophetic literature, see chap. 6, "Prophets and Prophetism in the Old Testament."

2. Cf. G. von Rad, *Old Testament Theology*, I (New York: Harper & Brothers, 1962), pp. 309 ff.

3. R. H. Pfeiffer, *Introduction to the Old Testament* (New York: Harper & Brothers, 1948), p. 438.

4. O. Eissfeldt, *Einleitung in das Alte Testament*, 1. Aufl. (Tübingen: J. C. B. Mohr, 1934), pp. 358 f. English translation, *The Old Testament: An Introduction* (New York: Harper and Row, 1965), pp. 318 f.

5. L. Köhler, *Theologie des Alten Testaments* (Tübingen: J. C. B. Mohr, 1936), pp. 227 f.

a certain extent, it can be said that its foundations were already laid in the anti-royalistic (and probably also anti-Davidic) "Deuteronomic circle," which has given us the so-called Deuteronomic historical work, Deuteronomy-II Kings.[6] But even so, this does not keep the idea itself from being essentially wrong.

According to a different view, the origin of the idea of a messiah is to be sought, for example, in a general hope of restoration which originated in the post-Exilic period and was anchored in the historical David. This belief was never held by the great prophets, who were predominantly prophets of doom; but its foundation was laid by the prophet-priest Ezekiel. In the earlier strata of his Book, we find the belief in the rebirth of the *nation*, but in the later strata, chapters 40–48, the belief in the "prince," who (in spite of his rather insignificant role, originally) was gradually developed into a messianic savior-king. In reality, Ezekiel represents a final stage in the ancient battle of the priest *against* the king; the prophet seems consciously to avoid the title *king*, which he reserves for Yahweh himself.[7] Subsequent stages of this development are represented by the secondary portions of Jeremiah ("Deutero-Jeremiah"), chapters 30 and 33, and even later by secondary portions of Ezekiel, chapters 34 and 38, by Hos. 3:5; Hag. 2:23; Zech. 3:8 ff.; 6:19 ff.; Isa. 55:4 f. According to this view, of course, *Ebed Yahweh*, "the Servant of the Lord," has nothing to do with the Messiah, much less with the Davidic Messiah. Finally, this development appears in Isa. 11:1 ff., which is dated in the second century B.C. This reconstruction being true, there is "no pre-exilic messianic hope," and "strictly speaking there is no exilic messianic hope," according to Aytoun.[8] Von Gall and Mowinckel—still, in 1955[9]—also reached approximately the same conclusion. Von Gall[10] recognized the connection with the sacral king, but identified him with the figure of the *Persian* king and thus rejected all messianic oracles in the pre-Exilic period as secondary.

The literary-critical concept of the Jewish confession also leads to the same conclusion, even though the line of argumentation is some-

---

6. See chap. 4, "The Pentateuch." Cf. Judg. 8:23; I Sam. 8:4 ff.

7. E. Hammershaimb, "Ezekiel's View of the Monarchy," *Studia Orientalia Ioanni Pedersen* (Hauniae: E. Munksgaard, 1953), pp. 130–140.

8. W. R. Aytoun, "The Rise and Fall of the 'Messianic' Hope in the Sixth Century," *Journal of Biblical Literature*, 39 (1920), pp. 24–43.

9. S. Mowinckel, *He that Cometh* (Oxford: Blackwell, 1955), pp. 17 f.

10. A. von Gall, *Basileia tou Theou* (Heidelberg: C. Winter, 1926).

what different. According to this view, the sayings concerning the Messiah in Isa. 9:1 ff., 11:1 ff., etc., cannot be pre-Exilic because the idea of the Messiah "includes a claim to world domination, which is not really characteristic of the messianic hope until a later stage of development," according to Buttenwieser.[11] Against this, it may be pointed out that "world domination" is an integral element in the ideology of the sacral kingship and, thus, is primitive. It was maintained in theory by lesser Canaanite city kings. Such a picture of the Messiah in the pre-Exilic period seems wholly impossible to literary critics who attempt to work out a consistent reinterpretation of the literary prophets in modern ethical and universalistic categories. For this same reason, they also consider passages like Mic. 5:1 ff., etc., to be secondary. In other words, the psychological prerequisites for a belief in a Messiah or a *David redivivus* do not appear until the post-Exilic period. The nearest parallel to this concept is found in the Barbarossa Myth, which originated after the fall of the medieval Germanic Roman Empire. Nor do these prerequisites occur in "Deutero-Isaiah": its exalted universalism, the final stage in the religious development of the prophetic ideas, has no room for the belief in a personal Messiah. *Ebed Yahweh,* "the Servant of the Lord," is personified Israel, the people of God, who suffer for others. The same is true in "Trito-Isaiah," Malachi, and Joel (all of which are, of course, post-Exilic): in these books, it is Yahweh himself who is the savior, and he has no need of help from a weak man. Similarly, there is no individual Messiah in the Apocrypal Literature or in the Book of Daniel, where the "Son of Man" in 7:13 "according to the author's own explanation is the nation of the holy ones of God."[12] The same is true of the Books of Enoch and the Book of Jubilees. But after the fall of the Maccabean dynasty, amidst the experiences of tryanny at the hand of Herod and the Romans, the belief in a personal Messiah, which previously had occurred in sporadic glimpses, bursts forth like a shooting star. We encounter this false belief suddenly in a fully developed form in Jesus, Josephus, and Philo. Its final shape runs along two parallel lines: the Davidic national and the apocalyptic. The former occurs in I Enoch 85–90, the Sibylline Oracles, the Psalms of Solomon, II Baruch, and the Testaments of the Twelve Patriarchs; and the latter,

11. M. Buttenwieser, "Messiah," *The Jewish Encyclopedia* (New York: Funk and Wagnalls, 1904), vol. 8.

12. Cf. E. Sjöberg, "Människosonen och Israel i Dan. vii," *Religion och Bibel,* 7 (1948), pp. 1–16.

in I Enoch 37–71 and IV Esdras. In a later period, both of these emphases are found in the Rabbinic apocalyptic literature. In surveying this view, it is interesting to notice how anti-messianic Jewish exegesis (which reflects strong a priori presuppositions) and Protestant exegesis agree in detail after detail. This raises serious questions about the objectivity of the latter, which is represented by such literary-critical scholars as Wellhausen, Stade, Nowack, Marti, Budde, Duhm, Volz, Hölscher, Eissfeldt, and Pfeiffer.

However, it must be admitted that there have also been Protestant exegetes who have realized that this negative attitude toward the idea of the Messiah and toward the literary importance of messianic oracles in Old Testament texts is untenable. Catholic scholars have taken a different position because of the tradition which they have inherited. On this issue, at least, this tradition seems to have been a real asset. The Protestant exegetes who have taken a positive attitude toward the concept of the Messiah represent a reaction to extreme literary-critical views. They have been motivated by a somewhat more conservative attitude in general, on the one hand, and by the emergence of new comparative religio-historical insights deduced from the discovery of new material, on the other. This reaction is represented by scholars like Gressmann,[13] Gunkel, Kittel,[14] and Sellin,[15] but the most important figure is the Catholic scholar, L. Dürr.[16]

The starting-point for *the new interpretation* is a correct understanding of the meaning of the "day of Yahweh"[17] in Amos 5:18 ff.; Hos. 2:18; Isa. 2:20. Gressmann (and in conjunction with him, Gunkel)[18] explained this expression in light of a widespread ancient Near

---

13. H. Gressmann, *Der Ursprung der israelitisch-jüdischen Eschatologie* (Göttingen: Vandenhoeck & Ruprecht, 1905); see also Gressman, *Der Messias* (Göttingen: Vandenhoeck & Ruprecht, 1929).

14. R. Kittel, *Die Religion der Volkes Israel*, 2 Aufl. (Leipzig: Quelle & Meyer, 1929), pp. 88, 90.

15. E. Sellin, *Die israelitisch-jüdische Heilandserwartung* (Berlin: E. Runge, 1909); see also Sellin, *Israelitisch-jüdische Religionsgeschichte* (Leipzig: n.p., 1933), pp. 52 and *Theologie des Alten Testaments* (Leipzig: Quelle & Meyer, 1933), pp. 122 ff.

16. L. Dürr, *Ursprung und Ausbau der israelitisch-jüdischen Heilandserwartung* (Berlin: C. A. Schwetschke & Sohn, 1925).

17. S. Mowinckel, *Psalmenstudien*, II (Oslo: J. Dybwad, 1922), pp. 229 ff.; see also Mowinckel, *The Psalms in Israel's Worship*, I (New York: Abingdon Press, 1962), p. 116.

18. H. Gunkel, *Zum religionsgeschichtlichen Verständnis des Neuen Testaments* (Göttingen: Vandenhoeck & Ruprecht, 1903).

Eastern popular mythical eschatology, at the center of which was the *Urmensch* (First Man), or King of Paradise, and which, in turn, was connected with an inherited formal "court style." However, when we trace the concept of the Messiah back to a "mythical" stage, we do not solve the problem but only make it more complicated. Still, it is certainly true that such a popular view including the belief in a messianic figure must have had a distinct origin. Therefore, Sellin, von Rad, Eichrodt, and Bleeker[19] have sought the origin of this idea in Israel in the specific historical and religious experience of this people, especially in the fundamental event at Sinai, and in Israel's unique idea of God. But in taking this position, these scholars do not deny that Israel's eschatology and belief in a Messiah have affinities with other ancient Near Eastern religions or that they reflect peculiarities which were drawn from these religions. On the other hand, Mowinckel[20] has sought the root of Israel's eschatology in the cult; for, in the world view of eschatology, he sees the actual cultic event projected into the future; but in that of mythology, he sees it pushed back into the pre-historic age. Even though this view contains an essential truth— the realization of the pronounced priority of the cultic event—still, the solution to the problem is not so simple. As to the figure of the Messiah, Mowinckel wants to make a clear distinction between a cultic messiah and an eschatological messiah.[21] However, in light of his understanding of the relationship of the cult and eschatology, this view must appear just as full of contradictions as it is erroneous. Like Sellin, Eichrodt, Bleeker, and Pidoux,[22] Dürr traces Old Testament eschatology back to "Israel's unique idea of God"; but at the same time, he is the first (if we leave Von Gall out of consideration) to suggest a new interpretation of the origin of the figure of the Messiah: essentially, it is to be sought *in the person of the sacral king*. And yet, Dürr does not draw the necessary conclusions of his discovery but is content with a compromise that stops halfway, namely, ancient "genuine Israelite" tradition complexes, such as we find in Genesis,

19. Sellin, *Theologie des Alten Testaments*, pp. 122 f.; G. von Rad (reference not identified); W. Eichrodt, *Theologie des Alten Testaments*, I (Leipzig: J. C. Hinrichs, 1933–1939), pp. 271 ff.; L. H. Bleeker, *Over inhoud en oorsprong van Israels heilsverwachting* (n.p.: n.p., 1921).

20. Mowinckel, *Psalmenstudien*, II, pp. 211 ff.

21. Mowinckel, *He that Cometh*, pp. 3 ff.

22. G. Pidoux, *Le Dieu qui vient* (Paris: Delachaux & Niestlé, 1947).

chapter 49, Numbers, chapter 24, are connected with the historical David and his house; in a later period, the Israelite picture of the Messiah is shaped by secondary influences drawn from the ancient Near Eastern "court style," in which a king is always described as the righteous one, an eternally powerful personification of the right, who inaugurates a messianic age of prosperity, fruitfulness, and abundance. However, according to Dürr, the perfection of the picture of the Messiah which appears in the figure of the Servant of the Lord in "Deutero-Isaiah" is a brilliant and absolutely new creation. It originated as an *antithesis* to the Babylonian-Assyrian king in his character of expiator and savior, and was subsequently eschatologized. There can be no doubt that, to some extent, Dürr's view is apologetic, but in spite of his inadequate treatment, he has pointed in the right direction for a correct historical understanding of messianism.

However, the assumption that a mythological and eschatological primitive stage *lies behind* the actual kingship cannot be proved, nor is it necessary. In any case, there is no evidence for this view—actually, idea and cultic form go well together (against Mowinckel). The most important premise for Israel's religion is that the sacral kingship and the royal Messiah[23] and everything associated with him *are already present in the Canaanite, pre-Israelite period.* Thus, the connection between the two is primary, not secondary; eschatology represents a later stage, not the first, contrary to Gressmann's opinion. Finally, several critics, including the French scholar A. Lods,[24] have sought to combine the various explanations, suggested from different quarters, into a synthesis: the mythological (that is, the common ancient Near Eastern belief in the return of the paradisiacal golden age), the historical-national (memorable events from the glorious days of David and Solomon), the cultic (the messianic belief originally rooted in the cult in the New Year Festival, but gradually eschatologized), and the royal-ideological (belief in the divine character of the king).

However, it must be maintained as a principle that the royal-ideological motif is absolutely central, as is now beginning to be admitted in many quarters, for example, in the works of Bentzen and

23. Cf. I. Engnell, *Studies in Divine Kingship in the Ancient Near East,* 2d ed. (Oxford: Basil Blackwell, 1967), p. 43, note 3.

24. A. Lods, "Le divinisation du roi dans l'Orient méditerranéen et ses répercussions dans l'ancien Israël," *Revue d'historie et de philosophie religieuses,* 10 (1930), pp. 209–221.

Patai.[25] The numerous detailed analogies between the idea of the sacral king and the idea of the Messiah preclude the possibility that the similarities merely represent parallel phenomena. They are also too detailed for us to be able to assume a common *form* but different contents. This explanation poorly reflects the situation of ancient times; and in light of the fact that active religious ideas actually connected with the sacral king, especially his role as expiator and "savior," correspond to religious ideas connected with the belief in the Messiah, it is impossible. As the different aspects inherent in the idea complex centered in the figure of the sacral king grew, essentially three points of view emerged. One is the "positive" aspect, which takes the term *messianic* in its literal sense. It is more or less thoroughly nationalistic and is the most common or the standard view, especially in Israel.

Another is the "negative" aspect, which is more esoteric and is characterized by an emphasis on the *aspect of suffering* in the royal ideology.[26] In Israel, the most far-reaching ideological consequences of this aspect are summed up with extraordinary clarity, both in the concept of the "suffering servant of the Lord" and in the figure of the Son of Man,[27] which is dominated by the eschatological-apocalyptic element.

A third aspect is the idea of the *Urmensch* (First Man), which, in cultural settings where the sacral kingship does not appear, is represented to some extent by the "ancestor" and which in time attains its most characteristic feature in Gnosticism. This aspect plays a relatively subordinate rôle in ancient Israel, but the first two aspects are much more prominent. Thus, the idea that the *Urmensch* was the root of the figure of the sacral king, as, for example, Bentzen thinks,[28] is erroneous. But it is also clear that the idea of a savior and the idea of a king are mutually interdependent. It cannot be maintained that the idea of a king was prior to the idea of a savior, or that it was the first and *original* root of the idea of a savior. We cannot tell which preceded the other in time, because this carries us back to a prehistoric stage.

The Old Testament: Terminology and Contents.—In the ideology

25. A. Bentzen, *King and Messiah* (London: Lutterworth Press, 1955); R. Patai, *Man and Temple* (New York: T. Nelson, 1947), pp. 172 ff.

26. Discussed further in this chapter and in chap. 5, "The Book of Psalms."

27. See chap. 12, "The Son of Man."

28. Bentzen, *op. cit.,* pp. 39 ff.

prevalent throughout the ancient Near East, the sacral king was considered divine in origin and the incarnate god in the cult, where he played the rôle of the god according to the "cultic pattern" which appears in more or less similar form in the different regions of the uniform culture of the ancient Near East.[29] This sacral-divine kingship also existed in Israel and its ideology was valid: the king is of divine origin (Pss. 2:7; 89:29; 110:3; II Sam. 7:14); he is divine (Pss. 8:6; 45:7; II Sam. 7:9); he is the incarnation of "righteousness"; he is the perfect judge; and he functions in the cult in the dual rôle of suffering and victory, of expiator and savior.[30] Here, already, we find a messianic ideology connected with the living historical bearer of the kingship, which is taken over from the Canaanite, pre-Israelite period. As a matter of fact, this early Canaanite stage of the Old Testament belief in a Messiah is more or less fully found in extrabiblical West Semitic sources: the Amarna letters, the Panammu, Kalamu, and Zakir inscriptions,[31] and last, but not least, the texts from Ras Shamra.

As bearer of this whole cultic and ideological reality, the Israelite king is designated by the special name "Messiah" (Hebrew *māshîah*, Aramaic *mᵉshîhaʾ*, "the Anointed One"), due to the well-known fact that the king was consecrated to his office by a holy anointing with oil (compare I Sam. 10:1—Saul, 16:13—David, I Kgs. 1:39—Solomon, II Kgs. 9:6—Jehu, 11:12—Joash), by which he was made partaker of the Holy Spirit, that is, of the divine life, and thus became divine himself. Similarly, the Babylonian king can be designated as *pašišu*, "anointed," which is also a priestly title.[32] Historically speaking, the most important form of this world view, undoubtedly common in all Canaan, is to be found in Jerusalem, where the Jebusite-Amorite priest-kingdom (which is connected with the Zadokite priesthood),[33] along with its entire cultic and ideological form, was already taken over by David (compare Ps. 110:4; Gen. 14:18 ff.) and was further expanded under Solomon and his successors.[34]

29. See chap. 2, "The Science of Religion."
30. See chap. 3, "Old Testament Religion."
31. Engnell, *Studies in Divine Kingship*, pp. 71 ff.
32. Cf. T. Jacobsen in *Proceedings of the American Philosophical Society*, 107 (1963), p. 477, note 11.
33. Cf. H. H. Rowley, "Melchizedek and Zadok," *Festschrift Alfred Bertholet* (Tübingen: J. C. B. Mohr, 1950), pp. 461–472; H. Ringgren, *Israelite Religion* (Philadelphia: Fortress Press, 1966), p. 61.
34. See chap. 3, "Old Testament Religion."

The term "messianism" may already be used for this actual historical royal ideology, in which the king appears as savior of the people. It is primarily out of this ideology that there gradually emerges, by the process of eschatologization, an *"eschatological* messianism," or a messianism in a narrow, pregnant, or qualified sense, which goes beyond the idea of the king but at the same time preserves an absolute connection with the dynasty of David. This involves the belief in a coming Messiah in the fulness of time, an ideal king of the family of David, actually a *David redivivus.* This eschatologization of the idea of the Messiah is first accomplished through the prophets, who strongly contribute to the severing of the royal ideology from the cult and, consequently, to the development which was gradually emphasized more and more, especially after the historical kingdom was brought to an end by the Exile.

However, it is very difficult to say where to draw the line between the present aspect and the futuristic or eschatological aspect in various Old Testament contexts. This is due to the fact that, on the whole, the temporal aspect was not fundamental in the typical Israelite and general Semitic thinking, as it is in the modern world. In the messianic oracles of the Old Testament, past, present, and future time are all present, simultaneously; the past, by its anchor in history—especially in the figure of David; the present, primarily by the experience in the actual situation of the cult; and the future, by the assurance of the perfection of this event in the future. The Messiah *has been,* the Messiah *is,* and the Messiah *will be*—in these three aspects, which exist side by side simultaneously, the whole dynamic of the idea of salvation in the Old Testament is reflected in the Messiah. At the same time, it is clear that the present aspect represents that which is complete. The ideal Messiah belongs to the last time. He comes "in that day" (*bayyôm hahû'*), "in the latter days" (*bayyāmîm hahēm*), "at that time" (*bā·ēth hahî'*), "in the latter days" (*bᵉaḥᵃrîth hayyāmîm*). All of this is summed up in the idea of the "day of Yahweh," the day of the Annual Festival, which brings doom on the unfaithful and on all enemies but also brings salvation, once for all, for the "remnant"[35] of

35. According to Engnell, the remnant was originally a cultic concept: Israel as the people that was rescued from Yahweh's judgment in the New Year Festival when the powers of chaos were destroyed. As a consequence of this, the idea of the remnant is closely connected with the messianic king; cf. Isa. 6:13; 10:20 f.

the pious, who are preserved in the time of doom and who will experience the restoration of the paradisiacal primitive state under the sceptre of the Messiah.

It is certainly evident that the future aspect is already strongly emphasized in the literary prophets; but in general, it has not been pushed out into the future so far that we can speak of real eschatologization in their message. *Eschatology* in the strict, advanced sense is not found in the Old Testament, with the special exception of the Book of Daniel. Instead, the terminology to which we have just alluded must be interpreted primarily as similar in meaning to the analogous Accadian expression *ina arkāt ūmi*,[36] which is very similar to the Hebrew *beōrekh yāmîm* or *beaḥᵃrîth hayyāmîm*, in the sense of "in the future" or "in coming days" (compare also the Hebrew *miqēṣ yāmîm*, "after a lapse of time"). Often, the arrival of the "day of Yahweh" or the Messiah is thought to be very near (compare, for example, Isa. 9:6; Joel 2:1; Zeph. 1:7). As a matter of fact, certain prophets even seem to have attached messianic expectations to a historical figure, a living descendant of David: compare Jer. 23:5 (Zedekiah); Hag. 2:23 (Zerubbabel). The view in "Deutero-Isaiah" and Ezekiel is more clearly oriented toward the future and has cosmic overtones, but it still does not exhibit an advanced eschatology. We cannot speak of an almost completely eschatological *outlook* before Daniel; and, even at that, this outlook is not the same thing as a well-worked-out eschatology.

As has already been pointed out, with regard to the positive aspect of messianism, which is especially relevant to the present discussion, the qualities of the coming Messiah are described primarily in the prophetic texts, while the analogous ideology dealing with the sacral king is found primarily in the Psalms and also in "disintegrated" form— in royal categories which have been reapplied—in texts which deal with such figures as Adam, Abraham, Moses, and Joshua. In this material, the Messiah is described as the ideal ruler in the future divine kingdom, the spirit-filled bearer of wisdom and righteousness who shall fulfill the promises, give his people victory and prosperity, restore the Davidic kingdom as the material foundation for the messianic era

---

36. According to W. von Soden's *Akkadisches Handwörterbuch* (Wiesbaden: Otto Harrassowitz, 1959), *arkāt* was originally *warkāt* and thus not related to *'orek.*

(compare, Amos 9:11 f.; Ezek. 37:22), and re-establish the paradisiacal primitive state. We must not forget that, in spite of this positive task, the Messiah also clearly exercises a function of judgment: before the establishment of the messianic kingdom, doom will come on the wicked and unjust, especially on the national enemies of Israel, whose complete conquest and subjugation is a primary assumption of messianism, but also on the enemies within the people of Israel (see Isa. 11:4 in conjunction with Ps. 110:6).

However, there are also oracles of a clearly messianic character outside the prophetic books. In the "historical" books, we encounter such passages for the first time in the so-called Shiloh oracle in the "blessing of Jacob" (Gen. 49:8 ff.), where the Judean Davidic Messiah is described.[37] Outside of this passage, we probably find the oldest direct testimony to the concept of the Messiah in the Balaam traditions in Numbers, chapters 22–24. In 24:5 ff., Israel's messianic future is described as a return to the primitive paradisiacal state; and in 24:17 ff., the Messiah is depicted as a star: the astral aspect is very ancient and is inherent in the royal ideology (see, in the Old Testament, especially Isa. 14:12).[38] The Accadian *šarru*, "king," is cognate with *šarāru*, "to shine." He is also said to be a sceptre out of Jacob-Israel who subjugates the hereditary foes Moab, Edom, and Amalek. In these texts (which may go back to about 1200 B.C.),[39] the outlook is strongly nationalistic and the future aspect is quite clear, although it still cannot be called eschatological. In a later period, both Saul and David are described in "present" messianic categories. From this time on, the messiah is inseparably connected with David and his dynasty (compare II Sam. 7:11 ff.; 23:1 ff.). Here, messianism in the Old Testament undoubtedly receives its most characteristic feature, which is cultivated especially by the prophets.

37. Engnell does not offer a definite interpretation for this passage. He mentions the usual suggestions, including "new born" (the divine savior child) and "ruler," but takes no definite stand. See his article "Silo" (Shiloh) in *SBU*[2].

38. In his article "Morgonstjärna" (Morning Star) in *SBU*[2], Engnell says: "The background of this passage is the worship of [the king] in the shape of a star and a cultic lamentation for his fictitious fall and burial. Isaiah (sic!) has used this motif for political propaganda and given the passage a derisive character."

39. Cf. W. F. Albright, "The Oracles of Balaam," *Journal of Biblical Literature*, 63 (1944), pp. 207–233.

In the great number of different types of royal, messianic psalms, such as Psalms of Refuge, Thanksgiving Psalms, Psalms of Lament, and especially "Royal Suffering Psalms"[40]—which may be subdivided into Penitential Psalms and Psalms of Innocence—to a great extent, we find the typical fluctuation between the present and future aspects of messianism. However, one thing is certain: there are in the Old Testament absolutely no eschatological psalms (or "messianic" psalms, to use the most common expression), that is, psalms completely detached from the cult and looking forward to "the last day" exclusively. The present cultic situation which these psalms presuppose includes primeval history, the attack by the power of chaos (embodied in national enemies as well as religious and internal political enemies), and the repeated defeat of chaos through the royal Messiah (Pss. 2:2; 18:51; 20:7; 28:8; 84:10; 89:39, 52; 132:10, 17), who is called "the Son of God"[41] (compare Pss. 2:7; 110:3 according to the LXX; II Sam. 7:14) or "the Son of Man"[42] (compare Pss. 8:5; 80:18; 146:3); "the servant (of the Lord)"[43] (compare Pss. 18:1; 27:9; 36:1; 69:18; 89:4, 21, 40); "the Son of the handmaid" (Pss. 86:16; 116:16), and many other epithets and honorable titles. This present cultic victory over chaos and the new creation which follows it is the prototype of the final future victory.

However, as has already been suggested, it is the *prophets* who took over and developed the ideology of the Messiah in close connection with the dynasty of David and who fashioned an ideal Messiah. The prophets give much greater emphasis to the future aspect of messianism, as they set the idea of the Messiah free from its cultic connection. However, Haggai and Zechariah still apply the belief in the Davidic Messiah to the contemporary historical descendant of David, Zerubbabel (Hag. 2:23; Zech. 3:8; 6:12).

Actually, we already encounter the belief in the Messiah in Amos, although this prophet delivers no direct oracle concerning the personal Messiah. However, the idea of the "remnant" and the future messianic

---

40. See chap. 5, "The Book of Psalms."

41. Cf. H. Ringgren, *The Messiah in the Old Testament* (London: SCM Press, 1956), pp. 12, 19; Ringgren, *Israelite Religion*, p. 225.

42. See chap. 12, "The Son of Man."

43. Cf. Ringgren, *The Messiah in the Old Testament*, pp. 39–64; Ringgren, *Israelite Religion*, p. 232; Ivan Engnell, "The 'Ebed Yahweh Songs and the Suffering Messiah in 'Deutero-Isaiah,'" *Bulletin of the John Rylands Library*, 31 (1948), pp. 54–93.

kingdom associated with the dynasty of David (Amos 9:11 ff.) also includes the belief in the Messiah.[44] A correct interpretation of Hosea shows that the Davidic messianic line is even more clearly dominant in this prophet. Hosea inseparably connects the messianic future with the house of David, and its material basis consists of the reunited and indivisible Davidic kingdom (Hos. 1:7; 2:2; 3:5; 6:11; 14:5 ff.). He describes the messianic future in the Promised Land in 2:17 ff.; 11:10 f.; and 14:5 ff. However, a more personal description of the Messiah himself is not found in Hosea.

In reality, Isaiah is the first real messianist among the prophets. He proclaims an advanced understanding of the Messiah, along with the coming kingdom that he inaugurates, which the prophet describes as the return of paradise in the fulness of time (compare especially 9:1–6; 11:1–10; and 32:1–5, texts which are among the most elevated in Israelite religion). In the Immanuel prophecy, which is also messianic,[45] the connection between the messiah and the sacral kingdom is especially clear. It should be observed that here, as elsewhere in Isaiah (also in Mic. 5:1 ff.), the Messiah is described as a child, in accord with the ancient ideology concerning the royal divine-savior-child, which is well-known through comparative ancient Near Eastern material, most recently from Ras Shamra.[46] The classic description of the Messiah in Isa. 9:1 ff. (Heb. 8:23b–9:6) presupposes David's work of unification and, as usual, the Davidic Judean future kingdom. The detailed similarities of this passage with the so-called Merneptah stele—an Egyptian inscription from about 1200 B.C.[47]—which scholars have apparently overlooked, testifies to the ancient form of Isa. 9:1 ff. It should be pointed out that this text is not passively pacifistic in character, but actively nationalistic. Isa. 11:1 ff. outlines the picture of the coming Messiah in even more complete royal ideological categories: as possessed by the Spirit and thus divine; as the all-seeing, all-wise, perfect "judge" (ruler, king), "the rod of whose mouth smites to the ground, yea, the breath of whose lips kills the guilty" (as v. 4 may be translated). This is followed by the description of the return of

---

44. Cf. A. Carlson in *Religion och Bibel*, 25 (1966), pp. 77 f.

45. E. Hammershaimb, "The Immanuel Sign," *Studia Theologica*, 3 (1949), pp. 124 ff.

46. See Engnell, *Studies in Divine Kingship*, pp. 124, 130 f.

47. See J. B. Pritchard, editor, *Ancient Near Eastern Texts* (Princeton: Princeton University Press, 1955), pp. 376 ff.

paradise with its "truce of God" in vv. 6 f. The nationalistic limitation and the absolute connection with the dynasty of David in this passage are also typical.

In Micah, the severe prophet of doom, we also find the nationalistic, messianic future perspective and the messiah who shall come "when she who is in travail has brought forth" (5:2 ff.). This prophet also connects the Messiah with the dynasty of David (5:1), his basic view is strongly nationalistic, and he expects the Messiah as an actual savior-king within the near future. In the Book of Joel, we find descriptions of the messianic age in a number of passages. Some of these are positive descriptions of the paradisiacal fruitfulness of the future (2:21 ff.; 4:18), and some are negative descriptions in the form of doom oracles against Israel's enemies (4:1 ff.). But the Book of Joel says nothing directly concerning the Messiah himself. This is to be explained by its "setting in life." Hab. 3:13 deals with the present Messiah, because the Book of Habakkuk is actually a cult liturgy and is to be looked upon as equivalent to a psalm.

In Jeremiah, where the Messiah is clearly referred to in some of the messianic oracles—original, of course—he is described in terms similar to those found in Isaiah. He will be the descendant of David who shall rule the future kingdom in justice and righteousness (23:4 ff., with its parallel in 33:14 ff.), and who shall actually be the resurrected David (30:9). It is generally thought that 23:4 ff. alludes to King Zedekiah (Heb. *ṣidhqiyyāhû*, "Yahweh is my righteousness;" 23:6: *Yahweh ṣidhqēnû*, Yahweh is our righteousness.")

In harmony with the tendency which has already been suggested above, Ezekiel ascribes only very limited tasks to the actual ruling "prince" (Heb. *nāśî*) of the dynasty of David. However, he declares that a Davidide will be at the head of the priestly state, the ideal to which he looks forward, according to the picture in chapters 40–48. Furthermore, he also adopts the traditional belief in a Messiah in its advanced futuristic aspect (Ezek. 17:22 ff.; 34:23 ff.; 37:15 ff.), which is a strong witness to the fundamental central position of messianism in prophetic circles. This is the way in which the problem of the Messiah is to be solved in Ezekiel, rather than by maintaining, in a literary-critical way and on wholly insufficient grounds, that the messianic passages in this book are "unauthentic" and "secondary."[48]

48. Cf. chap. 13, "The Figurative Language of the Old Testament."

The whole problem of Old Testament messianism is concentrated in "Deutero-Isaiah." We can only outline our positive solution in this essay. It is generally admitted that, in "Deutero-Isaiah," "turning of destiny"[49] and the messianic future are described in the same way that they are elsewhere in the prophets Isaiah and Micah, although they are housed in even more characteristic liturgical literary forms (compare especially 41:18 ff.; 49:8 ff.; 55:12 f.). The assertion that there is no personal Messiah in "Deutero-Isaiah" is based completely on the literary-critical separation of the "Songs of the Servant of the Lord" from the rest of the Deutero-Isaianic tradition collection, which is wholly unwarranted and basically incorrect. We certainly do find the Messiah in "Deutero-Isaiah": in the figure of the Servant of the Lord, even if it is in a highly specialized form.[50]

It is clear that the figure of the Ebed Yahweh, the Servant of the Lord, is none other than the Israelite Messiah that we encounter elsewhere in the prophets: he is the coming savior-king of the dynasty of David. Thus, the Servant of the Lord is not a new creation in the sense that Dürr[51] and many others want to affirm. Rather, he reflects a genuine Israelite ideology, with its usual background in the figure of the sacral king. However, under the influence of the ideas from the Babylonian religious environment and of the distinctive cultic situation in which they functioned, naturally the characteristic of suffering, already inherent in the figure of the Messiah (as is well known, especially from the "Royal Passion Psalms")[52] came to be greatly emphasized and developed in "Deutero-Isaiah": the Servant of the Lord is the *suffering* Messiah and is described in ancient royal ideological categories. By his passion and death, he procures expiation for his people; by his victory over death and through his resurrection, he enables them to share in the coming glory. But in spite of the strong emphasis on suffering, we must be careful not to overemphasize this feature. Even in Isaiah, chapter 53, the Servant of the Lord is and remains the one who conquers and triumphs, who rises again and is re-enthroned.

In Israel, the concept of a resurrection was already connected with

49. Hebrew *shûbh sheᵇbhûth*. See chap. 5, "The Book of Psalms," note 88.
50. See Engnell, "The 'Ebed Yahweh Songs and the Suffering Messiah in 'Deutero-Isaiah.'"
51. Dürr, *op. cit.*
52. See chap. 5, "The Book of Psalms."

the reigning sacral king, as is clear, among other things, from the words quoted in Hos. 6:1 ff.[53] In the messianic world view, the resurrection comes to occupy a more and more central place and is clearly proclaimed already in "Deutero-Isaiah." In the resurrection of the Messiah (the Servant of the Lord), "the many" that he "makes righteous" (52:13; 53:10 ff.), i.e., the godly, the "saved host" of his people share with him the life of the messianic future, which is connected with the restored Zion, 54:1 ff. Thus, Dan. 12:1 ff. is directly connected with this material.

However, it is very difficult, if not impossible, to distinguish between the present and eschatological aspects of messianism in the passages dealing with the Ebed Yahweh. But one thing is quite clear: there is no basis whatsoever for the alleged fundamental "universalistic" view in "Deutero-Isaiah." Instead, we actually encounter a thorough-going nationalism (compare especially 45:14, 24). Of course, it is true that the Messiah, the Servant of the Lord, and consequently his people, Israel, constitute a "covenant to the people" (42:6; 49:8), "a light to the nations," in order that Yahweh's salvation may extend to the ends of the earth. But the purpose of this is to show Yahweh's power through Israel's victory and sovereignty over all other peoples. In "Deutero-Isaiah," the peace which the Messiah brings is virtually a *pax israelitica.* This is something entirely different from the idea that the *power* of Yahweh and of his anointed is "universal," extending over the whole world. It should also be pointed out that the application of the concept of the Messiah to Cyrus in Isa. 45:1 f. is merely a secondary motif, although, on the whole, it is quite peculiar that a foreign king should be characterized as "*Yahweh's* Anointed." And yet, actually, this expression is clearly titulary (compare "my servant Nebuchadrezzar," in Jer. 25:9; 27:6; 43:10; Dan. 9:25), and simply means that Yahweh took Cyrus into his service as his instrument in order to carry out his promises to Israel. Thus, great emphasis should be placed on the words "for the sake of my servant Jacob" in Isa. 45:4a, which cannot be interpreted as a "gloss". Cyrus can be understood as the Mes-

---

53. Here, "the idea of resurrection as connected with the king's rôle in the New Year festival, is applied to the people . . . Even the temporal qualifiers confirm the terminological connection with a cultic event. It should be observed, however, that the verse is a quotation and does not represent the prophet's own opinion." Taken from Engnell's article "Uppståndelse" (Resurrection), in SBU[2].

siah, the Servant of the Lord, the central figure in "Deutero-Isaiah," only by an interpretation which is basically incorrect.

In the period after "Deutero-Isaiah," the main messianic line is set forth positively, although the aspect of suffering is expressed more or less clearly in the prophetic texts: for example, the "peaceful Messiah" described in Zech. 9:9 f.[54] has strong affinities with the suffering Messiah, the Servant of the Lord; but in the rest of Zechariah, the prophet sets forth the Messiah in positive terms, describing him as the "Branch" mentioned in 3:8 and 6:12 and usually identified with Zerubbabel.

Finally, the concept of the Messiah appears in a remarkably significant way in the Book of Daniel. But here, the point of view has changed, to some extent. The Messiah is described in a form which corresponds to the term "Son of Man"[55] in fully developed transcendent heavenly categories (in itself original), which is characteristic of apocalyptic literature. However, there are traditional elements in the messianic passages of this book: the Messiah, or Son of Man, ushers in the eternal messianic kingdom, and in spite of the fact that this kingdom is said to be world-wide in scope, a typical national outlook is present (7:14).

But before we conclude our discussion of the concept of the Messiah within the period and framework of the Old Testament canon and pass on to a discussion of the messianism in Judaism, we would like to sum up and emphasize some special problems and facts. The cumulative evidence of the different arguments made in the essay on "Prophets and Prophetism in the Old Testament" shows that the messianic oracles—and thus, the concept of the Messiah in our literary prophets—are essentially original and primary, although there are some individual exceptions. As a matter of fact, messianism is actually the leitmotiv throughout the entire history of Old Testament religion, especially in the prophets. At the same time, we have already pointed out above that in spite of the recurrence of a "universal" and sometimes cosmic outlook, Old Testament messianism is never able to be completely separated from Israelite nationalism. The belief in the Messiah develops into universalism in the modern sense for the first time in

54. "This passage obviously refers to the coming of the messianic king and his installation in power in such forms as actually did occur in the ancient Israelite kingdom." Taken from Bo Reicke's article "Intåget i Jerusalem" (Entry Into Jerusalem) in SBU².

55. See chap. 12, "The Son of Man."

the New Testament and Christianity. It is also important to observe that there is no original antithesis between the rule of God and the rule of the Messiah. This antithesis is a secondary ideological construction, even if it is a very old one. The kingdom of the Messiah is the kingdom of God.

Two other questions are more difficult to resolve: Why did the specific type of messianic eschatology which appears in the Old Testament grow up in Israel? What is it ultimately that makes the Old Testament belief in the Messiah unique? For it is amply clear that Israel occupies a unique position among other ancient Near Eastern peoples, notwithstanding the fact that certain external presuppositions, especially the essential belief in the ideal savior-king, must be said to have existed to a greater extent among these other peoples, particularly in Egypt and Babylon. When everything has been taken into consideration, it is impossible to avoid the conclusion that ultimately it is the originality of the Israelite idea of God which produced the concepts of messianism and eschatology and caused them to develop in a transcendental, apocalyptic direction, although, of course, there were many historical, cultural, psychological, and other kinds of factors which influenced this development (without going beyond the limits of scientific criticism and expressing a faith judgment). This unique idea of God cannot be dissociated from man's deep feeling of need. For as the well-known and little-known people who were the real bearers of religious development reacted to the majesty, power, and holiness of God, they experienced a deep sense of sin and the need for forgiveness from sin, a need which is concentrated in the belief in a wholly dominant savior, the Israelite Messiah.

With regard to the problem of what really makes the Old Testament belief in the Messiah unique, we cannot give an unequivocal answer, but we can summarize some of the characteristic features of this belief. First, we must point out that the uniqueness of Israelite messianism is due simply to the firmness and intensity with which the idea of the Messiah was developed and brought to a dominant position throughout the entire religious and political history of Israel. Another aspect of this uniqueness is that the concept of the Messiah was "historicized" by its connection with Jerusalem and the dynasty of David. This connection was never broken, even when the Davidic dynasty came to an end and the belief in the Messiah and the Messianic cult were "deculticized" and "eschatologized." But this does not mean that deculticization and eschatologization are unique features in the Old Testament. They have counterparts in other cultures, for example, in the similar Persian culture. As a matter of fact, this culture may have influenced Israelite messianism in its very last phase, although not to the extent that some scholars have maintained. Furthermore, the universalistic, cosmological feature of the Old Testament belief in the Messiah—which, after all, is not very strong, as we have already seen—and its ethical character, which is often overemphasized, are not unique in the Old Testament. On the contrary, the royal savior often has the character of a *nómos émpsychos*, an incarnate "justice" and "righteousness," as, for example, in the Hellenistic Caesar cult.[56] However, the growing emphasis on the "passion" of the Messiah, the development of the aspect of suffering, must be characterized as very typical. The idea of suffering as such is certainly inherent in the concept of the Messiah and emanates from the royal cult and the royal ideology. But the manner in which this aspect was developed in certain circles in Israel finally gained the ascendency over the positive nationalistic form of messianism, and through Jesus Christ, the Messiah of Christianity, it became wholly unique. But it is very difficult to trace the process by which this happened, especially in the later period. It is clear that the negative aspect, the aspect of suffering, represents the esoteric line, which was maintained on a narrow but clear basis through the development of select circles in Judaism in the post-canonical period.

Messianism and the Messiah in Judaism.—As far as content is concerned, the fundamental issue in the development of the idea of the Messiah in the post-canonical period is the relationship of the suffering Messiah in Judaism to the apocalyptic Messiah, who is primarily represented by the figure of the *Son of Man*, which is discussed in the next essay. In this article, we point out only a few matters very briefly.

The positive national aspect of messianism is dominant in Judaism, in spite of the fact that the Jewish belief in the Messiah is only in part significantly expressed in the apocryphal literature as a result of the actual historical development. The Messiah is of little or no importance in such books as the Wisdom of Solomon, Judith, Tobit. How-

---

56. Cf. E. R. Goodenough in the *Yale Classical Studies*, 1 (New Haven, Conn.: Yale University Press, 1928), pp. 59, 68 f.; see also Goodenough, "Kingship in Early Israel," *Journal of Biblical Literature*, 48 (1929), pp. 169, 203; G. Östborn, *Tora in the Old Testament* (Lund: Ohlssons, 1945), pp. 76 ff.

ever, in other apocryphal books and earlier Jewish apocalyptic writings, there is ample and clear evidence of the continuing importance of the positive belief in the Davidic Messiah: in I Maccabees, I Enoch, IV Esdras, the Sibylline Oracles, the Psalms of Solomon, Baruch, and the Testaments of the Twelve Patriarchs. Actually, we would not be exaggerating if we affirmed that the Messiah is also the heart of apocalyptic literature, even though this material is very scattered, thus making it difficult to get a homogeneous picture. Sometimes the Jewish Messiah appears as an earthly king and sometimes as a heavenly, transcendent figure; and in both cases, his coming ushers in the future messianic kingdom. And yet, there is no more antithesis between the kingdom of God and the kingdom of the Messiah in Judaism than there is in the Old Testament. If we attempt to synthesize this material according to the ancient royal ideological pattern by combining the scattered features of the Messiah, we arrive at the well-known description of the ideal savior-king, God's "chosen one," his "beloved," his "only begotten son" incarnate in a Davidide and actually thought of as *David redivivus* (thus, for example, in the Psalms of Solomon, especially Ps. 17).[57] He is described as the Anointed One, as one possessed by the Spirit of God, and as the righteous and perfect judge. He combines in himself the three royal offices: the king, the priest, and the prophet. In other works of Judaism, the phenomenon usually referred to as the "disintegration" or "democratization" of the original "royal pattern" is predominant, and the characteristics originally applied to the king are transferred to other figures, especially to the high priest. This phenomenon was already at work in very ancient times; and from the Exile onward, it naturally became particularly common: in all applicable features, the high priest inherits the cultic and ideological characteristics which were associated with the sacral king.[58]

Judaism also applied messianism to other living historical persons: Josephus describes John Hyrcanus I in messianic categories which are very similar to those connected with the figure of the Ebed Yahweh.

---

57. Cf. Mowinckel, *He that Cometh*, pp. 308 ff.

58. The ritual of the Day of Atonement reflects an ancient royal ritual with two phases: (1) Aaron—the king purifies himself by washing parts of his priestly (royal) garment, sacrifices a bull as a royal substitute, and enters the Holy of Holies; (2) the scape-goat rite, with interesting extrabiblical parallels, is used as a substitute to remove the guilt of the people, a rite of passage, followed by the purification of the sanctuary.

236 *Essays of Ivan Engnell*

It is widely known that messianism played a very important rôle in the political life of the Jews. Messianic hopes were constantly kindled and were associated with different leading figures, of which the best known is Bar Cocheba, the leader of the messianic rebellion in 132–135 A.D.

The concept of a *suffering* Messiah was not foreign to Judaism, either. It is true that this idea appears in only a few texts, but they are unambiguous. The circles responsible for I Enoch and IV Esdras have preserved the feature of suffering—at least, to some extent—in their understanding of the Messiah. In such religious circles as these, the messianic ideology along the line of suffering has been kept alive in its Ebed Yahweh form, even though a certain transformation toward an emphasis on the positive aspect of messianism is admittedly present; and this background represents one of the most immediate and special prerequisites for the interpretation of the idea of the Messiah in Jesus and in the New Testament. However, Judaism pushed the more esoteric feature of suffering, which characterized messianism originally, further and further into the background, particularly in the Christian age because of its natural antithesis to the basic Christian concept of Jesus as the suffering Messiah. A typical example of this is the striking way in which the Targum interprets Isaiah, chapter 53, in a thoroughly nationalistic positive messianic spirit, which is generally in line with the development of Judaism from the Maccabean Age on.[59] This is one of the points at which the Christian idea of the Messiah differs most radically from the Old Testament; another is universalism. But of course, the most basic difference of all is the time of the Messiah's coming. According to Christian belief, the Messiah came in the person of Jesus of Nazareth. Judaism denies that he is the Messiah and, at most, esteems him as a late successor to the Old Testament prophets. Eichrodt has remarked: "At the close of its career the form of the OT hope cries out for a critique and a reconstruction."[60]

---

59. See J. Jeremias in *Deutsche Theologie*, 2 (1929), pp. 106 ff.; N. Johansson, *Parakletoi* (Lund: Hakan Ohlsson, 1940), pp. 110 ff.; but cf. E. Sjöberg, *Der Menschensohn im äthiopischen Henochbuch* (Lund: C. W. K. Gleerup, 1946), pp. 116 ff.; criticized by Engnell in *Bibliotheca Orientalis*, 8 (1951), No. 5.

60. W. Eichrodt, *Theology of the Old Testament*, I, trans. J. A. Baker (Philadelphia: The Westminster Press, 1961), p. 490.

12

✽

The Son of Man

FROM a linguistic point of view, the Hebrew (*ben 'ādhām*) and Aramaic (*bar nāshā'*) expressions meaning "son of man," with their literal but rather barbarian translation, mean simply "a man," in agreement with the special significance which the term "son" has in both of these Semitic languages.[1] But through the constant absence of the definite article, the Hebrew expression clearly shows linguistically that, in reality, "son of man" is used in a special way, as a *terminus technicus*, a title.

It might seem logical to assume that, when Jesus adopted the expression *Son of Man* as a designation for himself, to a great extent he wanted to emphasize his humanity; and even in the Early Church, this was the most common interpretation of this phrase. But Jesus meant the exact opposite of this, as more recent investigations have demonstrated fully and as is further confirmed by a correct interpretation of the Old Testament background.

Actually, in several passages in the Old Testament and especially

In *Svenskt Bibliskt Uppslagsverk*, 2d ed., where it appears in Vol. II, cols. 229–232, this essay is called "Människosonen."

1. For a discussion of the philological problem, see E. Sjöberg, "*Ben 'ādhām* und *bar 'aᵉnāsh* im Hebräischen und Aramäischen," *Acta Orientalia*, 24 (1953), pp. 57–65, 91–107.

in Pss. 8:5; 80:18; and 146:3, the term *ben 'ādhām*, "son of man" (in other contexts, simply *'ādhām*), is no less than a title for the king-Messiah and is parallel to other titles, such as "Son of God" (Pss. 2:7; 110:3 according to the LXX; II Sam. 7:14), "servant of the Lord" (Pss. 18:1; 27:9; 36:1; 69:18), "Son of the handmaid" (Pss. 86:16; 116:16), and other honorary titles worn by the king. In spite of the fact that "Son of Man" (like "Son of God") also belongs to the thought-world of late Judaism (I Enoch, IV Esdras, Psalms of Solomon), we are by no means justified in concluding that it is a new creation from this late period. On the contrary, it belongs to the earliest religio-historical stratum, the complex of ideas centering around the person of the sacral king. The use of the term for the prophet himself in Ezek. 2:1 (RSV "Son of Man") is secondary, reapplied, or "democratized."

It is true that the term "Son of Man" reflects the collective concept, in connection with the tradition of the divine origin of mankind, and thus indirectly reflects the special ideas associated with the figure of the First Man. But first and foremost, it is connected with the thought-world of the sacral kingship which also (on the cultural stage of the sacral kingship) includes the figure of the First Man as an integral element[2] and which gives rise to different lines of development, namely, the concept of the Messiah in both positive and negative aspects, the figure of the First Man, and the ideas connected with the "Son of Man."[3]

Of these concepts, the term "Son of Man" represents a clearly positive aspect; but from the first, a distinct meaning seems to be latent in it: the transcendental-cosmic, or if one prefers, the astral—in other words, "Son of Man" is used to express the idea that the king is a divine and heavenly primordial being. At any rate, as time goes on, this aspect is emphasized more and more. As the term "Son of Man" is set free from its original cultic mooring and transferred to an eschatological, apocalyptic context, the transcendental aspect is also developed: "Son of Man" comes to refer especially to the transcendent

2. Cf. I. Engnell, "Die Urmenschvorstellung und das Alten Testament," *Svensk Exegetisk Årsbok*, 22–23 (1957–58), pp. 256–289, with criticisms of Bentzen and Mowinckel.

3. See chap. 11, "The Messiah in the Old Testament and Judaism," and I. Engnell in *Bibliotheca Orientalia*, 8 (1959), pp. 187 ff. See also Engnell's "Die Urmenschvorstellung und das Alten Testament."

heavenly savior-figure whose coming ushers in the messianic age. This development is completed in the Book of Daniel.

In Dan. 7:13 f., we meet, for the first time, this heavenly messianic figure in the description of the downfall of the kingdoms of the world, the judgment of God, and the "Son of Man" who comes with the clouds of heaven to rule over his eternal kingdom and to be served by peoples and tribes. Of course, there are those who want to assert that, on the whole, this passage does not pertain to an individual messianic figure, but is simply a personification of or a symbol for the people of Israel, and they support this view by v. 27. But it is clear that this interpretation is incredible; or, to put it more exactly, impossible, because the "Son of Man" is described in very personal terms in vv. 13 f.; it is an ancient, individual messianic term associated with the savior-king or Messiah, as pointed out above; and in Jewish apocalypticism in the period after Daniel, the "Son of Man" appears as an individual messianic figure, the savior and judge of the last time. That the kingdom of the Messiah-Son of Man also signifies the empire of the messianic people, Israel (as the interpretation given in v. 27 indicates), is wholly natural. To play this collective aspect off against the individual is to misunderstand completely the Old Testament way of thinking, in general, and the way of thinking in messianic circles, in particular—not to mention the view, represented by Mowinckel,[4] which denies any connection between the Messiah in the Old Testament and the Son of Man in Daniel and I Enoch, on the whole. However, it should be observed that the outlook in Daniel is by no means universalistic, but is clearly consistently nationalistic, even if the perspective is universal and cosmic.

In the period after Daniel, the main source for our knowledge of the ideas surrounding the Son of Man is the so-called Ethiopic Enoch, I Enoch, especially chapters 37–71, the so-called Similitudes.[5] In details which resemble Daniel, chapter 7, here the Apocalyptist gives a description of the Son of Man as the judge of the world who will be prominent in the last time in terms which are well-known from the royal messianic ideology. The Son of Man is chosen already as a preexistent heavenly being and, after he has had a part in the creation of

---

4. S. Mowinckel, *He That Cometh* (Oxford: B. Blackwell, 1956), pp. 346 ff.

5. Mowinckel, *ibid.*, pp. 354 ff.; E. Sjöberg, *Der Menschensohn in äthiopischen Henochbuch* (Lund: C. W. K. Gleerup, 1946) with the criticism by Engnell in *Bibliotheca Orientalia*, 8 (1959), pp. 187 ff.

the world, remains hidden, being known only to the righteous, whom he shall deliver at the final judgment of the world, which shall come first upon all foreign oppressors, but also upon the sinners in Israel— which is not a new idea at all.[6]

It is also significant that the Son of Man in I Enoch clearly displays the characteristic of *suffering*, a characteristic which—even if some scholars deny it—plainly reflects influences from the figure of the Servant of the Lord in "Deutero-Isaiah."[7] There can be no doubt that here we have one of the few but—for this very reason—all the more important connecting links in the chain of development leading from the Servant of the Lord to Jesus and the New Testament. That the Son of Man in I Enoch has actually preserved this characteristic of suffering is not made impossible by the fact that he is a transcendent being. Scholars have made this argument as a result of their modern Western logic, which fails to take the cultic experience into consideration. From the standpoint of the phenomenology of religion, in reality, the Son of Man does not represent the idea of the First Man, but the figure of the Messiah-King, in a negative form, with emphasis on the aspect of "passion," although, of course, this has been developed along eschatological, apocalyptic lines. Instead, it is Enoch himself who represents a form of the idea of the First Man, which has been gnosticized, to some extent. Therefore, it is no coincidence that the Son of Man in the "Similitudes" is simply identified with and has the title of Messiah.[8] Accordingly, the influence of the positive concept of the Son of Man has also left its trace, resulting in a de-emphasis on the aspect of suffering. Thus, the Son of Man in I Enoch represents the two ancient parallel lines in the royal ideology and the messianism which grew out of them: both the positive and the negative aspects. But it is because it has preserved the negative feature at all that the religious circle responsible for I Enoch is most significant, especially for New Testament studies.

The same is also true of the figure of the Son of Man in IV Esdras 13, where we find another variant on the Daniel motif. But in this

6. Engnell is here alluding to judgment as a motif in the New Year Festival.
7. Cf. Engnell, "The 'Ebed Yahweh Songs and the Suffering Messiah in 'Deutero-Isaiah'," *Bulletin of the John Rylands Library*, 31 (1948), pp. 54–93.
8. I Enoch 48:10; 52:4; cf. Sjöberg, *Der Menschensohn in äthiopischen Henochbuch*, pp. 140 ff.

work, the aspect of suffering has been pushed aside even more. We are now at the end of the first century A.D., and the national positive messianic aspect has been greatly strengthened. The heavenly, pre-existent Son of Man rises up out of the sea, meets an attack by all the heathen peoples headlong on Mount Zion, destroys them without sword simply by his powerful judicial word, and gathers the people of Israel around him for the messianic future. But in spite of the fact that the idea of the Son of Man became more and more nationalistic, still, the term *Son of Man* was obviously not (at least, not as thoroughly) involved in and tainted with nationalism as was the term *Messiah*. This must have been at least one of the reasons why Jesus adopted the term *Son of Man*.

Although the sources available to us are sporadic and weak, they are sufficient to let us see that the origin of the idea of the Son of Man came from within Israel and was ancient, and to let us hypo-thetically reconstruct its development. At first, the emphasis was pre-dominantly positive, but with a minor negative aspect. As time went on, this negative feature with its emphasis on suffering became more and more prominent. Later, the nationalistic aspect again came to pre-vail, along with the growing emphasis on eschatology and the develop-ment of the heavenly aspect of the Son of Man (which was present from the very beginning) into the concept of transcendence. Thus, we cannot accept the widely held view that the Son of Man in the New Testament came directly from the seventh chapter of Daniel, which, in reality, just happens to contain an ancient and consistent Israelite concept, or that Daniel, chapter 7, borrowed the idea of the Primordial Man from Persia.

13

❦

The Figurative Language of the Old Testament

FIGURATIVE language is a necessary human prerequisite to any presentation of spiritual reality in speaking or writing, especially in conscious literary forms, whether prose or poetry—in which it appears even more often. Thus, even in different cultures, figurative language has certain common fundamental characteristics. As to form, it can be divided into four groups: comparison, parable, metaphor, and allegory. But personification and typology are not usually considered to be figurative language. And yet, the distinctions between the various types of imagery are very flexible and, on the whole, a modern logical classification can hardly be applied to ancient languages, or the like, found in the Bible, especially in the Old Testament. It is usually assumed that comparison and parable refer to putting the figure beside the thing being symbolized, and that metaphor and allegory imply substituting the figure for the thing being symbolized. Accordingly, allegory can be characterized as a combination of metaphors. A metaphor can be based on the similarity between the concrete thing and the abstract concept or, using what is called *synecdoche*, it can be made part of a group of concrete things: for example, the crown may be a symbol for power.

This essay appears in *Svenskt Bibliskt Uppslagsverk*, 2d ed., Vol. I, cols. 283–312, under the title of "Bildspråk."

One thing that all forms of imagery are thought to have in common is some similiarity between the concrete reality and the figure, either a similarity in form or in content or in sentiment or in association or in something else. Figurative language is an obvious and necessary style form for prophetic, apocalyptic, and mystical literature, and especially for cultic liturgies and hymnic texts. In addition to these universal factors, there are others of a more special kind which may have a bearing on imagery, such as the special life situation of a particular culture, the artistic talent of the speaker or writer, the often very conservative impact of the tradition, or the conscious theological use of figurative language.

The imagery of the Bible clearly reflects these factors. This is one of the best criteria in support of what is usually called the unity of the Bible. But behind this unity, bearing the clear stamp of the tradition, the figurative language of both the Old and New Testaments has each its own peculiar fundamental characteristics. And no matter how much religious reality and manner of expression the two testaments have in common, the many different types of literature found in the Bible have their own individual characteristics. It is quite evident that, to a great extent, the Christian mode of expression is marked by its biblical heritage.

One thing that the different parts of the Old Testament have in common is that the figurative language which they use is Semitic. Although the reality lying behind the terms *Semites* and *Semitic* is hard to define, it is obvious that the Semitic languages, as vehicles for expressing certain attitudes toward reality—such as the ways in which Semitic people feel, think, and evaluate—are the most important common element and unifying bond lying behind these terms. Few linguistic groups are as uniform as the Semitic, and the most characteristic feature of Semitic people is their distinctive talent for oral and written literature, while their religious outlooks may differ radically. An obvious example of this is the contrast between the religiously untalented Arabs and the thoroughly religious Israelites, which has a definite impact on their respective literatures.

One feature which can be said to be common and characteristic in the various Semitic literatures is that the outlook is not logical and objective, but very subjective and emotional. Therefore, the purpose for using imagery is not aesthetic but practical. The intention is not to draw a logical parallel between the figure and the reality, but to argue and persuade by multiplying references, examples, and repetitions. This is done in a very traditional way, making use of stereotyped phrases and figures which often approach a kind of literary cliché. In this way, the speaker demonstrates his knowledge and "wisdom," the most important proof of which is his familiarity with the tradition. This is quite different from the modern individualistic ideal. Another characteristic of Semitic expression is that its imagery builds on the identity between the figure and what it symbolizes. The result is that, at times, the figure is actually substituted for the reality, in a way which is surprising and shocking and sometimes even incomprehensible to us. However, the phenomenon called *parallelismus membrorum* often helps us to resolve the difficulties. Here, it may be pointed out that the closest parallels we find in the Semitic world to the figurative language of the Old Testament, especially that found in the cultic psalm texts, are in Accadian and of course in Northwest Semitic materials, whereas the similarities with the imagery found in Arabic sources (which is often artificial) are not as numerous. The Arabic literature is much later than that which occurs in the Old Testament, and it is essentially different because it belongs to a different *Sitz im Leben.*

But that which makes the figurative language of the Old Testament distinctive is much more striking than these similarities with other Semitic literatures and is of much greater importance. As has already been pointed out, this distinctive mark takes on different forms of expression in different types of Old Testament literature, so that if we wish to get a clear impression of its true nature, we must examine the various portions of the Old Testament. Actually, we should begin with the poetic material, especially the cultic texts; but in order to make a broad survey, we will follow the Old Testament's own order and, thus, we will begin with the narrative literature, first with the "P work," Genesis-Numbers.[1]

Throughout the "P work," the first of the Israelite so-called historical works, it is most striking that the narrative technique is realistic, the style is concrete, and there is very little imagery. Of course, occasionally, we encounter figures such as the one in Yahweh's promise

---

1. See chap. 4, "The Pentateuch" and chap. 1, "The Traditio-Historical Method in Old Testament Research."

to Abram that his seed would be "as the dust of the earth" (Gen. 13: 16), but this is virtually a stereotyped phrase approaching a cliché. The statements that Ishmael "shall be a wild ass" (16:12) and that the smoke from Sodom is like the smoke from a furnace (19:28) can hardly be said to be very original figures. Actually, the same is true even in the poetic sections of the "P work": Gen. 27:27 ff., the story of Jacob's blessing of Isaac, and the narrative of the so-called Exodus Legend in Exodus, chapters 1–15, which originally had a cultic setting. And this includes the description of the plagues in Egypt in chapters 7 ff. and the so-called Song of Victory in chapter 15, even though the latter is a splendid piece of poetry from a literary point of view and contains isolated similes and metaphors. The imagery which occurs in the symbolism that characterizes the series of dreams in the cycle of the Joseph tradition (Genesis, chapter 37 ff.) is an exception. Quite naturally, there are poetic passages of the "P work" which use figurative language more abundantly: the so-called Testament of Jacob in Genesis, chapter 49, which characterizes Reuben as "boiling over as water," Judah as "a lion's whelp," Issachar as "a strong ass, crouching between the sheepfolds," Dan as "a serpent in the way, a viper by the path," Joseph as "a fruitful bough by a spring," this last figure being an oft-repeated motif in the symbolism of the so-called Tammuz type. However, in the songs of Balaam in Numbers, chapters 22 ff., the poetry is of a realistic type and very effective, at that, and thus contains very little imagery. Summing up, it can probably be said that the type and use of figurative language in the "P work" is due to the *Sitz im Leben* of the traditionist circle responsible for it, to this circle's purpose in putting forth its tradition work, and to the tendency which permeates this work. When we compare the imagery in the "P work" with analogous phenomena in other so-called historical works, we find one good argument among many (which are themselves convincing) for preferring the traditio-historical approach to the narrative literature of the Old Testament.

When we examine the figurative language in the next historical work, the "D work" (Deuteronomy-II Kings), it is clear that the literary outlook and distinct linguistic form differ fundamentally from that which we find in the "P work." One obvious difference is that imagery plays a much more prominent rôle in the "D work" than it does in the "P work." Even in the prose material, in Deuteronomy, we encounter a much greater use of figures of speech, which is due at least partly to the fact that the entire book is presented in the form of a speech by Moses. Naturally, there is very little figurative language in the legal material; but in ritual texts, such as the one in chaps. 27–28, the section concerning Ebal and Gerizim, we find, "And the heavens over your head shall be brass, and the earth under you shall be iron" (28:23, RSV). However, the most extensive use of imagery occurs in the numerous poetic passages. For example, we read, in what is called "Moses' Song of Resignation" (32:2, RSV):

> May my teaching drop as the rain,
> My speech distil as the dew,
> As the gentle rain upon the tender grass,
> And as the showers upon the herb.

A little further on in this section, we find other figures, such as Yahweh spreading out his wings like an eagle and carrying Israel on his pinions, making Israel suck honey out of the rock and oil out of the flinty rock, and causing Israel to drink the blood of the grape (vv. 11 ff.). And Yahweh's wrath is described in this way in v. 22:

> For a fire is kindled from (in) my nose,
> . And it burns to the depths of Sheol,
> Devours the earth and its increase,
> And sets on fire the foundations of the mountains.

In the narrative portions of the Book of Joshua, there is less use of figurative language; but in the Book of Judges, it is more frequent. But there is also poetic material of a realistic type in the Book of Judges, especially the extremely powerful and picturesque Song of Deborah, whose dramatic style includes scarcely a single genuine metaphor. In the description of the dream of the Midianite, in the story of Gideon (Judg. 7:13 ff.), we find a piece of dream symbolism; but at the same time, it is clear that, actually, we are dealing with something much more than imagery: the dream as a creative reality. The same may be said of what is called Jotham's Fable in Judg. 9:7 f., which, to a great extent, also has a so-called magical purpose: its intention is to create a reality; it is no less than a curse and, as such, is very effective (compare vv. 22 ff., 57). In the Samson tradition cycle, there is an example of figurative language in Judg. 14:14, in the developed *mashal* (proverbial or enigmatic) style:

> Out of the eater came something to eat.
> Out of the strong came something sweet.

The situation in I and II Samuel is similar to that found in the Book of Judges. When Saul is hunting David in the wilderness and David asks, "After whom do you pursue? After a dead dog! After a flea!" (I Sam. 24:14), he is essentially repeating a proverb which expresses humility. When Nabal's wife, Abigail, says to David, "The life of my lord shall be bound in the bundle of the living in the care of the Lord your God; and the lives of your enemies he shall sling out as from the hollow of a sling" (I Sam. 25:29), she is doing much more than using imagery: she is uttering a word symbol designed to create reality, a desire for blessing, which indeed was not without its reward. The so-called Song of the Bow in II Sam. 1:17 ff. is also of the realistic type and is very reserved in its use of figurative language. Nathan's parable in II Samuel, chapter 12, is the only one in its genre in the Old Testament, but it is all the more typical. It is so veiled that the king does not understand that it is he himself and what he has done to Uriah that is meant by it and, precisely for that reason, he pronounces his own doom. I and II Kings, which form the conclusion of the "D work," use the same type of literary style and figurative language. Here we may cite a couple of passages in particular. In I Kgs. 15:4, there is a very negative evaluation of King Abijam, which says that it was only "for David's sake" that he was given "a lamp in Jerusalem," that is, a son to succeed him on the throne. This is not purely figurative language, but refers to a cultic reality, the so-called lamp of David, a lamp which was always kept burning in the temple, symbolizing the continuation of the dynasty.[2] A similar example of this special relationship between cultic reality and imagery is the rhetorical question of the prophet Elijah to the Israelites, "How long will you limp on both sides?" (I Kgs. 18:21), because this is an allusion to

---

2. "From several allusions it is clear that in the pre-exilic temple the king and his covenant were represented by an always burning 'eternal lamp' (*nēr tāmîd*), e.g. I Kgs. 11:36; II Kgs. 8:19; II Chron. 21:7; cf. I Kgs. 15:4; Pss. 18:29; 132:17." Taken from H. Riesenfeld, "Lampor," in *SBU*². Cf. Riesenfeld, *Jesus transfiguré* (København: E. Munksgaard, 1947), p. 100 with note 19.

the cultic dance of the prophets of Baal. The reply of King Jehoash of Israel to Amaziah of Judah when Amaziah, self-confident because of his victory over Edom, challenges him to a battle: "A thistle on Lebanon sent to a cedar on Lebanon, saying, 'Give your daughter to my son for a wife'; and a wild beast of Lebanon passed by and trampled down the thistle" (II Kgs. 14:9), belongs to the same type as "Jotham's Fable." Summarizing, we can say that figurative language is not only used much more extensively in the "D work" than in the "P work," but also that it has a greater vividness and effectiveness in the former. This is due not only to the fact that the "D work" contains a large amount of poetic material, but also to the fact that its traditional material is of northern origin and, thus, has a very high literary quality.[3]

We may refer to the Chronicler's work only briefly. On the whole, this work does not use figurative language except in isolated cases, and then in passages which can be traced back to the "D work" or related sources. To illustrate this, we may cite II Chron. 10:10 f., where Rehoboam is urged by his young friends and advisers to treat the people even more severely than his father Solomon had done, and says, "My little finger is thicker than my father's loins," which is a quotation from I Kgs. 12:10 f. The style of the Chronicler's work, which has very little imagery, is in complete harmony with the type of traditionist circle responsible for it and with the purpose of the narrative.

For all practical purposes, the Book of Esther, a late pseudo-historical work which has the character of historical novel and festival legend at the same time, does not use figurative language at all. Perhaps this may seem surprising, but it is due to the conscious historicizing style of this work.

As has already been suggested, one should actually begin his investigation of the figurative language in the Old Testament with the Book of Psalms. The reason for this is that, in these cultic texts, we find not only the most plentiful, but also the most original imagery. In the psalms more than anywhere else we are faced with the most difficult problem involving figurative language, the problem of the

---

3. This translation renders exactly what Engnell has written. No other known statement by him could serve as a justification.

relationship between imagery and the cult. In other words, one must distinguish between cultic reality, figurative language influenced by cult, mythology, or ideology, and pure metaphors. This problem can be solved only by an examination of each separate case and, even then, the result is often very uncertain and, to a great extent, decided by subjective judgment, which is ultimately dictated by the scholar's over-all interpretation of the psalms, their date, types, and *Sitz im Leben.*[4]

But we may begin by observing that even in the Book of Psalms there is a rather conventional use of stereotyped terms, phrases, and figures. Thus, we find the expression "my glory" (*kebhōdhî*) for the spirit or the personal *I*; "my rock" (*sal'î*), for God; "shepherd," for both the king and God (Ps. 24). Here, we may also mention figures from the world of nature: one psalmist speaks of Yahweh's voice as that "which breaks the cedars of Lebanon. He makes Lebanon to skip like a calf, and Sirion like a young wild ox." (Ps. 29:5 f., RSV). This imagery has something to say about the phenomenology of the idea of God (Psalm 29 is now generally thought to go back to a Phoenician original). Another figure drawn from nature is found in a description of adversity in Ps. 102:7 f. (essentially, RSV):

> I am like a vulture of the wilderness,[5]
> Like an owl (*kōs*) of the waste places;
> I lie awake,
> I am like a lonely bird (who sits) on the housetop.

The figure of the tree has a unique position in the psalms. It is used both positively and negatively. In a positive sense, we find it in Ps. 1:3, which has to do with the "tree of life" and the "water of life."[6]

4. See chap. 5, "The Book of Psalms."
5. Hebrew *qā'āt*, possibly also "jackdaw." The translation "pelican" is certainly incorrect.
6. "Tree of life" is taken here in the wide sense of any tree or plant that is used as a symbol of life. Symbolic or real "trees of life" are said to have played an essential rôle in the cult. Ideologically, there was identity between the king and the tree of life or between the fertility god and the tree of life. See I. Engnell, *Studies in Divine Kingship in the Ancient Near East,* second edition (Oxford: Basil Blackwell, 1967), Index, *s.v.* "Tree of life" and "water of life." Cf. E. O. James, *The Tree of Life* (Leiden: E. J. Brill, 1966). Engnell's view on Psalms, chapter 1, is set forth in his " 'Planted by the Streams of Water,' Some Remarks on the Problem of the Interpretation of the Psalms as Illustrated by a Detail in

These motifs are, at one and the same time, cultic realities and symbols for an ideology manifest both in mythology (Gen. 2:9 ff.) and in messianism, mostly in a futuristic sense that at least approaches eschatology. This use of figurative language focusing on the tree of life was also originally connected with the Tammuz (the sacral king) complex.[7] And it is very difficult—in fact, impossible—to say where the distinction between cultic reality, ideology, and pure imagery should be made. We find this figure connected with the person of the king in a typical way in Ps. 80:16 ff., but we also find it used of "the righteous" in a "disintegrated" and "democratized" form in 92:13 f., where it can hardly refer to the Messiah-king. In its negative aspect, tree symbolism has much more the character of pure figurative language. The tree (or vegetables and flowers) as a figure for corruption and destruction is used of the unrighteous, the enemies, or mankind in general, in such passages as Pss. 37:35 f.; 90:5 ff.; 103:15 f. Tree symbolism is also used in this way in the Prophets and the Wisdom Literature.

As recent psalm research has made inescapably clear, the sacral king plays a very prominent rôle in the psalms, both cultically and ideologically. In a positive sense, the rôle of the king involves being an assurance for "blessing," fruitfulness, and annual crops, and in a negative sense, "humiliation" and "passion." The positive aspect is illustrated in Psalm 72, where it says of the messianic king (Solomon, according to the heading): "May he be like rain that falls on the mown grass, like showers that water the earth" (v. 6). Later, in this psalm (vv. 16 f.), this description is resumed in a manner which immediately reminds us of a Babylonian royal "Self-Praise Inscription."[8] We meet the negative aspect in pronounced "Tammuz style" in Ps. 129:3, where it says, "the plowers plowed upon my back; they made long

---

Ps. 1," *Studia Orientalia Ioanni Pedersen* (Hauniae: E. Munksgaard, 1953), pp. 85–96; cf. also his "'Knowledge' and 'Life' in the Creation Story," *Supplements to Vetus Testamentum*, 3 (1955), pp. 103–119.

7. Insofar as Tammuz and/or the king were supposed to be symbolically identical with the tree of life, see the preceding note.

8. It is not quite clear whether the reference is to one specific inscription or to the type of royal self-praise in general; for the latter, see A. L. Oppenheim, *Ancient Mesopotamia* (Chicago: University of Chicago Press, 1964), pp. 147 ff.; W. H. Ph. Römer, *Sumerische Königshymnen der Isin-Zeit* (Leiden: E. J. Brill, 1965), pp. 29 ff.

their furrows."[9] This is by no means to be interpreted as advanced imagery alone, but also must reflect a cultic reality of some sort or other. The same must also be said of the much-disputed passage in Ps. 2:7, which contains the divine oracle, "You are my son, today I have begotten you." The kernel lying behind the figurative language here is a cultic ideology. It is quite clear that a cultic reality lies behind Ps. 51:9, "Purge me with hyssop, and I shall be clean," in spite of the fact that the following line changes to a pure figure, "Wash me, and I shall be whiter than snow." Ps. 68:14, "The wings of a dove covered with silver, its pinions with green gold," must also be based on some sort of concrete reality, perhaps a cultic idol.[10]

These examples could be multiplied. But here we shall emphasize only one other special phenomenon, the "animal symbolism" found in the descriptions of enemies. The enemies are described in many psalms, especially in the Royal Psalms, under the figure of wild beasts, lions, wild bulls, dogs. Perhaps Ps. 22:13 ff. offers the best example of this. Here, again, we are dealing with something completely different from the use of imagery in the modern sense, for these are terms used in the tradition for what used to be called a primitive or magical way of understanding and describing reality, and they come from a cultic background which has a highly dramatic ideology. In its relationship to the cult, Psalm 22 belongs to a type that is different from the so-called fourth Ebed Yahweh Song in Isaiah, chapter 53 (and the difference is reflected in the figurative language of Psalm 22), where the whole complex, centered around the figure of the Messiah, appears in a purely ideological form. Thus, we make a big mistake when we treat the figurative language of the psalms the same throughout and reduce it to purely symbolic language. It is this erroneous practice in particular which has led scholars to reinterpret the Book of Psalms in an anachronistic *interpretatio europaeica moderna* in a spiritualistic, aesthetic, psychological, didactic, or historical direction. But at the same time, it should be pointed out that the descriptions

9. The reference is to those parts of the Tammuz liturgies which describe the suffering of the god, although there does not seem to be any literal parallel to this passage. Engnell seems to imply that some kind of ritual plowing could have symbolised this suffering.

10. For a somewhat different interpretation, along similar lines, see A. Haldar, *The Notion of the Desert in Sumero-Accadian and West-Semitic Religions* (Uppsala: Lundequist, 1950), pp. 46 ff.

of adversity in the psalms actually reflect a situation of the "chaos-cosmos battle" type, which in itself may be felt as real enough, even when they apparently speak of real illness.[11] And yet, there is no reason to deny that figurative language in the modern sense can also be used in these descriptions of affliction and of enemies, which often end with so-called curse formulae. As a matter of fact, Ps. 58:9 seems to do just this:

> Let them be like a snail which dissolves into slime,
> Like the untimely birth that never sees the sun.

This may be called imagery of the pure comparison type, and it has a good deal of originality and spontaneity about it.

The problem with the figurative language in the Song of Songs is that, while it reminds us of the imagery in the psalms, it differs from it in a typical way. Again, the way in which we deal with this problem inevitably depends on our basic understanding of the Song of Songs, that is, whether we think of it as an allegory, a drama, a collection of popular love poems, or (at least, originally) a royal *hieros gamos* text—a ritual text of the so-called Tammuz type, with a cultic *Sitz im Leben*. But irrespective of its meaning, the language in which it is expressed is unique and extremely beautiful, just because of the imagery. Still, it should be observed that the form alternates between figurative and realistic style. The Song of Songs contains both concrete statements and strong poetic language. And comparisons and genuine figures alternate with each other throughout the book. We read the comparison in 2:2:

> As a lily among brambles,
> So is my love among maidens.

But in 1:15, there is this genuine figure:

> Behold, you are beautiful, my love;
> Behold, you are beautiful;
> Your eyes are doves.

11. Cf. chap. 5, "The Book of Psalms."

This latter passage is also found in 4:1, where it is followed by a series of figures of speech that actually amount to a series of comparisons—which also occur in 6:4 ff.:

> Your hair is like a flock of goats,
> Moving down the slopes of Gilead.   (black, billowing)
> Your teeth are like a flock of shorn ewes
> That have come up from the washing,   (whiteness)
> All of which bear twins,
> And not one of them is bereaved.   (none of the upper or
>   lower teeth are missing)
>
> Your lips are like a scarlet thread,
> And your mouth is lovely.   (color and form)
> Your cheeks are like halves of a pomegranate
> Behind your veil.   (color, form, dimples)
> Your neck is like the tower of David,
> .Built for an arsenal,
> Whereon hang a thousand bucklers,
> All of them shields of warriors.   (her stature, the ornament
>   around her neck is compared
>   with bucklers on the tower of David)

This description is an integral part of the *waṣf* (the praise of the beauty of bride or "sister") which constitutes chap. 4:1–15 that ends with the imagery of the "vegetation type" in vv. 12 ff. and with the assurance that the bride is "a sealed-up Garden of Eden," "a sealed-up well," "a sealed-up spring" (i.e., a virgin). After the figurative language in 5:1 ff. (which many scholars consider to be obviously erotic, although this is not necessarily the case), there is a *waṣf* of the bride over the bridegroom in 5:10 ff., the most important part of which is vv. 14 f. (RSV):

> His arms are rounded gold,
> Set with jewels.
> His body is ivory work,
> Encrusted with sapphires.
> His legs are alabaster columns,
> Set upon bases of gold.

There must be some sort of cultic image behind these metaphors,[12] as parallels from Ras Shamra also indicate. For the sake of comparison, we may cite here a portion of the famous so-called Legend of King Keret, taken from a scene in which the king is expressing his ardent desire to marry:

> Give me Lady Hurriya (*ḥry*),
> The fair, the first-begotten;
> Whose fairness is like Anath's fairness,
> [Whose] beau[ty] like Ashtoreth's beauty;
> Whose eyeballs are the pureness of lapis,
> Whose pup[ils] the gleam of *jet;*
> ... *Let me bask in the brightness of* her eyes.[13]

The same may be said of the figurative language in the *waṣf* concerning the bride in 7:1 ff., where, among other things, we read in v. 7 (RSV):

> You are stately as a palm tree,
> And your breasts are like its clusters

—a description which corresponds to the well-known ancient figures of Astarte.[14] Summarizing, it may be said that, more than anywhere else in the Old Testament, the imagery in the Song of Songs is of what one might call a common Oriental type. This implies, among other things, that it becomes an end in itself, is separated from its original starting-point, and gets lost in details. These characteristics may be observed in several passages in the Song of Songs. At any rate, the Song of Songs incontestibly maintains its unique position from the point of view of imagery. And it contains passages like this (8:6 f., RSV):

> For love is strong as death,
> Jealousy is cruel as the grave.

12. This argument is taken up and developed by G. Gerleman, "Ruth, das Hohelied," *Biblischer Kommentar Altes Testament,* XVIII (Neukirchen-Vluyn: Neukirchener Verlag, 1965), pp. 68 f.

13. This translation is taken from J. B. Pritchard, editor, *Ancient Near Eastern Texts* (Princeton: Princeton University Press, 1955), p. 144.

14. Especially the statues of Artemis from Ephesus and other places in Asia Minor.

Its flashes are flashes of fire,
A most vehement flame.
Many waters cannot quench love,
Neither can floods drown it.

As far as the sentiment is concerned, the Song of Songs and
Lamentations are as far apart as any two pieces of literature could
be. But actually, there are several points of contact between them,
as far as imagery and its function is concerned. In Lamentations, we
find the same mixture of concrete and figurative language that we
find in the Song of Songs, as well as realistic descriptions of affliction
(compare, for example, 2:20; 4:10) and picturesque figures. This is
partly due to the fact that "the virgin, the daughter of Zion" is the one
who laments in chapters 1–2, a motif connected with an ancient cultic
literary pattern in which the goddess is the one afflicted. Also, all the
"virgins" of Jerusalem mourn with Zion (1:4, 18; 2:10) in a way that
reminds us of the ancient Greek choir and corresponds to the appearance of the "virgins" who witness to and celebrate the *hieros
gamos* of the bride and groom in the Song of Songs. In Lam. 2:6,
RSV (cf. also 2:4), we even find an allusion to the function of the
"booth" in this context:[15]

> He has broken down his booth like that of a garden,
> Laid in ruins the place of his appointed feasts.

On the whole, the style and structure of Lamentations are quite
similar to what we encounter in the Psalms of Lament—in fact,
Lamentations ends with a prayer for restoration (5:21 f.). Therefore,
it is natural for Lamentations to have many points of contact with the
Psalms of Lament, such as Psalms 22 and 48. Lamentations, chapter 3,
in particular may be designated as a Psalm of Lament containing a
traditional detailed description of the enemy. Lamentations also reminds us of the Book of Job and of several of the prophetic books,
especially Jeremiah—who, indeed, the Jewish tradition declared to

---

15. A booth of leaves is supposed to have been the place where the sacred
marriage was performed: Engnell, *Studies in Divine Kingship*, p. 157, note 2;
G. Widengren, *Sakrales Königtum im Alten Testament und im Judentum* (Stuttgart: W. Kohlhammer, 1958), p. 78; *Mesopotamian Elements in Manichaeism*
(Uppsala: Lundequist, 1946), pp. 119 f.

be the author of Lamentations. Imagery occurs throughout the book, and even the beginning (1:1) is typical:

> How lonely sits the city
> That was full of people!
> How like a widow has she become,
> She that was great among the nations!
> She that was princess among the cities
> Has become a vassal.

A good example of the mixture of concrete and figurative language is offered in 4:7 f.: it says that Zion's princes had formerly been "purer than snow, whiter than milk," but now, after the visitation, their color has become black and

> Their skin has shriveled upon their bones,
> It has become as dry as wood.

Finally, in 4:20, we find a piece of advanced royal ideology (apparently still wholly alive) in the form of figurative language:

> The breath of our nostrils, the Lord's anointed,
> Was taken in their pits,
> He of whom we said, "Under his shadow
> We shall live among the nations."

Actually, the Book of Job is completely unique and *sui generis* in the Old Testament. And yet, from many points of view, it can be said that this work occupies a middle position between the Psalms of Lament and the so-called Wisdom Literature. The Book of Job contains imagery of the more "profane" type characteristic of wisdom poetry and, thus, it often reminds us of the literary style of a more modern period. But it also contains figurative language similar in style and tradition to the Psalms of Lament and is often rather conventional. However, in harmony with its uniqueness, this poetic masterpiece often rises above these types to an original and exceedingly powerful imagery of its very own.

Naturally, there is no figurative language in the framework of the book (1–2; 42:7–17). But as soon as the poetic dialogue begins in chapter 3, the imagery begins. In his first speech, Job curses the day of his birth:

> That night—let thick darkness seize it! ...
> (Let it not) see the eyelids of the morning,

He "praises" Sheol:

> There the prisoners are at ease together ...
> And the slave is free from his master,

Finally, he concludes with these words (3:3 ff., 13 ff., 24):

> My sighing comes as my bread,
> And my groanings are poured out like water.

This kind of figurative language continues in the first speech of Eliphaz, whose theme is: seek grace from God, in order that it may be well with you, in chapters 4–5 and in Job's reply, in chapters 6–7, where, according to Bildad, the words come forth from Job's mouth as "a great wind" (8:2), and where Job complains about his friends abandoning him, using this imagery (6:15–17):

> My brethren are treacherous as a torrent-bed,
> As freshets that pass away,
> Which are dark with ice,
> And where the snow hides itself.
> In time of heat they disappear;
> When it is hot, they vanish from their place.

Figures like this, drawn from nature, as well as figures drawn from animal life, often occur in the Book of Job. In his first speech, Zophar describes Job's rebellious stubbornness in this way (11:12):

> But a stupid man will get understanding,
> When a wild ass's colt is born a man.

It should be mentioned that the language of the Book of Job is very compressed and expressive. In addition, it is a northern dialect and very difficult to understand. Consequently, to a great extent, a translation of this book must be a paraphrase and must greatly expand the wording in the Hebrew text in order to be intelligible. As an example, in his insolent reply to Zophar, Job says (13:14):

> I will take my flesh in my teeth,
> And put my life in my hand,

which is actually a traditional figure for mental composure. Further, he asks God (13:25):

> Wilt thou frighten a driven leaf
> And pursue dry chaff?

and accuses God of persecuting him (13:28):

> Man wastes away like a rotten thing,
> Like a garment that is moth-eaten.

In his second speech, Eliphaz uses this famous figure to describe the wicked (15:35):

> They conceive mischief and bring forth evil
> And their heart prepares deceit.

All these words have a highly "magical" character. Further, we encounter this description of the wicked in 18:16:

> His roots dry up beneath,
> And his branches wither above.

This "vegetation figure" is stereotyped, as is clear from Amos 2:9, as well as from the fact that it also occurs in the Ras Shamra literature.[16] In Zophar's second speech (20:24 f.), we find a powerful figure describing the fate of the wicked drawn from military life. The imagery from mining found in Job's concluding speech to his friends in 28:1 ff. is original: products like gold, silver, and costly stones cannot be

---

16. I D, 159; cf. Engnell, *Studies in Divine Kingship*, p. 142.

compared with wisdom. But is wisdom to be found in a mine? Job gives no answer to this question. God alone knows. The figurative language here is close to that which we find in the Wisdom Literature. Again, the imagery in the descriptions of adversity, which occur at regular intervals in the Book of Job, are of the same type as the descriptions of adversity in the Psalms, especially those in the Royal Psalms. An example of this is Job's reply to the second speech of Eliphaz (16:9 ff.). Sheol waits only for Job (17:14):

> I say to the pit, "You are my father,"
> And to the worm, "My mother," and "My sister."

Finally, passages such as chapter 38 may be used to illustrate another problem, that of the relationship between figurative language and mythology. It is certainly not easy to determine what is imagery and what is genuine mythology in this chapter, whose language and poetry is so splendid with its allusions to the wonders of creation and nature.

In contrast to the Book of Job, which is original and powerful, the figurative language of the Book of Proverbs is generally commonplace and traditional and belongs to what we might call an "everyday" type. As has already been suggested, the same thing may be said of all Wisdom Literature. For the sake of example, we may call attention to these statements concerning the treacherous woman (5:3 f.):

> For the lips of a loose woman drip honey,
> And her speech is smoother than oil;
> But in the end she is bitter as wormwood,
> Sharp as a two-edged sword.

The description of adultery and its consequences in 6:27 f. appears in more original imagery:

> Can a man carry fire in his bosom
> And his clothes not be burned?
> Or can one walk upon hot coals
> And his feet not be scorched?

The collection of the so-called Proverbs of Solomon in 10:1–22:16 is made up mostly of rather monotonous characterizations and maxims with little artistic quality. Quite often, these proverbs speak in pious platitudes, and the figurative language is colorless. The same must be said of the "Words of the Wise" in 22:17–24:22, which is usually considered to be a Hebrew version of the Egyptian "Wisdom of Amen-em-opet,"[17] although it is more parenetic. The "Proverbs of the Men of Hezekiah" in chapters 25–29 perhaps represent a somewhat more elevated type of literature. Among other things, these proverbs deal with the "fool" and the sluggard. We read, concerning the sluggard (26:14 f.):

> The door turns on its hinges,
> The sluggard turns on his bed.
> The sluggard buries his hand in the dish;
> It wears him out to bring it back to his mouth.

A more original comparison appears in 26:23:

> Like the glaze covering an earthen vessel
> Are smooth lips with an evil heart.

(This translation is supported by material from Ras Shamra).[18] The collection of the "Words of Agur" in chapter 30 is of great value. To a great extent, it uses a numerical-increase technique which is well-known from many other sources, not only in so-called "numerical proverbs," but also in texts of a completely different type, for example, from Ras Shamra.[19] As an example, we may cite these lines:

> The leech has two daughters:
> "Give, Give!"
> There are three which cannot be satisfied,
> Yea, four which never say, "It is enough":
> Sheol and the wailing of the barren,
> The land which cannot be satisfied with water
> And the fire which never says, "It is enough."

17. Cf. Pritchard, *op. cit.*, pp. 421 ff.
18. See W. F. Albright, "Some Canaanite-Phoenician Sources of Hebrew Wisdom," *Supplements to Vetus Testamentum*, 3 (1960), pp. 12 f.
19. E.g., II AB, III, 14–20 [cf. W. M. W. Roth, "Numerical Sayings in the Old Testament," *Supplements to Vetus Testamentum*, 13 (1965), p. 82]; I AB V, 8 f., 20 f. I D I, 42 f.

But there is one passage in Proverbs which should especially be mentioned: 8:22 ff. It belongs to that portion of Proverbs (chapters 1–9) which is usually considered to be the latest. In this passage, Wisdom is described as a pre-existent being who was created before the world and through whom it was created: "set up (Heb. *nissakh,* literally, "set up by anointing," the same expression used in Ps. 2:6 concerning the king, "the son of God") from the beginning" and "nurtured by God as a child" (Heb. *'āmôn,* probably, literally, "darling, intimate friend") (8:23, 30). Along with several other features, these expressions indicate that originally this passage was a piece of advanced royal ideology coming from an early date and associated with the idea of the king as the "Son of God," while its present form, with the feminine "Wisdom" as its central figure, is the work of the later period. This should be of some interest, because the passage is basic to the Logos speculation in the Prologue of the Gospel of John.[20]

The Book of Ecclesiastes is characterized by rather commonplace every-day wisdom, a strong dose of pessimism, and the motto: enjoy what you can as long as it lasts, but not to excess, because excess carries with it its own punishment. This book contains very little figurative language; 12:1 ff. has a certain poetic excellence, and the imagery in this passage which describes "the evil days," the time when "the spirit returns to God who gave it," is not devoid of a certain originality.

Turning now to the figurative language of the prophets, the first thing to be pointed out is that, from a literary point of view, scholars today have a completely different understanding from that of two or three decades ago. There are several reasons for this radical change. Today, we are much more conscious of the importance of discovering the *Sitz im Leben* of prophetic literature. It is now clear that the prophets drew heavily upon ancient cultic traditions. Recently discovered comparative material has contributed greatly to our under-

---

20. The pre-existence of the king is argued by Engnell on the basis of Isa. 49:2, "certain allusions in some characteristic royal psalms," and Ezek. 28:1 ff.: "in accordance with common Near Eastern ideology, according to which the sacral king exists as a divine being before his birth." See his article on "Pre-existens" (Pre-existence) in *SBU²*. In his *Studies in Divine Kingship,* p. 16, this is stated only for kingship in general.

standing of the external forms of the prophetic message, as is the case to an even greater extent of the Psalm literature. The fallacy of interpreting the prophets according to western standards, whether they be early or late, has been clearly demonstrated. The prophets were not literary men or conscious, individually creative, professional writers. The different prophetic "books" are predominantly collections of traditions handed down orally over longer or shorter periods of time. These books contain units of tradition modelled after inherited prototypes, and they have been put together according to traditional principles, especially association and the "alternating scheme." Not only the formal structure of the oracles, their introductory and concluding formulae, but also the literary phraseology and especially the figurative language are, to a large extent, dependent on a definite tradition which is often several centuries old and whose origin is undoubtedly to be sought in sacral contexts. Thus, "cultic language" is primary in relationship to "prophetic language," to the extent that prophetic language is not simply cultic language. The varying degrees to which different portions of prophetic literature depend on an original cultic background is reflected in the two main types of prophetic literature, the liturgy and the *dīwān*. Of course, this emphasis on the prophetic use of tradition is not to be taken as a denial of the individuality and uniqueness of the different prophets or in the language that they employ. On the contrary, we must exert every effort to find this uniqueness. In evaluating the imagery in the prophets, one must also consider other important factors, including the question of the originality of the so-called messianic oracles,[21] and especially the difficult question of the differences between imagery and reality, that is, cultic reality and the reality of the so-called symbolic acts.[22] Figurative language can also be of utmost importance as a criterion for determining the unity of a prophetic book or collection. This criterion was greatly neglected by literary critics in their analyses of so-called literary problems of the various books.

Scholars generally agree that the Book of Isaiah is a composite work consisting of three different "books" (or better, "collections"). The first, the so-called Proto-Isaiah, is thought to include chapters 1–39.

21. Cf. chap. 6, "Prophets and Prophetism in the Old Testament."
22. Cf. chap. 6, "Prophets and Prophetism in the Old Testament."

(In reality, there seems to be a division between chapters 34 and 35.[23]) It is in this collection, which is predominantly of the *dīwān* type, that we may expect to meet the prophet Isaiah himself and his imagery. This section is linguistically very rich and greatly varied and gives the overwhelming impression that Isaiah was a master of language and style. As might be expected, the oracles of doom are predominantly of the concrete type. They contain very powerful language and are characterized by intensive poetic afflatus. In several passages, the prophet uses tree symbolism, well-known from poetic texts, in its negative aspect in referring both to foreign nations and to Israel (compare 1:30; 10:33 f.; 17:10 f.; 18:5 f.). This same symbolism is found in its positive "tree of life" aspect in messianic oracles, for example, in the reference to the "shoot from the stump of Jesse" in 11:1 ff. The same figure, undoubtedly based on cultic realities, is also presupposed in Isa. 6:13, which refers to the "stump" which is the "holy seed."[24] In the famous "Song of the Vineyard" in 5:1 ff., it is clear that Isaiah is well acquainted with the theme and form of the Tammuz liturgy, for this is a cultic and stylistic presupposition lying behind this parable. It is quite possible that the introduction of this parable is a direct reference to Song of Songs 8:11.[25] Isaiah also uses other literary categories with special *Sitz im Leben*, as, for example, the watchman's song in 21:11 ff. and the harlot's song in 23:15 ff., in the oracle against Tyre. Also, this prophet often uses the theme of "the work and the master" (29:16), particularly to emphasize that the instrument—the ax, the saw, the rod—cannot boast itself against its lord (10:15). The fact that the contrast between darkness and light plays a big rôle in the oracles of Isaiah, especially in messianic contexts (compare, for example, 9:1 ff.),[26] also bears witness to his idea of God. Chapters 7–8 are very important and contain several symbolic

23. A similar position is now held by J. D. Smart, *History and Theology in Second Isaiah* (Philadelphia: Westminster Press, 1965), and J. L. McKenzie, *Second Isaiah. The Anchor Bible*, 20 (Garden City, N. Y.: Doubleday & Co., 1968).

24. Cf. I. Engnell, *The Call of Isaiah* (Leipzig: Otto Harrassowitz, 1949), pp. 49 f.

25. Thus, already, K. Marti, *Das Buch Jesaja* (Tübingen: J. C. B. Mohr, 1900), p. 52; cf. A. Bentzen in *Archiv für Orientforschung*, 4 (1927), pp. 209 f.

26. Light represents life and order, while darkness means chaos and death. God and his messiah, the king, stand for light, life, and order fighting the powers of darkness: Engnell, in "Ljus" (Light), in *SBU²*.

acts.[27] In these chapters, we encounter refined figures of speech alternating with bold and drastic ones. In 7:2, referring to King Ahaz, it says: "His heart and the heart of his people shook as the trees of the forest shake before the wind," while in vv. 18 f., it speaks of the flies from Egypt and the swarms of bees from Assyria, and of the king of Assyria as the razor with which Yahweh shall shave off "the hair of the head and of the feet." In 8:7 f., the impending doom is described under the figure of an all-enveloping flood. Behind this figure lies the primitive idea of the waters of chaos, which is of central importance in cultic contexts. The statement in 12:3, "with joy you will draw water from the wells of salvation," also comes from a cultic background, although the reference in this passage is to the "water of life." However, the figure of the broken potter's vessel in 30:14 (compare Jer. 19:10 f.) is wholly "profane," in contrast to the use of this "figure" in Ps. 2:9.[28] Chapters 24–27, the so-called Isaiah Apocalypse, which belong to the liturgy type, are unique in the Proto-Isaianic collection. That this section contains Isaianic material should not be denied, even though its final form is relatively late. The allegory of the great feast on Mount Zion in 25:6 ff. is of special interest. It seems certain that Isaiah is responsible for the message in chapter 28, with the possible exception of the "Parable of the Farmer" in vv. 23 ff. It is impossible to say whether the same is true of chapter 34. Be that as it may, the Proto-Isaianic collection concludes at chapter 34 with a prophecy of doom whose character is essentially cosmic and whose outlook approaches the eschatological. In this chapter, a suggestive figure is placed side by side with a dismal realism: the skies will roll up as a scroll (Mohammed has taken over this figure), the sword of Yahweh has drunk its fill, the streams shall be turned into pitch and the soil to brimstone, the strongholds shall be laid waste and shall become

27. Engnell here inserts a reference to his article on "Immanuel" in *SBU²*, in which he argues for a positive interpretation of the Immanuel oracle. In that article, Engnell contends that the young woman is probably the queen, who, in the cultic drama of the New Year festival, "impersonated the goddess and was called 'virgin' (*'almāh*)." "The oracle itself is a quotation from a cultic formula which has been found in a Ras Shamra text, where it is denoted as *bśrt* (=Hebrew *beśōrāh*), good news," viz., of the birth of the royal-divine child. (This is not quite correct, since the formula occurs in NK I, 7 and the word *bśrt* in IV AB III, 33; the reference in IV AB being, however, to the birth of a divine being). "Immanuel is the savior-name of this child."

28. The quotation marks around the word *figure* seem to imply that the expression reflects some ritual action, such as the breaking of a vessel, to symbolize and bring about the destruction of enemies.

the haunt of hyenas and jackals, snakes and vultures. And as the representative of all foreign nations, Edom, Israel's hereditary foe, is relegated to doom.

The Deutero-Isaianic collection begins with a prophecy of salvation for Israel in chapter 35, which is the direct antithesis of chapter 34: the wilderness shall blossom; Lebanon, Carmel, and Sharon shall be clothed with splendor; the eyes of the blind shall be opened and the ears of the deaf unstopped; the lame shall leap as a hart and the tongue of the dumb shall sing for joy; the wild beasts shall disappear, and the way through the wilderness shall be made smooth for the redeemed, whose heads shall be crowned with everlasting joy. This is more than classical imagery. An ancient messianic ideology lies behind it, actualized by the belief in an approaching transformation of reality. In chapters 36–39, two traditional units are of special interest. One is the lampoon against the king of Assyria in 37:22 ff., where we read:

> I will put my hook in your nose
> And my bit in your mouth,

imagery which is certainly typically Isaianic. The other is the so-called Psalm of Hezekiah in 38:10–20, the nucleus of the complex chapters 36–39. This is undoubtedly a Royal Psalm of Lament taken from a distinctly cultic context. It contains characteristic features of the Tammuz type, such as the shepherd's tent that has been plucked up, the web of life cut off from the loom, and it ends with a *descensus ad inferos*, a descent into Sheol. In 40:6 ff., we encounter a typical use of the "vegetation figure" in its negative aspect. The lampoon against the "virgin daughter of Babylon" in chapter 47, set forth in consistent allegorical style (it declares that "loss of children and widowhood" shall come in full measure in one and the same night upon the "secure and rich") is much like 37:22 ff. Also, the so-called Ebed Yahweh Songs in 42:1 ff.; 49:1 ff.; 50:4 ff.; and 52:13–53:12 reflect the ideology of the "Psalm of Hezekiah," although in a more advanced form and without the cultic connection so obviously the background of Isa. 38:10 ff. On the whole, the figurative language in these songs can be understood only against the background of the ancient royal ideology.[29] This is reflected partly in its negative form, with motifs

29. Cf. I. Engnell, "The 'Ebed Yahweh Songs and the Suffering Messiah in Deutero-Isaiah," *Bulletin of the John Rylands Library*, 31 (1948), pp. 54 ff.; and

such as vicarious suffering under the symbol of the lamb, smiting the cheek and public scourging, the disfigured appearance and the descent into Sheol; and partly in its positive form, with the title of Servant, the figure of the "young plant," the call from the womb, the administration of justice, the possession of the Spirit, the victory over the enemies, the justification of "the many" after the *ascensus,* the rising up from Sheol, and the exaltation.[30] Summarizing, it must be admitted that, in spite of the different themes and purposes of the collections, the imagery in Deutero-Isaiah is so similar in character to that in Proto-Isaiah that the only explanation which can do justice to the material is that offered by the traditio-historical approach: we must assume that there were direct personal lines of communication from the Deutero-Isaiah work to the prophet Isaiah, and that the man or circle responsible for this collection was not only thoroughly influenced by the message of the prophet—his ideology, style, and imagery—but also had available traditional material handed down directly from Isaiah himself.

To a great extent, this is also true of the Trito-Isaianic collection in chapters 56–66 and of the traditionist circle lying behind it: to the extent that it is necessary and correct to consider chapter 56 the beginning of a new section. In light of the fact that its structure is of the *dīwān* type and that it contains many detailed characteristics which are very similar to Isaiah, chapters 1–34, in a way, the Trito-Isaianic collection is closer to Proto-Isaiah than it is to Deutero-Isaiah. We may cite chapter 59 as an example. To some extent, the imagery in this chapter is typically Isaianic, as when it says of the unrighteous:

> They hatch adders' eggs,
> They weave the spider's web;
> He who eats their eggs dies,
> And from one which is crushed a viper is hatched.

The powerful and suggestive description of Yahweh as the "one who treads the winepress in bright red garments," that is, as the judge and avenger sprinkled with blood, in the allegory at the beginning of

H. Ringgren, *The Messiah in the Old Testament* (London: SCM Press, 1956), pp. 54 ff.

30. Engnell, "The 'Ebed Yahweh Songs and the Suffering Messiah in Deutero-Isaiah."

chapter 63, is a good example of very consistent figurative language. Finally, in chapter 66, the regeneration of Israel and Zion is described under the figure of a childbirth which happens so quickly that the child, the new Israel, is born the very moment that the travail pains begin, whereupon the mother, Jerusalem, caresses her "son," carries him in her arms, and consoles him. In the last verses of this chapter, the scene again changes quickly: the new heavens and the new earth are characterized not only by Israel's faithful observance of the new moon and sabbath, but also by the faithful "going forth and looking on the dead bodies of the men that have rebelled against me (Yahweh); for their worm shall not die, their fire shall not be quenched, and they shall be an abhorrence to all flesh" (66:24). Thus, the Book of Isaiah ends with a passage of startling realism, for that is certainly what is intended here, and not figurative language.

The imagery used by Jeremiah, who was "appointed a prophet to the nations, to pluck up and to break down, to destroy and to overthrow, to build and to plant" (1:5, 10), undoubtedly bears the strong personal stamp of the prophet, in spite of the fact that, to a great extent, Jeremiah drew upon inherited style forms, traditional phraseology, and stereotyped figures, and that he can be very concrete and caustically realistic in proclaiming his main theme: the apostasy of Israel and Judah from Yahweh and their worship of foreign gods. There is one figure of speech which Jeremiah uses repeatedly in speaking of this apostasy: the marriage between Yahweh (the groom) and Israel (the bride), in which the bride is an adulteress who practices her fornication "upon every high hill and under every green tree" (2:20; also Hosea), referring to the Baal cult on the high places and in the groves of trees, and who "commits adultery with stone and tree" (3:9), that is, worships images of foreign gods. The expressions "Israel, the faithless one" and "Judah, the false one" occur again and again (3:6 f.). In several passages, Yahweh also addresses Israel-Judah as "daughter," or "the daughter of my people." These terms are vestiges of an original ideological stage bound up with the cult, in which it was assumed that the god was married to a goddess, who is replaced in Jeremiah by "the daughter-the people." Therefore, the figures of the wife and the daughter are so interwoven that it is hardly possible to separate them (8:19 ff.). Sometimes, the imagery used to describe this apostasy is drastically intensified, as in 2:23 ff., where

Israel is compared with a camel mare and a wild ass passionately in heat. Jeremiah uses a number of figures in speaking of the visitation and punishment. In most cases, they are traditional. Thus, the oft-recurring theme of "the foe from the North" (1:4 ff., 10) appears under the figure of a lion, or a shepherd or many shepherds with their flocks (both are symbols for a king; Jeremiah uses the figure of the shepherd quite often), a sword, pestilence, scorching wind, or a tempest. The lament of Judah is often compared with the travail of a woman in childbirth having her first child (4:31 f.; 22:23). The same figure is also used of foreign nations, Syria, for instance (49:24). Jeremiah often declares with bitterness and resignation that the judgment of purification is in vain, as in 6:29:

> The bellows blow fiercely,
> The lead is consumed by the fire;
> In vain the refining goes on,
> For the wicked are not removed.

This imagery from the world of mining occurs rather frequently in Jeremiah; for example, in 11:4, Egypt is appropriately referred to as "the iron furnace." Quite different is the prophet's description of the visitation in 9:16 ff., which has many affinities with the situation in life and form of the lament for the dead. Here we find the famous words:

> For death has come up into our windows,
> It has entered our palaces,
> Cutting off the children from the streets
> And the young men from the squares . . .
> The dead bodies of men shall fall
> Like dung upon the open field,
> Like sheaves after the reaper,
> And none shall gather them.

Another well-known figure occurs in 13:23, where the prophet illustrates Judah's intrinsic sinfulness by asking:

> Can the Ethiopian change his skin
> Or the leopard his spots?

Jeremiah also uses the familiar figure of the tree, in both its positive and negative senses. Examples of the positive aspect are found in 2:21, where Israel is compared with a choice vine planted by Yahweh as a figure for election, and in 11:16, where Israel is compared with "a green olive tree, fair with goodly fruit." Examples of the negative aspect appear in 8:13 and in 17:5 ff., where Yahweh says, through Jeremiah:

> Cursed is the man who trusts in man
> And makes flesh his arm . . .
> He is like a shrub in the desert.

A genuine figure of speech is used here: "flesh" refers to man in his weakness, while "arm" is a standard metaphor for the saving power of God. This passage could be characterized as a paraphrase of Ps. 1:3.

Although, in time past, it was generally thought that the Psalms drew upon Jeremiah, Jeremiah is greatly influenced by the style, language, and imagery of the Book of Psalms, not only in the sections of lament which occur in this at regular intervals, but also in the hymnic passages, such as the ones in 31:35 ff. and 51:15 ff. But the most characteristic are the oracles of lament, which express the deep individual sympathy of Jeremiah for the affliction of his people and his grief over the catastrophe he had to proclaim. A couple of typical examples may be cited. In 8:23, Jeremiah says:

> O that my head were waters
> And my eyes a fountain of tears,
> That I might weep day and night
> For the slain of the daughter of my people!

And in 23:9, he laments:

> My heart is broken within me,
> All my bones shake;
> I am like a drunken man,
> Like a man overcome by wine,
> Because of the Lord
> And because of his holy words.

This feeling of sympathy is often typically intensified in the prophet, to such an extent that he curses himself and the day of his birth (20: 15 ff.):

> Cursed be the man
> Who brought the news (*bissar*) to my father,
> "A son is born to you,"
> Making him very glad.
> Let that man be like the cities
> Which the Lord overthrew without pity;
> Let him hear a cry in the morning
> And an alarm at noon,
> Because he did not kill me in the womb;
> So my mother would have been my grave,
> And her womb for ever great.
> Why did I come forth from the womb
> To see toil and sorrow,
> And spend my days in shame?

But in spite of all his oracles of doom, Jeremiah does not want the people to be destroyed, any more than any of the great prophets did; he wants them to be converted and to repent. He uses many figures in his passionate appeals to the people. In 4:4, he says:

> Circumcise yourselves to the Lord,
> Remove the foreskin of your hearts,
> O men of Judah and inhabitants of Jerusalem.

After this conversion, for which Jeremiah hoped in both Israel and Judah (compare especially chapter 3), the prophet announces that Yahweh will inaugurate a new age. He describes the return from Exile in a way that is very reminiscent of "Deutero-Isaiah" (compare especially Jer. 31:7 ff.) and the new age in conventional messianic terminology, especially with regard to the role which "the true shepherd," "the righteous branch" of the lineage of David, plays in this age: 23:4 ff. (compare Isa. 52:13 ff.); 33:14 ff. But 31:31 ff., the description of the new covenant with the law "written upon the hearts of the Israelites" and put "within them," is characteristic of Jeremiah. Scholars usually date the emergence of individualism with Jeremiah; but this is erroneous, because individualism is just as old as collectivism. And yet, it is true that emphasis on the individual is characteristic of Jeremiah. Another indication of this, besides 31:31 ff., is that the prophet takes up the proverb (Heb. *māshāl*) about the fathers who ate sour grapes which set the children's teeth on edge (compare Lam. 5:7; Ezek. 18:2) to combat the doctrine of retribution upon the children for evil deeds done by their fathers (31:29 f.). In the collection of oracles against nations, which is found in Jeremiah, chapters 46–51, there are passages in traditional style, that is, in the form of the so-called *qînāh* or lament for the dead, such as those concerning Egypt in chapter 46 and Moab in chapter 48; but there are also passages which use imagery of a more original and individual sort. Finally, Jeremiah also enacts numerous so-called symbolic acts: the waist-cloth at the Euphrates (13:1 ff.) and the broken potter's vessel in the Valley of Hinnom (chapter 19). Actually, the writing down of the collection of Jeremiah's oracles, as it is related in chapter 36, is also a symbolic act in a special situation. Ultimately, we might say that Jeremiah's whole life, in the way that the Book of Jeremiah describes it (Jeremiah has no wife or family, and he functions outside the social community), is designed to illustrate the apostasy of the people from Yahweh and their isolation and doom. The figurative language in the Book of Jeremiah is uniform throughout and thus testifies to the unity and integrity of the book.

In Ezekiel, the call vision in chapter 1 already reflects this prophet's highly visionary and very peculiar disposition. This vision has been characterized as symbolic, as well as grotesque, abstruse, and formless. No prophet has been the object of psychological analysis to the extent that Ezekiel has. Scholars have used the entire arsenal of technical terms taken from psychology in describing his actions: parapsychic and hypnagogic states, clairvoyance, photisms, levitations.[31] However, Ezekiel is by no means exclusively eidetic; like other prophets, he also experiences numerous auditions; not only does he see, he also hears the divine revelation. Moreover, he repeatedly performs symbolic acts, even though scholars are sometimes undecided as to whether these actually reflect concrete acts or experiences of a purely

31. G. Widengren, *Literary and Psychological Aspects of the Hebrew Prophets* (Uppsala: Lundequist, 1948), pp. 94 ff.

psychical nature, such as the enactment of the siege of Jerusalem in 4:1 ff. On this point, the distinctions may be fluid. In any case, his literary style has a highly concrete character, while imagery is found only to a relatively small extent. But still, the prophet can say, in the description of the day of doom in chapter 7, that the redeemed "will be like doves of the valleys, all of them moaning" (v. 16). And in the Jerusalem cycle in chapters 8–11, Ezekiel has the "princes among the people," Jaazaniah and Pelatiah, say: "The time is not near to build houses; this city is the caldron, and we are the flesh," but then he himself changes the figure so that, while the caldron still represents the city, the flesh now represents all the slain (11:3 ff.). Further, in his sharp invectives in chapter 13, he characterizes the false prophets in this way: "Your prophets have been like foxes among ruins, O Israel" (v. 4). In chapter 15, Ezekiel uses the well-known tree motif in its negative aspect: Israel is a dry vine branch, burned with fire and doomed to destruction. The same motif is found in its original connection with the person of the king in 19:10 ff. This applies, to an even greater extent, to the oracle against Egypt in chapter 31, where Pharaoh is depicted as the tree of life with the water of life, but still is doomed to descend into Sheol forever. The figurative language here is very impressive, in spite of the traditional motif, and the whole narrative constitutes a piece of truly great poetry. The same may be said of the kindred oracle in 28:1–10, with its variant in vv. 12–19, both of which are directed against the king of Tyre. This chapter contains in a very advanced (but also polemical) form a description of the king as a divine, pre-existent being on the mountain of the gods in paradise, who is doomed nevertheless, because of his self-deification and hubris, to be cast down into Sheol to remain there forever. The collection of prophecies against foreign nations in chapters 25–32 ends with a veritable vision of hell in 32:17 ff. The description of the massacre of Gog in the last days, in chapters 38–39, is parallel to this, although it uses warlike, ruthless, and bloody terminology.

One style form very characteristic of Ezekiel is the allegory, which at the same time contains a traditional and yet highly distinctive imagery. The first real, well-developed example of this type appears in chapter 16. This passage begins with an obviously proverbial statement—Ezekiel often uses a proverb as his theme—concerning the sinful nature of Israel, which she inherited as the offspring of an Amorite father and a Hittite mother (16:3, compare v. 45). Ezekiel then sketches the religious history of the people of Israel: her election, as a new-born child whom Yahweh nurtures in spite of her miserable condition —unwashed from the blood of her birth and cast out in the open field —so that she grows up to be a beautiful maiden and a queen adorned in gold; and her apostasy from Yahweh the groom, under the figure of reckless fornication in drastic, realistic detail: Israel is a harlot so enflamed by her passion that she gives her harlot's hire instead of receiving it. Finally, this passage ends in a merciless oracle of doom. Not only does this allegory with its figurative language appear unusually harsh and rancid to modern man, but no doubt it also appeared the same way to the prophet's own contemporaries. Another allegory of the same type is found in 16:44 ff. It begins with the proverb "like mother, like daughter," and has the same ethnic background as 16:1 ff. According to this passage, after the period of disgrace, Judah-Jerusalem and her "sisters" (the older Samaria and the younger Sodom) shall be rehabilitated and restored in harmony with "the everlasting covenant" and its promises. Still another allegory on the same theme occurs in chapter 23, where the sisters Oholah (Samaria, the older) and Oholibah (Jerusalem, the younger) and their "fornication" (that is, apostasy from Yahweh) are described in imagery whose realism and rabidity even exceed that found in chapter 16. The presupposition and background for these recurring allegorical descriptions are both the figure of the "marriage" between Yahweh and Israel and especially the actual cultic practices in the time of the prophet, which include a far-reaching syncretism and religious disintegration which received perhaps its most powerful impetus from the widely prevalent cultic prostitution. But even beyond this, the prophet's own highly sentimental personal disposition must have been an important contributing factor in these allegories. Many scholars understand this disposition as an abnormal weakness, but this is by no means necessary or even likely.

Even though Ezekiel's proclamation of doom is very intensive, he also maintains a firm belief in a restoration after doom and in a prosperous messianic future under a righteous "shepherd" of the lineage of David, as we have already suggested. He expresses this belief in several passages, but especially in chapters 34 and 36 ff. In 34:23 ff., we find a description in classical style of the blessing and fruitfulness of the messianic age during the time of the "covenant of peace" in the "plantations" over which "Yahweh's servant David" rules. Here we read: "A new heart I will give you, and a new spirit I will put within you; and I will take out of your flesh the heart of stone and give you a heart of flesh" (36:26). This belief in the future reaches its climax in the very important chapter 37, where in a vision the prophet sees a valley full of dry bones given new flesh and a new spirit and then raised to a new life. Here, Ezekiel declares that the graves shall be opened and Israel's dead shall arise and be gathered again into the land of Israel (37:1 ff., 12 ff.). This proclamation, which approaches eschatology, is further affirmed by a symbolic act: two sticks, representing Ephraim and Judah, are joined together in a figure intended to create reality, symbolizing the restoration of the Davidic kingdom (37:15 ff.). We should also interpret chapters 40–48 against this background. These chapters consist of a visionary and programmatic outline of the restored temple, detailed ordinances concerning the form of its cult, including typical compromises involving the status of the Levites (44:9 ff.), and especially duties of the Davidic "prince" (chapters 45 f.). This portion of the book contains a special combination of concrete and figurative language in ancient classical style, for example, in the passage concerning the water of life and the tree of life (47:12). There can be no doubt, especially in light of the imagery, that the prophet-priest Ezekiel also speaks in these chapters. Indeed, the style and composition reflected in these chapters go back to a remote period in the ancient Near East, as is shown by King Gudea of Lagash about 2000 B.C.[32]

The figurative language in the Book of Daniel is dictated by the apocalyptic character of this writing in its pseudo-historical disguise. The main character, Daniel, is modelled after a figure well known in the popular tradition, a sage, a primitive king described as divine, whose divine character is manifested especially in his gnosis to interpret dreams.[33] As is to be expected, this theme of interpreting dreams occurs often in the book, and it has left its mark on the imagery,

32. S. N. Kramer, *The Sumerians* (Chicago: The University of Chicago Press, 1963), pp. 137 ff.

33. The reference is to the Daniel or Danel of the Ugaritic Aqhat texts. Engnell argues that the Daniel of the biblical book represents a transformation of popular traditions preserving the memory of the mythical king of the Ras Shamra epic. Daniel is "described in royal categories," including the descensus motif, the death and resurrection motif, and the wisdom and oracular function of Daniel. Based on his article "Daniel" in *SBU²*.

which is surprisingly uniform, both in the Hebrew and the Aramaic sections, in spite of the fact that the book—or, rather, collection of traditions—lacks uniformity. Since the central figure, Daniel, is described in "distintegrated" royal categories, and since different kings play a prominent rôle in this writing, it is not surprising that we find a great number of ancient royal ideological motifs in the book. These include the peculiar form of the ancient tree symbolism in chapter 4, in close connection with original mythological motifs, the king being identified with the tree of life or cosmic tree. The motif of the stump that remains, from whose roots a new kingdom shall spring up, which is well known from Isaiah's call vision (Isa. 6:13), also occurs here (Dan. 4:12, 23). Moreover, Joseph, as he is presented in the Joseph tradition cycle in Genesis, is the obvious prototype of Daniel as an interpreter of dreams. Typical is the dream of the statue composed of gold, silver, bronze, iron, and clay, which falls down and becomes "like the chaff of the summer threshing floors" which the wind carries away so that no one can find any trace of them (Dan. 2). Chapter 3 is a variant on the statue theme, and ends with the familiar story of the three men in the furnace whose object is to glorify the God of Israel. The symbolism in which this apocalyptist operates is imaginative, but also bound to tradition, and it is clear that real imagery does not occur to any great degree in these chapters. This is also true of chapter 6, where, actually, the motif of the king's *descensus ad inferos* or sojourn in Sheol lies behind the story of Daniel in the lion's den. (In 6:20, Daniel is typically called the "servant of God," a variant of Ebed Yahweh, "the Servant of the Lord," and in 11:33 ff., the term *hammaskîlîm*, "those who are wise," is modelled after Isa. 52:13.) The relative absence of figurative language in dream symbolism is further exemplified in the description of Daniel's dream of the four wild beasts (world kingdoms) and the Son of Man in chapter 7.[34] The style of this passage naturally reminds us of Ezekiel, and the same is often the case with other passages in Daniel. Chapter 10 is best described as a dialogue between God and a figure who is described in disintegrated royal categories. Concerning this royal angelic figure, v. 6 says: "His body was like beryl, his face like the appearance of lightning, his eyes like flaming torches, his arms and legs like the gleam of burnished bronze." This manner of expression clearly recalls the description of

34. Cf. chap. 12, "The Son of Man."

the groom in the Song of Songs, and there can hardly be any doubt
that ultimately a concrete idol or imagery inherited from such a context lies behind this passage. Chapter 11 describes the destiny of the
"glorious land" in the course of the war between the kings of the South
and the kings of the North, which reaches its climax when the "abomination that makes desolate" is set up. It states that the king (Antiochus IV Epiphanes) shall respect neither the gods of his fathers nor
"the one beloved by women," that is, Tammuz-Adonis, nor any god
at all other than himself—he is the very incarnation of human hubris
in asserting that he is god. But after the time of visitation, there
shall be a period of restoration and resurrection, especially for Daniel,
the "king", in which the *hammaskîlîm*, "those who are wise"—that
is, the righteous who follow the example of the Ebed Yahweh and lead
others to "righteousness" in order that they might be resurrected—
"shall shine like the brightness of the firmament; and those who turn
many to righteousness (shall then shine) like the stars for ever and
ever" (12:3 ff.). On the basis of these observations, we are justified
in drawing two conclusions concerning the Book of Daniel. First, in
content and ideology, this work is important as an example of the
apocalyptic religion later to be a vital factor in the New Testament.
Second, the dream symbolism in this book, which is abstruse and
bound to tradition, predominantly makes use of concrete style and not
of imagery in the usual literary sense.

While the Book of Daniel reflects the very latest style in the Old
Testament, the prophetic books which make up the so-called Book
of the Twelve Prophets contain the oldest known prophetic language,
interspersed with a good deal of later material. This is especially true
of the first book in this group, Hosea. As far as we know, this is the
first prophet who consistently describes the relationship between
Yahweh and Israel under the figure of a marriage. As has already been
suggested, this figure was further developed later, especially by
Jeremiah and Ezekiel. However, this hardly justifies the conclusion
that these prophets took over this figure directly from Hosea. It is
more likely that all three of these prophets are representatives of a
definite tradition which undoubtedly had an origin, but not one which
can be definitely determined chronologically. At any rate, the imagery
which Hosea uses in employing this figure is sharp and rancid.
Throughout the book, Israel's apostasy is spoken of under the figure

of fornication and lewdness: the bride Israel "goes after her lovers" (2:7 ff.), the Baals, which Israel erroneously considers to be the ones that give fertility to the land of Canaan. But there is also another side to this figure. Israel is an unfaithful mother with unfaithful children (2:6). It is this which Hosea portrays in his symbolic acts when he marries an unfaithful wife and an adulteress (chapters 1 and 3),[35] and when he gives his children names which illustrate and effect the coming doom: Jezreel, Lo-Ruhamah, and Lo-Ammi. The peculiar intensity of Hosea's language is due to the fact that, from the very moment that he appears, he opposes a widespread cultic apostasy in the northern kingdom, and his preaching is directed almost exclusively against this apostasy. He describes the present situation with very concrete terminology; but at the same time, he also uses a group of different figures to depict the coming divine judgment: a wind shall "wrap them in its wings" (4:19), or Yahweh is "like a moth" and as "rot in the bones" (5:12); as a lion, a young lion who seizes his prey and "carries it off and none shall rescue" (5:14); he lurks beside the way like a leopard (13:7); or he intervenes as a bird-catcher who spreads out his net over Ephraim and "brings them down like birds of the air" (7:12). The fire is standard imagery which Hosea adopts to describe the visitation which Yahweh sends on the cities of the northern kingdom and which shall devour its palaces (8:14; compare Amos 1:4; Jer. 49:27). He also uses the figure of travail of a woman in childbirth (13:13). On the whole, it may be said that the imagery of Hosea is unusually rich and diversified in his description of doom.

But Hosea speaks not only of apostasy and doom, but also of Yahweh's election, love, and covenant faithfulness, and he also uses a rich figurative language to depict this facet of his message. In 9:10, Yahweh says, in an anomaly with a positive meaning:

> Like grapes in the wilderness
> I found Israel,
> Like the first fruit on the fig tree,
> In its first season,
> I saw your fathers.

---

35. Engnell adheres to the theory that Hosea married twice; his first wife was of foreign descent and religion (*'ēsheth z⁽e⁾nûnîm*); the second was Gomer, a cult prostitute. See his article on "Hosea" in *SBU²*.

Furthermore, in 10:1, we find the simile of the tree, as well as in 14:6 ff., where it says, concerning Israel:

> He shall blossom as the lily,
> He shall strike root as the poplar (Heb. Lebanon);
> His beauty shall spread out;
> His beauty shall be like the olive,
> And his fragrance like Lebanon.

This is because Yahweh "will be as the dew to Israel," a figure for life-giving which has its origin in Hosea's concept of God with its strong emphasis on his function as giver of fertility. This concept is found in 6:3:

> His going forth is sure as the dawn;
> He will come to us as the showers,
> As the spring rains that water the earth.

The oracle in 7:3 ff. apparently has the form of a brief allegory. Actually, it has a special background: the royal ideology. The imagery of the baker is based on the rôle of the sacral king as provider for the people, which was acted out in the cult with appropriate rites.[36] The background of the much disputed oracle in 6:1–2 (which is an integral part of the tradition unit 6:1–5) is also the royal ideology:

> Come, let us return to the Lord;
> For he has torn, that he may heal us;
> After two days he will revive us;
> On the third day he will raise us up,
> That we may live before him.

The imagery in this oracle is based on the language of North Israelite psalms, and v. 2 is clearly a direct quotation from this material. The meaning of the passage is that the people participate in the "passion" and "resurrection" of the king, a concept which gradually became an important aspect of messianism: compare Isaiah, chapter 53, part of which uses terminology conspicuously similar to that of Hosea,

---

36. See Engnell, *Studies in Divine Kingship*, pp. 155 f.

chapter 6. There can be no doubt that this Hoseanic oracle—or, at least, the setting and ideology of the royal *descensus* which it presupposes—lies behind Luke 24:7 and I Cor. 15:4, where the concept is preserved in a living messianic tradition.

We could cite many other well-known passages to illustrate Hosea's imagery, such as "sowing the wind and reaping the whirlwind" (8:7), and the compulsion arising from shame and the fear of doom to

> say to the mountains, Cover us,
> and to the hills, Fall upon us (10:8),

and especially 13:14, quoted by Paul from the LXX in I Cor. 15:55:

> O death, where is thy victory?
> O death, where is thy sting?

How the Massoretic text should be rendered here is an open question. It would hardly be an exaggeration to say that no other prophet is Hosea's equal in the use of effective, expressive, and diversified figurative language. Unfortunately, the translations, to some extent, obscure the expressive, compressed, and living character of this prophet's language, and we say this in full cognizance of the unusually large number of difficulties to be found in the text of the Book of Hosea.

It may be said, certainly, that the Book of Joel is to be regarded as a homogeneous liturgy, whether we interpret it as a real cult liturgy (which is likely) or as a prophetic poem imitating a cult liturgy. In either case, a form-critical analysis shows that this work is a unit. The central theme is the "day of Yahweh." Therefore, it is very important, in studying the rôle of imagery in this book, to determine whether the visitations of grasshoppers which Joel describes are real or whether they are figures of speech for the doom to come on the day of Yahweh.[37] If we take the entire book into consideration, the latter view is certainly more reasonable. And this is by no means discredited by the fact that concrete and realistic language continually

---

37. See the translation of Engnell's article on "Joel" in *SBU*[2] to be found in A. S. Kapelrud, *Joel Studies* (Uppsala: Almqvist & Wiksell, 1948), pp. 193 ff.

alternates with figurative language in this book in the traditional way. Thus, Joel can speak of the swarms of grasshoppers as "a nation powerful and without number," with "lions' teeth" (1:6), as "warriors," "soldiers," and "thieves" (2:7 ff.). But he also uses other figures to describe the visitation, especially the figure of fire, a devouring fire (1:19; 2:3); he speaks of the day of doom as

> a day of darkness and gloom,
> a day of clouds and thick darkness (2:2);

in 3:3 f., he alludes to "portents in the heavens and on the earth, blood and fire and columns of smoke" and to how "the sun shall be turned to darkness, and the moon to blood"; and in 4:15, he tells how

> the sun and the moon are darkened,
> and the stars withdraw their shining,

a figure which later becomes standard in apocalyptic literature. In order to depict the doom which is about to come upon the people, Joel uses the figures of the scythe which passes over the ripened harvest and of the winepress which overflows with the "blood" of grapes, that is, of the enemies. He also compares Israel with a vine and a fig tree (1:7) which are laid waste, and thus exhorts the "virgin" Israel to lament "for the bridegroom of her youth" (1:8). On the other hand, he declares (4:18) that during the coming messianic age

> the mountains shall drip sweet wine,
> and the hills shall flow with milk.

On the whole, the imagery of Joel is strongly influenced by the Canaanite syncretistic cultic environment in which the prophet lived and which he undoubtedly opposed. There is a striking similarity between Joel and Hosea, at this point. This might indicate that these two prophets were contemporaries, although there is actually no reason why Joel could not have prophesied almost a hundred years earlier than Hosea.[38] However, there is an important difference be-

---

38. Engnell does not seem to maintain this early date for Joel elsewhere. In his article "Joels bok" (The Book of Joel), in *SBU*[2], he says ". . . it is certainly pre-exilic; so far as its contents are concerned it is timeless." (Cf. Kapelrud, *op. cit.*, p. 195.)

tween these two prophets: Hosea directs his oracles against the northern kingdom, while Joel directs his oracles against the southern kingdom. The fact that the figurative language in the Book of Joel is not particularly rich or diversified is due primarily to the *Sitz im Leben* and limited purpose of the Joel liturgy.

In Amos, we meet one of the foremost masters of words and figures in the Old Testament. This prophet had the unique ability to take over material which had been handed down to him in the tradition and to combine it skilfully and use it in his own message. This point is very important, because when we analyze Amos along with comparative material, we find that the prophet is not what he was formerly thought to be, that is, an individual creative master of language in the modern sense. Thus, the introductory oracle in 1:2, concerning Yahweh who roars from Zion, is obviously a *shāhid* verse— a verse quoted from a Jerusalemite cultic context, as is made clear by comparing it with Joel 4:16 and Jer. 25:30. The imagery in the series of oracles of doom against foreign nations in 1:3–2:3 is also strongly bound by traditional style, especially in the proclamations concerning the manner of punishment (1:4):

> So I will send a fire upon the house of Hazael,
> And it shall devour the strongholds of Ben-hadad

(Compare 1:10, 12, 14; Hos. 8:14; Jer. 49:27.) In spite of—or, rather, thanks to its rigid traditional style, this section of the book is very impressive, even from a purely linguistic point of view. After Amos begins his real theme, his proclamation of doom against North Israel (2:6), we find an oracle against the Amorites, who had been high as the cedars and strong as the oaks, but whose "fruit above and roots beneath" Yahweh had destroyed (2:9). The same figure occurs in the Old Testament in Job 18:16; but, as has already been pointed out, we now know of the existence of this metaphor very early in the Ras Shamra literature. Amos 3:3 ff. has sometimes been cited as typical proof that the prophet Amos had the ability to create his own figures:

> Does a lion roar in the forest,
> when he has no prey?
> Does a young lion cry out from his den,
> if he has taken nothing?

But in reality, there are striking ancient Near Eastern parallels to this figure in a collection of Nergal Hymns, first published in 1904.[39] Still, it is true that the way in which this tradition complex is put together is very impressive from the standpoint of imagery and is well suited to the purpose of the prophet: to show that Yahweh himself stands behind everything that takes place, that he reveals it to his prophets, and that, consequently, they are confronted with the inescapable, inspired compulsion to proclaim the divine message. Also, as is now generally recognized, the most poetic passages in Amos (4:13; 5:8; and 9:6), where Yahweh is described as the sovereign creator God, the sustainer, and the giver of fertility, are undoubtedly verses quoted from a Jerusalemite Annual Festival Psalm. On the other hand, as far as we can tell, the oracle of doom against the women of Samaria who are compared with cows of Bashan prepared for slaughter (4:1 ff.) is the prophet's own creation. This oracle is so drastic in Hebrew—which, to be sure, is hard to interpret—that a translation can only give a poor rendering of it. The prophet's famous *qînāh*, or lamentation, over the "virgin Israel" (5:1 f.) is actually only a brief allusion to a well-known motif which he uses as an introduction to the proclamation of doom against the northern kingdom in the verses that follow. The brief allegory in 5:19 reminds us of 3:4 f. It describes the "day of Yahweh" and its inescapable visitation under the figure of a man who

> fled from a lion,
> and a bear met him;
> or went into the house and leaned with his hand against the
>   wall,
> and a serpent bit him.

In other passages, the standard figure for the theme of the "day of Yahweh" is that of "darkness and not light" (5:18), which is undoubtedly an intentional reversal of the general concept and experience of joy at the Annual Festival. In line with this, 5:13 says that *hammaskîl* "must be silent in that day." Some versions render this: "Therefore the wise are silent at this time, for it is an evil time," but this points in an entirely wrong direction, because in this passage

---

39. J. Böllenrücher, *Gebete und Hymnen an Nergal* (Leipzig: J. C. Hinrichs, 1904).

Amos is thinking of a specific element in the ritual of the Annual Festival: the recitation of the psalm which is also called *maskil*.[40] Some translations have also given the concrete description of "those who are at ease in Zion, those who feel secure on the mountain of Samaria," that is, in Samaria (6:1–10), a profane character throughout, whereas, in reality, its character is sacral; or, more specifically, it has the character of the so-called Tammuz liturgy. The proclamation of doom which concludes this section of the book (6:11 ff.) begins in this typical way:

> Do horses run upon rocks?
> Does one plow the sea with oxen?
> But you have turned justice into poison
> And the fruit of righteousness into wormwood.

The last few words in this figure also occur in Hosea in a somewhat different form (10:4), and seem to be standard.

The visions of Amos concerning doom in the form of locusts, fire, the plumb line, and the sword in chapters 7–9 may serve as our point of departure in attempting to describe the mixture of concrete and figurative language in these chapters. This portion of the book contains powerful mythological features: on the "day of Yahweh," He will make "the sun go down at noon, and darken the earth in broad daylight" (8:9); then no one will be able to escape, neither they who "dig into Sheol" nor they who "climb up to heaven" nor they who "hide at the bottom of the sea," for Yahweh shall "command the serpent, and it shall bite them, and the sword and it shall slay them" (9:2 ff.). Here again the prophet uses standard figures: there are parallels to this not only in the Psalms (Ps. 139:8 ff.), but also in the Ras Shamra texts and in the Canaanite psalm fragments in the Amarna letters.[41] The very consistent and undoubtedly authentic conclusion of the Book of Amos (9:8 ff.) describes the judgment as a judgment of purification: figuratively, a sifting. This judgment will be followed by a restoration, depicted in a traditionally messianic way: when "the booth of David (that is, the kingdom of David) that is fallen" is restored,

---

40. Cf. chap. 5, "The Book of Psalms," Headings.

41. Amarna letter No. 244 II 15–19 (edited by Knudtzon); the Ras Shamra reference is not quite clear, possibly I AB II, 2; SS 62.

The plowman shall overtake the reaper
And the treader of grapes him who sows the seed;
The mountains shall drip sweet wine,
And all the hills shall flow with it.

This may be compared with Exod. 3:17; Joel 4:18; and especially one Ras Shamra text (I AB III: 16 f.). Seen against this concrete background, some have supposed that the statements in 8:11 are much too spiritualistic and therefore secondary:

"Behold, the days are coming," says the Lord God,
"When I will send a famine on the land;
Not a famine of bread, nor a thirst for water,
But of hearing the words of the Lord."

But this view is due entirely to an anachronistic spiritualization of the expression "word of Yahweh." Actually, this expression refers to revelations from Yahweh through the prophets in the form of oracles. By every right, Amos stands in this succession of prophets, even from the standpoint of his use of imagery.

The one chapter of the Book of Obadiah is a favorite object of literary criticism. A careful form-critical analysis indicates that this book actually is a uniform liturgy like the Book of Joel. This is completely confirmed by a linguistic analysis including the figurative language, which is uniform and almost entirely stereotyped throughout, as is shown by comparing it with relevant passages in the Psalms, Lamentations, Amos, Jeremiah (especially chapter 49), and Ezekiel. In the day of doom, the heathen nations, personified in the hereditary enemy, Edom, shall "drink and stagger and shall be as though they had not been" (v. 16), whereas "the house of Jacob shall be a fire, and the house of Joseph a flame" which consumes the house of Esau (Edom) which is as "stubble" (v. 18). This will be carried out by "saviors" going up on Mount Zion, and thus "the kingdom shall be the Lord's" (v. 21).

Sometimes the Book of Jonah is interpreted as a consistent allegory in which Nineveh is used as a disguised name for Jerusalem, but nothing could be more erroneous. To be sure, Jonah is a pseudonymous writing and, to a large extent, its author makes use of different types of ancient traditional material, such as popular legend motifs, the fish and the castor oil plant; but especially does he make use, in 2:3–10, of an original psalm of the Royal Passion Psalm type. The over-all purpose of the book is to oppose prevalent Jewish particularism and consciously to defend universalism, a doctrine unique here in the Old Testament. All the imagery in the book is concentrated in the psalm in chapter 2; it belongs to the traditional *descensus* type: the floods of Sheol encompass the speaker and he "sinks to the bottom of the mountains, and the bars of the (under) world close upon him forever"; here, the whole psalm changes into a traditional motif of trust, which is characteristic of the Royal Passion Psalms.

In his use of figurative language, Micah exhibits many characteristics which we find in other prophets, especially Hosea and Amos. This is to be expected, because they belong to approximately the same time period. Micah describes Israel's apostasy under the figure of a harlot. In 1:16, he uses these words in calling upon his hearers to mourn over the visitation:

> Make yourselves bald and cut off your hair,
> For the children of your delight;
> Make yourselves as bald as the eagle,
> For they shall go from you into exile.

This is one of the more expressive figures in Micah's oracles, which are usually harsh and rough and whose imagery is not very rich in nuances. Some stereotyped figures occur in the book, such as that of the pain and anguish of a woman in travail (4:9 f.), but most of the descriptions of doom and desolation are clearly written in realistic language: for example, in 3:12, it says that Zion shall be plowed as a field, Jerusalem shall become a heap of ruins, and the temple mountain a wooded height. And yet, we find in Micah a limited use of figurative language. Micah describes the doom which is to come upon the "false prophets" (3:6 f.) under the figure of night and darkness. Speaking of the existing destruction (7:5), the prophet recommends the expediency of silence in this way:

> Guard the doors of your mouth
> From her who lies in your bosom.

Jesus quotes v. 6, which has to do with the insubordination of a son to his father, in Matt. 10:35 f. and Lk. 12:53. But along with his concrete language, Micah shows great fondness for and proficiency in assonance and plays on words; compare, for example, the *qînāh* of the prophet over the cities and villages of Judah in 1:8–16. No translation can do justice to the original Hebrew of this passage. However, Micah uses imagery in his oracles of salvation in an entirely different way, which may suggest the rôle that positive preaching actually played in the prophet's message. As we would expect, these oracles also often contain stereotyped material. For example, the description of the future in 4:1–5 is obviously a variant of Isa. 2:2–4 and, yet, neither of these prophets borrowed from the other; but this is a *shāhid* verse which originally belonged to the cultic context of the Jerusalemite Annual Festival. However, the description of salvation in the future messianic kingdom in 4:4 is classical and captures the prophetic ideal in a nutshell:

> But they shall sit every man under his vine and under his
>   fig tree,
> And none shall make them afraid.

Also, the mysterious statement concerning the virgin-mother: "when she who shall bring forth has brought forth," which is found in the oracle concerning the Messiah from Bethlehem Ephrathah (5:1 ff.), is well known and important. In the verses which follow, Israel's future powerful position is described (5:7) under this figure: "the remnant of Jacob" shall be

> like a lion among the beasts of the forest,
> like a young lion among the flocks of sheep.

Finally, in 7:7–10, we find a typical "disintegrated" Royal Psalm of Trust, which, in v. 11, passes over to a tone which can almost be called eschatological.

The usual alternation between concrete and figurative language appears in the Book of Nahum, especially in the enemy motif which dominates its three chapters. The concrete language, which is also impressively poetic, is found in such passages as 2:3 ff. and 3:2 ff., while the imagery occurs in such passages as 1:8 ff. and the central portion of chapter 2 on the fall of Nineveh. For example, in 2:8 (Heb. 2:9), Nineveh is compared with a pool whose waters run away, and in 2:11 f. (2:12 f.) with a lion's den. In 3:4, we find the well-known figure of a harlot. The imagery in 3:12 is very expressive:

> All your fortresses are like fig trees with first-ripe figs—
> If shaken they fall into the mouth of the eater.

Finally, in 3:17, Nineveh's merchants, princes, and scribes are compared with grasshoppers which settle on the fences in a day of cold but fly away when the sun rises, a figure which means essentially the same thing as that of mice leaving a sinking ship.

In Habakkuk, we find the same alternation between concrete and figurative language, even in chapter 3, where the hymn and the prayer motif are combined and where the liturgy of the Book of Habakkuk reaches its climax. Sometimes the thought approaches the apocalyptic: the sun and moon stand still in their habitation, when Yahweh bestrides the earth in fury and tramples the nations in anger (3:11 f.).

Occasionally, Zephaniah also approaches the apocalyptic, as in this description of the "day of Yahweh" (1:15):

> A day of wrath is that day,
> A day of distress and anguish,
> A day of ruin and devastation,
> A day of darkness and gloom,
> A day of clouds and thick darkness.

In chapter 3, the prophet describes the situation in Jerusalem, "the rebellious and defiled city," in these words (3:3):

> Her officials within her are roaring lions;
> Her judges are evening wolves that leave nothing till the morning.

But he depicts the future which belongs to the preserved "remnant" in traditional messianic terms (3:16 ff.).

For all practical purposes, there is no imagery in the two chapters of the Book of Haggai at all, but figurative language does play a very prominent rôle in Zechariah. To a great extent, the dream symbolism in the "night visions" of this prophet is reminiscent of the Book of Daniel, and it also provides the immediate background for analogous portions of the Book of Revelation in the New Testament. As in Daniel, an angel explains to Zechariah the meaning of the visions of the four riders on different-colored horses (actually, the passage mentions only one rider and many horses), the four horns and the four smiths (chapter 1; 2:1 ff.), and the four chariots (chapter 6). In chapter 3, which is based on the motif of the "passion" of the sacral king, we encounter "the Accuser" (Satan), as in the Book of Job. This scene concludes with Yahweh's promises that he will send his "servant the Branch," who will inaugurate the messianic age, when everyone "will invite his neighbor under his vine and under his fig tree" (3:10; compare Mic. 4:4). In chapter 4, "the two anointed ones," Zerubbabel and the high priest Joshua, appear figuratively as two olive trees, a typical application of the ancient symbolism of the tree of life in a context which may still almost be characterized as royal. In 8:12, we have a description of the messianic future in traditional concrete language. In 9:9, which belongs to what is usually called "Deutero-Zechariah" (that is, chapters 9–14)—a very debatable designation[42]—the prophet exhorts the "daughter of Jerusalem" to rejoice greatly over the Messiah-king, who comes

> triumphant and victorious . . . ,
> humble and riding on an ass,
> on a colt the foal of an ass.

Jesus clearly intends to imitate this passage when he makes his entry into Jerusalem (Matt. 21:1 ff. with parallels). The imagery in chapters 9 ff. is richer than it is in the earlier chapters, but there is no typological or qualitative difference between the two parts of the book. The figures in chapters 9–14 are traditional; for example, in describing the fate of Israel's enemies, the prophet uses the figure of a devouring fire (9:3 f.), tree symbolism, the figure of the lion and the shepherds

---

42. Since Engnell did not write the article on the Book of Zechariah in SBU[2], there is no way of developing his view further. Cf. B. Otzen, *Studien über Deutero-Sacharija* (Copenhagen: Munksgaard, 1964).

(11:1 f.); and he says that Judah's princes (RSV, clans) are "like a blazing pot in the midst of wood, like a flaming torch among sheaves" (12:6). When he speaks of the doom to come upon the chosen people, he uses the figure of the sword and of fire which purifies metal (13:7 ff.). He describes the "day of Yahweh" as a day "when the light is gone, because the light of heaven is darkened," "when there is neither day nor night," "when at evening time there shall be light" (14:6 f.)—a typical apocalyptic description of chaos. Chapters 9–14 also use traditional imagery in hope oracles: Israel is Yahweh's flock (9:16) from which the "cornerstone," the Messiah, is to come (10:4). The opening words of 12:10 clearly recall Joel 2:28: "And I will pour out on the house of David and the inhabitants of Jerusalem a spirit of compassion and supplication." Furthermore, the ideas which appear in the verses following this are based on the royal passion motif and are connected with the figure of the "Servant of the Lord" and its ideology: they shall look on "him whom they have pierced," they shall mourn for him, as one mourns for an only child and weep bitterly over him, as one weeps over a first-born. The figurative language ends in chapter 14 with an allusion to the "water of life" (RSV, "living waters") which flows out of Jerusalem to the East and to the West, "in summer as in winter"; then "the Lord will become king over all the earth," then "the Lord will be one and his name one" (14:8 f.).

Finally, in the Book of Malachi, the last book of the Old Testament, Levi, the "ambassador of Yahweh of hosts"—that is, the Levites—and Yahweh's covenant with them, is the central theme. It is significant that we encounter several times, in this book, the idea that Yahweh is the father of all (compare 1:6; 2:10; 3:17), as this shows that we have now come a long way in the process of "disintegration" and "democratization."[43] In speaking of the Levites, the Book of Malachi uses the figure of refining metal (3:3). Last but not least, in connection with the concept of the "day of Yahweh," before which the prophet Elijah shall come (3:23), we encounter in this book what is perhaps the most beautiful and poetically expressive imagery in the entire Old Testament, in the description of the salvation of the righteous: "But for you who fear my name the sun of righteousness shall rise, with healing in its wings" (3:20). Here, we have an excellent example of

43. Cf. chap. 5, "The Book of Psalms."

how an idea rooted in the cult and in mythology grew into a purely religious and ideological concept, while retaining the original figure. The following verses are less poetic: "you shall go forth leaping like calves from the stall." Perhaps this is to be designated as characteristic, for, thus, in the last chapter of the Old Testament, we find the two types of imagery which stand side by side throughout the entire Old Testament: one which occurs in the best type of poetry and the other which draws on concrete, everyday language. Summarizing, we may say that our remarks at the beginning of this essay are confirmed by the character of the Old Testament material itself: the figurative language of the Old Testament is uniform and bound to tradition; but at the same time, it is enriched by the way in which individual writers used it and so has a peculiar uniqueness.

Index

Aaron, 125, 176, 194, 198, 204, 211, 235n
Abib. *See* Nisan
Abigail, 247
Abijam, 247
Abimelech, 78
Abiram, 212
Abital, 191n
Abner, 81
Abraham, 54n, 176, 197, 202, 225, 245
Accadian (Akkadian) literature, 9, 76, 84, 87, 88, 89n, 90–92 *passim*, 94, 106, 121n, 125, 155, 159, 181, 191, 192, 225, 226, 244
Acrostic. *See* Psalms, types of
Adam, 225
Aetiological material, 22, 189, 190
Agur, 260
Ahab, 131
Ahaz, 264
Ahijah, the prophet, 44, 131
Ahura Mazda, 20
Akītu Festival, 113n, 180n, 181, 182, 183n11, 183n12, 191
ᵃlāmôth. *See* Psalms, headings of
'al 'ayyéleth hashshạ́har. *See* Psalms, headings of
'al haggittîth. *See* Psalms, headings of
'al hashshᵉmînîth. *See* Psalms, headings of

Allah, 19, 20, 149
'al maḥᵃlath. *See* Psalms, cultic terms
'al mûth labbēn. *See* Psalms, headings of
'al ('el) shōshannîm ('ēdhûth). *See* Psalms, headings of
'al tashḥēth. *See* Psalms, headings of
'al yônath 'elîm rᵉḥōqîm. *See* Psalms, headings of
Amalek, 211, 226
Amarna letters, 111, 125, 155, 201, 202, 223, 283, 283n
Amaziah, king of Judah, 248
Amaziah, priest at Bethel, 132, 133
Amen-em-opet, Wisdom of, 260
Amorites, 82, 223, 272, 281
Amos, 44, 128, 132, 139, 147, 149, 152, 153, 160n, 162, 163, 170, 175, 176, 227, 277, 281–284, 285
Amphictyony. *See* Israelite religion
Amraphel, 202
Anath, 254
Animism. *See* Religion
Anthropomorphisms, 56
Anti-cultic psalms. *See* Psalms, types of
Antiochus IV Epiphanes, 109, 276
Apocalypticism, 29, 176, 216, 218, 222, 232, 233, 235, 238, 240, 243, 274, 275, 280, 287
Apocrypha, 218, 234, 235

291

Apokatastasis. *See* Life after death
Aqabah, Gulf of, 200
Aqhat, 82, 274n
Arabians, 38, 243
Arabic: language, 125, 126n, 167, 200, 212; literature, 165, 167, 168, 244; religion, 189
Aramaic language, 122, 126n, 237, 275
Aramaisms, 107, 110, 111
Araunah, 131
Ark, 89
Arnon river, 210
Artaxerxes III Ochus, 111
Artemis, 254n
Asa, 44
Asaph. *See* Psalms, authorship of
Ascents, Songs of. *See* Psalms, types of
Asherah, 126
Ashtoreth, 254
Assyria, 46, 144, 221, 264
Astarte, 254
'Atira festival, 189
Atonement, 46, 184, 186, 191n
Avaris, 202

Baal, 82, 88–89n, 126, 131, 173, 205n, 248, 267, 277
Baal Berith, 183
Baal-Melkart, 131
Baal-peor, 136
Baal-zephon, 204, 207
Babylon, 144, 164–165, 180n, 182, 190, 202, 221, 223, 230, 233, 250, 265
Balaam traditions, 63, 226, 245
Bāmāh (high place) cult. *See Canaanite* religion
Bamoth (place name), 210
Baptism, 206
Barbarossa myth, 218
Bar Cocheba, 236
Baruch, books of: First, 99; Second, 218, 235
—the man, 164, 168
Bashan, 87, 282
Bathsheba, 78
Beer (place name), 210
Ben-hadad, 281
Ben Sira, book of, 69, 99
Bethel, 40, 128, 132, 139
Bethlehem Ephrathah, 286
Biblical traditions, arrangement of: alternation, 70, 115n; association, 70
Bildad, 257
Binghînôth. *See* Psalms, headings of
Bitter Lakes, 200
Book of the Covenant, 65, 209

Caesar cult, 234
Canaan, 38, 40, 128, 136, 165, 183, 190, 198, 201, 202, 202n, 203, 277
Canaan, conquest of: nature of, 199–200, 203–204; date of, 201–203; mentioned, 110, 207. 208, 211, 214
Canaanite religion: official, 35; Bāmāh (high place) cult, 35, 44, 130n; popular, 35, 173; Yahwistic opposition to, 43–45, 137, 173, 178
Carmel, 265
Casuistic laws, 47
Chaos, and Cosmos, 22, 23, 36, 41, 93, 115n, 118, 138, 159, 159n, 167n, 180, 181, 182, 205, 205n, 211, 224n, 227, 252, 289
Chiaroscuro, 149
Chronicler, Chronicler's work, 10, 51, 69
Church fathers, 51, 114n
Circumcision, 46, 192
Community (Collective), and individual, 21–22, 31–33, 46–47, 84, 114, 115n, 117–118, 120, 152–155, 161–162, 270–271
Conversion, 45, 48, 113n, 130n, 158, 160, 170, 178, 270
Corporate personality. *See* Israelite religion
Cosmic mountain, 93, 93n
Cosmos. *See* Chaos
Court prophets. *See* Prophets, types of
Covenant, 38, 45, 60, 64, 80, 89, 106, 113, 120, 139, 140, 144, 160, 171, 174, 180, 183, 188, 198, 209, 231, 247n, 270, 273, 277, 289
Creation epic. *See* New Year festival
Cult: cultic acts or rituals, 22, 144, 198–199; cultic drama, 22, 93, 104, 118, 159n, 181, 193, 194, 208, 212, 213, 214, 264n; purpose of, 22, 94, 118; sacrifice in, 22–23, 46, 91, 112, 182, 188, 190, 193, 195, 235n; ritual sham battle in, 23, 36, 115–116n, 118, 181, 181n, 192, 192n, 203, 204n, 211; sacred marriage or *hieros gamos* in, 23, 36, 182, 191, 195, 252, 255; righteousness, 45, 137–140; official Israelite (royal), 94, 104, 108, 130n, 141–142, 145n, 161, 172–173, 195; cultic dance, 190, 193, 205, 248
—centralization of: in P work, 52, 57, 60; in D work, 52, 57, 174, 187, 188; and dating Pentateuchal sources, 57–58, 60; in prophetic

literature, 174
Cultic texts, and sacral acts, 73, 85, 182, 191, 193, 199, 205, 208
Culture hero, 21
Cush, 78
Cyrus. *See* Messiah

D circle, 59, 106
D work: North Israelite origin of, 58, 185–186, 248; anti-Canaanitism in, 61, 131; characteristics of, 61–62, 174, 179, 185–187; anti-royalism in, 62, 174, 217; date of, 62; and reactionary prophets, 62, 173–174, 179; and P work combined, 62–63; nationalism in, 174. *See also* David
Dan, 245
Dance, cultic. *See* Cult
Danel, or Daniel, 274n
Dathan, 212
David: in D work, 61–62; a title, 82; and Jebusite cult traditions, 131; mentioned, 36, 42n, 46, 62, 80–83 *passim*, 89, 91, 129, 216, 217, 221, 223, 225, 226, 227, 247, 253. *See also* Psalms, authorship of
David redivivus. See Messiah
Davidic dynasty: in P circle, 59–60; in prophetic literature, 161–162, 174, 274; mentioned, 107. *See also* Messianism
Day of Yahweh. *See* New Year festival
Dead, the: attitudes toward, 28; disposal of, 28; communion with, 28, 183
Dead Sea scrolls, 10
Death: avoidance of, 28; highest good, 28; myths concerning origin of, 28; and mourning customs and rituals, 28, 167n; caused by prophets, 145
Deborah, 134
Deborah, Song of, 43, 72, 97, 246
Decalogue, 39
Deculticization, 75, 99, 193, 213, 233, 234, 235. *See also* Psalms
Democratization. *See* Disintegration
Descensus ad inferos. See King, sacral
"Deutero-Isaiah", 42, 48, 107, 135, 140, 143, 143n, 144, 162, 170, 218, 225, 230–232 *passim*, 240, 265–266, 270
Deuteronomic history. *See* D work
Deuteronomist, The, 170, 174, 210
Deuteronomy. *See* D work
Dew, 190, 191n, 278
Diaspora, 107, 144, 188
Disintegration (or Democratization),

64, 85, 100, 104, 104n, 121, 145n, 150, 193, 205, 225, 235, 238, 250, 273, 275, 286, 289. *See also* Patternism
Dīwān. *See* Prophetic literature
Documentary hypothesis. *See* Pentateuch
Dōd, 83
Dura synagogue, 206n

E work, 52, 57, 59, 209
Ebal, Mount, 57, 246
Ecstasy: and the cult, 30; definition of, 30; and hallucination, 30; and revelation, 30, 148, 271; and shamanism, 30; and inspiration, 30–31, 123–124, 147–148, 152, 154–155, 159–160, 179; and mysticism, 31; and the prophets, 124–126 *passim*, 127n, 129, 130, 145–152, 271; prophetic means of inducing, 129–130
—types of: auditory, 30, 147, 148, 271; levitation, 30, 147, 271; motory, 30, 126; photism, 30, 147, 271; quietistic, 30, 126, 129; visionary or eidetic, 30, 147, 148, 149, 150, 271; mixed, 147
Edom, 210, 226, 248, 265, 284
Egypt, 64, 93, 93n, 123, 191, 192, 197, 199–202 *passim*, 204, 205n, 207, 211, 264, 268, 271
Egyptian literature, 121n, 199, 200, 202
Egyptian religion, 104, 123n, 126, 151n, 159, 233, 260
Egyptians, the, 38, 188, 197, 204, 208
El. *See* God, names of
El Elyon. *See* God, Yahweh
Elephantine papyri, 188
'el hann°ḥilôth. *See* Psalms, headings of
Eli, 134
Elijah, 44, 67, 126, 129, 132, 163, 194, 247, 289
Elim, 209
Eliphaz, 257, 258
Elisha, 44, 67, 132, 133, 145, 151, 163
Elohim. *See* God, names of
El-Shaddai. *See* God, names of
Enemies (and adversity): in the Psalms, 84, 103, 107, 109, 110, 115–119, 122, 249–252 *passim*, 259; in the cult, 145, 151n, 191, 192, 204, 205, 211, 214, 224, 226, 255, 263, 264n, 265, 280, 284, 286, 288; animal symbolism for, 251–252
Enoch, books of, 218, 235, 236, 238–240 *passim*

Enthronement festival. *See* Israelite festivals; King, sacral; New Year festival

Enthronement psalms. *See* Psalms, types of

Enūma eliš, 182

Ephesus, 254n

Ephraim, 87, 274, 277

Eschatological psalms. *See* Psalms, types of

Eschatology, 29, 46, 115–116n, 122, 286. *See also* Messianism

IV Esdras, 219, 235, 236, 238, 240

Etham, 204, 207

Ethan. *See* Psalms, authorship of

Ethics. *See* Prophets, reactionary

Euphrates river, 271

Evil-merodach, 62

Evolution of thought. *See* Religion

Exile, the: and Israelite exclusivism, 45–46; mentioned, 151, 177

Exodus from Egypt: and Passover, 186, 188–189, 198, 206, 207–208; historicity of, 197–203 *passim*, 205–206, 208; in D work, 198–199; in prophetic literature, 198–199; in the Psalms, 198–199; in P work, 199: in the cult, 199, 203–206, 207–208, 212n; geographical problems of, 199–200, 208; date of, 200–203; and the Ten Plagues, 203–204, 204n, 206; intinerary of, 204–205. *See also* Passover

Exodus Hymn, 72, 198, 205, 208, 245

Ezekiel: founder of Judaism, 46, 47, 217; mentioned, 107, 141, 142, 147, 148, 150–152 *passim*, 162, 165, 175, 229, 271–274

Ezra: and post-Exilic Judaism, 47, 50, 53, 61; and authorship of Pentateuch, 50

Fixing of destiny, 36, 42, 180, 182, 197, 230

Forgiveness, 157, 233

Form-criticism, 63, 65. *See also* Traditio-historical method

Gad, 129, 131

Gera, 78n

Gerizim, Mount, 57, 195, 246

Gibeah, 128

Gideon, 43, 134, 246

Gilead, 87, 140, 253

Gilgal, 128, 132

Gnosticism, 21, 29, 31, 222, 240

God, High: primitive belief in, 5, 18, 36–38, 39–40, 143–144; war god, 18; god of fate, 18, 40, 49, 80; characteristics of, 18–20 *passim*, 37–38, 139, 171; giver of fertility, 18–20 *passim*, 38, 39, 83, 87, 167n, 249n, 277, 282; youthful god, 18–20 *passim*; resting god or *Deus otiosus*, 19, 38; hypostatization of, 21; death and resurrection of, 23, 167n, 190, 251n
—names of: El, 20, 20n, 36, 37; El of the fathers, 20, 37–38, 144; El-Shadday, 37, 52; Peace, 40; Righteousness, 40, 140; Elohim, 56, 71, 71n
—Yahweh: creator, 16, 18, 40, 79–80, 113, 282; and El Elyon, 16–18 *passim*, 19n, 36, 40, 40n, 44, 49, 140, 144, 171, 172, 174, 212n; god of judgment, 38, 40, 45, 48, 144, 144n, 154, 224n, 239, 266, 277; national diety, 39, 45, 56, 108–109, 144; and Israel, 45, 79–80, 118, 120, 144, 153, 171, 180, 194; god of salvation, 45, 118, 120, 218, 269; controller of history, 46, 109, 112, 162, 282, 289; omnipotent, 49, 118, 144, 162, 173, 231, 232–233; king, 105–106, 183n; and sacrifice, 113; and Kenite hypothesis, 203

Godly, the, 119, 120, 231, 240

Gog, 272

Golden calf, 66, 136

Golénisheff papyrus, 126n

Gomer, 141n, 277n

Greek literature, 9, 189

Gudea, 274

Habiru, 201, 202

Hadad, 89

Hades. *See* Sheol

Haggadah, 206

Hallel. *See* Psalms, types of

Hallucination. *See* Ecstasy

Hammurabi: code of, 191n; the man, 202

Hannah, Song of, 72

Haphtārôth, 279

Hasidim. *See* Pharisees

Hazael, 281

Hazeroth, 210, 211

Hebron, 59

Heman. *See* Psalms, authorship of

Henotheism or Monolatry. *See* Religion

Hermon, Mount, 98

Herod the Great, 218

Hezekiah, 44, 187, 260

—Psalm of, 72, 97, 265
Hieros gamos. See Cult
Higgāyôn. *See* Psalms, headings of
High god. *See* God, High
Hinnom, Valley of, 271
Hittites, 272
Holiness Code, 53, 56
Holofernes, *See* Orofernes
Holy of holies, 235*n*
Hor, Mount, 210
Horeb. *See* Sinai
Hosea, 44, 136, 140, 141*n*, 147, 151,
  152, 162, 175, 228, 267, 276, 279,
  283, 285
Huldah, 57
Hurriya, 254
Hymns. *See* Psalms, types of

"I". *See* Prophetical literature; Psalms,
  Book of
Idolatry, 144–145
Immanuel, 151, 228, 264*n*
Inanna and Shukalletuda, Myth of, 204*n*
Individual. *See* Community
  (Collective); Prophetism, Yahwistic
Inspiration. *See* Ecstasy
Intercessors. *See* Prophets
Iranian and Persian religions, 29
Isaac, 202, 245
Isaiah, 45, 140, 141, 150–152 *passim*,
  160*n* 162, 175, 228, 264–266
Ishmael, 245
Ishtar, 88*n*
Isogloss argument. *See* Pentateuch
Israel: election of, 45, 60, 64, 160, 171,
  174, 197, 198, 206, 273, 277, 289; in
  D work, 61; in Egyptian bondage,
  198; mentioned, 114, 117, 119, 121,
  122, 153, 172, 180, 182, 185, 187,
  189, 200, 202*n*, 205, 206, 211, 213,
  226, 230, 233, 239, 240, 248, 267,
  269, 270, 272, 274, 278, 280, 282,
  285, 286, 289. *See also* God, Yahweh;
  Messiah
Israelite festivals: Sukkôth (Feast of
  Booths), 36, 181, 184, 185, 186, 195,
  196; day of Atonement, 41, 184, 195,
  235*n*; feast of Harvest or Fertility,
  92, 182, 184; enthronement, 183,
  183*n*; feast of Unleavened Bread,
  183, 186–189 *passim*, 193, 198, 204.
  See also New Year festival; Passover
—religion: and the amphictyony, 13,
  19, 38, 144; and ancient Near Eastern
  religions, 13, 144, 155, 162–166
  passim, 172–173, 199, 215, 219–223

passim, 261*n*, 274, 282; primitive
  monotheism, 17, 39, 143; and
  corporate personality, 20, 41, 120,
  161; and pantheism, 21; and
  Canaanite religion, 35, 36, 39, 48,
  51, 94, 109–111 *passim*, 126, 127,
  133, 135, 140, 155, 165, 184, 186,
  187, 215, 218, 223, 280, 281; tribal,
  37; and pre-Israelite or desert
  religion, 37, 40, 43, 48, 64, 66, 81*n*,
  134–137, 139, 165, 189, 194, 214,
  221, 223; post-Exilic exclusivism, 45;
  and retribution, 48; and Hellenism,
  49; skepticism in, 49; fertility motif
  in, 119; and the Jerusalemite-
  Deuteronomistic line, 171–174. *See
  also* Canaanite religion
Issachar, 245
Iye-abarim, 210

J work, 52, 57, 59, 209
Jaazaniah, 272
Jacob, 79, 87, 174, 197, 202, 231, 245,
  284, 286
—Blessing of, 226, 245
Jebusites, 82, 131, 223
Jeduthun. *See* Psalms, authorship of
Jehoash of Israel, 248
Jehoiachin, 62
Jehoshaphat, 129, 131
Jehu, king of Israel, 43, 223
Jephthah's daughter, 88*n*
Jeremiah, 47, 138, 140, 141, 150–152
  passim, 162, 164, 168, 174, 175, 229,
  255, 267–271
Jericho, 132, 201, 202, 210
Jerusalem, 36, 40*n*, 45, 52, 53, 57–62
  passim, 70–75 *passim*, 80–83 *passim*,
  89, 107, 109, 133, 138, 140, 141,
  141*n*, 144, 151, 163, 171–174 *passim*,
  187, 194, 223, 233, 247, 255, 267,
  270–273 *passim*, 281–289 *passim*
Jesse, 71, 263
Jesus, 20, 42, 48, 51, 121, 122, 178,
  218, 234–237 *passim*, 240, 241, 286,
  288
Jethro (Reuel), 198, 202
Jezreel, 151, 277
Joash, 223
Job, book of, 48, 69, 255, 256–259
Joel, 141, 162, 279–281, 284
John the Baptist, 178
John Hyrcanus I, 235
Jonah, 284–285
Jonathan, 81, 91
Jordan river, 210

Joseph, 64, 79, 87, 197, 203, 245, 275, 284

Josephus, 51, 194, 218, 235

Joshua, the high-priest, 288

—successor of Moses, 191n, 198, 202, 225

Josiah, 44, 52, 57, 187

—reform of. *See* Passover

Jotham's fable, 246, 248

Jubilees, Book of, 188, 218

Judah, 111, 153, 187, 201, 203, 245, 267–268, 270, 273, 274, 286, 289

Judges, the, 42n, 66, 187

Judith, Book of, 111, 234

Kadesh, 59, 64, 209, 210

Kaiwan, 136, 139

Kalamu inscription, 223

Kenites, 38

Keret text, 82, 204, 254

Kibroth-hattaavah, 210, 211

King, sacral: in Israel, vii, viii, 5, 20, 21, 26, 36, 41–46 *passim*, 59, 83, 85, 89, 104, 183; divine, 20, 41, 106, 221, 223, 228, 261n, 272, 274; in ancient Near East, 23, 36, 41, 44, 104, 109, 182, 183; passion, death (*descensus ad inferos*), and resurrection of, 35–36, 40–42 *passim*, 48, 91, 92, 105, 113, 119–122 *passim*, 181–182, 183n, 195, 223, 230–231, 231n, 234, 250, 265–266, 274n, 275, 278, 288, 289; enthronement of, 36, 182, 183, 230; as expiation for sin, 41, 46, 89, 105, 222, 223, 230; son of God, 41, 92, 261; and victory over chaos and enemies, 41, 95, 118, 120, 182, 222, 225, 227, 240; servant of Yahweh, 41, 105, 222, 230, 235, 266; responsibilities of, 41, 105, 150, 278; savior, 41, 108, 174, 204, 222, 223, 224, 234, 235; lawgiver and judge, 41, 223, 228, 235, 239, 240, 266; and the prophets, 62, 131, 138, 141, 145, 150, 153, 161–164 *passim*, 172–173; and the Psalms, 82–83, 85, 100, 104, 225, 250; Yahweh's anointed, 109, 115n, 216, 223, 231, 235, 256; as mediator, 115: representative of Israel, 115, 162n, 180; representative of Yahweh, 115n, 216; in the Passover, 186, 187, 191, 193; and Moses, 191, 191n, 194, 204, 211, 225; as priest, 217, 223, 235; and universalism, 218, 231, 232, 234, 236, 239; and Abraham, 225;

and Adam, 225; and Joshua, 225; and the son of man, 238; pre-existence of, 261n, 272; as shepherd, 268, 270, 273. *See also* Messiah; Son of man

Kingu, 192

Kish, 78n

Korah, the priest, 66, 212

—Sons of. *See* Psalms, authorship of

Lachish, 201

Laments. *See* Psalms, types of

Lamnaṣṣēaḥ. *See* Psalms, headings of

Leah tribes, 201, 202, 202n, 203

Lᵉʿannôth. *See* Psalms, cultic terms in

Lebanon, 248, 265, 278

Lᵉhazkîr. *See* Psalms, cultic terms in

Lᵉlammēdh. *See* Psalms, headings of

Lᵉthôdhāh. *See* Psalms, cultic terms in

Levi, 203, 289

Levitation. *See* Ecstasy, types of

Levites, 187, 198, 274, 289. *See also* Psalms, authorship of

Lidhûthûn. *See* Psalms, headings of

Life after death: views of, 28–29, 191n; apokatastasis, 29; the second death, 29; transmigration of souls and reincarnation, 29

Literary criticism. *See* Traditio-historical method

Liturgy. *See* Prophetic literature; Psalms, types of

Lo-ammi, 151, 277

Logos, 261

Lord's Supper, 206

Lo-ruhamah, 151, 277

Maccabean age, 97, 105, 107, 218, 236

Maccabees, Books of, 68, 235

Magic. *See* Religion

Maher-shalal-hash-baz, 151, 164

Malachi, 177, 289

Man, views of, 27, 179

Mana, 15

Manasseh, 87

    —Prayer of, 99

Man of God. *See* Prophet, definition of

Marah, 211

Mari, 81, 82

Maśkîl. *See* Psalms, types of

Massah, 211

Maṣṣôth. *See* Passover

Matriarchy. *See* Religion, sociology of

Mattanah, 210

Mediterranean Sea, 200

Meribah, 211

Merneptah, Pharaoh, 203

    —stele, 201, 202, 228

Mesopotamian religions, 104
Messiah: servant of Yahweh, 42, 46, 48, 122, 217, 221, 227, 230–232 *passim*, 235–236, 238, 251, 275, 289; cultic, 42, 108, 118, 161, 195, 220–223 *passim*, 227, 233–235 *passim*, 238, 240; transcendent, 46, 233–235 *passim*, 238; and sacral king, 140, 161–162, 173, 174, 204, 215–236 *passim*, 238–240 *passim*, 263n, 288; savior, 162, 171, 216, 217, 223, 228–235 *passim*, 239; spiritualization of, 162, 176; son of God, 162, 227, 235, 238; and Moses, 191, 204, 225; and Israel, 216; and the Patriarchs, 216; and Cyrus, 216, 231; and the high priest, 216, 235; *David redivivus*, 218, 224, 229, 235; personal, 218, 228, 230, 239; and Primal Man (*Urmensch*), 220, 222, 238; and nationalism, 222, 226–236 *passim*, 239–241 *passim;* and the son of man, 222, 227, 232, 234, 237–240 *passim;* and the star, 226, 226n; son of the handmaid, 227, 238; a child, 228, 264n, 286; in Judaism, 232, 234–236, 238. *See also* King, sacral; New Year festival
Messianic oracles, authenticity of, 45–46, 155–162, 215–218, 229, 232, 262
Messianism: and sacral king, viii, 35, 36, 42–46 *passim*, 122n, 161n, 161–162, 174, 235; eschatological, 42, 105, 122, 161n, 162, 176, 216, 220–226 *passim*, 231–234 *passim*, 238–241 *passim*, 250, 264, 274, 286; in the prophetic literature, 42, 108, 132, 136, 140, 145n, 155, 157–162, 173–175 *passim*, 217, 224–232 *passim;* and the Davidic dynasty, 42, 161–162, 174, 217, 221, 223–235 *passim*, 270, 273–274, 283, 289; origin of, 42, 219–220, 223, 241; and the remnant, 45, 108, 120n, 154, 160, 160n, 224, 224n, 227, 287; in the Psalms, 86, 105, 106, 118, 119, 120n, 235; in the New Testament, 178, 215, 232–233, 236, 240, 241; in the post-Exilic period, 216, 217, 235; in the Pentateuch, 226. *See also* King, sacral; Son of man
Meter. *See* Textual emendations
Micah, 128, 150, 175, 229, 285
Micaiah, 43, 131
Midian, 198, 202

Midianites, 38, 246
Midrash, 78, 107
Mikhtām. *See* Psalms, types of
Miriam, 205, 211
Mishna (or Mishnah), 9, 47, 74, 76
Mizmôr. *See* Psalms, headings of
Moab, 210, 226, 271
Modern anachronistic view of the Old Testament, 137–141 *passim*, 146, 155, 159–160, 163, 172, 240, 251, 262, 284
Mohammed, 20, 264
Monotheism. *See* Israelite religion; Religion
Mosaic religion, 34, 36–40 *passim*, 44, 143–144, 173
Moses: in P work, 60, 60n, 210; in D work, 61, 63, 208, 210, 245–246; and prophetic religion, 135; intercessor for Israel, 191n, 211; mentioned, 19, 38, 50, 60, 63–65 *passim*, 176, 188, 198, 202–205 *passim*, 210–212 *passim*. *See also* King, sacral; Messiah; Psalms, authorship of
Môt, the god, 92
Mustamli, 168,
Mysticism: sufism, 31; types of, 31; the *unio mystica*, 31, 175. *See also* Ecstasy
Myth, 5, 22, 185

Nabal, 247
Nabis. *See* Prophets, types of
Nahaliel, 210
Nahum, 141, 286
Naphtali, 87
Nathan, 129, 131, 247
Nationalism. *See* D work; Messiah; Prophetic preaching; Psalms
Nebuchadrezzar (or Nebuchadnezzar), 231
Nehemiah, 47, 53, 61
Nehushtan, 191n
Nergal hymns, 282
New Year festival: and the creation epic, 18, 22, 23, 144, 145, 180, 182, 205, 227; in the ancient Near East, 26, 145n, 180–184 *passim*; and the Enthronement festival, 36, 41, 89, 90, 90n, 92, 93, 95, 105–106, 144n; the messiah in, 106, 108, 221, 231n; and the day of Yahweh, 108, 219, 224, 279, 282, 287, 289; and the sacrificial (communal) meal, 183, 189, 190, 194, 204; and passover, 191, 194; mentioned, 110, 113, 113n, 115–116, 118, 119, 159n, 160, 205,

240n, 264n, 282, 286
Nineveh, 284, 287
Nisan (or Abib), 186, 191

Obadiah, 284
Obed-edom, 89
Oboth, 210
Oholah, 273
Oholibah, 273
Oral tradition: and *Sitz im Leben,* 6–8 *passim;* and fixation of Old Testament traditions, 6, 9, 65, 70, 73, 74, 168, 169, 179; reliability of, 7, 8, 66, 168–169, 179; mentioned, viii. *See also* Traditio-historical method
Orofernes (or Holofernes), 111

P circle, 26, 52, 58, 59, 66, 67, 174–175, 185–186
P code, 109
P work: anti-Canaanite tendency of, 61; date of, 61; and D work combined, 62–63; genealogies in, 66; and the Patriarchs, 174; mentioned, 7, 11, 52, 53, 56–61 *passim,* 63, 66
Panammu inscription, 223
Pantheism. *See* Israelite religion
Parallelism. *See* Textual emendations
Paran, wilderness of, 210, 211
Paronomasia, 149
Passover: in the ancient Near East, 26; and Josiah's reform, 58, 187; in P work, 185–188 *passim,* 194, 203, 208; observance of, 186; in D work, 186–188 *passim;* in the Chronicler's work, 187; historicity of, 189–193 *passim;* cultic interpretation of, 189–193, 203–207 *passim,* 213; Samaritan, 195; mentioned, 36. *See also* Exodus from Egypt; King, sacral; New Year festival
—festival: in the post-Exilic period, 186; and the feast of unleavened bread, 192–195 *passim,* 198, 204, 208; origin of, 192–193, 203; and the wilderness wandering, 213; mentioned, 110, 183, 189, 194
—legend: in P work (Exod. 1–15), 60, 64, 188, 193, 203, 206–208 *passim,* 211, 245; historical development of, 194
Patriarchal religion, 143
Patriarchs: and Israel, 162n; in the prophets, 174–175; in P work, 175; mentioned, 197. *See also* Messiah
Patternism: myth-and-ritual, viii, 5,

22–24; elements in cultic pattern, 23, 36–37; common cultic pattern, 23–25 *passim,* 36, 182, 184, 222, 234, 254; diffusion theory, 24; opposition to a single pattern, 24–25, 33–34, 182; disintegration and reintegration, 25, 25n; comparative method, 25, 26, 182, 184
Pax israelitica, 231
Peace. *See* God, names of
Pelatiah, 272
Pentateuch: Mosaic authorship of, 50–51, 61; and humanism, 51; divine names in, 51, 52, 55, 56; documentary hypothesis, 51–55 *passim,* 59; and Hebrew syntax, 54; and the "isogloss" argument, 55; and the division of the Book of Psalms, 71. *See also* D work; E work; J work; P work
Persian language and culture, 167, 234, 241. *See also* Iranian and Persian religions
Pesaḥ. *See* Passover
Peshitta, 76, 86
Pharaoh of the Exodus, 191–192, 197, 198
Pharisees (Ḥasidim), 47, 48, 116, 119n, 120
Philistines, land of, 198
Philo, 51, 194, 218
Philology. *See* Textual emendations
Photism. *See* Ecstasy, types of
Pi-ha-hiroth, 204, 207
Pisgah, Mount, 210
Pithom (Tell el-Mashuta), 197, 201
Plagues, the ten. *See* Exodus from Egypt
Polydemonism. *See* Religion
Polytheism. *See* Religion
Priest. *See* King, sacral; Prophet, cult
Primal man (*Urmensch*): mediator, 21; redeemer, 29; and the son of man, 237–240 *passim. See also* Messiah
Prophet, definition of: man of God, 43, 131, 134; inspirational, 123, 126; institutional, 123, 126, 129; foreteller, 124–125, 154; forth-teller, 125, 154
Prophetic: books: nature of, 45, 153, 157–158, 166–168, 262, 266; growth of, 157–158, 164, 167–168, 179, 262, 266; canonization of, 179
—literature: "I" in, 149; liturgy type, 166–167, 175, 179, 230, 262, 264, 279, 281, 283, 287; dīwān type, 166–168, 262, 263, 266

—master, 126, 128, 145, 153, 157, 159, 166, 168, 169

—oracles, arrangement of: alternation, 156–159 *passim*, 167, 168, 262; association, 158, 167–168, 262; catchword, 158; chronological similarities, 168; similarities of situations or audiences, 168; similarities of content, 168, 262; similarities of introductory formulae, 168, 262

—oracles, dating of: oracles of salvation, 127, 129, 155–160 *passim*, 178; difficulties involved in, 149, 169

—preaching: main themes of, 45–46; and nationalism, 109, 109n, 132, 156, 162, 174, 176; and monotheism, 143; and idolatry, 144–145, 267

—schools or guilds (sons of the prophets), 43, 26–133 *passim*, 153

Prophetism: in the ancient Near East, 43, 134; and later Judaism, 45, 176; primitive, 125–129 *passim*, 145, 176; reactionary- or doom-prophetism, 127–134 *passim*, 142, 154–160 *passim*, 164, 177, 178, 217, 229; development of, 176–177, 218; decay of, 178

—Yahwistic: and Mosaic religion, 44, 135, 172; diversification of, 134, 138, 162, 171–172; Bedouin character of, 135–136, 178; and individualism, 152–155, 270–271; literary character of, 163–169; and fulfilment of prophecy, 169–170; and Israel's God, 171, 233. *See also* Messianism; Universalism

Prophets: of Baal, 126, 248; calls of, 129, 130n, 133, 141, 150; and the divine word, 129, 146, 149, 150, 163–164; disciples of, 141, 143n, 153, 157–159 *passim*, 160n, 164, 166, 168, 169, 172, 176, 179; Yahweh's instruments, 145; and the Spirit, 146, 178; symbolic acts of, 150–151, 164, 165, 262, 271, 274, 277; intercessors, 154; and traditional material, 155, 172, 262, 266, 271–275 *passim*, 279, 281, 285. *See also* Ecstasy; King, sacral; Psalms; Universalism

—cult: and priest, 123–124, 142; mentioned, 95, 108, 108n, 126–128 *passim*, 134, 141, 142

—reactionary: and North Israelite cults, 44, 139, 140, 141n, 175; and the D work, 62, 170–171, 179; anti-cultic statements in, 128, 138–142 *passim*;

and the wilderness line, 134–137; and the cult, 138–142, 152, 153, 159, 160, 165, 166, 172, 176, 179, 262–267 *passim*, 273, 279, 281, 286; and ethics, 138–144 *passim*, 154, 160n, 162n, 175, 178, 218, 234; and foreign cults, 139, 173; and cults of wicked men, 140; response of people to, 140, 142, 153–154; and the Patriarchs, 174–175. *See also* King, sacral; Sacrifice

—types of: nabis, 43, 125–133 *passim*, 141, 141n, 142, 145, 151, 155; seers, 43, 126, 133, 152; visionaries, 43, 126; court prophets, 127, 129, 131, 134, 161; transitional figures, 130–132, 145, 163, 177; false, 150, 156, 161, 162, 170, 176, 272, 285

Psalms: cultic setting of, 69–76 *passim*, 80–82 *passim*, 87, 88, 91–103 *passim*, 107–109 *passim*, 110n, 112–115 *passim*, 118, 119, 244, 248, 250–251; outside the Book of Psalms, 72; origin of, 73, 75–76, 104; deculticization of, 75, 99; historical setting of, 77, 78, 81, 96–97, 119; and guilds of singers, 80, 112; classification of, 94; structure of, 94–95; and wisdom circles, 100; and prophetic circles, 100, 102, 106–109 *passim*, 112, 114; nationalism in, 108–109, 118, 119; and Jeremiah, 269. *See also* Traditio–historical method; Universalism

—approaches to: historical, 96–98, 107, 111, 112, 119; aestheticizing, 98; didactic, 98–99, 100; spiritualistic, 98, 101, 112, 116, 118n; royal-sacral, 104, 122; figurative, 118, 118n

—authorship of: David, 68, 71, 74, 78, 80–82 *passim*, 85, 86; Asaph, 71, 74, 79, 80, 87, 110n; sons of Korah, 71, 72, 74, 78, 80, 82, 87; Jeduthun, 74, 78, 90; Ethan, 74, 79, 80; Levites, 74, 80; Heman, 79, 80; Moses, 79, 80; Solomon, 79, 80, 250

—Book of: arrangement of, 70; division of, 70–71; doxologies in, 71; duplicates in, 71; the Elohim psalter, 71–72; and traditionist circles, 74, 99; final redaction of, 75; "I" in, 114–120 *passim*

—canonization of: and the Chronicler's work, 69; date of, 69, 72, 101, 104–108 *passim*, 111; and ben Sira, 69,

99; and oral tradition, 70; and the Jerusalem temple, 72, 80, 85–87 *passim*
—cultic terms in: 'al maḥ°lath, 90; l°°annôth, 90; l°hazkîr, 90; l°thôdhāh, 90
—date of: criteria for determining, 106–114, 119; post-Exilic dating, 109–112 *passim*, 117, 119
—headings of: primary, 77; secondary, 77–78, 81, 83, 85; musical terms, 77, 87, 92; lamnaṣṣēaḥ, 79, 86; sh°mînîth, 86; °ªlāmôth, 86, 88, 88–89n, 92; 'al ('el) shōshannîm ('ēdhûth), 87; binghînôth, 87; 'el hann°ḥîlôth, 87; higgāyôn, 87; 'al haggittîth, 88; 'al hashsh°mînîth, 88; mizmôr, 88; shîr, 88; l°lammēdh, 90; lidhûthûn or 'al y°dhûthûn, 90; 'al 'ayyéleth hashshâḥar, 91; 'al yônath 'ēlîm r°ḥôqîm, 91; 'al mûth labbēn, 92; 'al tashḥēth, 92
—origin of: in North Israel, 79, 80, 83, 86, 110, 278; in royal cult, 104, 108; in post-Exilic period, 106–107, 110, 111
—types of: royal passion, 48, 92, 119, 122, 227, 230, 285; laments, 70, 80, 87, 89, 91, 95, 96, 101, 107, 110, 113, 116, 118, 122, 227, 255, 265, 269; hymns, 70, 89, 95, 96, 101, 107, 269; Hallel, 71; songs of ascents, 71, 72, 88, 92, 93; wisdom, 76, 99–101 *passim*; royal, 82–86 *passim*, 95, 96, 101, 104, 105, 113, 118, 122, 227, 251, 259, 265, 286; maśkîl, 89, 89n, 90n, 282; mikhtām, 89; prayers, 89; shiggāyôn, 89; enthronement, 89, 95, 96, 101, 105n, 183; penitential, 90, 95, 110, 113, 227; liturgical, 94, 95, 101, 108, 115n, 121; hymns of Zion, 95; royal protective, 95, 96; thanksgiving, 95, 96, 101, 112, 227; innocence, 95, 227; anti-cultic, 99, 101, 106, 112–114 *passim*; acrostics, 100; torah-liturgy, 100, 101; mixed, 101; psalms of blessing and curse, 101; psalms of entrance, 101; non-cultic, 101; reflective lyrics, 101; imprisonment, 117n; prayers of the accused, 117n; psalms for special occasions, 118n; eschatological or messianic, 225–226; psalms of refuge, 227
Psalms Scroll at Qumran, 69n
Puah, 204
Purim festival, 78n

Qînāh, 282, 286
Qumran, 69, 69n

Raamses, 197, 198, 202, 204, 207
Rabbinic thought, 170, 191–194 *passim*, 219
Ramah, 128
Ramses II, king, 201
Ras Shamra. *See* Ugaritic literature
Rechabites, 43, 136, 173
Reeds, Sea of (Red Sea), 191n, 198, 200, 205, 208, 209
Rehoboam, 248
Religion: origins of, 14; animism, 14–16 *passim*, 19; evolutionistic approach to, 14–16 *passim*, 19, 25, 32–33, 56, 95, 106–107, 112, 114, 126–128, 130, 132, 143, 146, 151, 152, 157–158, 163, 172, 175, 176; holiness, 15; magic, 15–16, 100, 117, 118, 122, 150, 164, 189, 204, 246, 251, 258, 264n; polydemonism, 16; henotheism or monolatry, 16, 18, 143; polytheism, 16, 18, 143; monotheism, 16–18 *passim*, 142–145. *See also* Cult
—sociology of: task of, 32; interest fellowship, 32, 32n; life fellowship, 32, 32n; matriarchy, 32, 33; totemism, 32, 33; primitive mentality, 33
Remnant. *See* Messianism
Repentance, 153n, 270
Rephidim, 209, 211
Resting god or *Deus otiosus*. *See* God, High
Resurrection, 26–27, 145
Reuben, 203, 245
Reuel. *See* Jethro
Revelation. *See* Ecstasy
Righteousness: and the cult (the ṣ°dhāqāh table), 45, 100, 113, 120, 138, 160n, 180, 223, 225, 229, 233, 276; and salvation, 122n. *See also* God, names of
Rite of passage (Rite de passage). *See* Wilderness wandering
Ritual sham battle. *See* Cult
Rome, 123
Royal psalms. *See* Psalms, types of

Sabbath, 46, 181
Sacral acts. *See* Cultic texts
Sacral king. *See* King, sacral
Sacrifice: aspects of, 22–23; expiatory- or trespass-offering, 92; not needed by Yahweh, 113; thank-offering, 114; prophetic attitude toward, 129, 139,

143; sin-offering, 186. *See also* Cult
Sacrificial (communal) meal. *See* New Year festival
Sadducees, 116, 120
Sakkuth, 136, 139
Salvation, 27, 122, 122n, 158–160 *passim,* 179, 197, 206, 214, 224, 231, 289
Samaria, 52, 128–129, 273, 282
Samaritans, 53, 195
Samson, 246
Samuel, the man, 130, 130n, 177, 187, 198
Ṣaphon, 205n
Satan, 288
Saul, 42n, 78, 81, 91, 129, 223, 226, 247
Savior. *See* King, sacral; Messiah
Scapegoat rite, 235n
Seba, 81n
Ṣᵉdhāqāh table. *See* Righteousness
Seers. *See* Prophets, types of
Selah, 88
Semitic languages, 243
Septuagint (LXX), 55, 68, 70, 76, 81, 86–89 *passim,* 91n, 97, 98, 114n, 199, 209, 227, 238, 279
Serapeum, 200
Servant of Yahweh: Moses as, 60n, 191; in "Deutero-Isaiah", 89n, 90n, 218, 221, 230–232 *passim;* in the psalms, 92, 105, 119, 122; Israel as, 218. *See also* King, sacral; Messiah
Shāhid verse, 281, 286
Shamanism. *See* Ecstasy
Sharon, 265
Shear-jashub, 151
Shechem, 183
Shemaiah, 131
Shᵉmînîth. *See* Psalms, headings of
Sheol (Hades), 29, 78, 116, 119, 122, 136, 182, 192, 205, 214, 253, 259, 260, 265, 266, 272, 275, 283, 285
Shepherd. *See* King, sacral
Shiggāyôn. *See* Psalms, types of
Shiloh, 44, 131, 134, 226
Shimei, 78n
Shiphrah, 204
Shîr. *See* Psalms, headings of
Shur, Wilderness of, 209, 211
Sibylline oracles, 218, 235
Sidrā', 179
Simeon, 203
Sin: expiated by suffering and death of sacral king, 41, 48; mentioned, 157, 183, 191n, 214, 233

—a god, 91
—Wilderness of, 209, 211
Sinai (or Horeb), 38, 64, 207–211 *passim,* 220
Sirion, 249
Skepticism. *See* Israelite religion
Sociology of Religion. *See* Religion, sociology of
Sodom, 245, 273
Solomon, 36, 79, 80, 81n, 221, 223, 248, 259. *See also* Psalms, authorship of
—Psalms of, 69, 99, 218, 235, 238
—Wisdom of, 234
Son of God. *See* King, sacral; Messiah
Son of the handmaid. *See* Messiah
Son of man: in Daniel, 218, 239–241 *passim,* 275; transcendent or cosmic concept of, 238–241 *passim;* development of idea of, 241. *See also* Messiah; Primal Man
Song of the Bow, 247
Sons of the prophets. *See* Prophetic schools or guilds
Soul: several souls in one person, 26; twin-soul, 26; functional soul, 26, 27; life- or body-soul, 26, 116; collective soul, 27; dream-soul, 27; eternal existence of, 27; image- or ghost-soul, 27, 28
Spirit, 145, 146
Succession history, 67
Succoth, 204, 207
Suez, Gulf of, 200
Suffering, 48
Suffering servant. *See* Servant of Yahweh
Sufism. *See* Mysticism
Sukkôth (Feast of Booths). *See* Israelite festivals
Sumerian literature, 9, 76, 84, 88–92 *passim,* 121n, 155, 159, 204n
Symbolic acts. *See* Prophets
Synagogue: and the post-Exilic form of the Israelite cult, 47, 112, 205; and the Book of Psalms, 70, 75, 112; and the prophetic literature, 179; mentioned, 110
Syncretism, 131, 134, 173, 187, 273, 280
Synecdoche, 242
Syria, 268

Taberah, 211
Tabernacle, 53, 60, 210
Tabu, 15

Talmud, 9, 47, 56

Tammuz-liturgy, 87, 92, 167, 167n, 182n, 245, 250, 251n, 263, 265, 276, 283

Targum, 86, 236

Tehom, 191, 205

Tekoa, 133, 152

Tell bet-Mirsim, 201

Temple: First: and canonization of the Psalms, 70, 72, 75, 94, 102, 112; and canonization of the prophetic books, 179; mentioned, 47, 52, 53, 57–60 *passim*, 66, 70, 72, 81n, 93, 127, 133, 141, 164, 185, 194, 202, 247, 247n, 285

—Second, 46, 70, 99, 110, 112, 274

Testaments of the Twelve Patriarchs, 218, 235

Tetrateuch, 58, 63, 203, 208, 213. *See also* P work

Textual criticism. *See* Traditio-historical method

Textual emendations: and philology, 77; and meter, 77, 94, 94n, 96; and parallelism, 77, 94, 244

Timsach, Lake, 200

Tobit, Book of, 234

Tôrāh, 39, 66

Torah-liturgy. *See* Psalms, types of

Totemism. *See* Religion, sociology of

Traditio-historical method: and oral tradition, 3–9 *passim*, 53–54, 59, 62, 65–67 *passim*, 73–75 *passim*, 154, 163–169, 174, 179; composition-analysis, 4; and context, 4; and form-criticism, 4, 5, 10, 58, 59, 63, 64, 73, 84, 95, 96, 101, 103, 121, 149, 154, 158, 166, 203, 211, 214, 279, 284; an analytical method, 4–6 *passim*, 96, 103, 211, 214; and literary criticism, 4, 9–11, 45, 51–53, 58, 64, 114, 116, 127, 135, 154–158 *passim*, 163, 169, 176–177, 194, 199, 200, 208, 213, 215, 217–219 *passim*, 230, 262, 284; synthesis, 5; and written tradition, 5, 65–67 *passim*, 73–75 *passim*, 153, 156–157, 163–164, 169, 177–178; and cultic *Sitz im Leben*, 7–9 *passim*, 68–73 *passim*, 96–97, 103, 121, 166, 169, 199; and internal investigation of Old Testament material, 7–8, 58, 101, 120, 124, 166, 171; and comparison of Old Testament literature with non-Israelite literature, 8–9, 73–77 *passim*, 81–84 *passim*, 103, 104, 117, 120, 125–127 *passim*, 155, 165–166, 183, 199, 219–220, 261–262; and textual criticism, 9–10, 54, 55, 73–77 *passim*, 95–96, 120, 149, 177, 205; and the Psalms, 70, 73–74, 98–99

Transmigration of souls. *See* Life after death

Tree symbolism, 249–250, 249–250n, 263, 269, 272, 274, 278, 288

Tumilât, Wadi, 200

Tyre, 131, 263, 272

Ugaritic literature, vii, 20n, 74–75, 81, 82, 85, 87, 91, 111n, 125, 133, 155, 166, 181, 182, 186, 190, 191n, 204, 223, 228, 254, 258, 260, 264n, 274n, 281, 283

Unio mystica. See Mysticism

Universalism: in the Psalms, 106, 108, 109, 122; in the prophetic literature, 108, 109, 155–162, 175, 218, 231, 285. *See also* King, sacral

Unleavened Bread, Feast of. *See* Passover

Ur, 181

Uriah, 247

Urmensch. See Primal Man

Uruk, 181

Vegetation, Rite of, 113–88

Vintage festival, 89

Virgin, 88n, 92

Visionaries. *See* Prophets, types of

Vulgate, 68

Waṣf, 253

Wenamun, 125

Wilderness wandering: and the rite of passage (*rite de passage*), 136, 192, 206, 214, 235n; length of, 202–203, 214; *Sitz im Leben* of, 205, 211–214; Kadesh complex, 209; Sinai complex, 209; itinerary of, 209–212; historicity of, 210–214; historicization of, 213; and the Passover, 213; in the Psalms, 214. *See also* Passover

Wisdom literature, 49, 175, 250, 256, 259

Wisdom psalms. *See* Psalms, types of

Yahweh. *See* God, Yahweh

Zadokite priesthood, 223

Zakir inscription, 223

Zalmon, 87

Zarathustra, 20

Zebulun, 87
Zechariah, 141, 148, 232, 288
Zedekiah, 151, 225, 229
Zelophehad's daughters, 66
Zephaniah, 287
Zered, Valley of, 210
Zerubbabel, 225, 227, 232, 288

Zin, Wilderness of, 210
Zion, 47, 113n, 171, 173, 241, 255, 256, 264, 267, 281, 283–285 *passim*
Zipporah, 198
Zoan, 202
Zophar, 258